COMMERCIAL SATELLITE IMAGERY AND UNITED NATIONS PEACEKEEPING

To Meeta and Shabnam

Commercial Satellite Imagery and United Nations Peacekeeping

A View From Above

DISCARDED

DISCARDED

Edited by

JAMES F. KEELEY
Centre for Military and Strategic Studies

ROB HUEBERT
Department of Political Science, University of Calgary

ASHGATE

Published by
Ashgate Publishing Company
Gower House
Croft Road
Aldershot
Hants GU11 3HR
England

Ashgate Publshing Company
Suite 420
101 Cherry Street
Burlington, VT 05401-4405
USA

Ashgate website: http://www.ashgate.com

British Library Cataloguing in Publication Data
Commercial satellite imagery and United Nations
    peacekeeping : a view from above
    1. United Nations - Congresses 2. National security - Canada
    - Congresses 3. Artificial satellites in remote sensing -
    Congresses 4. Military surveillance - Congresses 5. Remote
    sensing equipment industry - Military aspects - Congresses
    6. Peacekeeping forces - Congresses 7. Security,
    International - Congresses 8. Canada - Military policy -
    Congresses
    I. Keeley, James F. II. Huebert, Robert N. (Robert Neil),
    1960-
    327.1'72

Library of Congress Cataloging-in-Publication Data
Keeley, James F.
    Commercial satellite imagery, and United Nations peacekeeping : a view from above /
    James F. Keeley and Rob Huebert.
        p. cm.
    Includes bibliographical references and index.
    ISBN 0-7546-1072-1
        1. Space surveillance. 2. Artificial satellites in remote sensing--Political aspects. 3.
    National security. I. Huebert, Robert N. (Robert Neil), 1960- II. Title.

UG1520.K44 ~~2003~~ 2004
327.12--dc22   2003063652

ISBN 0 7546 1072 1

Printed and bound in Great Britain by Antony Rowe Ltd, Chippenham, Wilts.

Contents

List of Figures

List of Tables

List of Contributors

Steve Adam is a Senior Data Analyst with Canadian Geomatics Solutions, Ltd., Calgary, Alberta, Canada.

Michel Bourbonnière is Professor of International Law at the Royal Military College, Kingston, Ontario, Canada.

Dana G. Clarke is a Major in the Canadian Forces, Section Head of Plans, Strategy and Doctrine in the Directorate of Space Development, Department of National Defence, Ottawa, Ontario, Canada.

Corey Michael Dvorkin is an analyst in the Directorate of Western Hemisphere Policy, Department of National Defence, Ottawa, Ontario, Canada.

Richard C. Gorecki is Manager, Marketing and Client Support, with Pixxures Canada, Ltd., Calgary, Alberta, Canada.

Louis Haeck is Adjunct Professor at l'Ecole Polytechnique, University of Montreal, and at the Royal Military College, Kingston, Ontario, Canada.

Mryka Hall-Beyer is an Assistant Professor in the Department of Geography, University of Calgary.

Alvin L. Hanks is a founder and Principal with Chesapeake Analytics.

Rob Huebert is an Associate Professor in the Department of Political Science and Associate Director of the Centre for Military and Strategic Studies, University of Calgary.

Ram Jakhu is a Professor of International Law at McGill University, and Director of the McGill Centre for the Study of Regulated Industries.

James F. Keeley is an Associate Professor in the Department of Political Science and a Resident Fellow of the Centre for Military and Strategic Studies, University of Calgary.

Robert S. Macleod is a Lieutenant-Colonel in the Canadian Forces, with the North American Aerospace Defence Command, Colorado Springs, Colorado, U.S.A.

Alex Morrison is the Former President of the Lester B. Pearson Canadian International Peacekeeping Training Centre, Cornwallis Park, Clementsport, Nova Scotia, Canada.

Jean-Pierre Paquette is President of ImStrat Corporation, Carleton Place, Ontario, Canada.

Ulric Shannon is in the Regional Security and Peacekeeping Division, Department of Foreign Affairs and International Trade, Ottawa, Ontario, Canada.

C. Vincent Tao contributed to the conference while an Assistant Professor in the Department of Geomatics Engineering, University of Calgary. He is currently holder of the Canada Research Chair in Geomatics and Associate Professor of Geomatics Engineering in the Department of Earth and Atmospheric Science, York University, Toronto, Canada.

Q.S. (Bob) Truong is a Program Manager in the Safeguards Support Program of the Canadian Nuclear Safety Commission, Ottawa, Ontario, Canada. He has a PEng in Mechanical Engineering from the University of Toronto.

Preface and Acknowledgements

The conference which generated the chapters in this volume arose from a recognition of the rapidly developing interest among both international organizations and non-governmental organizations in the possibilities for the use of increasingly available, and increasingly capable, commercial satellite imagery in a variety of roles typically associated with peace-keeping and similar humanitarian operations. Given Canada's significant and complex involvement in the field of satellite imagery as a producer and consumer of this imagery, and as a home to a significant associated commercial industry, its historically strong connection to UN peacekeeping operations which have been subject to a tide of criticism and introspection, and the significance of its industrial, technological, military and political ties to the United States, the relationship of CSI to Canada's security requirements, and particularly with reference to UN peacekeeping, seemed a natural and important, if large, area of inquiry. The release of the Brahimi Report (*Report of the Panel on United Nations Peace Operations*) shortly before the conference provided at least an indirect confirmation of this.

In organizing the conference, we tried to bring together a variety of concerns and perspectives: technical, commercial-industrial, political, legal and military. We drew on a wide range of individuals – academics from a variety of disciplines, government personnel (including military), and from the private sector. We are particularly grateful for the interest shown by our private-sector participants in the conference.

A number of people and organizations contributed significantly to the conference, in terms of support, time and money. We are grateful for their interest and encouragement. The Centre for Military and Strategic Studies at the University of Calgary, headed by David Bercuson, provided essential institutional support and drive, and the Centre's Administrative and Budget Officer, Shelley Wind, gave us crucial 'back office' support, as did the Research Associate and Events Co-ordinator, Nancy Pearson-Mackie. A number of graduate students at the Centre contributed their services as rapporteurs and assistants: Steven Heard, Chris Bullock, Mike Schlueter, Ray Szeto, and above all Dylan Kirk. Dr. Ron Keith and Dr. John Ferris, of the Departments of Political Science and History respectively, served as panel chairs for the conference, as did Dr. Hall-Beyer. Kari Roberts of the Department of Political Science and Jillian Dowding of the Centre for Military and Strategic Studies prepared the index. We wish to acknowledge the support of the Departments of National Defence and of Foreign Affairs and International Trade, and the North American Aerospace Command, which contributed paper-givers (in an individual capacity). We also wish to thank Anne Keirby of Ashgate Publishing for her interest, support and patience.

Essential financial support was provided by BCT TELUS, the Security and Defence Forum Special Projects Fund of the Department of National Defence, the University of Calgary Research Grants Committee, and the Departments of Political Science and History of the University of Calgary.

List of Abbreviations

ABM	Anti Ballistic Missile
AIAC	Aerospace Industries Association of Canada
AMTI	Air Moving Targets Indication
ARTEMIS	Africa Real Time Environmental Monitoring Information System
ASTER	Advanced Spaceborne Thermal Emission and Reflection Radiometer
AVHRR	Advanced Very High Resolution Radiometer
BMD	Ballistic Missile Defence
C4I	Command, Control, Communications, Computers and Intelligence
CCUNPROFOR	Canadian Contingent of the United Nations Protection Force
CNSC	Canadian Nuclear Safety Commission
CIA	Central Intelligence Agency
CIC	Commercial Imagery Coordinator
CNES	Centre Nationale d'Etudes Spatiale
COPUOS	Committee on Peaceful Uses of Outer Space (UN)
CSA	Commercial Space Agency
CSI	Commercial Satellite Imagery
CTBT	Comprehensive Test Ban Treaty
DAAC	Distributed Active Archive Centers
DEM	Digital Elevation Models
DFAIT	Department of Foreign Affairs and International Trade
DGRS	Deployable Ground Receiving Stations
DND	Department of National Defence
DOD	Department of Defense
ECOWAS	Economic Community of West African States
EOS	Earth Observing System
EOSAT	Earth Observation Satellite Company
EROS	Earth Resources Orbiting Satellite
ERS	Earth Resources Satellite
ERTS	Earth Resources Technology Satellite
ESA	European Space Agency
EUMETSAT	Exploration of Meteorological Satellites
FAS	Federation of American Scientists
FMC	Field Mapping Coordinator
GAC	Global Area Coverage
GIS	Geospatial Information System

GLONASS   Global Orbiting Navigation Satellite System
GMTI   Ground Moving Targets Indication
GOES   Geosynchronous Operational Environment Satellites
GPS   Global Positioning System
GSD   Ground Sample Distance
HDF   Hierarchical Data Format
HUMINT   Human Intelligence
IAEA   International Atomic Energy Agency
ICTY   International Criminal Tribunal for Yugoslavia
IFOR   Implementation Force
IFSAR   Interferometric Synthetic Aperature Radar
ISMA   International Satellite Monitoring Agency
ISRO   Indian Space Research Organisation
JERS   Japanese Eearth Resources Satellite
KOMPSAT-2   Second Korean Multi Purpose Satellite
LAC   Local Area Coverage
MCOT   Maritime Combined Operational Training
MEF   Marine Expeditionary Force
MODIS   Moderate-resolution Imaging Spectroradiometer
MONUC   United Nations Mission in the Democratic Republic of
                 Congo
NASA   National Aeronautic and Space Administration
NATO   North Atlantic Treaty Organization
NCSA   National Center for Supercomputer Applications
NGO   Non-governmental Organization
NIMA   National Imagery and Mapping Agency
NOAA   National Oceanographic and Atmospheric Adminstration
NORAD   North Amercian Aerospace Defence
NPIC   National Photographic Interpretation Center
NRO   National Reconnaissance Office
NRSA   National Remote Sensing Agency
NTDB   National Topographic Data Base
NTM   National Technical Means
OST   Outer Space Treaty
PDD   Presidential Decision Directive
RDBMS   Relational Database Management Systems
RMA   Revolution in Military Affairs
RMS   Remote Manipulator System
RRES   Rwanda Refugee Exodus Situation
RSI   Radarsat International
RUF   Revolutionary United Front
SADC   Southern African Development Community
SAR   Synthetic Aperture Radar
SDI   Strategic Defence Initiative
SHIRBRIG   Standing High Readiness Brigade
SPOT   System Probatoir d'Observation de la Terre
UAE   United Arab Emirates

UK	United Kingdom
UN	United Nations
UNDHA	Department of Humanitarian Affairs
UNDOF	United Nations Disengagement Observer Force
UNEF II	Second United Nations Emergency Force
UNFICYP	United Nations Force in Cyprus
UNGA	United Nations General Assembly
UNHCR	United Nations High Commission for Refugees
UNIFIL	United Nations Interim Force in Lebanon
UNITA	National Union for the Total Independence of Angola
UNMOGIP	United Nations Military Observer Group in India and Pakistan
UNPROFOR	United Nations Protection Force
UNSCOM	United Nations Special Commission
VSATs	Very Small Aperture Terminals
WMC	World Meteorological Congress
WMO	World Meteorological Organisation
WWW	World Wide Web

Introduction: Commercial Satellite Imagery, UN Peacekeeping/Making and National Security: A Canadian Perspective

James F. Keeley and Rob Huebert

This volume presents papers from the conference, 'The Need to Know: The Use of Commercial Satellite Imagery and Canadian Security Needs', held at the University of Calgary on November 17–18, 2000. The principal focus of the conference was to understand the impact that commercial satellite imagery is having on the international system. For our purposes, 'commercial satellite imagery' (CSI) is defined as unclassified satellite imagery publicly offered for a fee on a routine basis, whether by a public agency or a private firm. CSI represents one of the most exciting new forms of technology that is reshaping the manner in which international relations are conducted.

The conference examined two developing trends that increasingly will shape the conduct of international security policies through the use of CSI. The first is the increasing capabilities of the commercial satellite imaging industry, including both the satellite operators and various service or value-added providers. The technology associated with the industry continues to expand at a prodigious rate. The second trend investigated is the growing use, and awareness of the possibilities of use, of that imagery in peacekeeping/peacemaking and humanitarian operations in the international realm as well as for the protection of national security for states.

These issues are approached from a Canadian perspective. Canada is both an imagery and a service provider and has significant security interests affected by the development of the commercial satellite imagery industry. While the two themes are distinct, they also overlap, given Canada's historical involvement in UN operations, specifically peacekeeping and peacemaking. This intersection points to a number of issues in both the UN's use of commercial satellite imagery in peacekeeping and peacemaking and in Canadian governmental approaches to the industry. The advantage of providing a Canadian focus is found in the fact that while Canadian industry is capable of producing technology that is the best in the world, as a medium power, the ability of Canada to exploit this technology is limited. Thus many of the problems that Canadian policy makers face are similar to those facing many other states which are now developing similar capabilities.

1

For the United Nations, the application of CSI in its peacekeeping and peacemaking operations raises a number of issues. In narrow terms, the range of relevant questions includes: specific information requirements for its peacekeeping and peacemaking operations and the ability of CSI to address these requirements; specific systems for acquiring, analysing, interpreting and using the imagery, including such considerations as hardware, software, communications, organizational issues, and integration with other information and information technology; costs; relations between the UN and imagery (and imagery service) providers in the commercial sector and from governmental suppliers; and legal issues arising from the use of CSI. Various larger issues are also opened up by considering the use of CSI in peacekeeping and peacemaking operations: the need for and impediments to more effective peacekeeping and peacemaking operations; attitudes towards the gathering and use of intelligence and other information by the UN in these operations; the adequacy of the UN's approach to and capabilities in modern information technology (including Geographic Information Systems) especially in its peacekeeping and peacemaking operations; command and control within peacekeeping and peacemaking operations; the conduct of 'complex humanitarian operations' (i.e., operations with both a significant humanitarian assistance component and a significant peacekeeping and peacemaking component), including relations between the UN and UN peacekeeping and peacemaking operations on the one hand and nongovernmental organizations on the other; and broad relations between the UN and its member states, especially on questions touching on the possession by the UN of potentially significant independent information capabilities.

For a state such as Canada, which has both a CSI capability in RADARSAT and imagery services and strong links to and dependence on other technologically-capable states such as the United States, a similarly lengthy list of considerations might arise: Canada is both a supplier and a user of CSI and related services; it has a security interest, both narrowly in terms of defence and more broadly in terms of economic and technological factors, in the CSI field; it has strong economic, technological and defence links to the United States and to other allies, so that co-operation with these is valued on a number of fronts, including technological compatibility in the military sphere, access to technology and markets, and so on. In addition, however, Canada has a strong interest in peacekeeping and peacemaking operations by the UN, and in ensuring that these become more effective. To this end, indeed, the Canadian government participates in the Standing High-Readiness Brigade now available for deployment, has stand-by troop arrangements with the UN, and has proposed a UN rapid reaction capability. A strong UN and effective peacekeeping and peacemaking capability looms large in Canadian security interests.

It is this Canadian interest in peacekeeping and peacemaking and the UN that serves as our area of intersection, though not necessarily of compatibility. Some Canadian interests and concerns could be jeopardized by some forms of a UN CSI capability, if not by a UN CSI capability as such. If this is the case, constraints placed upon the approach even of a state presumed relatively supportive of a more effective UN could present a useful threshold for considerations of efforts to improve UN capabilities. If, on the other hand, there are possibilities for a positive

Canadian response to the question of a UN CSI capability, this could also serve as a base for the improvement of the UN's peacekeeping and peacemaking effectiveness. Canada also must be alert to sharing a continent with the sole remaining superpower. The events of September 11, 2001 have resulted in a substantially different American approach to security than was the case before the attack. As a result Canada must be much more aware of American concerns for the protection of the North American continent. This includes both an increased need for better surveillance of North America and to ensure that the enemies of North America do not have access to these surveillance capabilities. In both regards the role of CSI assumes greater significance.

Commercial Satellite Imagery and UN Peacekeeping and Peacemaking

The various issues which must be addressed in considering the possibilities and problems in the use of CSI for UN peacekeeping and peacemaking have been broadly indicated above. They fall in general terms into the categories of technical, commercial supply and legal issues, issues more narrowly focused on the integration of imagery into UN peacekeeping and peacemaking operations, and finally broader, more political questions about the UN as such.

Technically, a wide variety of satellites, sensors and associated systems are available. Relevant characteristics of these satellites include the following:

1 The sensors: panchromatic, multispectral, thermal or radar; whether the sensors can be moved to increase the swath which can be covered or to provide stereoscopic images; available resolutions.
2 Revisit times over a given location.
3 Whether the imagery is on film or, now the more usual case, stored and downloaded as digital data. If the latter, what are the storage capabilities of the satellite? Must it download to a regional array of ground stations, or can it retain data and download to a smaller number of ground stations?
4 What are the capabilities and the requirements for the communication and analysis of the imagery? Developments in communications technology, such as the Internet, and in computer hardware and software are making imagery more readily available and more readily manipulable for analysis.
5 How fast can required imagery products be made available to a user?
6 How readily can the imagery and its products be integrated with other information, for example in a Geographical Information System suitable for the user's needs?
7 How readily might imagery from one satellite be substituted for or integrated with imagery from another satellite, or with aerial imagery?

In commercial and supply terms, companies and agencies which provide imagery and related products are proliferating. The market for satellite imagery is growing, and its range of civilian (or at least non-military) applications is expanding. However, the relationship between a user and the CSI industry depends on how certain issues are handled:

1   Imagery costs may vary considerably from one provider to another, and depending on the characteristics of the imagery sought: high-resolution versus low-resolution, archived versus new, "rush" versus less hurried acquisition, and so on.
2   Contractual relationships with suppliers may also vary, with price implications: is a user a bulk purchaser or an occasional purchaser? Could it negotiate for a bundle of services, or would it spread its contacts or perform some services itself?
3   What copyright or licensing requirements would come into play? How would these affect the intended use, including possible sharing among users?
4   Given that the satellites in question are owned by governmental agencies and/or consortia of firms subject to varying national regulations, what controls over access to or the use of imagery exist, how might these affect the intended use, and could alternative sources be found as and when needed to bypass restrictions placed on any one source?

Some of these commercial issues touch on national laws and regulations. Others arise within international law, concerning rights to acquire and use imagery data, access to the imagery, and ability to control the dissemination of the data.

With respect to applications to UN peacekeeping and peacemaking operations, a further set of concerns arises. In the narrower, technical sense, these include the following:

1   What are the requirements for information and timeliness of delivery? How well do these match the capabilities of the imagery industry? How might requirements – and their match with capabilities – vary by the size, nature and phase of the mission? How might they vary by the location of the user: in the UN's New York headquarters, or in the field command centre of an operation?
2   How would imagery and/or imagery products be delivered to users (since delivery times are affected not only by the revisit times of a satellite but also by the characteristics and capabilities of the organization)?
3   Would primary analysis, interpretation and product generation be provided by industry or by the user? If the latter, would this occur in the field or at headquarters? What are the technical and personnel capability requirements in either location? How would these requirements be met?

These do not, however, exhaust the possibilities even within a focus simply on peacekeeping and peacemaking. In order to address the full potential for the use of the imagery, much less to address some of its problems, other questions can be raised, such as:

1   Is the United Nations organized appropriately, in its headquarters and its field commands, to use the imagery? In particular, what problems must be dealt with in multinational C4I (command, control, communications, computers and intelligence)? These issues cannot be taken for granted even in the most technologically capable states.
2   Might this imagery also raise possibilities for stronger cooperation with non-governmental organizations in 'complex humanitarian operations'? If so, how

could these possibilities be developed, and what problems would have to be addressed?

More broadly still, the possible use by the United Nations of commercial imagery raises some very basic and profoundly political questions. The United Nations is an association of sovereign states, not a transcendental actor that stands above and apart from its member states. It is limited by the sensitivities, the prejudices, the interests, and the range of tolerance and support of those states. Satellite imagery, especially higher-resolution imagery, is historically and psychologically associated with politically dominant states and with espionage. Even as high-resolution imagery in particular becomes commercially available, this association will be hard to shake and will pose a basic political limitation on the willingness of states to accept its use by the UN. 'Intelligence' is a sensitive word, however properly it might describe information-gathering and however legitimate it might seem even in a peace-keeping and peacemaking context. States might be very reluctant to allow the UN to develop an autonomous 'intelligence' capability, even though they may also be deeply distrustful as well of the other probable alternative: UN dependence on the willingness of individual states to supply imagery, imagery products and/or imagery-derived information when needed.

Canadian Policy

CSI offers Canadian policy-makers a powerful tool. The ability of systems such as RADARSAT can provide an important surveillance system that is currently unmatched in northern Canada. It can also be used as a Canadian contribution to multilateral operations with the United Nations and other international collations. It can also serve to protect Canadian national interests over Canadian territory. However, the technology is not cheap or technologically simple. It required substantial resources and requires careful planning to best utilize it to its fullest capacity. In order to achieve the optimal use of CSI for Canadian policy the following questions need to be addressed:

1   How does Canada ensure that the development of CSI will best serve its national interests? Not only does Canada have to define its 'national interests', it must also take into account the interests of a wide range of actors. First, the commercial interests that are developing CSI must be allowed to maintain their economic viability. Any policy that the Government of Canada develops must remain sensitive to this requirement. The Government also needs to ensure that the needs and requirements of its allies are protected. The relationship with the United States must be given particular attention. The challenge for Canada is to ensure that American concerns are met in a manner that does not interfere with Canadian interests. Third, the Canadian Government must also ensure that the various needs within its own departments are met in a coherent and rational fashion. How are these various interests to be balanced?

2   The Canadian Government must also ensure that CSI adjust to a changing international environment. The events of September 11, 2001 and its aftermath

demonstrate how quickly events can change the international security environment. The development of CSI and its means of distribution require long-term actions and planning. However, the assumption governing this planning can change radically and quickly. How can this best be done?

Canada faces a complicated set of factors in developing an international security policy that utilizes CSI to its fullest capacities. Further complicating this challenge is the absence of comprehensive space policy that includes national security. Canada has preferred to limit its space policy to commercial considerations that downplay the importance of space assets in it foreign and defence policies.

The Chapters

The chapters are organized into three broad groups. The first set addresses a variety of legal, technological and commercial issues. Together, they lay an essential foundation for an understanding of the capabilities and limits of CSI, the nature of the commercial imagery industry, and some overarching issues and problems in relevant international law.

Ram Jakhu provides an overview of the general legal principles governing the acquisition and dissemination of satellite imagery. These activities, he notes, have been carried out under the general international legal principle of freedom of outer space. The rights to launch remote sensing satellites and to acquire remote sensing imagery, he argues, are enjoyed by all. In particular, the right to acquire the data without the consent of the sensed state is established. The right to disseminate remote sensing imagery without the consent of the sensed state is also established, but in practice so, too, is the right of the sensing state not to disseminate that data, or to put such restrictions on its dissemination as it sees fit. Some of the states which initially championed the principles of free acquisition and non-discriminatory dissemination of imagery have now started imposing restrictions on the collection and release of some imagery. Finally, a sensed state does not have a right under international law to seek or demand satellite imagery of its territory.

Much of the attention to the possible use of CSI has been aroused by the commercial availability of high-resolution imagery – imagery of 1 m resolution or less. This offers to the general public imagery of a sort until recently the exclusive province of the governments of the most technologically capable states. However, as a consequence the possible contribution of lower resolution imagery to UN operations goes unremarked, at least among non-specialists. *Mryka Hall-Beyer* focuses on the possibilities and the issues associated with low-resolution imagery. While it may be limited in what it can see, it also presents various advantages: it tends to be very inexpensive, is often extensively archived, and repeat images of an area may be obtained in a short period of time (cloud cover permitting). Even with its low resolution, it may still be useful for disaster management purposes, and for some purposes pertinent to peacekeeping and peacemaking operations, such as general monitoring and coverage of an area, locating large groups of displaced persons, and pinpointing areas which deserve closer attention. Hall Beyer also notes some factors in the acquisition and analysis of this imagery.

Jean-Pierre Paquette presents an overview of the many satellite systems currently available or likely to be available in the near future. While some of these are low-resolution, others have resolution down to 1 m for panchromatic sensors and 4 m for multispectral sensors. He also notes the characteristics of Canada's RADARSAT –1, which has an all-weather capability. The major advantages and disadvantages of the various systems are briefly noted from the perspective of peacekeeping and peacemaking operations. All provide some capacity for the mapping of road and rail networks, identification of terrain, identification of regions of destruction, and assessment of urban area displacement, and the tracking of large refugee populations. Many add to this list an ability to assess agricultural capacity, to track large refugee populations, and to detect changes. Disadvantages vary from one system to another, but may include an inability or limited ability to task sensors, limitations on the ability to extract information for military applications due to low resolution, and in some cases slow revisit times. Basic image costs – that is, without taking into consideration elements such as additional processing and value-added – may also vary considerably, from a low of US$600.00 for LANDSAT to a high of US$3800.00 for SPOT.

Vincent Tao and *Bob Truong* illustrate how information from satellite and other imagery may be combined with other data through the use of Geographic Information Systems technology. Interest in the use of CSI in nuclear safeguarding applications has developed very significantly in both the International Atomic Energy Agency and in various states over the last decade. It has been recognized that substantial work is required to develop new safeguard techniques to meet effectiveness and efficiency objectives at both the State and the Agency level. The new technologies of GIS and remote sensing have changed the way information is captured, stored, processed and distributed. Their chapter describes research work conducted at the University of Calgary in conjunction with the Canadian Nuclear Safety Commission (CNSC). A system, GeoATOMS[a], has been developed based on the GIS technology for nuclear data management and reporting. A unique feature of the system is that both geospatial data such as maps and images as well as texture data such as reports and documents can be managed seamlessly.

The cost of high-resolution satellite imagery has often been cited as one serious obstacle to its use. *Steve Adam* examines some of the financial considerations involved in the use of this imagery. He notes the variability in pricing, depending on factors such as resolution, needs, and the level of processing. He suggests a degree of price stability, based on growing demand. Commoditization of imagery, based on its evolution into relatively standardized product types, may exert downward pressures on prices, but this will be among like products. Acquiring new imagery, especially if the need is time-sensitive, will cost more than acquiring archived imagery. He also explores briefly the sorts of purchasing agreements which a user might seek to develop with imagery suppliers.

Alvin L. Hanks and *Richard C. Gorecki* address issues of data acquisition and distribution. They note that some systems have a data storage capability which reduces their dependence on ground stations, but in other cases the pattern of several ground stations and accompanying regional distributors is still followed. They particularly note the possibilities presented by advances in communications and in computer technology: the internet, high-speed data transfer, and deployable receiving stations. In regard to pricing, they also suggest that a user should carefully define its needs and approach these as constituting a 'bundle' with various characteristics. They describe a hypothetical case of the application of CSI by a peacekeeping and peacemaking mission, laying out one model of an organization to define the needs, interact with potential suppliers, receive and distribute the data.

The second set of chapters turns directly to the peacekeeping and peacemaking application. The emphasis here is especially on the organizational and political issues which would be faced by the UN in attempting to exploit CSI.

James F. Keeley notes that government, non-profit and private users (including the media and researchers) are making increasing use of commercial satellite imagery (CSI), or are increasingly considering its use. There have been instances of use, and studies of the potential use, of satellite imagery and of CSI more particularly, by the United Nations. The recent Report of the Panel on United Nations Peacekeeping Operations has called for marked improvements in UN capabilities for such operations, including more extensive use of information technology and geographic information systems technology. In this general context, it makes sense to consider in more detail issues arising from the possibility for the use of CSI and the implications of the more organized use of CSI by the United Nations in support of its peacekeeping and peacemaking operations. The chapter also briefly notes some issues which the use of this imagery raises for Canadian security policy. These include policies on access to imagery, relations with the US, responding to the Revolution in Military Affairs, and support for UN peacekeeping and peacemaking.

Alex Morrison addresses the use of CSI within the broader context of the role of 'intelligence' in UN peacekeeping and peacemaking operations, and speaks from the perspective of the peacekeeper. He calls for a stronger UN capability in the area of 'intelligence' or 'military information' for the sensitive, including the use of CSI. He also points, however, to the considerable resistance which one might expect from states anxious to guard their sovereignty.

Sovereignty and resistance are principal themes of *Ulric Shannon's* chapter, which focuses on the political obstacles to increasing the UN's capacity to use commercial satellite imagery. He notes some of the doubts which states might have about certain claims for the use of this imagery. For example, its high cost might offset any personnel reductions which it could permit, and indeed a reduction in personnel on the ground might be undesirable in its own right. A detailed, clear and persuasive demonstration of benefits would be necessary to overcome political obstacles – and even then might not suffice. These political obstacles must be addressed. He closes by suggesting that the benefits of using CSI in peacekeeping and peacemaking might be modest, and certainly would not be a panacea. Above all, however, financial and political problems must be dealt with.

Another set of issues in the use of commercial satellite imagery in UN peacekeeping centres on how certain organizational matters will be addressed. *James F. Keeley* briefly surveys some of these, in two larger contexts: first, the matter of a UN intelligence or 'information' capability; and, second and still more broadly, the problem of C4I in United Nations operations. Five scenarios are used to present some of the problems which must be addressed. The first is a composite of some classic complaints about UN operations; the second turns to a "leading nation" model of peacekeeping; the third considers the possibility of a UN CSI capacity at its New York headquarters; the fourth looks at a CSI capacity in the field; and the fifth at the combination of a headquarters and a field capacity.

The third set of chapters looks more closely at Canadian security interests. These extend beyond peacekeeping and peacemaking applications, and indeed beyond purely military applications of CSI, to include technological and commercial factors, and relations with allies. All of these factors would, however, bear on how Canada might approach the use of CSI in UN operations.

Michel Bourbonnière and *Louis Haeck* provide an overview of Canadian security concerns affected by commercial satellite imagery. The Federal Government's involvement in the RADARSAT-1 and RADARSAT-2 projects is perceived as an important strategic investment, to develop a key sector of the Canadian economy and industrial base as a part of an information-based economy. It is also very important to Canada's defence capabilities in monitoring threats, maintaining sovereignty over the Canadian north and maximizing effective military operations abroad. The key to continued Canadian prosperity in commercial space-based imaging rests on maintaining and improving commercial alliances and military interoperability with our American allies. Future Canadian regulatory structures in commercial space-based earth imaging face a creative challenge. To ensure access to American technology and markets Canadian legislators will have to balance US security needs while maintaining a competitive environment for Canadian companies to operate in. In this sense, Canadian interoperability between the Canadian military and Canadian civil space industry will be the determining factor ensuring our place in the international markets for spacebased earth imaging.

Rob Huebert examines the policy challenges faced by the Canadian Government as it attempts to develop policy governing the use of CSI. He traces the development of Canadian space policy since the end of the Second World War and argued that the Canadian government has preferred to avoid the development of a holistic policy that includes defence and foreign policy issues. Nevertheless, the development of commercial satellite imagery has created a wide range of new and exciting possibilities for Canada. For example, Canadian peacekeeping and peacemaking operations stand to make considerable gains through the utilization of CSI. CSI is also playing an increasingly important role in determining the impact of climate change on Canada. It is also evident that CSI requires a complex mix of industry and government in order to establish the technology and fully use it. The partnership between the Canadian Space Agency and MacDonald-Dettwiler to develop RADARSAT-2 demonstrates this need for co-operation. The fact that Canada must subsequently rely on the US to launch the satellite underlines the need for bilateral co-operation. The recent agreement reached between Canada and the US on the operation of commercial remote sensing satellite systems underscores the reality that Canada cannot operate such systems in isolation from international realities. The challenge increasingly facing the Canadian government is to manage these various actors and requirements to produce a coherent foreign and defence policy. At the same time, the government must be sensitive to the problems that they will create. This chapter will initiate a consideration of these challenges.

Robert S. MacLeod also addresses the general issues for Canadian security raised by commercial satellite imagery. He notes the trade-off between security and commercial concerns which must be addressed. Canada has a strong historical and commercial involvement in commercial satellites. It also has a strong interest in their security applications,such as surveillance, tracking, law enforcement and general support to military operations.

In a sense, *Corey Michael Dvorkin* picks up, in his review of American policy towards commercialization, from Ram Jakhu's observation that some early supporters of openness are now moving towards more restrictive policies. The United States, like Canada, must resolve the potential contradictions between commercial and more classic security concerns: on the one hand, preserving and extending a strong American presence in a growing market, and on the other preserving American information dominance in a crucial high technology sector. As the impact of the French SPOT system on US policies demonstrates, efforts to achieve the latter objective may work to its disadvantage in the former, and thus also, in the longer term, compromise its information dominance. This circle can be squared if the United States manages to achieve and maintain a very strong commercial dominance, such that others are essentially driven from the field, or if it obtains a more subtle hold, through regulation of its own industry and through exploitation of the technological linkages of others with American firms, and of their dependence on American private and government services. If the United States is unable to achieve 'shutter control' through commercial access control domination, or through the exploitation of industry networks in which US firms dominate, or through its own provision of certain essential services (e.g., launching), what effects would follow? If the US is dominant, this affects the Canadian position towards its own industry (e.g. the RADARSAT example) and the Canadian policy stance vis-à-vis UN use. If the US cannot dominate, it cannot stop others from eroding its information advantage, and this rationale for hindering a UN capability could decline. However, if the US must approve peacekeeping operations, this could support its policy. It could be in the American advantage to have a UN with this capability if others can also supply it, anyway, in order to strengthen UN peacekeeping effectiveness.

Dana G. Clarke also addresses the security issues posed by CSI. He reviews the development and the functions of access controls, as means of limiting the resolution of available imagery, limiting distribution of images, or limiting the ability to image certain locations or areas, and of preserving preferential government access to imagery as needed. He briefly covers both American and Canadian efforts to develop regulations.

Chapter 1

International Law Governing the Acquisition and Dissemination of Satellite Imagery

Ram Jakhu

Introduction

Definition and technology

Satellite imaging or space remote sensing denotes the collection of data (images, information) acquired, in photographic or digital form, by space-based devises, instruments or sensors without any physical contact with the sensed object(s), but using electromagnetic radiation (radio waves).[1] Before the space age began on 4 October 1957, human beings gathered information, on any part of the Earth, on the ground or from air using balloons and aircraft carrying cameras. However, the way humans gathered information on the surface of the Earth changed radically when the first artificial Earth orbiting satellite was launched on 18 August 1960 specifically designed to photograph the Earth's surface. Since then, the technology has advanced considerably both in the military as well as the civil domain.

Remote sensing satellites are of two types, which correspond to the functioning characteristics of their sensors; i.e. passive and active. While passive satellites (with optical sensors) observe merely radiation emitted by the sensed object, active satellites (with radar sensors) emit radiation toward the object being sensed and measure the energy reflected or 'backscattered' by that object.[2] Currently both types of sensors are being used for various applications. However, active satellites using radar or synthetic aperture radar (SAR) sensors are becoming popular because of their advantages as they can take images or 'see' at night and through clouds. The 'seeing' capability of a satellite is described in its spatial resolution, which corresponds to the size of the smallest object that can be observed by that satellite. For example, a satellite image of one meter (m) resolution indicates that objects measuring one-meter across or more are depicted in that image. This means that the higher the resolution of satellite imagery the more detailed and precise the information gained about the sensed objects.[3]

However, high resolution or quality of satellite images cannot exclusively and automatically result in high quality of and readily use-able information. Operating space systems and taking images, which essentially occur in outer space, must be supplemented by ground–based activities for appropriate data processing and

11

interpretation in order to make the satellite imagery practically useful. Satellites collect first imagery in the form of raw data, which is also known as unprocessed data. 'Primary data' or 'unenhanced data', derived from raw data after some processing, consists of radio signals that have been pre-processed or not yet processed enough to make them useable images or other products.[4] Primary data is processed with the use of sophisticated computer and other technologies and expertise to produce useable products.[5] Data interpretation techniques are used to obtain information from images that convey ideas or impressions. Therefore, the term 'analysed information' is used to indicate the facts and figures, which result 'from the interpretation of processed data, inputs of data and knowledge from other sources'.[6] The degree of accuracy and completeness of the information depends largely upon the interpreter's experience and the knowledge of objects being analysed and their surroundings, which are collected from the material in literature, such as maps, books, articles and reports.

Satellite systems and their capabilities: Commercial opportunities and security threats

Since the launch of the first remote sensing satellite in 1960, significant technological advances have been made as active satellites are routinely launched and used, imagery of one-meter resolution is readily available and highly accurate information is being derived by using sophisticated data interpretation techniques and expertise. A large number of remote sensing satellites are currently in orbit and more are expected to be launched in the near future by several counties like Brazil, China, Canada, France, India, Israel, Japan, Russia and the US. They currently provide and will continue providing imagery at various details for numerous civil and military applications.[7] For example, it is recently reported that by tripling its military space spending Canada will be enhancing its 'intelligence-gathering and surveillance of and from Space'.[8] Canada's RADARSAT-1 remote sensing satellite was launched in 1995 and is currently being used for civilian and military applications. It will be replaced possibly in 2003 by RADARDSAT-2, which will produce images with 3 m resolution and RADARSAT-3 is also expected to be planned soon.[9]

The Indian Space Research Organisation (ISRO) currently markets worldwide 5.8 m resolution imagery from its Indian Remote Sensing (IRS) satellite series. It has also planned to launch in 2002 its new remote sensing satellite called CARTOSAT, which will produce 2.5 m images and help meet growing demand for satellite imagery in India and abroad.[10]

An Israel-US private joint venture called ImageSat will launch and operate the company's Earth Remote Observation Satellite (EROS) which would be derivatives of Israel's OFEQ-3 surveillance satellites. ImageSat, which replaced West Indian Space Company of Cayman Islands, is incorporated in the Netherlands Antilles. The company plans to complete by 2005 the launch of all its satellites, two of which will have 1.8 m resolution capability and others would take images with 0.82 m resolution for commercial purposes.[11]

The US Government's LANDSAT-7 remote sensing satellite, launched more than a year ago, produces 18 m resolution imagery, which is distributed globally.[12] An

American private company, Space Imaging, has launched in September 1999 the world's first commercial remote sensing satellite, called IKONOS, that takes black-and-white images with 1 m resolution and colour with 4 m resolution.[13] For its extensive global commercial operations, Space Imaging has already established business offices in Athens, Tokyo, Seoul and Dubai. It has entered into an agreement with a Turkish company to sell high-resolution images to Turkish industry and to the Turkish military, which could buy 'intelligence and mapping data at world commercial sale prices'.[14] A similar agreement has been concluded with India's Antrix Corporation, the commercial arm of the ISRO, under which IKONOS's 1 m resolution data will be distributed in India.[15] If approved by the US Government, Space Imaging is planning to launch in 2004 its second satellite that will take images with half-meter resolution.[16]

The French SPOT (*System Probatoir d'Observation de la Terre*) satellite has a 10 m resolution. The European Space Agency (ESA) has also launched two Earth Remote Sensing (ERS1 and 2) satellites carrying a SAR. Russia has also been marketing its remote sensing products. At present the best quality data are obtained from the Russian sensor KVR1000 on board some of the Cosmos satellites which have photographic resolution of about 2 m (or an equivalent of about 1 m pixel size). This is considerably better than that acquired from either the French or the Indian satellites.

Historically, remote sensing was exclusively developed and used for military purposes prior to the launch of the first civilian the American LANDSAT-1 in 1972. It has been estimated that at least 75 per cent of all satellites are launched for military purposes, mainly to increase the effectiveness of terrestrial forces by utilising advanced photographic, electronic and ocean surveillance satellites employed to acquire information on military targets. The early warning, meteorological and highly accurate navigation systems together with the ability to communicate via satellites providing rapid, efficient and reliable capabilities have enhanced the sophisticated modern weapons systems. Such satellite capabilities have been employed in actual wars, e.g. in the Persian Gulf area and Yugoslavia.[17] The most significant impact in the military field has been the application of reconnaissance technology to verification of compliance with the terms of arms control treaties and confidence building measures. Only the US and Russia operate early warning spacecraft. The Russian satellites use the Molniya orbits, in which a satellite takes about 12 hours to go round the Earth once. In contrast, the US early warning spacecraft are put into the geostationary orbit. The new generation of the US photographic reconnaissance satellites are capable of resolution between 0.10 m and 0.15 m. France has also developed a reconnaissance satellite called HELIOS with a resolution of about 1 m.[18] Germany's interest in photoreconnaissance satellites was revived in April 1989 as Chancellor Helmut Kohl said that: 'European observation satellites could enable us, in the future, to monitor compliance with arms control agreements using our own resources.'[19]

Since the end of Cold War, military remote sensing technology and techniques are being increasingly applied for civilian applications. Consequently, the capabilities of civil remote sensing satellites are increasing to such an extent that they could now be applied to military tasks to a large extent. Besides better resolution of modern systems on board satellite, another significant improvement has been the ability to point the camera sideways. For example, the French SPOT satellite can tilt its optics 30 degrees on either side of its ground track to observe any site within a 950 km swath. This reduces the revisit time of the spacecraft to 2.5 days compared to 16 days. In this way an object could also be viewed from different angles enabling the acquisition of stereoscopic images and, thus, facilitating interpretations. Other recent developments in the remote sensing field include (a) advanced commercial data interpretation techniques and fast distribution channels,[20] and (b) better and long-lasting cameras and sensors.[21] The US military satellites have the capability to provide remote sensing imagery on a very short notice, but such data were not available to the public for civilian applications.[22] Recently, the Canadian and European experts developed a new system to prove that 'commercially available remote sensing and communication satellites can be used together in a challenging, real-world application' like fighting forest fires with a response time as little as 10 to 15 minutes.[23]

There are numerous applications of satellite imagery both for civilian and military purposes. Civilian uses could include: meteorology and weather forecasting, crop monitoring, pollution monitoring and environmental protection, cartography and land use, marine and Earth resources discovery and management, natural disaster assistance, news gathering etc. Military applications of satellite imagery include: reconnaissance, missile launch detection, arms control treaty verification, strategic and tactical planning etc. Increased capabilities of civilian remote sensing satellites and readily availability from commercial sources of satellite imagery are fast developing new applications and a huge worldwide market. However, these developments have started giving rise to security concerns as well. It has rightly been pointed out by Colleen Hanley that:

> As the commercial availability of detailed, unclassified imagery increased, so did the concern that commercially available imagery would be used for non-sanctioned military or terrorist activities. High-spatial resolution imagery can reveal the precise location of roads, railways, airport layouts, military installations, and other structures. It can be used to gather intelligence, assist in battlefield mapping, or, in some cases, used in conjunction with cruise missile technology for precise weapons delivery.[24]

In view of the increasing security concerns, various countries have started changing their traditionally held regulatory policies on the acquisition and distribution of the remote sensing satellite imagery. This chapter, discusses the relevant issues of international law with respect to the following three aspects:

1   Right to acquire remote sensing imagery: right to launch remote sensing satellites;
2   Right to disseminate remote sensing imagery (without the prior consent of the sensed State);
3   Right to seek remote sensing satellite imagery (from the sensing State).

In addition, the chapter will discuss and examine newly adopted regulations and policies to determine whether or not they are consistent with the applicable principles of international law.

International Law

Right to acquire remote sensing imagery: Right to launch remote sensing satellites

Even before the launch of Earth's first artificial satellite on October 4, 1957, legal scholars were advocating that it would not be logical and desirable to extend a State's sovereignty beyond the air space above its territory. Moreover, after the launch of first satellites both by the Soviet Union and the US, no State protested the passage of these satellites over its territory. Such a failure to protest was considered to be a 'tacit or implied consent or agreement' among States to allow the free passage of satellites over their territories. This 'consent or agreement' was given a formal recognition in the United Nations General Assembly (UNGA) Resolution No. 1721 XVI of 1961 and also Resolution No. 1962 XVII of 1963. These Resolutions are viewed as having enunciated legally binding principles (including the freedom of outer space principle) as they have been incorporated in toto in the 1967 Outer Space Treaty.[25] Article I paragraph 2 of the Treaty clearly specifies that: 'Outer space, including the Moon and other celestial bodies, shall be free for exploration and use by all States without discrimination of any kind, on a basis of equality and in accordance with international law.'

Although the terms 'exploration' and 'use' are not defined in the Outer Space Treaty, they are generally understood to include exploitation of outer space for all scientific, military and commercial purposes. The phrase 'all States' does not mean that only 'States' are allowed to explore and use outer space. This freedom extends to States, their private natural or legal persons under their authority and supervision, and to the international organisations of which they are members.[26] However, the freedom of use of outer space is not absolute, but rather an attribute of State sovereignty which may be referred to as freedom of action.[27] Since this sovereignty is not outside or above the law, freedom of action can thus be exercised only within the limitations prescribed and to the extent allowed by law.[28] As noted earlier, the Outer Space Treaty entitles all States to freedom of action, but such freedom is allowed to be exercised only 'without discrimination of any kind', 'on a basis of equality', and 'in accordance with international law'. The phrase 'without discrimination of any kind', read in conjunction with the Preamble and other provisions of the Outer Space Treaty, implies that if certain States are able, only at a later stage, to make use of outer space, their freedom shall not be circumscribed by those States that have already placed their satellites in orbits around the Earth. The phrase 'on the basis of equality' refers to the equal rights of all States to explore and use outer space. The term 'equality' must be understood to mean de jure equality or 'sovereign equality' as recognised in Article 2(1) of the Charter of the United Nations.[29] Since absolute freedom of action may lead to chaos, emphasis on the equality of States serves to guarantee the protection of the rights of all States. Space activities must be carried out 'in accordance with international law, including the Charter of the United Nations'. One of the most important rules of international law that applies to the use of outer space is that States must exercise their rights in such a way as not to abuse their rights[30] and not to adversely interfere in the enjoyment of similar rights by other States.[31] In other words, the right of freedom of use of outer space by States is limited by analogous rights of other States.

It is generally considered that the legal principle of freedom of exploration and use of outer space has become a part of customary international law (in fact *jus cogens*[32]) that is binding upon all States, whether or not they are Parties to the Outer Space Treaty.[33] Irrespective of the challenge posed by the so-called Bogota Declaration,[34] the universal validity of the freedom of exploration and use of outer space re-mains unaffected.[35]

It is pertinent to note here that remote sensing by aircraft has been carried out before the advent of satellites. Such activity has always been governed by the principles of State sovereignty over the airspace above a State's territory as recognised under international law.[36] Remote sensing by satellite, on the other hand, is a space activity carried out under the legal regime of freedom of use of outer space. Therefore, the use of satellites for remote sensing has not been seriously questioned because a satellite, not being an aircraft,[37] would not be subject to the legal regime of State sovereignty. Temporary passages of satellites through air space of States while 'going to' or 'coming from' outer space have also been accepted by States without any significant protest.[38]

An obvious conclusion drawn from the above discussion is that every State is equally entitled to launch remote sensing satellites to acquire all sorts of imagery without discrimination of any kind. Each State is prohibited to abuse its rights and is obliged to respect the corresponding rights and interests of other States. Therefore, each State is entitled to launch remote sensing satellites for acquiring imagery for scientific, military and commercial purposes without any kind of prior authorisation or consent from the sensed State(s). Since the provisions of the Outer Space Treaty provide general legal regime for the exploration and use of outer space, the United Nations General Assembly's Committee on Peaceful Uses of Outer Space (COPUOS) has been attempting to adopt a specific legal regime to govern the acquisition and distribution of satellite imagery. Since the freedom of use of satellites for acquiring remote sensing data imagery generally recognised, the main focus of the debates in the COPUOS has been on the distribution of remote sensing imagery acquired with the use of satellite(s).[39]

Right to disseminate remote sensing imagery (without the prior consent of the sensed state)

The legality of dissemination of the satellite imagery has been the subject of controversy in the COPUOS for over two decades. There essentially were two opposing views: one stressed sovereignty in the form of freedom of action of the sensing State and the other pleaded sovereignty over natural resources of the sensed State. The first view was presented by the States (i.e. the US and some of the Western countries) that advocated the unrestricted use of satellites for remote sensing and freedom of distribution of satellite imagery. The second view, advanced mainly by the Socialist and developing countries, stressed that the reception, processing and distribution of the imagery acquired with satellites are essentially earth-based activities and thus must be governed by State sovereignty, especially the universally recognised principle[40] of permanent sovereignty over natural resources within a State's territorial jurisdiction.[41] They advocated the need of prior consent of the sensed State for distribution of satellite imagery to third State(s). This view is well expressed in the following position, which was jointly propagated by the Soviet Union and France:

> A State which obtains information concerning the natural resources of another State as a result of remote sensing activities shall not be entitled to make it public without the clearly expressed consent of the State to which the natural resources belong or to use it in any other manner to the detriment of such State. Documentation resulting from remote sensing activities may not be communicated to third parties, whether Governments, international organisations or private persons, without the consent of the State whose territory is affected.[42]

This view was not shared by other delegations to the COPUOS. However, after lengthy discussions in the COPUOS, the UN General Assembly, on the recommendation of the COPUOS in 1986, finally adopted unanimously a Resolution containing the Principles Relating to Remote Sensing of the Earth from Outer Space.[43] Principle IV of the Resolution recognises the interests of the sensed State(s) as it provides that remote sensing activities,[44]

> shall be conducted on the basis of respect for the principle of full and permanent sovereignty of all States and peoples over their own wealth and natural resources, with due regard to the rights and interests, in accordance with international law, of other States and entities under their jurisdiction. Such activities shall not be conducted in a manner detrimental to the legitimate rights and interests of the sensed State.

However, it is nowhere mentioned in the Resolution that the sensing State should seek the consent or authorisation of the sensed State prior to the distribution of the imagery acquired with the use of a satellite. As noted earlier, the principle of full and permanent sovereignty of all States over their natural resources is a principle of customary international law. However, the information about these resources acquired by remote sensing satellite becomes the property of the sensing State, which remains free to use or disseminate this information. Moreover, it should be kept in mind that the launching State (i.e. State of Registration) retains jurisdiction, control and ownership over its satellites launched into outer space[45] and consequently over the benefits accrued, including imagery acquired with the use of satellite(s). In other words, the right of control over and ownership of satellite imagery are based on the principle of State sovereignty,[46] though within the parameters of international law. Thus, a State, in its relations with others, is authorised to both positive and negative rights over its property (including property belonging to its nationals); i.e. a State can use or dispose of its property as well as not to use or not to distribute to others. It is well known that only a State is the best judge, within the parameters set by international law, of its actions and thus it may decide not to disseminate all or certain types of satellite imagery to others. In this regard, the latest regulatory policy initiatives of the US and other countries are enlightening and relevant.

In 1997, on the request of Israel, the US has decided, by adopting a law, for not allowing any American satellite operator to collect or distribute a certain type of satellite imagery of Israel's territory.[47] This prohibition applies to such imagery, which is no more detailed or precise than the satellite imagery of Israel which is routinely available from commercial sources. The US has also decided not to declassify or otherwise release satellite imagery with respect to Israel unless the satellite imagery of Israel is no more detailed or precise than what is routinely available from commercial sources. It is important to note that similar prohibitions on the collection and distribution of satellite imagery of any other country or geographical area can be imposed by the President of the US. Though the phrases like 'no more detailed or precise' and 'routinely available from commercial sources' are ambiguous and could create problems in the future, yet from the international law perspective it is important to note that this American decision demonstrates two points: Firstly, the sensing State controls the collection and distribution of satellite imagery and secondly, the sensing State has the right to distribute as well as not to distribute satellite imagery with or without the agreement with the sensed State(s), but subject to its obligations under international law.

In order to further expand and implement the above-mentioned prohibitions, the National Oceanic and Atmospheric Administration (NOAA) of the US Department of Commerce, has issued new Interim Final Regulations relating to the 'Licensing of Private Land Remote Sensing Space Systems'.[48] These Regulations have been issued on 31 July 2000 under the Land Remote Sensing Policy Act of 1992,[49] as amended by the 1998 Commercial Space Act[50] and the Presidential Policy announced March 10, 1994.[51] The Regulations provide for require-ments for the licensing, monitoring and compliance of operators of private Earth remote sensing satellite systems. They also include provisions that are considered necessary for the promotion of the collection and availability of satellite imagery, while preserving US national security interests, foreign policy and international obligations.

Under Section 960.4 of these Regulations, a license is required by a person subject to the jurisdiction or control of the United States who operates or proposes to operate a private remote sensing satellite system, either directly or through an affiliate or subsidiary. The phrase 'person subject to the jurisdiction or control of the United States' has been defined very broadly and can include foreign entities that, for example, use a US launch vehicle and/or platform; operate a spacecraft command and/or data acquisition or ground remote station in the United States; and process the data at and/or market it from facilities within the United States.[52] Each licensee is required to comply with the Land Remote Sensing Policy Act of 1992, these Regulations and the conditions of his license. These conditions would include that:

a) The licensee shall maintain operational control from a location within the United States at all times, including the ability to override all commands issued by any operations centers or stations. (the so-called shutter control right of the US government).

b) The licensee could be required by the US Secretary of Commerce to limit data collection and/or distribution as determined to be necessary to meet significant national security or significant foreign policy concerns, or international obligations of the United States.[53]

The terms 'significant national security' and 'significant foreign policy concerns' are nowhere defined in the Regulations and thus can be used arbitrarily, depending upon the political convenience of the American Administration in power at a given time. It is not difficult to see that because of these Regulations, the US policy and law, in practice, will have an extensive extraterritorial application with respect to the collection and/or distribution of satellite imagery by not only American satellites but also by non-American systems like, the Canadian RADARSAT system.[54] (As discussed in Chapter 15 in this volume.)

In fact, Canada has already declared to follow the American approach in developing national controls on the collection and distribution of satellite imagery. On 9th June 1999, the Canadian Ministers for Defence and Foreign Affairs jointly issued a policy statement according to which Canada will develop new legislation to control commercial remote sensing satellites.[55] The new law will enable the processing, analysis, exploitation and distribution of data collected by high-performance satellites but subject to the Canadian national security and foreign affairs interests.[56]

India is trying to control the distribution of satellite imagery but to its own nationals. Under a July 2000 agreement between the Government of India and Space Imaging company of the US, 'sensitive Indian installations such as military bases and airfields will be blotted out of Ikonos images before they are distributed' in India.[57] The usefulness and effectiveness of this approach are questionable.[58] However, this example provides further evidence of State practice to control the distribution of satellite imagery at least about its own territory and to its own nations. India's control practice, undoubtedly, is quite limited as compared to that of the US.

Meteorological data has always been considered to be a public good to be used to benefit all. This was one of the main reasons that even the US did not privatise meteorological satellites when it opened the Earth resources remote sensing satellites for private operation. Meteorological data has always been exchanged freely on a nondiscriminatory basis and without any fee. However, the World Meteorological Organisation (WMO) at its 12th Congress in 1995, for the first time in its history, adopted a Resolution that imposed a restriction, though limited, on the exchange of meteorological data among the member States of the WMO.[59] The Resolution includes a provision that allows member States to place conditions on the re-export of meteorological data for commercial purposes. It has been rightly observed that the Resolution 'has hampered the free flow of meteorological data for weather services world-wide for the largest operational application of remote sensing.'[60]

The European Organisation for the Exploration of Meteorological Satellites (EUMETSAT), an intergovernmental European organisation, has been established with the primary objective of acquiring, maintaining and exploiting operational meteorological satellites. EUMETSAT retains 'world-wide exclusive ownership of all data' produced by its satellites. Since 1994, EUMETSAT has been encrypting its satellite data with the intention of restricting the availability of the data only to those who have been specifically authorised. Thus its data distribution practice has become more restrictive.

The 1998 Agreement between EUMETSAT and NOAA provides for guiding principles for the dissemination of satellite meteorological data from the merged US

and European satellite systems.[61] Under these guiding principles a certain type of
satellite data could be denied to an enemy country during crisis or war. The phrase
'crisis or war' includes 'a peacemaking or peacekeeping operation involving US and
Allied personnel and resources.'[62]

A brief discussion in this section shows that (a) subject to applicable principles
of international law, each State is entitled to distribute or not to distribute all or
certain type of satellite imagery to others without the consent of the sensed State(s),
(b) the distribution or denial of satellite imagery is essentially determined by
national laws and policies of the sensing State(s), and (c) an increasing number of
States have started adopting their laws and policies to restrict the distribution of
satellite imagery while maintaining their right to acquire such imagery without the
consent of the sensed State(s).

Right to seek remote sensing satellite imagery (from the sensing state)

A State cannot be considered legally entitled to a right to seek from the sensing State
satellite imagery of a third country in view of the right of the sensing State, as
discussed above, to deny distribution of such imagery. However a question arises:
does the sensed State have a right under international law to seek or demand from
the sensing State the satellite imagery of its own territory? In this regard, one must
discuss Principle XII of the 1986 UN Principles on Remote Sensing, which provides
that:

> As soon as the primary data and the processed data concerning the territory under its
> jurisdiction are produced, the sensed State shall have access to them on a non-
> discriminatory basis and on reasonable cost terms. The sensed State shall also have access
> to the available analysed information concerning the territory under its jurisdiction in the
> possession of any State participating in remote sensing activities on the same basis and
> terms, taking particularly into account the needs and interests of the developing countries.

Does this Principle on non-discriminatory access (.i.e. open skies) entitle the sensed
State to a right to demand satellite imagery about its territory? An answer to this
question depends upon the legal status of the 1986 UN Resolution on Principles on
Remote Sensing. However, the legal status of the Resolution still remains somewhat
controversial as there are two schools of thought on the issue: one strongly believes
that the Resolution has become part of customary international law, thus binding all
States;[63] and the second acknowledges its value as merely a recommendation,
without any legal obligations.[64] Even if one accepts that this Resolution is not part
of customary international law, one must not ignore the fact that this Resolution,
particularly its Principle on nondiscriminatory access, has often been cited by
various nations and their entities as an authoritative principle applicable to their
satellite imagery distribution policies.[65] Of particular interest here is the provision
in the currently applicable US Land Remote Sensing Policy Act of 1992, which
expresses the American position on the issue as it obliges each private remote
sensing satellite operator to 'make available to the government of any country
(including the United States) unenhanced data collected by the system concerning
the territory under the jurisdiction of such government as soon as such data are
available and on reasonable terms and conditions'.[66] Thus the US legislation

appears to maintain its consistency with the 1986 UN Resolution, except that it adds conditions to such non-discriminatory access, as discussed below.

Principle XII of the 1986 UN Resolution under its mandatory wording (e.g. 'shall have access') clearly recognises the legal right of the sensed State to seek from the sensing State satellite imagery of its own territory. This Resolution, as noted earlier, has been the result of lengthy discussions and compromises between the member States of the COPUOS and seems to have achieved a good compromise as it was finally adopted unanimously.[67] While the Resolution has accepted the position of the Western States by recognising the right of the sensing State to acquire satellite imagery without the consent of the sensed State, it has also incorporated the position taken by the Socialist and developing countries as it recognises their interests in having non-discriminatory access to satellite imagery of their respective territories. It is therefore expected of the sensing State(s) to positively respond to the requests by the sensed States for satellite imagery of their respective territories.[68] A denial of such a request would likely be considered contrary to the provisions of the 1986 Resolution, particularly of its Principle XII. It must however be recognised that this right of the sensed State may be limited in scope because of the following reasons:

1   The UN Principles apply only to satellite imagery acquired for 'the purpose of improving natural resources management, land use and the protection of the environment'. This does not include imagery for meteorological and military purposes.
2   The sensed State could have access 'on a non-discriminatory basis and on reasonable cost terms'. This phrase is not defined and is open to several inconsistent interpretations, which could possibly make it an ineffective right.
3   As noted above, the sensing State (or its relevant entity) maintains ownership over imagery acquired by its satellites and determines the distribution or denial of such imagery, though in accordance with international law.

Therefore, the practical implementation of the right to non-discriminatory access might run into some problems. A brief discussion of the applicable US law gives us a sample of such problems. The US data policy for remote sensing satellite systems has been specified in Section 960.12 of the 2000 Regulations on Licensing of Private Land Remote Sensing Space Systems. It *inter alia* provides that:

1   If the US government has financially supported a satellite system, the licensee will be obligated that 'all of the unenhanced data from the system be made available on a non-discriminatory basis except on the basis of national security, foreign policy or international obligations'.
2   If a satellite system has been funded by private sources, the licensee may provide access to its unenhanced data in accordance with reasonable commercial terms and conditions, subject to the requirement of providing data to the government of any sensed state.
3   If the US Government has (either directly or indirectly) funded a licensed system, the US government reserved the right to determine, subject to national security concerns, whether wide-spread availability of remote sensing data on reasonable cost terms and conditions requires that some or all of the

unenhanced data from the system be made available on a non-discriminatory basis.

Therefore under the US law, the sensed State may have access to unenhanced data, but non-discriminatory access may be allowed only subject to the US national security concerns, foreign policy interests or international obligations. On the basis of these restrictions (exceptions), the US may deny a sensed State the satellite imagery of its territory, but such denial would be considered contrary to the 1986 UN Resolution as it does not entitle any sensing State to such exceptions. Canada is planning to adopt a data distribution policy and law similar to that of the US.[69] Other countries, thus, could also be expected to follow a similar approach in the future. This trend would certainly upset the balance of interests that was painfully achieved under the 1986 UN Resolution and the availability of satellite imagery for all purposes, including for commercial and peace-keeping missions, could depend upon pure discretion of the sensing State(s) rather than on an international principle of non-discriminatory access.

Conclusions

The observing capability of remote sensing satellites is increasing and their operation is being privatised rapidly. These developments have given rise to some serious security concerns.

International law entitles all States to freely acquire satellite imagery without the consent of the sensed States. Subject to the applicable principles of international law, a sensing State is entitled to determine the distribution or denial of satellite imagery. The 1986 UN Resolution recognises the right of the sensed State to have access, on a non-discriminatory basis, to satellite imagery of its own territory. However, contrary to the provisions of this Resolution, several States have started making such access subject to their national security concerns, foreign policy interests or international obligations.

Ironically, the United States that has always and ardently advocated the freedom of acquisition and non-discriminatory dissemination of satellite imagery (i.e. open skies policies) has started imposing the most detailed, complex and extensive national legal prohibitions on the collec-tion and distribution of such imagery. These prohibitions apply not only to the American private remote sensing satellite operators but also to almost all foreign operators and satellite imagery distributors that have any link with the US. Any unilateral application of such prohibitions universally, purely on the basis of national interests, will be contrary to the principles of the 1986 UN Resolution and will seriously impede non-discriminatory access to any satellite imagery even for peaceful commercial purposes and peace-keeping missions. Moreover, because of a close affinity between the civilian uses of remote sensing satellites and military reconnaissance, there is a strong possibility that these satellites could become the first targets for anti-satellite strikes not only during actual war or crisis but also in anticipatory attacks. Therefore, it is suggested that an international agreement be reached, at least initially amongst the satellite imagery producing States, (a) to ensure the readily and non-discriminatory availability of satellite imagery in all forms for civilian, commercial and peace-keeping purposes, and (b) to prohibit the use of any force against all remote sensing satellites (i.e. a prohibition similar to the one under Article XII (2) of the 1972 Treaty on the Limitation of Anti-Ballistic Missile Systems, which forbids interference with 'national technical means of verification' that include early warning satellites). Such agreement should be negotiated as soon as possible because an un-reasonable delay would seriously hinder the expansion of the satellite remote sensing industry, which currently struggles to become a commercially viable space activity.

Notes

1   The UN Principles Relating to Remote Sensing of the Earth from Outer Space, (General Assembly Resolution 41/65 adopted without vote on 3 December 1986) (hereinafter the UN Resolution on Remote Sensing) define the term 'remote sensing' as 'the sensing of the Earth's surface from space by making use of the properties of electromagnetic waves emitted, reflected or diffracted by the sensed objects, for the purpose of improving natural resources management, land use and the protection of the environment' (Principle I. a). The US National Oceanic and Atmospheric Administration (NOAA) defines 'remote sensing space systems' under 15 C.F.R. 960.3 (31 July 2000) as 'any device, instrument, or combination thereof, the space-borne platform upon which it is carried, and any related facilities capable of actively or passively sensing the Earth's surface, including bodies of water, from space by making use of the properties of the electromagnetic waves emitted, reflected, or diffracted by the sensed objects'.

2   Passive sensors like optical imagers measure emitted radiation at any wavelength producing high spatial resolution images and multispectral sensors, using several radio frequency bands, can produce false colour images. On the other hand, active sensors, like radars or synthetic aperture radars, using 'backscattered' radiation can measure distance, altitude or velocity and produce high-resolution images. For details, see Staelin, D.H. and Kerekes, J. 'Remote Sensing Capabilities' in Dallmeyer, D.G. and Tsipis, K. (eds), *Heaven and Earth: Civilian Uses of Near Earth Space* (Kluwer, 1997), 163, at 165.

3   Comparing satellite resolutions, John Pike indicates that '1-meter resolution imagery permits the identification of buildings, and the recognition of vehicles. 2.5-meter resolution imagery is marginally adequate for the identification of buildings, and the detection but not recognition of vehicles. 5-meter resolution imagery permits the recognition but not the identification of buildings, but not the detection of vehicles. Ten meter resolution imagery is marginally adequate for the detection of larger buildings, but not the detection of vehicles.': John Pike: http://www.fas.org/ irp/imint/resolve3.htm (date accessed: 6/11/00).

4   The terms 'primary data' and 'unenhanced data' are synonymous. The UN Resolution on Remote Sensing, *supra note* 1, defines the term 'primary data' as 'the raw data that are acquired by remote sensors borne by a space object and that are transmitted or delivered to the ground from space by telemetry in the form of electromagnetic signals, by photographic film, magnetic tape or any other means' (Principle I. b). The US, under 15 C. F. R. 960.3 (31 July 2000), defines 'unenhanced data' as 'remote sensing signals or imagery products that are unprocessed or subject only to data pre-processing. Data pre-processing may include rectification of system and sensor distortions in remote sensing data as it is received directly from the satellite; registration of such data with

respect to features of the Earth; and calibration of spectral response with respect to such data. It does not include conclusions, manipulations, or calculations derived from such data, or a combination of such data with other data. It also excludes phase history data for synthetic aperture radar systems or other space-based radar systems.'

5   'Processed data' according to the UN Resolution on Remote Sensing, *supra note* 1, means 'the products resulting from the processing of the primary data, needed to make such data usable' (Principle I. c).

6   Ibid. Principle I. d.

7   For a detailed information about numerous remote sensing satellite systems belonging to various countries, visit: http://www.fas.org/spp/guide/index.html (date accessed: 6/11/00).

8   Pugliese, L., 'Canada Plans to Triple its Military Space Spending', *Space News*, 6 November 2000, 3.

9   Ibid.

10   Jayaraman, K.S., 'Indian Imagery Business Expected to Boost Profits', and 'Antrix Sets its Sights on Commercial Satellite Market', *Space News*, 7 August 2000, 36.

11   Opall-Rome, B., 'ImageSat International Plans Initial Public Offering', *Space News*, 14 August 2000, 16.

12   Iannotta, B., 'Landsat 7 Satellite Maintains Resolution Quality', *Space News*, 7 August 2000, 34; also by the same author, 'Several Firms Promote Global Distribution of Landsat 7 Data', *Space News*, 7 August 2000, 36.

13   Bekdil, B.E. and Enginsoy, U., 'U.S. Satellite Operator Offers Imagery to Turkey', *Space News*, 11 September 2000, 4.

14   Ibid.

15   Jayaraman, K.S., 'India, U.S. Firm Agree to Sale of 1-Meter Imagery', *Space News*, 17 July 2000, 1.

16   Bekdil, B.E. and Enginsoy, U., *supra* note 13.

17   In the Gulf War, the US and allied powers, had extensively relied on space capabilities, which included (a) seven military remote sensing making 12 passes a day over the area of war, (b) civilian remote sensing satellites like SPOT and US Landsat, (c) 15–20 signal intelligence satellites, (d) 3 weather satellites, (e) 4 military communications satellites, and (f) 16 navigation satellites (GPS). According to the US Air Force Chief of Staff, Merril McPeak, 'Desert Storm was the first space war, since it was the first occasion on which the full range of modern military space assets was applied to a terrestrial conflict': Cited in Vlasic, I., 'Space Law and the Military Applications of Space Technology', in *Perspectives on International Law*, (1995). In his written Testimony Presented to the Senate Armed Services Committee Strategic Forces Subcommittee (March 22, 1999, Peterson AFB, Colorado), the US General Richard B. Myers expressed that 'the successes of DESERT FOX and, for that matter all future military operations, are directly linked to on-orbit assets that are operated by my Component Commanders. ... Space capabilities are so integral to successful operations that we will never again execute a contingency operation or war plan without the benefit of the space-based systems providing weather, warning, navigation, communication, and intelligence information': http://www.spacecom.af.mil/usspace/speech14.htm (date accessed: 10/04/01). Denise N. Shorb, 'Space Technology Enhances Allied Force Bomber Missions [in Yugoslavia]', *Air Force News*, 14 April 1999: http://www.fas.org/man/dod-101/ops/docs99/n19990414_ 990673.htm (date accessed: 10/04/01).

18   'France begins work on Helios reconnaissance satellite', *Aerospace Daily*, vol. 141, no. 34, 20 February 1987, 270. Also see, 'Ariane Sends French Spysats Into Orbit', http://www.spacedaily. com/spacecast/news/ariane-99x.html (date accessed: 6/12/99).

19   'Address by Dr Helmut Kohl', *European Space Agency Bulletin*, No. 58, May 1989, 22.

20   Recently, Eastman Kodak Co. declared that it would enter into remote sensing commercial market in order to provide, via Internet, information which it will extract from satellite imagery. Bates, J., 'Kodak Aggressively Chasing New Market in Remote Sensing', *Space News*, 28 August 2000, 26.

21   Ibid. Also, see Singer, J., 'Sensor May Lengthen Life of Missile Warning Satellites', *Space News*, 6 November 2000, 10: 'The US Air Force is developing a new type of infrared sensor that could lengthen the life of missile-warning satellites while reducing their weight and cost.'

22   Innotta, B., 'Remote-Sensing System to Help Fight Forest Fires', *Space News*, 28 August 2000, 28.

23   Ibid.

24   Hanley, C., 'Regulating Commercial Remote Sensing Satellites Over Israel: A Black Hole in the Open Skies Doctrine?', 52 *Administrative Law Review* (Winter 2000), 423, at 427. In his article on 'Moving Towards a Transparent Battlespace', General Richard B. Myers stated that 'The proliferation of near real-time, militarily-significant imagery is a major concern for us, a concern that would have to be magnified in times of crisis. The debate over distribution of commercial imagery during periods of national crisis is an issue that will take on increasing importance': *Defence Review Magazine*, (1999 Spring), http://www.spacecom.af.mil/usspace/defrev.htm (date accessed: 10/04/01).

25   The Treaty on Principles Governing the Activities of States in the Exploration and Use of Outer Space, including the Moon and Other Celestial Bodies (entered into force on 10 October 1967). Currently there are over ninety States Parties to this Treaty. (hereinafter referred to as the Outer Space Treaty).

26   Article VI, the Outer Space Treaty.

27   Adams, T.R., 'The Outer Space Treaty: An Interpretation in Light of the No-Sovereignty Provision', 9 (1) *Harvard International Law Journal*, (1968), 140, at 141.

28   Jenks, C.W. and Larson, A., (ed.), *Sovereignty within the Law* (1965), 433: the 'sovereignty of the State consists of its competence as defined and limited by international law and is not a discretionary power which overrides the law'. Similarly, Sir Gerald Fitzmaurice said that 'States are sovereign; but this does not imply for them an unlimited freedom of action', in 'The General Principles of International Law Considered from the Standpoint of the Rule of Law', 92, *Recueil des cours* (1957), at 49.

29   'International persons (States) are equal before the law when they are equally protected in the enjoyment of their rights and equally compelled to fulfil their obligations': Dickinson, E.D., *The Equality of States in International Law* (1920), 3.

30   Under international law, the concept of 'abuse of rights' provides that States are responsible for their acts 'which are not unlawful in the sense of being prohibited' but cause injury to other States. See Brownlie, I., *Principles of Public International Law*, (1998), 446–447. Also according to Lauterpacht, 'There is no legal right, however well established, which could not, in some circumstances, be refused recognition on the ground that it has been abused': cited in Brownlie, ibid, 448.

31   At its 1980 session, the International Law Commission has opined that 'a universe of law postulated that the freedom of each of its subjects should be bounded by equal respect for the freedoms of other subjects; that States engaging in an activity which might cause injurious consequences internationally should take reasonable account of the interests and wishes of other States likely to be affected': UN Doc. A/CN.4/334/Add.2, paras 52, 56 and 60 (cf. UN Doc. A/AC.105/C.2/SR.369, February 15, 1982, 4). See the decision of the International Court of Justice in Anglo-Norwegian Fisheries, United Kingdom vs. Norway (1951), International Court of Justice, *Reports of Judgements and Advisory Opinions*, 116 et seq.; also in Lachs' opinion, 'There can be no doubt that the freedom of action of States in outer space or on celestial bodies is

neither unlimited, absolute or unqualified, but is determined by the right and interest of other States. It can therefore be exercised only to the extent to which as indicated it does not conflict with those rights and interests. There should therefore be no antinomy between the freedom of some and the interest of all': Lachs, M., *The Law of Outer Space: An Experience in Contemporary Law-Making* (1972), 117.

32   According to Article 53 (Treaties conflicting with a peremptory norm of general international law (*jus cogens*)), Vienna Convention On The Law Of Treaties (signed at Vienna on 23 May 1969 and entered into force on 27 January 1980): 'A treaty is void if, at the time of its conclusion, it conflicts with a peremptory norm of general international law. For the purposes of the present Convention, a peremptory norm of general international law is a norm accepted and recognised by the international community of States as a whole as a norm from which no derogation is permitted and which can be modified only by a subsequent norm of general international law having the same character'.

33   Vlasic, I.A., 'The Growth of Space Law 1957–65: Achievements and Issues', (1965), *Yearbook of Air and Space Law*, 365, at 379–380. See also Matte, N.M., *Aerospace Law: Telecommunications Satellites* (1982), 30–31, fns. 60 to 62.

34   'Declaration of the First Meeting of Equatorial Countries', signed in Bogota, December 3, 1976, by Brazil, Colombia, Congo, Ecuador, Indonesia, Kenya, Uganda, and Zaire. The Declaration is reprinted in Jasentuliyana, N. and Lee, R.S.L. (eds), *Manual on Space Law* (1979), vol. II, 383 et seq.

35   Under Bogota Declaration, ibid., a number of equatorial States had declared their sovereignty over those portions of the geostationary orbit that are above their national territories. These claims have generally been dismissed as contrary to the established principles of international law. For a detailed discussion, see Jakhu, R.S., 'The Legal Status of the Geostationary Orbit', VII, *Annals of Air and Space Law* (1982), 333 et seq.

36   Convention on International Civil Aviation, signed on 7 December 1944, (hereinafter referred to as the Chicago Convention), Article 1 of which provides that 'The contracting States recognise that every State has complete and exclusive sovereignty over the airspace above its territory.'

37   An 'Aircraft' is a 'machine which can derive support in the atmosphere from the reaction of the air': Annex 6 to the 1944 Chicago Convention, ibid.

38   Goedhuis, D., 'The Question of Freedom of Innocent Passage of the Space Vehicle of One State Through the Space Above the Territory of Another State which is not Outer Space' (1960) 2 *Colloquium on the Law of Outer Space*, 42, at 42–43; Haley, A.G., *Space Law and Government* (1963), at 62–63; McDougal, M.S., Lasswell, H.D., Vlasic, I.A., *Law and Public Order in Space* (1963), at 203; Cooper, J.C., in Vlasic, I.A. (ed.), *Explorations in Aerospace Law: Selected Essays by John Cobb Cooper 1946–1966* (1968), at 274. However, the Council of the International Civil Aviation Organisation has been of the opinion (at ICAO Doc. C-WP/8158 of 15/1/86 as presented by the ICAO Observer to the Legal Subcommittee of the COPUOS at its 1986 session) that '(d) The right of innocent passage of spacecraft through the sovereign airspace is proposal *de lege ferenda* (i.e. a legislative proposal not reflecting the existing law); such right does not exist under the present international law of the air; an unconditional right of passage through the sovereign airspace does not exit even with respect to the civil aircraft and is specifically subject to a special authorisation with respect to State aircraft and pilot-less aircraft; (e) The operation of spacecraft in the airspace may require operational co-ordination with air navigation services to ensure the safety of air navigation.'

39   Vlasic, I.A., 'Principles Relating to Remote Sensing of the Earth from Space' in Jasentuliyana, N. and Lee, R.S.K. (eds), *Manual on Space Law* (1979) vol. I, 303, at

309: '... the principal concern of States in relation to remote sensing was not so much the lawfulness of the observation activity conducted from space, which few contested, as the question of the disposition of data gathered by remote sensing satellites'.

40 The 1962 UN General Assembly Resolution No. 1803 (XVII) containing the 'Declaration on Permanent Sovereignty over Natural Resources'.

41 This principle is considered to have become a part of *jus cogens* applicable to all States. Brownlie, I., *supra* note 30, 515.

42 UN Doc. A/AC.105/C.2/L.99 (1974).

43 See *supra* note 1.

44 The term 'remote sensing activities' as defined by Principle I (para f) of the UN Resolution on Remote Sensing means 'the operation of remote sensing space systems, primary data collection and storage stations, and activities in processing, interpreting and disseminating the processed data'.

45 Article VIII, the Outer Space Treaty.

46 State sovereignty implies the existence and the freedom of action of States, as limited by international law, in their international relations as well as with respect to their internal affairs; especially, the freedom of exclusive jurisdiction over their territory, their personal jurisdiction over their citizens and legal persons established under their jurisdiction, things present and maters happening in their jurisdiction.

47 See the National Defense Authorization Act for Fiscal Year 1997 (S. Rep. No. 104–278, 104th Cong. 2nd Sess., s. 1745 (1996), s. 1044. Authorizing appropriations For Fiscal Year 1997 For Military Activities of the Department of Defense, For Military Construction, And For Defense Activities of the Department of Energy, To Prescribe Personnel Strengths For Such Fiscal Year For The Armed Forces, And For Other Purposes:

PROHIBITION ON COLLECTION AND RELEASE OF DETAILED SATELLITE IMAGERY RELATING TO ISRAEL AND OTHER COUNTRIES AND AREAS

COLLECTION AND DISSEMINATION – No department or agency of the Federal Government may license the collection or dissemination by any non-Federal entity of satellite imagery with respect to Israel, or to any other country or geographic area designated by the President for this purpose, unless such imagery is no more detailed or precise than satellite imagery of the country or geographic area concerned that is routinely available from commercial sources.

DECLASSIFICATION AND RELEASE – No department or agency of the Federal Government may declassify or otherwise release satellite imagery with respect to Israel, or to any other country or geographic area designated by the President for this purpose, unless imagery is no more detailed or precise than satellite imagery of the country or geographic area concerned that is routinely available from commercial sources.

48 15 C.F.R. Part 960 [Docket No.: 951031259-9279-03] RIN 0648-AC64. The date for public comments on this interim final rule was extended until 30 October 2000. National Oceanic and Atmospheric Administration, 15 C.F.R. Part 960 [Docket No. 951031259-9279-03] RIN 0648-AC64. [Federal Register: September 18, 2000 (Volume 65, Number 181)]. (hereinafter referred to as the 2000 US Remote Sensing Regulations).

49 15 U.S.C. 5601 et seq.; Public Law 102–555, 106 Stat. 4163.

50 Bill H.R. 1702.

51 Entitled, 'US Policy on Foreign Access to Remote Sensing Space Capabilities' (PDD 23).

52   See Sec. 960.3 of the 2000 US Remote Sensing Regulations: 'Person means any individual (whether or not a citizen of the United States) subject to US jurisdiction; a corporation, partnership, association, or other entity organized or existing under the laws of the United States; a subsidiary (foreign or domestic) of a US parent company; an affiliate (foreign or domestic) of a US company; or any other private remote sensing space system operator having substantial connections with the United States or deriving substantial benefits from the United States that support its international remote sensing operations sufficient to assert US jurisdiction as a matter of common law'. Further more, 'beneficial owner' means 'any person who, directly or indirectly, through any contract, arrangement, understanding, relationship, or otherwise, has or shares: the right to exercise administrative control over a licensee; and the power to dispose of, or to direct the disposition of, any security interest in a license. All securities of the same class beneficially owned by a person, regardless of the form which such beneficial ownership takes, shall be aggregated in calculating the number of shares beneficially owned by such person. A person shall be deemed to be the beneficial owner of a security interest if that person has the right to acquire beneficial ownership, as defined in this definition, within sixty (60) days from acquiring that interest, including, but not limited to, any right to acquire beneficial ownership through: the exercise of any option, warrant or right; the conversion of a security; the power to revoke a trust, discretionary account, or similar arrangement; or the automatic termination of a trust, discretionary account or similar arrangement.'

53   Ibid., Sec. 960.11.

54   Bates, J., 'NOAA Lifts Cap on Foreign Investment in Satellite Imaging', *Space News*, 14 August 2000, 1, at 20: 'Radarsat-2, imaging satellite also could fall under US jurisdiction. Radarsat-2 is being built by MacDonald Dettwiler and Associates, a Canadian subsidiary of Orbital Sciences Corp. , Dulles'.

55   'Canada To Control Imaging Satellites', *News Release No. 134*, Department of Foreign Affairs and International Trade, Ottawa, June 9, 1999.

56   Ibid: 'As modern remote sensing satellites can produce imagery whose quality approaches that obtained from specialized intelligence satellites, we must ensure that the data produced by Canadian satellites cannot be used to the detriment of our national security and that of our allies'.

57   Jayaraman, K.S., 'India, U.S. Firm Agree To Sale of 1-Meter Imagery', *Space News*, 17 July 2000, 1. According to the Executive Director of Antrix (commercial arm of the ISRO), 'This is a security requirement even for the 5.8-meter resolution imagery from India's own remote sensing satellites', Ibid.

58   'India's Futile Imagery Policy', *Space News*, 24 July 2000, 22.

59   Resolution 40, World Meteorological Congress (CG XII, 12th Meeting), 'WMO Policy and Practice for the Exchange of Meteorological and Related Data and Products Including Guidelines on Relationships in Commercial Meteorological Activities' (1995).

60   Gabrynowicz, Joanne Irene, 'Expanding Global Remote Sensing Services', in *Proceedings of the Workshop on Space Law in the Twenty-First Century*, organised by the International Institute of Space Law and the UN Office for Outer Space Affairs (2000), 97, at 108.

61   Agreement Between the United States National Oceanic and Atmospheric Administration and the European Organisation for the Exploration of Meteorological Satellites on an Initial Joint Polar-Orbiting Operational satellite Systems, signed on 19 November 1998, Washington, D.C.

62   Ibid, Annex 1.

63   Gabrynowicz, Joanne Irene, *supra* note 60, at 100–104; Christol Carl, cited in Ramey, Robert A., 'Armed Conflict on the Final Frontier: The Law of War in Space' (48) *Air*

Force Law Review, (2000) at fn. 501; Gaudrat, P. and Tuinder, H.P, 'The Legal Status of Remote Sensing Data: Issues of Access and Distribution', in Lafferranderie, G & Crowther, D. (eds.) *Outlook on Space Law over the Next 30 Years* (1997), 351, at 353.

64 Bourbonnière, M. and Haeck, L., 'Canada's Remote Sensing Program and Policies', in Baker, J.C., O'Connell, K.M. and Williamson, R.A., *Commercial Observation Satellites: At the Leading Edge of Global Transparency* (RAND, 2001) 263, at 287, fn. 4.

65 Gabrynowicz, Joanne Irene, *supra* note 60, at 101, in fn. 26 cites the following legal documents that contain references to the 1986 UN Principles on Remote Sensing: The US Commercialization Act (14 U.S.C. §§ 4201–4292 (1984)), now repealed and replaced with the US Land Remote Sensing Policy Act of 1992 (5601–5642; Canadian RADARSAT Data Policy, Document no. RSCA-PR0004, Sec. 10.1 b. (Canadian Space Agency), July 13, 1994, at 11; ESA Envisat Data Policy, ESA/PB-EO (97) rev. 3, Paris (European Space Agency), 19 Feb. 98; Principles of the Provision of ERS Data to Users, ESA/PB-EO (90) 57, rev. 6 Paris, 9 May 1994 (European Space Agency, Earth Observation Programme Board), Sec. 2 General Principles, 2.1 Legal Principles, para. 2, at 2.

66 15 U.S.C. 5601 et seq. (Public Law 102-555, 106 Stat. 4163), Sec. 202 (b) 2. The provisions of this subsection are repeated in Sec. 960.11(b) 10 of the 2000 US Remote Sensing Regulations, *supra* note 48.

67 Gorove, Stephan, *Developments in Space Law: Issues and Policies*, Utrecht Studies in Air and Space Law, vol. 10 (1991), at 300: 'The long negotiations accompanying the drafting of Principles on Remote Sensing revealed strongly held political convictions and ideological beliefs frequently at loggerhead positions. It was quite a feat to bridge the seemingly irreconcilable views and come up with a text that the countries in the North and South, East and West could live with. The reason for the final success may be attributed ... to the hard work and willingness of COPUOS members to go an extra mile, resulting in a give and take ...'. Also see Gaudrat, P. & Tuinder, H.P, *supra* note 63, according to whom the Principles in the 1986 UN Resolution, 'which can now be considered as being part of customary international law, provide for a balance between the freedom of observation for the sensing states and the right of having access to these data by the observed state'.

68 It must also be noted that Principle XII recognises particular 'needs and interests of the developing countries' with respect to non-discriminatory access to satellite imagery of their respective territories. Such recognition of legitimate or special interests of the developing countries seem to provide an extra protection of their non-discriminatory access right, which must not be constrained by the sensing State(s) since international law accommodates different interests of states and often requires an element of appreciation: Brownlie, *supra* note 30, at 29.

69 The following is one of the several principles that will guide the Canadian Government in the drafting and adoption of the law to regulate the distribution of satellite imagery by the Canadian remote sensing satellite operator, 'The Government of Canada reserves the right to ... make available to the government of any country, including Canada, data acquired by its system concerning the territory under the jurisdiction of such a government (sensed state) in accordance with the United Nations A/RES/41/65 Principles Relating to Remote Sensing of the Earth from Space. However, such data shall not be provided to the sensed state if its uncontrolled release is determined to be detrimental to Canada's national security and foreign affairs interests': 'Canada To Control Imaging Satellites', *supra* note 55.

Chapter 2

Availability and Potential Use of Low Spatial Resolution Satellite Imagery for Peacekeeping and Disaster Management

Mryka Hall-Beyer

Introduction

The biological eye functions so that it can vary how much detail is perceived, depending on the distance to the object in focus. If human interest is piqued by what it sees, the eye is brought closer and adjusts its focus to 'zoom in' on the object. Much of optical technology is geared to extending the eye's capacity to zoom in and out, to satisfy the need for various kinds of information. Satellite imagery fits within this conceptualization. The earliest LANDSAT sensors (1972) viewed the earth's surface in discrete pixels 80 m square, and this was soon augmented by the TM sensor (1984), viewing at 30 m. LANDSAT imagery approximates what the eye will see during a commercial airline flight, though with greater detail and sensitivity to a wavelength range larger than that of the eye. We want to see greater detail from space. Increasingly fine spatial[1] resolution has been sought, culminating so far in satellite imagery in the 1 to 4 m pixel size range.[2] Classified specialized images improve on this even further.[3]

Obtaining fine spatial resolution has tradeoffs. One is in the amount of spectral detail: the finest resolution imagery is panchromatic. The most obvious tradeoff is data quality. There are limitations in data storage on board, in transmission rates to ground receiving stations, in area included in a file of a size compatible with processing technology capacity, and in cataloguing, archiving and distributing data. This means that fine resolution sensors do not record the entire earth's surface continuously, but instead are directed to specific locations on request. The process is costly, both in execution and to allow companies to recoup their investment in innovative technology. In addition, a single scene is only a few kilometers wide, with larger areas requiring mosaicing and its inherent problems. Fine resolution imagery demands highly sophisticated techniques to achieve precise geometrical correction. Obtaining repeat imagery of a given area at a short time interval is not a routine matter. Despite these cautions, this kind of detailed imagery is needed in specific critical situations. Other chapters in this volume provide details on this kind of imagery and its uses.

The other need for information is the 'zoomed out' view, acquiring an overview of a piece of ground. Overviews look for temporal or spatial trends in ground cover, pinpoint areas where we would profit by more detail, and monitor rapidly changing situations such as flooding. The payoffs of this kind of imagery are nearly the reverse of the disadvantages of fine resolution. Overview imagery has a very high repeat rate. It permits a synoptic view of a large area. It is easy to geolocate. It is routinely obtained for most areas, and it is archived for most areas over long time periods. Finally, it is very low cost. Until very recently, low spatial resolution imagery had a resolution of 1 km pixels or less. It has served mainly for weather forecasting and for large-area vegetation monitoring, such as tracking the northward progression of spring.[4] However, recent launches (1999) have conjoined improved spatial resolution (250 m or 500 m pixels) with large area global coverage and free access to make this imagery worth a second look.

Applications Approach to Imagery

A useful approach to assessing the kind and information content of imagery for particular applications uses the following set of questions:

1 What is it we want to know (final information product required)?
2 What objects appear on the surface that will contribute to providing this information?
3 Are there objects on the surface that will act as surrogates for hidden objects of interest: for example, disturbed earth in certain patterns, or differential soil wetness, suggesting the presence of underground buildings or mass grave sites?
4 What are the physical and spectral characteristics of the surface objects: overall size and individual dimensions; colour, including the entire spectrum available to sensors; temporal variability; other characteristics that can be used in identification, such as association, texture, or pattern? Can these potentially be automatically detected (and what level of personnel training is required to do so)? Or do they require human judgement?
5 What are the resources brought to bear on producing the information: automation, hardware, personnel expertise, and the like?

Illustration of this approach applied to low-resolution imagery

Limiting consideration to low-resolution imagery, defined as that with a pixel size of 250 m or larger, this chapter will illustrate the decision-making process concerning peacekeeping and disaster management. This is a single case, not a complete listing. Such a listing must be supplied by field experts in the individual situation.

Information content required Overview allowing identification and situation of sites requiring more detailed imagery. Case: an overview of population displacements and camp formation/growth.

Surface objects required to do this Existence of new camps, created by forest clearing; presence of new roads.

Surrogates on the surface for subsurface object   Road traffic is not directly visible at this resolution, but large dust clouds stirred up by traffic on dirt surface roads may be visible. Nighttime heat or light readings might allow interpretation of population or activity of camps.[5]

Physical and spectral characteristics of objects   Size of camps would be much larger than individual pixel sizes, whether 250 m or 1000 m. Roads would most likely not be this wide. The visibility of sub-pixel sized objects depends on the degree of spectral contrast between the object and its surroundings. If the road surface is sufficiently distinct – for example, bare dirt surrounded by dense vegetation – the contribution of the road reflectance to the pixel in which it is situated may be sufficient to make it visible. On the other hand, a narrow dirt road in a desert area will probably not be visible on 250 m imagery.

As for spectral properties, cleared areas will be bright in most visible and near infrared bands. Man-made materials such as tents or metal roofing are most often also bright in most bands. A large agglomeration of people will in some situations have a thermal signature distinct from their background, at least at night and in cold weather. Whether this signature is sufficiently different from background to be recorded on low-resolution imagery would need investigating.

How does a non-specialist learn about spectral properties? One advantage of low spatial resolution imagery is its low cost. If an item similar to the one in question can be positively identified in a geographical area the interpreter knows well, an image can be acquired for the known area and simply examined to find out the object's spectral properties. Also, commonly known spectral 'signatures' can be referenced in many textbooks.[6] It suffices to overlay the spectral sensitivity bands of the sensor on the spectral response curves of the object to see if it will be distinguishable.

With respect to temporal variability, can we tell if a clearing or road is new, or how rapidly it has been growing? Low spatial resolution imagery is high temporal resolution. The images can be acquired daily or more often. Some caveats exist. First is the presence of clouds over the site of interest? While thin cirrus can be 'removed' from an image, the only remedy for thick cloud is active microwave (radar) imagery. This is sufficiently different in its properties to require a separate treatment, and it is not freely available.[7] Clouds lower the effective temporal resolution, particularly in tropical areas or areas subject to cloud-related disasters such as flooding or volcanic eruption. Second, vegetation phenology over the site must be thoroughly understood to eliminate false positives during change detection. Third, any automated change detection procedure requires consistent radiometric, geometric and atmospheric treatment so that the same information is being conveyed in successive images. Radiometric treatment is generally not a problem for images closely spaced in time, as the sensors only change properties very slowly. Geometric treatment (co-referencing) may be a problem in some images, but is increasingly automated. It is less of a problem in low spatial resolution images where high geometric precision is less possible anyway. This leaves varying atmospheres on successive images. This topic is too complex to treat here.[8] A simple solution is to require a high degree of change to trigger an interpretive response.

Temporal variability also includes the question of long-term monitoring. One km imagery is archived and freely available starting in 1978. Archived moderate resolution imagery such as LANDSAT, if it is more than 10 years old (1972–1991) may be available for minimal cost for some areas. No continuous global coverage is available, however. This imagery also has a much lower repeat time, which combined with cloudiness may make appropriate images unavailable.

Other characteristics of an object, such as association of roads with clearings, or a regular rectilinear pattern (or lack thereof) might be clues. Some of these can be flagged by automated digital image processing techniques, or queried within a Geographic Information System[9] if sophisticated processing software is available. They can also be used to set up keys for human interpreters.

More information will be given below about resource requirements. However, the primary requirement is bandwidth and communications facilities to acquire the imagery. Numerous image viewing software products are available as freeware.[10] If this is the extent of software, interpretation would depend on the trained operator. Low-cost systems allow a fair degree of automated analysis.[11] Central organizations with site licences for more complex software can allow field teams to do further analysis, or alternatively a central processing facility could transfer interpreted products to field teams.

This analysis indicates that the problem taken as an example can use low-resolution imagery effectively.

Low Spatial Resolution Imagery Before 2000

Before 2000, most low-resolution imagery came from the various NOAA programs.

Weather imagery is most familiar to most people and comes from the geostationary satellites that view a sixth or more of the earth's surface and continuously update the information. This material is ubiquitous from weather organizations worldwide. The panchromatic visible band, with 1000 m spatial resolution, may be useful for general surveys although its spectral resolution makes it less than choice data. Products are available back to 1979, but only the most recent 3 week period is available online.[12] Nonetheless, knowledge of cloud cover at particular times and places can be very useful in streamlining acquisition procedures for other imagery by limiting the time periods searched. The AVHRR instruments on a series of NOAA polar orbiting satellites have been operational since 1978. These have a resolution at nadir of 1.1 km. Progressive distortion occurs toward the edges of the image due to the large differences in angle (up to 55° off the vertical). Designed partly for vegetation monitoring worldwide, it carries both a red and nir reflectance channel besides several thermal bands. A single image has a swath 2350 km wide, and images are obtained many times a day for a given location. The best images of a given area occur when it is near nadir (directly below the satellite), and these are obtained twice a day. Numerous products have been produced from AVHRR imagery, including time period composites (to eliminate clouds), and geometrically corrected and atmospherically corrected images. For periods before 2000, these are the most useful low-resolution images available.[13]

The EOS AM-I System and Follow-on

An integrated system of earth observation was initiated aboard the TERRA (EOS AM-1) spacecraft launched in December 1999. This satellite platform contains five instruments that target various science issues. Many of these are related to global change investigations. All of the data obtained, including derived scientific products, is made available free of charge over the web. As of June 2001, many of these products are still experimental, but extensive validation has made at least the basic imagery fully operational.

The instruments most useful for the kind of ground monitoring required for peacekeeping and disaster monitoring are primarily MODIS, and to some extent ASTER. ASTER is not low resolution (the pixel footprint ranges from 15 m to 90 m depending on the band). However, its science mission does not include continuous coverage of the earth's surface, nor extensive archiving. Once fully operational, however, it will be worth searching for an area to see if anything is available.[14]

MODIS includes 250 m resolution bands in the red and nir spectral regions, useful for vegetation and soil. Five 500 m bands track other visible, nir and mir spectral regions, and 1000 m bands exist in several thermal wavelengths, for a total of 36 bands.[15] This combination is ideal for viewing surface vegetation changes, and provides sufficient spectral resolution to differentiate by colour most objects that the eye can see. The blue and green bands also provide information about water clarity and quality (plankton blooms are quite visible) that might affect the viability of a water supply for large encampments. These have not been present on low-resolution imagery in the past.

Thermal bands may be used to monitor large fires during the daytime. Their utility to track thermal islands during night acquisition has not yet been proven. MODIS does, however, acquire and transmit nighttime images. To date, these are being used experimentally to track population data and link this to CO_2 emissions in areas where ground-gathered data is not readily available.[16] It is possible that these images could be used for similar evaluations of population movements once the technique is validated. It relies primarily on the various thermal bands, which have only 1000 m resolution.

MODIS presently acquires an image of each ground position once a day, in the morning (hence EOS AM-1). Follow-on launches will provide afternoon imagery as well.

Direct reception

Data from the EOS AM-1 system can be directly downloaded from the satellite to properly equipped stations. Only data actively acquired while the satellite is above the horizon, not data from elsewhere on earth will be available in this mode. Downloading now requires a 3 m or larger antenna, and a technically difficult installation, although it can be mounted on mobile vehicles. Software to convert data to usable products is available free of charge, but requires a highly skilled technician to operate. Direct download is still experimental, and is being done by about 10 stations worldwide. However, experience with similar direct downloads of

AVHRR and data indicates a good possibility for future products permitting lower cost and greater ease of operation after the prototype period is past.[17]

Practicalities: accessing imagery

Two search engines control access to free low-resolution data.[18] Both provide search capacity for guest or registered users. Registration is free and apparently unrestricted, and allows users to save and recall searches, remember data delivery preferences, and order data without filling out a form each time. The search engines, particularly at the EROS address, are very complex due to the large amount of data archived.

Search criteria include a sensor (e.g., MODIS), data product (e.g., 250 m reflectance), date range, and geographical coordinates. Some products allow further narrowing of the search, for example by time of day, number of images (called 'granules') returned, or percent of cloud cover. Once search criteria are set, the actual search time varies from a few seconds (more typical of NOAA) to several minutes (more typical of EROS). This time does not depend on connection bandwidth. The results returned give much more extensive data for each image, and sometimes allow the user to view a browse image or a map showing the area covered. From the results page, the user selects the images to be put into the 'shopping cart' and checks out. There may be a choice of image media, although ftp pull (initiated by the user) is the most usual and rapid way to obtain data.

Following checkout, the user will be notified immediately (within minutes) by e-mail that the order has been received. A follow-up e-mail, usually within 15 minutes to a few hours, provides the necessary information to download the files. Since file numbering systems are complex and cryptic, it is a good idea for the user to save all image data from both the search results page and the confirming e-mail, at least until the file has been received and processed. In some image processing software, this metadata can be added to the image file itself to avoid loss.

Practicalities: using imagery

A common problem with 'free' data is that many potential users may not have the facilities to use it. This is not generally the case with low-resolution images. The EOS data, in common with LANDSAT and other NASA missions, uses a common file format called HDF. Working with the EOS mission, the NCSA has developed free software that allows both the images themselves and their accompanying data to be viewed.[19] These are either command line or JAVA based. They allow some data manipulation and conversion to other formats. Since the HDF format is so widespread, most commercial image analysis packages have routines that recognize and read the data. Nevertheless, many of these lose some detailed metadata contained in .hdf files, so the NCSA software should be used to find it and add it to the commercial software image file.

Many commercial software companies provide free software that can be used to view and do simple manipulations of imagery, although they do not include advanced processing.[20] Discussion of image processing systems commercially available is beyond the scope of this chapter.

Caveat: web jpeg files

In promoting the use of imagery for various purposes, both NOAA and NASA provide many examples of images on their websites. These do provide excellent appreciation of the images. However, these images have been chosen to illustrate particular phenomena, they are largely cloud-free, and they have been enhanced for best viewing. They are usually in jpg format for web viewing. These images can be saved. However, the jpeg format is lossy to various degrees. The enhancements applied mean that the original pixel values are not recoverable. Often metadata provided with these images is incomplete, so that the exact location, bands, and time may not be available. This can create problems. First, they show only data obtained in visible bands. Second, most of the 250 m 'resolution' jpegs provided at the MODIS image gallery[21] are combinations of bands 1, 4 and 3 (red, green and blue). Of these, only the red band is received at 250 m resolution. It is not stated how the final 250 m sample was processed, and these images may not give a proper appreciation of the detail available in the red and nir 250 m bands.

Hardware requirements

The primary limiting factor in using free low spatial resolution imagery is the availability of high speed download capacity. Images can range from a few megabytes to more than 300 megabytes for multi-band MODIS images. Where rapid download is not available in the field, it would be prudent to establish central locations where trained personnel can search, download and distribute data to the organization's field personnel as needed. Until recently, data storage capacity was a problem, but the ready availability of CD writers has greatly alleviated it.

Until about 1995, image processing on a personal computer was a tedious and frustrating occupation. Improvement in computer speed has relieved this problem. Today, image processing software can be run on ordinary personal computers and is available for all the common operating systems. Computer power, RAM and disk capacity will influence the ease with which various operations can be carried out and the maximum size of images that can be processed at one time.

Conclusion

Low spatial resolution imagery is readily available with free access. The main constraint to its use in the field or in remote areas is rapid web data connection. Processing this data is becoming ever easier. This imagery has the great advantage of providing sufficient spatial detail for many peacekeeping applications, while having very high temporal resolution needed for near real time monitoring and tracking change. It provides the broad view of an area, and can be used as reconnaissance to pinpoint areas and times where resources can be most effectively allocated to higher resolution imagery.

Notes

1	Acronyms and technical terms are defined in Appendix I. Colour illustrations have not been reproduced, but are accessible at http://www.ucalgary.ca/geog/~mhallbey.
2	See other articles in this collection. One, but not the only, source of such data is Space Imaging Inc., http://www.spaceimaging.com/
3	See other articles in this collection.
4	M.D. Schwartz. 1998. 'Green wave photography'. *Nature*, Vol. 394, pp.839–840.
5	J.P. Muller, C. Doll and C. Elvidge. 2000. 'Nighttime 36-band MODIS data for mapping global urban population, GDP and $CO2$ emissions'. http://ltpwww.gsfc.nasa.gov/ MODIS/MODIS.html. While this reference investigates all bands, including vis, nir and swir, the MODIS handbook (http://modarch.gsfc.nasa.gov/MODIS/RESULTS/DATAPROD/MOD_02.pdf) states that only tir bands are collected at night.
6	Cf. J.R. Jensen. 2000. *Remote Sensing of the Environment: An Earth Resource Perspective*. Upper Saddle River, NJ: Prentice-Hall. T.M. Lillesand and R.W. Kiefer. 2000. *Remote Sensing and Image Interpretation*. Toronto: John Wiley and Sons. J.B. Campbell. 1996. *Introduction to Remote Sensing*. New York: The Guilford Press. F.F. Sabins. 1997. *Remote Sensing: Principles and Interpretation*. New York: W.H. Freeman and Co. A spectral library containing primarily geological surfaces and human artifacts can be found at http://asterweb.jpl.nasa.gov/speclib.
7	A very simple radar tutorial is http://www.ccrs.nrcan.gc.ca/ccrs/eduref/ sradar/indexe.html. A more detailed treatment, based on Canada's RADARSAT, can be downloaded at http://www.rsi.ca/classroom/RSIUG98(499).pdf.
8	For more extensive information and case studies, see R.S. Lunetta and C.D. Elvidge. 1998. *Remote Sensing Change Detection*. Chelsea, Mi. Ann Arbor Press.
9	See references in note 6.
10	See the PCI, ESRI and ERMapper references in Appendix II. This is not intended to be an exhaustive list, and the author does not endorse any of these products.
11	For an example, see http://www.idrisi.com/04order/04order.htm.
12	At http://www.goes.noaa.gov.
13	AVHRR imagery is archived at http://www.saa.noaa.gov.
14	http://asterweb.jpl.nasa.gov.
15	MODIS band listings can be found at http://ltpwww.gsfc.nasa.gov/MODIS/ MODIS.html. Choose 'About MODIS' and then 'Technical specifications'.
16	Muller et al., 'Nighttime 36-band MODIS data.'
17	Direct download extensive documentation is available at http://rsd.gsfc.nasa.gov/eosdb.
18	NOAA handles GOES and AVHRR data: http://saa.noaa.gov for AVHRR, and http://www.goes.noaa.gov/index.html for GOES. The various EOS-AM1 images and their derived products are available from the EROS Data Gateway: http://edcimswww.cr.usgs.gov:80/~imswww/pub/imswelcome/plain.html.
19	http://hdf.ncsa.uiuc.edu.
20	See note 10.
21	http://modarch.gsfc.nasa.gov/cgibin/texis/MODIS/IMAGE_GALLERY/modimgview/ allimages.html.

Appendix 2.1 Acronyms and Glossary

ASTER: Advanced Spaceborne Thermal Emission and Reflection Radiometer. Sensor aboard TERRA. Available starting in 2000.

AVHRR: Advanced Very High Resolution Radiometer aboard NOAA's polar orbiting satellites. Returns 1.1 km data in red, near infrared and three thermal bands. Available since 1978.

DAAC: Distributed Active Archive Centers. The source of most spatial datasets, including imagery from NASA sites.

EOS AM1: Earth Observing System AM (morning) satellite. It will be joined in 2001 by EOS PM-1.

EROS: Earth Resources Observation System.

GAC: Global Area Coverage. AVHRR data resampled to 4 km resolution but covering very large areas in a reasonable file size.

HDF: Hierarchical Data Format.

HRPT: Directly downloaded AVHRR data – the most common data.

LAC: Local Area Coverage. AVHRR data recorded onboard for later download to receiving stations. Otherwise identical to HRPT.

LANDSAT: NASA series of six pioneering earth observation satellites, beginning in 1972. Earlier satellites returned 4-band MSS data at 80 m resolution, since1984 6-band TM data at 30 m resolution and thermal at 120 m resolution, and since 1999 ETM+ 6-band data at 30 m + 15 m panchromatic band and 60 m thermal band in both high-gain and low-gain format.

MODIS: Moderate-resolution Imaging Spectroradiometer. A sensor aboard TERRA. Provides 250, 500 or 1000m data in 36 bands.

NCSA: National Center for Supercomputer Applications. Nir: near or 'photographic' infrared, wavelengths longer than the edge of human sight to about 1 micrometre.

NOAA: (US) National Ocean and Atmospheric Service. Source for AVHRR images.

TERRA: See EOS AM-1.Tir: Thermal infrared: wavelengths between approximately 3 and 14 micrometres.

Chapter 3

Commercial Satellite Imagery in Peacekeeping Sensor Capabilities – Present and Near Future

Jean-Pierre Paquette

Introduction

The applications of commercial satellite imagery (CSI) have been wide-spread in non-peacekeeping domains such as mining, agriculture and forestry management, environment assessment, natural disaster damage assessment and urban planning for at least 25 years. Airborne sensors have been employed for almost a century. These applications were previously performed using a combination of the low- and medium-resolution imagery from the satellite borne systems for general information extraction and the high-resolution images from airborne sensors for detailed information.

With the successful launch of the IKONOS-2 high-resolution satellite borne sensor in September of 1999, the benefit of a high resolution sensor is now available from a commercial satellite platform. This satellite is only the first of several planned high-resolution systems to be launched within the next 4 years.

The UN has used commercial satellite imagery in several operations. These include the Gulf War in Iraq (1990–91), Rwanda Refugee Exodus Situation (1996), Bosnia and Herzegovina (1996–present day) and Kosovo (1999), agricultural and environmental assessment for Africa and emerging nations, as-well-as arms control and non-proliferation assessment, just to name a few.

Present Day Operational Sensors – Overview

There are 12 operational commercial imaging satellite systems available today. These do not include the geo-stationary weather satellites. Of these 12 commercial earth observation systems, this chapter discusses only the 10 operational systems that have the highest spatial and spectral resolution and timely acquisition benefits to UN operations. They are:

LANDSAT-5 and 7 TM	(USA)
SPOT-1, 2 and 4	(France)
RADARSAT-1 SAR	(Canada)

IRS-1C/D Pan & LISS-3 MS   (India)
KVR-1000   (Russia)
IKONOS   (USA)

Figure 3.1, Satellite Launches and Lifetimes, provides a review of the operational and near-future systems.

Additional historical imagery is available from archives collected by several previous systems including LANDSAT 1–4 (1975– program continues), SPOT (1986–program continues), JERS (1992–1998), ERS-1 (1991–2000), and KVR-1000 (1986–program continues) platforms.

The combination of these sensors provides coverage of approximately 80 percent of the globe's surface, in several regions of the electro-magnetic (EM) spectrum[1] at several different spatial and spectral resolutions. Optical sensors acquire imagery in the regions that include the visible range of blue, green and red, and selected portions of the infrared region. Synthetic Aperture Radar (SAR) collects data in the microwave region of the EM spectrum.

Common terms used to identify the sensor technical specifications within this chapter include:

1   Spatial Resolution or Ground Sample Distance (GSD). The detail discernible in an image is dependent on the spatial resolution of the sensor and refers to the size of the smallest possible feature that can be detected.

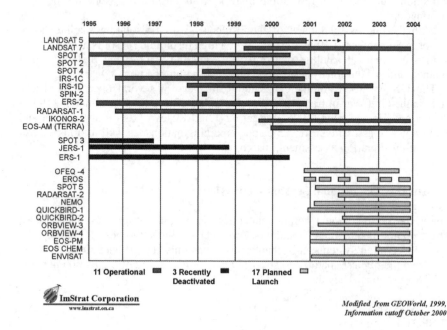

Figure 3.1   Satellite Launches and Lifetimes

2 Spectral Resolution. Spectral resolution describes the ability of a sensor to define fine wavelength intervals of the visible and infrared portions of the EM spectrum.
3 Panchromatic imagery, often referred to as grayscale imagery or black and white imagery. Many panchromatic sensors detect and collect data from the reflected light energy in the blue, green, red and near infrared (0.45μm to 0.75μm) regions of the EM spectrum. This data is visualized as a single grayscale image.
4 Multispectral Imagery. Imagery collected by sensors that detect reflected and radiated light energy in the individual bands of blue, green, red and near infrared, short wave, and thermal infrared (0.45μm to 100μm) regions of the EM spectrum.

Present Day Operational Sensors – Technical Capabilities

The following technical information is provided to assist in identifying the CSI sensors that could best be used in a support role to UN operational peacekeeping and other assistance missions.

LANDSAT series satellites

Both the US government and US commercial entities have operated the LANDSAT series of earth observation satellites since 1972. The LANDSAT series is the oldest of the CSI systems and has a collected archive of world coverage dating back to 1972. Today, two satellites are in operation. They are the LANDSAT-5 Thematic Mapper (TM)[2] and the LANDSAT-7 Enhanced Thematic Mapper Plus (ETM+)[3] systems. Both satellites are multispectral sensor systems that provide spectral coverage of the visible, and portions of the infrared, and thermal infrared regions of the electro-magnetic spectrum.[4]

These CSI sensors provide very large area coverage, nearly 32,000 sq km, at a reasonable spatial resolution (GSD) of 30 m. LANDSAT imagery collects data in the visible colour range of blue, green and red, three regions of the infrared range and one region of the thermal infrared. The differences between the LANDSAT-5 and the LANDSAT-7 systems are the improvement to each of the sensors acquisition capabilities, the increase in the GSD of the thermal sensor and the addition of a 15 m GSD panchromatic sensor. The thermal sensor on LANDSAT-5 has a GSD of 120 m and the improved thermal sensor of LANDSAT-7 has a GSD of 60 m. The addition of the 15 m panchromatic sensor allows for improving the final image product by fusing the spatial resolution of this channel with the combination of spectral resolutions of the colour bands to create a sharper, more detailed natural colour or false colour image.

The technical specifications for LANDSAT satellite borne sensors are:

Single image scene coverage:
Swath width: 185 km
Swath length: 172 km
Area Coverage: 31,820 sq km.

Spatial resolutions:
Bands 1 through 5 and band 7 is 30 m GSD.
Landsat-5, Band 6 is 120 m GSD
Landsat-7, Band 6 is 60 m GSD
Landsat-7, Band 8 is 15 m GSD

Spectral resolutions are:
Band 1 – Blue 0.45–0.52 micrometer (μm)
Band 2 – Green 0.52–0.61 μm
Band 3 – Red 0.63–0.69 μm
Band 4 – Near-IR 0.76–0.90 μm
Band 5 – Short wave IR 1.55–1.75 μm
Band 6 – Thermal IR 10.4–12.5 μm
Band 7 – Short wave IR 2.08–2.35 μm
Band 8 – Panchromatic 0.52–0.90 μm

The LANDSAT data is collected by the sensors and downloaded to one of the 13 regional ground station affiliates locate in several countries. These affiliates include: Argentina, Australia, Brazil, Canada, China, European Union, Indonesia, Japan and the USA. The LANDSAT-5 data is then sold via an exclusive license to Space Imaging LLP of Colorado, USA. The LANDSAT-7 imagery is archived and distributed by the United States Geological Survey.

The benefits of using LANDSAT imagery to support peacekeep-ing missions pertain to:

1   Large size area search and detection of terrain features;
2   Identify regions of destruction by war, fire, flood or other disaster;
3   Road and rail network identification and mapping;
4   Assessment of agricultural capacity;
5   Assessment of urban area displacement;
6   Potential tracking of very large groups of refugees;
7   Employing the large temporal archive for change detection assessment for disaster regions.

The disadvantages of the LANDSAT series satellites are:

1   There is no capability to task the sensors to collect over a specific region within a limited time period;
2   The Time over Target revisit period for either of the two LANDSAT satellites is 16 days.

RADARSAT-1 satellite

The RADARSAT-1 system was developed under the management of the Canadian Space Agency (CSA)[5] in cooperation with provincial governments and the private sector.

Unlike the passive collection optical systems listed in this chapter, RADARSAT-1 is an active emitter and collector Synthetic Aperture Radar (SAR) system. This active microwave sensor has the capability of penetrating haze and cloud cover that obscures optical sensors. The claim to fame of SAR sensors is stated as 'A Day or Night and all-weather data acquisition sensor'. RADARSAT-1 offers users a wide variety of beam selections. The satellite's SAR has the unique ability to shape and steer its beam from an incidence angle of 10 to 60 degrees, in swaths of 45 to 500 kilometers in width, with resolutions ranging from 8 to 100 m. RADARSAT-1 covers the Arctic daily and most of Canada every three days, depending on the swath selected. The archive created with RADARSAT-1 is 5 years old and continues to grow.

The technical specifications for the RADARSAT-1 satellite borne sensor are:

Beam Mode single image scene coverage:
Fine:	50 km x 50 km
Extended High:	75 km x 75 km
Standard:	100 km x 100 km
Wide:	150 km x 150 km
Extended Low:	170 km x 170 km
ScanSAR Narrow:	300 km x 300 km
ScanSAR Wide:	500 km x 500 km

Beam Mode spatial resolution:
Fine:	8 m
Extended High:	25 m
Standard:	25 m
Wide:	30 m
Extended Low:	35 m
ScanSAR Narrow:	50 m
ScanSAR Wide:	100 m

SAR Incidence Angle ranges:
Fine:	36.4°–47.8°
Extended High:	49°–59°
Standard:	20°–49°
Wide:	20°–45°
Extended Low:	10°–23°
ScanSAR Narrow:	20°–46°
ScanSAR Wide:	20°–46°

RADARSAT data are received in Canada and through an international network of receiving stations. These stations are located in Australia, China, Japan, Norway, Puerto Rico, Saudi Arabia, Singapore, South Korea, and the United Kingdom. Data can be made available to users within four hours of its acquisition. RADARSAT International (RSI), a private Canadian company, was established in 1989 to process, market and distribute RADARSAT-1 data on behalf of the CSA and Canada. RSI has a worldwide distribution network that provides regional contacts for its clients.

The benefits of using RADARSAT-1 imagery to support peace-keeping missions pertain to:

1   All weather and day/night acquisition capability;
2   Satellite system is task oriented, thus it is capable of performing rapid response actions;
3   Large to small size area search, detection, monitoring and analysis of terrain features;
4   Identify and monitor regions of destruction by war, fire, flood or other disaster;
5   Road and rail network identification and mapping;
6   Assessment of agricultural capacity;
7   Assessment of urban area displacement;
8   Potential tracking of large groups of refugees;
9   Employing the temporal archive for change detection assessment for disaster regions.

The disadvantages of the RADARSAT-1 satellite are:

1   The multiple beam modes make choosing the right product complex;
2   The Fine beam mode 8 m GSD is still insufficient to acquire detailed information extraction for some military applications.
3   SAR imagery is difficult to interpret by untrained personnel.
4   Image file sizes are very large and often difficult to manipulate.

SPOT series satellites

The SPOT[6] satellite Earth Observation System was designed by the CNES (Centre National d'Etudes Spatiales) in France, and developed with the participation of and Belgium. This system of sensors began in 1986 with the launch of SPOT 1. Follow-on sensors have kept the program going and plans are in place to continue with subsequent improved sensors. Presently the SPOT 2 and SPOT 4 satellites are operational. SPOT 1 is in a partial standby mode. This long-standing program provides a still growing archive of over 6 million images of the world's surface.

The SPOT satellites carry a sensor package that collects both panchromatic and multispectral imagery. The technical specifications for SPOT satellite borne sensors are:

Single image scene coverage:
Swath width: 60–80 km
Swath length: 60 km
Area Coverage: 3,600–4,800 sq km.

Spatial resolutions are:
Panchromatic imagery – 10 m GSD
Multispectral imagery – 20 m GSD

Spectral resolutions on SPOT 1, 2 and 3 are:
Band 1 – Green 0.5–0.59 μm
Band 2 – Red 0.61–0.68 μm
Band 3 – Near-IR 0.79–0.89 μm

SPOT 4 are:
Band 1 – Green 0.5–0.59 μm
Band 2 – Red 0.61–0.68 μm
Band 3 – Near-IR 0.79–0.89 μm
Band 4 – Short wave IR 1.58–1.75 μm

For all SPOT sensors the Panchromatic spectral resolution is 0.52–0.90 μm.

The SPOT data is collected by the sensors and downloaded to one of the 22 regional ground station affiliates locate in several countries. These affiliates include: Argentina, Australia, Brazil, Canada, China, Ecuador, France, Indonesia, Israel, Italy, Japan, Pakistan, Russia, Saudi Arabia, Singapore, South Africa, South Korea, Sweden, Taiwan, Thai-land, and the USA. The data is then sent to SPOT Image of France, and its regional distributors distribute the data worldwide to their clients via regional archives or direct from the main archive in Toulouse, France.

The benefits of using SPOT imagery to support peacekeeping missions pertain to:

1   Medium size area search, detection and analysis of terrain features;
2   Identify regions of destruction by war, fire, flood or other disaster;
3   Road and rail network identification and mapping;
4   Assessment of agricultural capacity;
5   Assessment of urban area displacement;
6   Potential tracking of large groups of refugees;
7   Using stereo pair images for very accurate mapping and charting;
8   Employing the large temporal archive for change detection assessment for disaster regions.

The disadvantage of the SPOT series satellites is:

1   The 10m GSD is insufficient to acquire detailed information extraction for some military applications.

IRS-1 C/D series satellites

The National Remote Sensing Agency (NRSA), India, designed the Indian Remote Sensing Earth Observation satellites IRS-1C and 1D[7] satellites. These satellites are owned and operated by the Government of India's Department of Space and have been in operation since 1995 and 1997 respectively.

The technical specifications for IRS-1C/D and LISS-3 satellite borne sensors are:

Single image panchromatic scene coverage:
Swath width: 70 km
Swath length: 70 km
Area Coverage: 4,900 sq km.

Single image multispectral scene coverage:
Swath width: 140 km
Swath length: 140 km
Area Coverage: 19,600 sq km.

Spatial resolutions are:
Panchromatic imagery – 5 m GSD
Multispectral imagery – 20 m GSD

Spectral resolutions on LISS-3 are:
Band 1 – Green 0.52–0.59 µm
Band 2 – Red 0.62–0.68 µm
Band 3 – Near-IR 0.77–0.86 µm
Band 4 – Short wave IR 1.55–1.70 µm

The IRS-1C/D sensors have a Panchromatic spectral resolution of 0.50 – 0.75 µm.

Collection of IRS-1C/D imagery data is through regional ground stations located in India, Germany, Taiwan, Thailand and the USA. Distribution of the imagery products is through the ANTRIX Corporation, the commercial arm of the Indian Government's Department of Space and via an exclusive International Sellers agreement with Space Imaging LLP of Colorado, USA.

The useful benefits of using IRS-1C/D imagery to support peacekeeping missions pertain to:

1   Medium size area search, detection and analysis of terrain features;
2   Identify regions of destruction by war, fire, flood or other disaster;
3   Road and rail network identification and mapping;
4   Assessment of agricultural capacity;
5   Assessment of urban area displacement;
6   Potential tracking of large groups of refugees.

The disadvantages of the IRS-1C/D series satellites are:

1   The satellites do not acquire imagery in many regions of the globe;
2   The revisit time over target is 24 days;
3   The 5m GSD is insufficient to acquire detailed information extraction for some military applications.

SPIN-2 series satellites

The Russian-designed Earth Observation SPIN-2 satellites[8] are owned and operated by the Russian Government's Ministry of Defense. The imagery archive has been in operation since 1984.

The SPIN-2 satellite has two sensors aboard. It includes the TK-350 mapping camera and the KVR-1000 high-resolution imaging camera. Both cameras are hard copy negative film format. The satellite is launched into a low earth orbit that lasts approximately 90 days. The exposed film canister is then ejected from the satellite and recovered on the ground. The film is then wet processed into negative format and digitized for distribution.

The technical specifications for the SPIN-2 satellite borne sensors are:

Single image panchromatic scene coverage for TK-350:
Swath width: 200 km
Swath length: 300 km
Area Coverage: 60,000 sq. km.

KVR-1000:
Swath width: 180 km
Swath length: 40 km
Area Coverage: 7,200 sq. km.

Spatial resolutions are:
TK-350 Panchromatic imagery – 10 m GSD
KVR-1000 Pan imagery – 2 m GSD

The SPIN-2 TK-350 and KVR-1000 sensors each have a panchromatic spectral resolution of 0.49–0.59 μm.

Collection and data distribution of SPIN-2 imagery is by agree-ment with the Russian Government's Interbranch Association SOVINFORMSPUTNIK and the two US based companies: Aerial Images and the TerraServer group.

The useful benefits of using SPIN-2 imagery to support peace-keeping missions pertain to:

1   Small size area search, detection and analysis of terrain features;
2   Identify detailed regions of destruction by war, fire, flood or other disaster;
3   Detailed road and rail network identification and mapping;
4   Detailed assessment of urban area displacement.

The disadvantages of the SPIN-2 series satellites are:

1   The satellites do not acquire imagery in many regions of the globe;
2   The revisit time over target may be months to years;
3   The very slow distribution network for the imagery;
4   The Russian government's policy does not permit distribution of all geographical regions of the archive to be releasable to most clients.

IKONOS-2 satellite

The Lockheed Martin Corporation of Colorado, USA, built the IKONOS-2 satellite system for Space Imaging LLP[9] of Colorado, USA. This totally commercially built, owned and operated satellite has been in operation since September of 1999. Space Imaging LLP was formed in 1994 as a totally commercial entity and was given license by the US Government to build and operate a high-resolution imagery satellite to acquire, collect, archive and commercially distribute these imagery products on an international basis.

The technical specifications for IKONOS-2 satellite borne sensors are:

Single image panchromatic scene coverage:
Swath width: 11 km
Swath length: 11–100 km
Area Coverage: 121–1,100 sq km.

Single image multispectral scene coverage:
Swath width: 11 km
Swath length: 11–100 km
Area Coverage: 121–1,100 sq km.

Spatial resolutions are:
Panchromatic imagery – 1 m GSD
Multispectral imagery – 4 m GSD

Spectral resolutions are:
Band 1 – Blue 0.45–0.53 μm
Band 2 – Green 0.52–0.59 μm
Band 3 – Red 0.64–0.72 μm
Band 4 – Near-IR 0.77–0.88 μm

The IKONOS-2 sensor has a Panchromatic spectral resolution is 0.45–0.90 μm.

Collection of IKONOS-2 imagery data is through exclusive regional ground stations located in United Arab Emirates, Greece, Japan, South Korea and the USA. Distribution of the imagery products is through Space Imaging LLP of Colorado, USA. The regional ground stations have an exclusive International Distributors agreement with Space Imaging for their specific regions.

Aside from image resolution, another major difference that the IKONOS system provides is the ability to task the satellite to acquire a specific area of interest on the earth's surface in a timely manner. Unlike the other optical sensors systems the IKONOS satellite is very maneuverable in its orbital path. The satellite can point obliquely in any direction, to any side or forward and backwards along the orbital path. This versatility allows for very quick acquisition and time over target revisit.

The benefits of using IKONOS-2 imagery to support peacekeeping missions pertain to:

1   Small size area search, detection, identification and analysis of terrain features;
2   Detailed identification of regions of destruction by war, fire, flood or other disaster;
3   Detailed road and rail network identification and mapping;
4   Detailed assessment of agricultural capacity;
5   Detailed assessment of urban area infrastructure;
6   Detailed assessment of urban area displacement;
7   Detailed detection and identification and assessment of military build up and deployments;
8   Damage assessment of road, rail and air transportation network infrastructure;
9   Potential tracking of large groups of refugees.

The disadvantages of the IKONOS-2 satellite are:

1 There is only one satellite available to perform the necessary tasks demanded by the worldwide commercial market.
2 Costly due to the small area coverage by the satellite in a single acquisition.

The two operational satellite systems not discussed in this chapter are the European Space Agency's ERS-2 (F) and the NASA operated EOS-AM (TERRA) satellite. Both these systems are considered as scientific research and evaluation test bed platforms. The ERS-2 imagery products are available commercially from the collected archive and are useful for creating Digital Elevation Models from the interferometric data.

Near Future Launch Sensors – Technical Capabilities

In light of the ever-expanding information collection market in remote sensing, several other high-resolution satellite sensors are planned for launch within the next 4 years. This new systems capabilities and scheduled launch are briefly described in the list below.

Canada plans another SAR system that is follow-on to the RADARSAT-1 program. RADARSAT-2 is the follow on system to the RADARSAT-1 sensor. The RADARSAT-2 SAR sensor will be an enhanced version of the RADARSAT-1 system and will have a 3 m high-resolution beam mode, as well as its present compliment of beam modes. The method of RADARSAT-2 data distribution is expected to continue through RADARSAT International and its international network of regional af-filiates.

In Europe, a consortium company called Astrium plans to launch and operate its own satellites by 2004. The 'TerraSAR' space system is based on a two-satellite constellation carrying a dual-frequency instrument in the X- and L-band. The active SAR system enables short revisit or site access times of two days or better, allowing rapid identification of changes on the Earth's surface. Resolutions of up to one meter will be offered.

The European Space Agency plans a successor to the ERS systems. The new satellite is called ENVISAT. This multi-sensor satellite will include a SAR instrument called The Advanced Synthetic Aperture Radar (ASAR), a high-resolution imaging radar instrument, which will be used for both detailed regional research and global land and ocean surveillance.

France plans a follow-on satellite to the SPOT series with SPOT 5. The SPOT-5 is planned for launch in early 2001. The SPOT-5 sensor will be an enhanced version of the previous SPOT systems and will have a 2.5–5 m panchromatic and a 10 m multispectral sensor package. The method of data distribution is expected to continue with the international network of regional affiliates.

India will continue with its IRS series systems with the launch of its IRS-P5. This is a follow-on system to the IRS-1C/D and LISS 3 sensors. It is planned for launch in early 2001. The P5 will have a 2.5 m panchromatic sensor, but is not expected to have a multispectral sensor on board. The method of data distribution has not been determined at this time.

Israel plans to launch and operate a commercial version of its indigenous spy satellite technology. The OFEQ-4 is to be launched in late 2000–early 2001. It will have a 1 m panchromatic sensor. A limited distribution of the data will likely be through a US distribution network.

A joint Israeli/USA commercial program called the West Indian Satellite System has its EROS-A The EROS Series. The EROS A is the first of this high-resolution series and planned for launch in late 2000. It will have a 1.8–2 m panchromatic sensor. The EROS-A series will have two systems in place and will be followed with the B1 to B6 Series. The EROS-B series will be launched between the years of 2001 and 2004. The method of data distribution has not been determined at this time.

In the US, there are two companies that have planned systems. EarthWatch, of Colorado, plans the QUICKBIRD 1 system for launch in late 2000. It will have a 1-metre panchromatic and a 4 m, 4 channel multi-spectral sensors aboard similar to IKONOS characteristics. QUICKBIRD 2 will launch approximately 9 months after the launch of QuickBird 1. The method of data distribution is by an international network of regional affiliates. OrbImage, of Virginia, plans to launch ORBVIEW 4 in early 2001. It will have a 1 m panchromatic and a 4 m, 4 channel multispectral sensors aboard similar to IKONOS characteristics. It will also include a 200-channel hyperspectral sensor with a spatial resolution of 8–16 m. Initially OrbImage had planned to launch ORBVIEW 3 in mid-late 2000, prior to ORBVIEW 4. OrbImage now plans to launch this system in mid-late 2001. The system will have a 1-metre panchromatic and a 4 m, 4 channel multispectral sensors aboard similar to IKONOS characteristics. The method of data distribution for both ORBVIEW systems is to be through an international network of regional affiliates.

Commercial Satellite Imagery – Basic Product Costs

Imagery data costs vary extensively between data providers. These variations in costs are generally based on: product type, size of area coverage, acquisition costs associated with international ground stations, data processing levels, and delivery response time and methods. The following list of imagery base product prices has been compiled directly from the satellite data operators or providers and is current as of 15 October 2000. These costs reflect only the base price of the base processed imagery and do not include added processing, value added interpretation or data analysis, or shipping costs. The figures given are in American dollars.

LANDSAT – 5 TM (Space Imaging, USA) $600.00.
LANDSAT – 7 ETM+ (USGS, USA) $600.00.
SPOT Image – 2 and 4 (SPOT Image, France) $3,800.00.
RADARSAT – 1 SAR (RSI, Canada) $3,000.00.
IRS – 1C/D Pan and LISS – 3 MS (Space Imaging, USA) $2,500.00.
KVR – 1000 (Sovinforumsputnik, Russia) $2,500.00.
IKONOS (Space Imaging, USA) $3,000.00.

Notes

1   Canadian Centre for Remote Sensing – Fundamentals of Remote Sensing Tutorial (http://www.ccrs.nrcan.gc.ca/ccrs/eduref/tutorial/indexe.html).
2   Space Imaging – IKONOS, IRS-1C/D, LISS-3 and Landsat-5 (www.spaceimaging.com).
3   USGS – Landsat-7 (http://landsat7.usgs.gov).
4   Canadian Centre for Remote Sensing – Fundamentals of Remote Sensing Tutorial (http://www.ccrs.nrcan.gc.ca/ccrs/eduref/tutorial/indexe.html).
5   Canadian Space Agency & RADARSAT International – RADARSAT-1 (www.space.gc.ca) and (www.rsi.ca), RADARSAT-2 (http://radarsat.mda.ca/).
6   SPOT Image – SPOT Panchromatic and SPOT XS (www.spotimage.fr).
7   Space Imaging – IKONOS, IRS-1C/D, LISS-3 and Landsat-5 (www.spaceimaging.com).
8   Sovinforumsputnik – KVR-1000 (http://www.spin-2.com/spin/default.htm).
9   Space Imaging – IKONOS, IRS-1C/D, LISS-3 and Landsat-5 (www.spaceimaging.com).

Chapter 4

Trends in Commercial Satellite Imaging with Implications for Defence and Security Applications

Alvin L. Hanks and Richard C. Gorecki

Introduction

The possibilities are immense. Imagine constellations of high resolution imaging satellites, circling the earth every ninety minutes and collecting endless streams of digital imagery. These systems are mapping the earth in ten or twenty kilometer strips, sending Gigabytes of image data to hundreds of ground stations and providing content to thousands of user nodes around the world.

Yes, the future of satellite imaging is exciting to contemplate. But, what are the practical matters of this business? How will these systems actually work? What drives the collection priorities? How is the data to be distributed? Will it be affordable? This chapter will examine practical matters such as these within the context of acquiring and using the new sources of commercial satellite imagery, and the opportunity for application to international military peacekeeping.

Satellite Imaging Systems

Traditionally, satellite imaging systems were government-initiated and supported, such as the US LandSat program, or quasi-government such as the French Spot Image program. These imagery collectors provided data in the 30 m and 10 m range of ground resolution and, in combination with their multi-spectral sensing capabilities, provided data useful primarily for wide area surveillance and scientific purposes. The positive effects of these operational systems were broadly based and important in the early stages of commercial satellite imaging. The LandSat and Spot programs stimulated early development in product standardization, the establishment of distribution systems and the creation of data exploitation techniques. All of these developments proved to be important and useful experiences to build on.

Dramatic changes in the world geopolitical structure, associated principally with the break up of the Soviet Union and the attendant decline of ideological polarization, has resulted in a reduction in international tension with respect to the threat of large scale, global conflict. This new perspective in international affairs has permitted increased commercial use of formerly restricted defense technology. The most revolutionary and visible change of this nature resulted when the US federal government approved the commercial deployment of imaging satellites capable of collecting images at 1 meter ground resolution.

Unique character of satellite imaging systems

The early history of commercial high-resolution imaging satellites has been characterized by a series of progressive steps, in contrast to the more continuous evolution of remote sensing systems and technology in general. This step-wise form of innovation has occurred because satellite imaging systems introduce several unique characteristics into remote sensing, including:

Worldwide Access Imaging satellites operate in sun synchronous, polar or near polar orbits that keep the satellites in optimal sunlight. A satellite completes an orbit approximately every 90 minutes. With an equatorial crossing time typically of around mid-day, the satellite is constantly collecting imagery and has direct access to any location on the earth's surface.

Rapid Revisit Times A single satellite typically re-visits any place on earth within two and a half days. The actual data collection opportunity depends on weather (i.e. cloud cover) in the target area. The satellite system has significant flexibility in collecting data for specific target areas because of the 'whisk broom' design. The imaging system normally operates in a stripping mode, covering a 10 to 20 kilometer continuous strip. Alternatively, it may operate in a spot mode, focusing on selected areas of a specific dimension (e.g. a 22km x 22km area). The sensor is gimbaled or the entire bus rotates so that the focal plane array may be pointed at targets within a wide field of regard (up to 35 or 40 degrees off nadir). These features, as well as the ability to vary the spatial resolution, increase the collection opportunity and the potential to revisit selected areas of interest.

Continuous Image Collection A modern satellite collection system such as Space Imaging's IKONOS system, constantly collects a strip of imagery eleven kilometers in width. The system has a high capacity, on-board data recorder that permits a 'store-and-forward' mode of operation. Image data is stored on the satellite until the system is in view of a ground station. Data is then transmitted to the ground station, clearing the on-board recorder for the next orbital pass.

Digital Data The imaging sensor on-board the satellite is a charged couple array of photo-sensitive cells. Imagery is collected, stored and transmitted all in a digital mode. This characteristic provides the advantage of preserving data resolution and fidelity. Typically the sensor collects data at 11 or 12 bits quantization, thereby retaining significant spectral detail and yielding more information for the exploitation process.

Current and planned satellite deployments

Several companies have applied for and received licenses to operate commercial imaging satellites. In September 1999, Space Imaging, a joint venture sponsored by Lockheed Martin and Raytheon, successfully launched its IKONOS satellite. It is currently collecting imagery at 0.87 m (at nadir). EarthWatch is poised to launch its

QuickBird1 in November 2000. Table 4.1 depicts the characteristics of these modern, imaging satellites.

Table 4.1   Satellite Imaging Systems

	IKONOS[1]	QuickBird 1[2]	ImageSat
Orbit Altitude:	423 Miles	372 Miles	480 km
Orbital Inclination:	98.1 degrees	66 degrees	'polar'
Orbit Frequency:	98 minutes	varies	90 min
Equator Crossing:	10:30am	varies	mid-day
Area Coverage:	11km x 11km	22km x 22km	
Spectral Coverage:	pan and MSS	same	pan
GSD:	1m and 4m	same	1.8m/0.82m
Image Quantization:	11 bits/pixel	11 bits/pixel	

Several companies have plans to launch comparable systems in 2001 including: OrbImage, a subsidiary of Orbital Sciences; EarthWatch (QuickBird 22), partly owned by Ball Aerospace; and, ImageSat International, an international consortia jointly sponsored by Israeli and US interests. This trend is irreversible, with several other governments supporting satellite programs, such as India, Turkey, Japan, China, Korea, Brazil and Thailand. Commercial ventures such as the German based RapidEye also have established programs that may soon result in operational imaging satellites.[3]

The Virtual Collection System

Consumers of spatial data, including those in the defense and security sectors, have special needs for information that can only be effectively derived from remote sensing systems. We recognize that the new generation of high resolution imaging satellites will fill a unique role in meeting these needs based upon special characteristics such as global access and rapid revisit opportunities. We also must recognize that aerial imaging systems and related technologies contribute significantly to the information needs of spatial data users. This combination of satellite imaging and aerial collection systems is highly complementary and can be said to represent a 'virtual collection system', offering a wide range of spectral, temporal and image resolution capabilities.

Complimentary airborne systems

There are significant technical trends to be noted in aerial imaging systems. In situations where the political or military environment permits operation of airborne systems, these sensors can provide extremely useful and timely information.

Several advances in this technology deserve particular attention. State-of-the-art metric quality mapping cameras are being integrated with inertial navigation and global positioning systems yielding real time geocoding of the collected imagery. This innovation reduces the time and cost of aero-triangulation and, therefore, reduces the delivery period and price of information derived from aerial imagery.

Significant advances have also been made in digital camera systems. The Z/I Imaging Digital Modular Camera, for example, will potentially offer a 4 to 8K pixel array, with a resolution of 5 cm.[4] This development will also reduce data collection and processing costs and expand the period during which imagery can be collected under lower light conditions.

High technology active sensors such as Interferometric SAR and LIDAR are being deployed at an increasing rate. These sensors have the capability of operating at night and under all weather conditions, producing precision DEM and radar derived digital orthophotos. These systems reduce the overall time to produce high-resolution topographic maps.[5]

Data archives and networks

The approach to data archiving and distribution is driven in part by the technology of the satellite. Modern systems have large capacity, onboard digital recorders that allow for continuous collection of imagery. Using this 'store and forward' technique, systems such as IKONOS and QuickBird need only two or three ground stations and a central processing facility. Space Imaging maintains ground control stations in Sweden, Oklahoma and Alaska. EarthWatch maintains ground control stations in Norway and Alaska. Both companies transfer the image data to their main facilities in Colorado for product finishing.

Lacking significant store and forward capacity, the early pioneer of commercial satellite imaging, Spot Image, required multiple, regional ground stations. Spot thus established the pattern of distributed ground stations for the collection, processing and distribution of image data and derived information. These ground stations, numbering about 20, serve as regional mapping centers, data storage archives and product generation facilities. The new satellite imaging company, ImageSat International, also follows this model. Their network of ground processing stations currently numbers about fifteen (including some overlap with the Spot Image network). These image archive and data distribution networks are integral to a company's commercial business model and have a bearing on how the customer orders and receives the image data.

The business model for each company varies somewhat, depending on its use of regional affiliates, distributors and value added re-sellers (VARs). Thus the process for ordering data and fulfillment of orders varies. It is common for the ground station, distributor or re-seller in the region where the imagery is derived to serve as the principal archive and order fulfillment agent. The primary company (e.g. Space Imaging) establishes a product catalogue, product standards, pricing and ordering policies along with policies and mechanisms for data delivery.

Data delivery commonly is achieved in the following manner:

The Internet In the age of the Internet, one would expect that much of the data would be transferred electronically. However, most image files exceed one

Gigabyte of data and to transfer these images using 56K modems is not practical.

Very Small Aperture Terminals (VSATs) These are increasingly used as wide area networks for the transfer of large amounts of data. Commercial VSAT technology, increasingly available on a subscription basis, has the theoretical capacity to transfer data at rates from 35 Megabits per second to 55 Megabits per second. Currently, capacities are on the order of 6 Megabits per second. Hughes Networks Systems is promoting a commercial system called 'SpaceWay' to be available in 2002.

Deployable Ground Receiving Stations (DGRSs) A number of government programs (5) have resulted in the development of this sophisticated technology. For example, Veridian ERIM International has developed a system called International Eagle and Raytheon has been marketing a commercial, deployable ground station for some time. The British Defense Evaluation and Research Agency has also developed a mobile ground station. Other companies such as Matra, MacDonald Dettwiler and Datron have competing technologies. One of the principal characteristics of these stations is the ability to ingest imagery from the several different commercial imaging satellites. These stations were initially built for government programs and typically cost several million dollars. However, there is a high likelihood and potential that these systems can be sold commercially for multiple applications. As a result, we expect these systems to be available for less than a million dollars.

Traditional Methods Commercial imaging companies will trans-fer data using a number of alternative methods. However the preferred and most common way to move large amounts of image data is still by means of CD-ROM via overnight courier.

Image data archives, whether data is derived from a satellite or an aerial system, represent a major asset for consumers. The commercial sector recognizes that all imagery has value, either as a source of immediate information, historical content or change detection information. As a result, companies will archive large volumes of image data in distributed production centers and satellite ground stations. These storage centers collectively represent a significant network of image data and image derived information.

The data volume generated by commercial, high resolution satellites is expected to grow from 77 Terabytes of raw imagery data in 2000 to 513 Terabytes by 2004.[6] Despite the excitement over this dramatic increase in data volume and area coverage, there will be significant challenges in archiving and managing these very significant and growing volumes of data.

Market Drivers and Trends: The Effects of Commercialization

It is important to recognize that modern commercial imaging systems are the result of commercial ventures. The stakeholders and investors in these companies are motivated to generate revenues and profits from satellite imagery and its derivative products. The world wide market for this imagery and derived products is predicted to exceed $1.5B in 2003.[7] The market demand is not only large and growing, but is diverse in terms of the types of applications. In our market research, we have identified more than 120 market segments and sub-segments that drive the demand for high-resolution satellite imagery. This imagery will have practical value in traditional markets such as environmental monitoring, local government planning, utility facilities management, forestry and mineral exploration. Important new markets are emerging in the areas of wireless telecommunications, agriculture, insurance, and disaster response.

Defense and security applications have always been a significant market for remote sensing data and related information products. How-ever, within the context of the current remote sensing industry, these ap-plications represent a relatively small segment.[8] As the overall market for high resolution imagery expands and matures, an industry structure is being created that includes (1) competition between a growing number of satellite imaging companies and (2) an evolving network of distributors and VAR's that serve the individual market segments. With this development, there is pressure toward the creation of product standards, lower prices and a common data distribution infrastructure.

Industry structure

Porter[9] has provided a classic definition of industry structure in terms of principal components such as the competitors, suppliers, buyers, intermediaries, etc. This model is a useful way to understand the roles of the participants, the relationships between the components and the dynamics within the industry.

The remote sensing industry is made up of components as illustrated in Table 4.2. As will be discussed further in the section, the industry is relatively stable and made up of older, well established companies. However, it is undergoing significant growth and change due to a number of factors. For example, the introduction of high-resolution, commercial imaging satellites is a discontinuous event, and represents a disruptive factor for the traditional aerial imaging companies. In addition, there are several areas of technical change creating dynamics within the remote sensing industry. These include the pervasive rise of the Internet, and price/performance improvements of enabling technologies such as desk-top processing, data storage and data transmission bandwidth.

With growth in markets and improved business opportunities, the industry is also seeing major capital investments. These investments permit the implementation of cost effective, advanced technologies and also result in some degree of industry consolidation. All of these factors affect the future of the remote sensing industry and the opportunity for any given market sector (e.g. military peacekeeping) to access image data and imagery derived products.

Market drivers

Market drivers are those factors that generally exist outside of a particular market or industry but have a direct or pervasive impact on it. Industry participants, especially buyers, may lack the ability to influence these factors but must be aware of their effects. Among the significant market drivers in the remote sensing industry are the following:

Evolving Changes in Enabling Technologies This factor includes primary systems such as sensors (e.g. 12K X 12K CCD arrays) and data management

Table 4.2   Key Components of the Remote Sensing Industry

MAJOR TECHNOLOGY SUPPLIERS
Cameras: Kodak, LH Systems, Z/I Imaging
Data Management Systems: H-P, IBM, Lockheed Martin, Sun
Ground Station Providers: Datron, MacDonald Dettwiler
Satellite Systems: Ball Aerospace, Lockheed Martin,
                                 Space Systems Loral, TRW
System Integrators: Core Software Technology, Orbital Sciences

IMAGERY ACQUISITION AND SERVICES COMPANIES
Regional Remote Sensing and Mapping Companies:
  3DiLLC, Aero-Metric, Analytical Surveys Inc., EarthData Inc., Triathlon
  Mapping
Satellite Imaging Companies: EarthWatch, ImageSat International, OrbImage,
  Space Imaging, Spot Image

BUYERS OF SATELLITE IMAGERY AND RELATED SERVICES
Organization   *Application*
Local Governments: environmental planning, infrastructure, regional
                                 development, taxation mapping, transportation
National Governments   national mapping, defense planning and operations
and Defense Agencies:
Petroleum and Mining: exploration and extraction
Regulated Utilities: electrical and gas distribution

technology, as well as overall trends in the performance of data systems such as processors and storage systems. For example, In-tel's next generation of processor, the PIV chip, will run at 1.4 Gigahertz. The common disk drive in desk-top computers will be 100 GB within two years.

One of the major drivers within information technology based industries is, of course, the ubiquitous nature of the Internet. It may be argued that in the remote sensing industry the simultaneous deployment of high resolution imaging satellites and the rise of the Internet as an e-commerce tool will be one of the most significant elements of change.

Image Exploitation Technology This technology represents a major factor driving our ability to derive useful information from remote sensing imagery. Several processing steps are necessary to remove geometric and spectral anomalies that naturally occur in the image collection process. These processes correct the image and result in a geocoded, ortho-rectified image that can be used for direct measurement and information extraction. Feature extraction of thematic data such as elevation, land use/land cover, roads, water/wetlands is a key process that is typically time and labor intensive. Changes in image collection systems such as the integration of GPS for geo-coding and the use of multi-spectral data for feature identification have drastically changed the imageprocessing model, resulting in improved performance and major cost reductions.

Government Regulation This is always a major external factor affecting industry structure. In the case of the remote sensing industry, government regulation generally creates opportunity through the licensing of new technology and the creation of new markets as a result of legislation. An example of the latter case is the establishment of new environmental rules that increase the demand for imagery being applied in the areas of forestry, agriculture, land development.

A current example of government regulation creating a market is the auctioning of wireless communications spectra. This has permitted commercial companies such as Sprint PCS, AT&T Wireless, etc., to own regions of wireless spectra and create a market for imagery derived in-formation for application in planning and wireless system deployments.

Government regulations establish the rules under which data may be collected and distributed. In this regard, all governments have security concerns that are manifested in either restrictions on collecting imagery over their own territory, or collecting and distributing imagery over other nations. These regulations are reflected in the commercial licensing agreements that govern use of the imagery.

Market trends

Proliferation of Data Collection Systems: Traditional remote sensing collection systems such as metric quality framing cameras have been improved and integrated with inertial measurement units and GPS, yielding real time geodetic positioning. Esoteric collectors such as LIDAR and Interferometric SAR have been added to airborne collection platforms. Satellite systems with high-resolution imaging capabilities, radar and hyper-spectral collectors add to the data source mix. All of these systems contribute to the variety of imagery derived information types available to meet user needs.

Growth in Market Demand: A greater variety of remotely sensed data and overall improvement in information content (e.g. resolution and spectral response) have resulted in more information to support more market needs. The result is an improved contribution to mission critical needs and applications, and the fueling of major growth in remote sensing data product markets. This process becomes synergistic as more demand fuels the development of new and better technology as well as the proliferation of service providers.

Product Commoditization: Increased market demand and data availability results in the emergence of product standards and the commonality of product offerings. Examples of where this is happening are in the case of digital ortho-photos and digital elevation models (DEMs). Consumers benefit from this trend through their ability to compare products, prices and competitive offerings whereas product providers benefit from standardizing on a small number of common formats.

Competitive Pricing: One of the most significant trends we see in the remote sensing industry is increased competition (between image data collectors and between value added re-sellers) leading to increased downward pressure on price. This pressure naturally benefits the consumer such that competitive pricing has become an important discriminator in the market.

Overlay of Commercialization and Defence/Security Applications

Access issues

One of the key attributes of satellite imaging is the opportunity to cover the entire earth and to re-visit areas of interest on a frequent and predictable basis. As the number of satellite collection systems increases, the total collection capacity or 'virtual collection system' will grow in its capacity to make imagery and image derived data accessible.

Past attempts to control area coverage over certain countries during peacetime have not been effective and seem less likely as systems proliferate. However, we should still expect that the national licensing rules under which the imaging companies operate will restrict distribution of data during periods of international conflict. Furthermore, host nation rules and sensitivity to the use of imagery and mapping products over their sovereign areas will continue.

As suggested previously, the remote sensing industry and, in particular, the satellite imaging sector is growing significantly. This is a result of rising demand in various market sectors, including the areas of defense and security. In the context of data access, therefore, the security (i.e. peacekeeper) customer has the opportunity to negotiate favorable treatment, as would any other major consumer.

Products and pricing

This chapter has previously discussed trends in product standardization and availability of image products as commodities, such as digital orthophotos and DEMs. These trends allow the user, including the military peacekeeping consumer, to define standard products that meet their needs and then compare products offered by different providers. The concept of product standardization for image data products also includes commonality of geodetic projections, data formats, and data transfer standards.

The military security force as a customer

A likely action by the security/peacekeeper customer when exploiting satellite imagery will be the negotiation of a pre-purchase agreement. Under this scenario, those organizations or agencies that have responsibility for the peacekeeping mission would (whether they are acting on an individual or joint basis) approach the major satellite imaging companies and establish preferred conditions under which they would purchase the satellite image products. This purchase arrangement could incorporate the following:

User Needs and Product Bundles: Let us assume that the peacekeeping application would require geo-coded, mosaiced images. These may be required in the form of digital ortho-photos or as color balanced, system corrected satellite images. Users may need temporal coverage (e.g. only during a given season) and /or a frequent revisit capability. (e.g., daily or weekly coverage over selected areas). Typically the needs for this application would include specialized products or specific types of information derived from the imagery such as roads, topography, hydrography, etc. These products and information types may be organized in bundles, designed to meet requirements for coverage over specific areas of interest.

Product Formats: The satellite imaging vendors offer standard projections and a number of common data formats. In order to expedite data ordering and delivery, peacekeeping agencies could predefine their required standards as these adhere to existing image exploitation systems.

Procedures for Receipt of Data: Satellite image data will be available out of archives or as a special collection request. Whether the imagery exists in archive or needs to be collected will affect the price of the imagery and the data delivery schedule. Each satellite imaging company will have established fees for these two conditions.

Furthermore, each company will have standard delivery and higher priced 'rush' delivery options. The definition of standard delivery may vary (e.g. from overnight to thirty days). As companies develop their pricing policies, we would expect to see delivery fee break points (e.g. next day, within three days, within seven days or less than 30 days). Obviously, the peacekeeper application has unique needs that can be specified.

Product Prices: The needs of the peacekeeper application could establish a unique product pricing model A number of variables unique to the peacekeeping application need to be considered such as multiple user licensing, product bundles, frequency of coverage, priority of new image collection and product delivery conditions. All of these can and should be pre-negotiated in order to achieve the best price for the customer.

A hypothetical case for the peacekeeping application

The following represents a hypothetical case where commercial satellite imagery is used in a peacekeeping mission. The specific scenario presented here is one of monitoring a cease-fire zone, however there are many other possibilities. We will assume that a no-fly buffer zone has been established along the border which precludes the acquisition of aerial imagery.

The purpose of presenting this case is not to elaborate on the specific application(s) of the imagery. Rather, we would like to focus on the process by which a peacekeeping requirement for imagery will be satisfied by means of accessing the virtual collection system.

The first step in this process is a request for imagery (Figure 4.1). This would likely originate within a UN monitoring agency, either at the headquarters or field level. However, it is conceivable that the request be made by one of the states being monitored.

A Field Mapping Coordinator (FMC) would carry the request forward. This individual would invariably be a representative of one of the UN monitoring agencies. In addition, this responsibility should be given to someone who has a good understanding of imagery/map applications at the field level.

The next step would be for the imagery request to be transferred to a Commercial Imagery Coordinator (CIC). This position would function outside the conflict zone and would have direct contact with the satellite imaging (acquisition) companies. At a practical level, however, this role would likely interface with a network of satellite

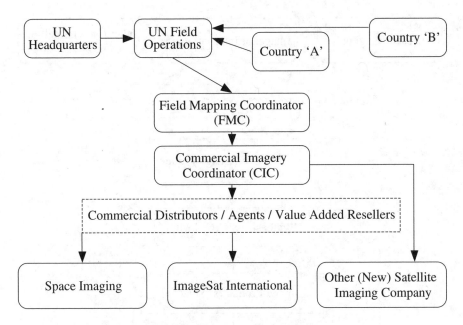

Figure 4.1   Processing of Initial Request for Imagery

imagery distributors, agents and value added resellers (collectively referred to as 'distributors'). The distributors accessed by the CIC would most likely be the regional representatives for their respective organizations.

The profile of the CIC would ideally be modeled after a military intelligence officer who is well versed in remote sensing as well as the commercial satellite imaging industry. The position would be permanent, where the individual is within the hierarchy of one of the deployed monitoring (i.e. UN) forces. He or she should be conversant with specialized Internet-based software tools to assist in an image search.

Within any given satellite imaging company or distributor (collectively referred to as an 'imagery supplier'), an Account Manager would be assigned to assist in responding to the needs of the CIC. The Account Manager would collect information on critical aspects of the image request including the intended application. Key issues that would need to be addressed include those pertaining to the area of interest, the required currency of the data, the necessary date of delivery as well as requirements for ground resolution, spectral resolution and positional accuracy. Analysis of these criteria will determine what level of image processing is needed, and whether archived imagery is suitable or new image acquisition is required.

Ultimately, this dialogue would lead to a recommendation by each Account Manager (assuming several are involved, representing different imagery suppliers) for one or more image products (Figure 4.2). These products would be 'packaged'

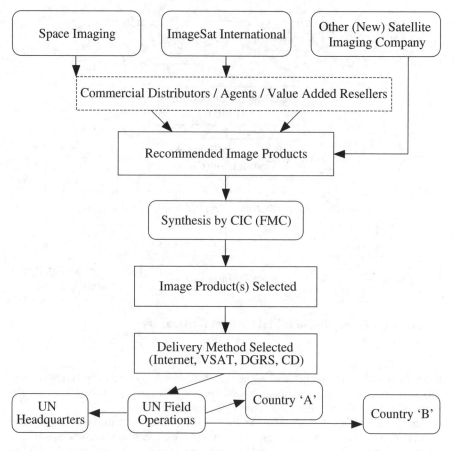

Figure 4.2   Selection and Delivery of Imagery

on the basis of the above order criteria. Pricing, for example, would reflect the area of image coverage (where this area may be polygonal), the urgency for delivery, ground resolution, the required level of processing and whether the imagery is in archive or not. Typically, a pricing model/purchase agreement would have been pre-negotiated with each imagery supplier.

The CIC would then synthesize input from the various imagery suppliers and be responsible for making the final selection of image products. The decisions reached by the CIC would likely involve further dialogue with the FMC.

The final task in this process is the actual delivery of the imagery product(s). The mechanism for this will depend on criteria such as urgency, file size, system availability and the communications/ transportation infrastructure. Delivering imagery to UN headquarters, for example, would be relatively expedient given the advanced level of communications/transportation infrastructure within North

America. The method of delivering imagery to a field command center, however, will depend on such things as the degree of Internet support (e.g. wireless capabilities, bandwidth capacity) as well as the availability of systems for data retrieval and post processing (e.g. DGRS or VSAT). In many cases, it will still be most expedient to air courier data on CD or in hard-copy format.

In summary, the goal of fulfilling the requirements for satellite imagery in a cease-fire monitoring scenario will be achieved most effectively through leveraging developments in the commercial satellite industry as well as related communications technologies. The key objectives of controlling costs while expediting delivery of useful image products will be achieved through efficiently accessing the virtual collection system.

Conclusions

This chapter has discussed the significant impact on the remote sensing industry of the new commercial, high-resolution satellite imaging systems. This is a discontinuous innovation within the industry that has drastically affected industry structure as defined by the relationships between competitors, suppliers and markets. This innovation in combination with additional factors such as improvements in enabling technologies (e.g. desk top processing and storage technology), image exploitation technology and the ubiquitous growth of the Internet, has insured that the remote sensing industry is robust and growing.

This chapter has also discussed the complementary nature of various image collection systems, such as advanced aerial imaging, LIDAR and IFSAR. These sensors all contribute appreciably to image data archives and subsequently to the information that may be derived from remotely sensed data.

In addition to growth in the commercial side of the remote sens-ing sector, the above factors have resulted in improved information and product availability, increased product standardization, growth of data archives, expansion of distribution networks and competitive pricing. Defense and security interests, including peacekeeping missions, have the opportunity to take advantage of these evolving trends within the remote sensing industry.

Military peacekeeping draws particular benefit from an extensive imagery collection system, common product formats, responsive delivery systems and commercial pricing. It has been suggested that these benefits can be optimized by pre-negotiating preferred purchase agreements with the satellite imaging companies and their distributors. In this fashion, the defense and security markets can be assured of achieving the full benefit of the commercial satellite-imaging sector.

Notes

1 http://www.spaceimaging.com/aboutus/satellites/IKONOS/ikonos.html.
2 www.digitalglobe.com QuickBird 2 was lost during a failed launch attempt on 20 November 2000, however, on 5 December 2000, ImageSat International was successful in launching the first of 8, planned satellites. This satellite has a ground sample distance of 1.8 meters.

3   'India Authorized to Build 1-Meter Imaging Satellites', *Space News*, 30 October 2000, and 'US Firms Enter Race to Build Spy Satellite for Turkey', *Space News*, 14 August 2000.
4   www.ziimaging.com.
5   Jason Bates. 'Data Delivery Drives Remote Sensing Industry', *Space News*, 30 December 2000, and 'GM Officials Consider Sale of Hughes', *Space News*, 23 October 2000, p.4.
6   'Market Intelligence Brief: Geospatial Image Data Management Systems', Chesapeake Analytics, Inc., Rev. 10/00.
7   'Ecommerce in Remote Sensing', Draft Report, Chesapeake Analytics, Inc., October 2000.
8   'Imaging Craft of Limited Utility, NIMA Chief Says', *Space News*, 25 September 2000.
9   Michael Porter (1985), *Competitive Advantage*, Harvard Business School Press, pp.4–11.

Chapter 5

Development of Geospatial Technology for Nuclear Information Management

C. Vincent Tao[1] and Q.S. (Bob) Truong

For 50 years, Canada has been involved in nuclear activities. These activities involve uranium mining, nuclear fuel fabrication, nuclear exports, nuclear power generation, nuclear research, and nuclear waste management. The CNSC (Canadian Nuclear Safety Commission), formerly the Atomic Energy Control Board (AECB), closely monitors these activities. Nuclear activity in Canada includes nuclear generation stations, research reactor licenses to universities, nuclear research and test establishments, active uranium mines, fuel fabrication plants, and waste management licences.[2] Canada has the richest uranium deposits in the world, and, it is the world's largest producer and exporter of uranium.

Information Circular (INFCIRC) 153 is a model safeguards agreement that countries can voluntarily adopt. INFCIRC/153 was produced in 1970 and has been used in Canada since 1972. The INFCIRC/153 agreement requires accountancy of nuclear materials. In 1997, the CNSC submitted 567 reports detailing 18,358 transactions in-volving nuclear material.

To strengthen safeguards, high priority has to be placed on in-creased access to information and increased access to facilities. In 1997, the Additional Protocol, INFCIRC/540, was adopted by the IAEA Board of Governors. The new protocol measures include:[3]

1   Information about and access to all aspects of the nuclear cycle from uranium mining to nuclear waste disposal;
2   Information about and access to fuel-cycle related research and development;
3   Information about all buildings on a nuclear site;
4   Short notice inspection to all buildings on a nuclear site;
5   Information on the manufacture of sensitive nuclear related technologies;
6   Inspection of locations that import or export nuclear related material or technologies;
7   Collection of environmental samples;
8   Administrative arrangements that improve the process of providing inspectors with multiple entry visas to allow for unannounced inspections;
9   IAEA use of modern means of communication (e.g., satellite phones) during inspection.

As discussed in Tao, et al.,[4] the current reporting system at the CNSC is not suitable for managing and archiving a vast amount of data as well as a variety of data types to meet the requirements set by the Additional Protocol. It is also realized that approximately 70 per cent of the data required by the Additional Protocol is geographically related. These include region and site maps, photos, plans, drawings and even videos. Moreover, in this new Protocol, the IAEA is requesting more than accounting information. It requires an increase in access to information. This information includes up-to-date maps of sites and information on activities that are related to the nuclear fuel cycle. From a data management and reporting point of view, it is very challenging to develop a system that meets all the requirements and supports spatial and dynamic functions based on a traditional database approach.

In order to address the Additional Protocol requirements, the University of Calgary in conjunction with the CNSC has investigated a new approach to nuclear information management and reporting. The new approach is developed based on a GIS (Geospatial Information System) approach. It provides a spatially enabled solution to data management and reporting. In this chapter, the GIS-based approach is introduced. The design and development of a GIS-based prototype system, GeoATOMS™, is then described. The system has now been fully implemented. Datasets including 1:50,000 and 1:250,000 National Topographic Database (NTDB) of Canada, aerial photos and satellite images pertaining to several important nuclear sites, detailed building plans and drawings, along with the related documents and video clips, have been integrated and populated into the system.

Spatially Enabled Information Management: A GIS-based Approach

A GIS is a software system that is capable of storing, manipulating, analyzing, and presenting geo-spatially referenced data. GIS technology integrates common database operations such as queries and statistical analysis with the unique visualization and geographic analysis of spatial data, such as maps and images. These abilities distinguish GIS from other information systems and make it valuable to a wide range of public and private enterprises for information collection, management and decision-making.

GIS records information about the real world objects as a collection of thematic layers that can be linked together based on the geo-referencing information. This simple but extremely powerful and versatile concept has proven invaluable for solving many real-world problems from tracking delivery vehicles, to recording details of planning applications, and to modeling global atmospheric circulation.

There are two information components in a GIS, namely the spatial component and the non-spatial (or aspatial) component. The spatial component is basically the geographical portion of the GIS. A unique feature of any GIS is its capability to manage the spatial data efficiently. There are two fundamental types of spatial data, namely vector data and raster data. The spatial phenomena can be represented using either of these two types. Vector data is normally represented using geometric feature entities such as point, lines and polygons. The topological relationships among these feature entities need to be established. Raster data – for instance, imagery – offers a good representation of the actual texture of the location being photographed. Due to the increasing use of remotely sensed images such as commercial high-resolution satellite images for remote monitoring and verification, integrating faster images and vector maps becomes of particular importance. The GIS data model idea is to manage the raster data and vector data in an integrated fashion.

The non-spatial component consists of data elements that are texture and descriptive. They are the attributes of feature entities in the real world. The data models of managing the non-spatial component have been highly standardized. The commonly used ones are the relational model and the object-relational model. In order to link the spatial and non-spatial components, a hybrid GIS data model is required. One of the key elements in any GIS is the design and implementation of its hybrid data model that handles the spatial and non-spatial data in an integrated manner. This hybrid data model makes GIS very powerful, as it can support integrated data query and spatial analysis.

Spatial analysis is a tool used to analyze information spatially. It supports functions such as spatial statistical analysis, network analysis and three-dimensional analysis. For example, a GIS can answer questions such as: where are the closest emergency services to the site? what is the quickest route from Toronto to the Bruce Generating Station? where is the best place to build a new generating station? and which is best routine in terms of safety to transport the nuclear materials?

GIS has been designed for offering these solutions. These functions are not only important for site managers for planning and decision-making, but also for inspectors to locate the events and navigate the routines. This is clearly advantageous in support of the increased access to facilities that is a stated priority in the new Protocol.

Data mining has been considered as an innovative tool for information extraction and knowledge discovery from mass data sets. Its significance for detecting undeclared nuclear activities has been recognized by the safeguards community. With the use of GIS, spatially enabled data mining can be developed to explore the spatially related hidden patterns or relationships among the sites and to track the nuclear materials. This technology is very promising but is still in a research stage.

Design and Implementation of GeoATOMS™

The design of the system focuses on the following factors: efficiency, ease of use, functionality, automation, information tracking, and database design.

With the inception of this system, every attempt has been made to create a database that manages the data, and creates reports that can be submitted under the INFCIRC/540 protocol. From a database management perspective, information is stored as a single record, such that there would be no redundancy or confusion to which record is the most current.

Organization of spatial data is crucial to maintaining an efficient program when querying for spatial data. For example, when a nuclear site is viewed in detail, all the other sites are not important; therefore the program should not have to draw graphics for spatial data that is out of context. One way to organize spatial data is to create a directory style hierarchy. The advantage of a hierarchy is to separate data with different map scales. Automation of the directory is another advantage of this style by checking to see if a map is within the boundaries of a larger map and classify it to where the map belongs. This type of hierarchy also contains databases and raster images in each level of the hierarchy.

There are three different types of spatial data in the system. A small-scale data set of Canada, including themes such as provinces, cities, lakes and primary road networks, is necessary for the initial map display and indexing. As the purpose of the system is to manage nuclear facilities within the main sites, it will be necessary to include large-scale data sets of the areas that are administered by the AECB. The data sets that were used in the system are the National Topographic DataBase (NTBD) data purchased from Geomatics Canada. In total, 39 layers at scales of 1:50,000 and 1:250,000 pertaining to the AECB administered sites were available. To assist in the monitoring of nuclear facilities and to detect any potentially important changes, it is necessary to have access to high-resolution aerial photos and satellite imagery of the selected sites. This raster imagery, obtained from the AECB, has been geo-referenced and integrated into the system.

There are many different ways to organize non-spatial data. Information stored in the database will be stored like an object. These objects include member states, nuclear sites, facilities, equipment, nuclear materials, and documents. Each type of object is grouped into one table, since objects of the same nature will have similar attributes. When the state of the object is changed, as in commissioning and decommissioning a nuclear site, a record of this change is made in a logging table specific to the object. The non-spatial data in the nuclear management system is hierarchical as well. Smaller objects belong to larger objects, and each smaller object can only belong to one larger object at one instant. A relational database management system is useful in this situation. Such an RDBMS can be found in Microsoft Access. First, there are many member states. Within these member states, there are sites. Facilities exist at these sites. Materials, equipment and documents exist in facilities. The site, equipment and facilities tables will have tables that will track the changes to these tables, while the materials table will log each time the material is traveling between facilities. There will be no physical accounting of materials in each facility, although an SQL command can determine this amount. To fulfill the requirements of INFCIRC/540, the tables that record changes will be the keys to reporting successfully to the IAEA.

In the system, there are three types of tables, which include permanent tables, changing tables and logging tables. Permanent tables are ones that have permanence and do not change over time. All the records in this table are finite. Examples of these kinds of tables are member state tables or facility type tables. Changing tables represent all the current objects in the system. Their current states are also kept in these tables and the record of the change of states is logged in logging tables. Logging tables are similar to changing tables except they are old records of previous states. Based on the use of this dynamic modeling design, the system is able to manage all the current records as well as track all the historic records. The third normalized form was used to create these tables.

Software has taken a new direction. Most software packages are now component-based and ActiveX, Plug-ins, Java Beans are examples of these types of packages. Components have different attributes, which deal with different data types. Each component handles word documents, spreadsheets, images, OLE objects, etc. GIS technology has different components as well. Some of these are the database component, spatial component, visual graphics component, spatial/non-spatial data link component, query component, data management and data analysis components, etc. When combining each of these components, it creates a program. All of these components work independent of each other, but work together to form a program. Furthermore, each of these components can be used in another program without any complications. This breaks down proprietary software, making component-based programming popular.[5]

Functionality and Applications of GeoATOMS™

The main functions of the GeoATOMS™ system can be grouped into four categories: (1) spatial functions such as zooming, panning, digitizing, identity, spatial finder, distance measure, properties, layer control etc.; (2) querying functions such as spatial query, facility query, database query, SQL query, etc.; (3) database functions such as viewing, editing and logging, as well as security functions; and (4) image archiving and manipulations. Due to the fact that there will be different types of users using the system, i.e., international inspectors, AECB staff and facility managers, three levels of security controls have been developed. Users with different security levels are only allowed to access certain functions.

GeoATOMS™ can be used for the following applications:

1   Integration with imagery for inspection. The incorporation of satellite imagery would assist change detection. This would provide inspectors with useful information for determining if a more detailed, or additional inspection is warranted.
2   Navigation tool for an inspector. The system can now be used for inspectors to create a plan of navigation, even when the inspector is not familiar with the site.
3   Linking the Protocol Reporter to the GIS. The Protocol Reporter is another database that requires a GIS link. This system has or will have the capability to link other database structures.
4   Training for the nuclear staff and the public.
5   Nuclear material accounting and tracking. Due to the structure of the database, the system can provide accounting and tracking of nuclear material.

An example of the system interface and some functions is shown in Figure 5.1. A Graphic User Interface (GUI) is designed based on the web browser standard with which most users are familiar. The user is able to edit and query the sites, facilities and equipment status through the GUI. In the example, the user clicked a building at a nuclear site. The system brought up a big window showing this building along with all the equipment information related to this building. The link to all the documents related to this building is also available. In fact, all non-spatial information is stored in the Microsoft Access database. The seamless link between the GIS graphic engine and the database has been constructed in GIS.

Figure 5.2 shows the function of the powerful spatial hyperlink. Once a site is clicked by a user, the detailed site map will be displayed and the relevant information about this site can be queried and accessed. Figure 5.3 shows the tracking record of nuclear materials. The system was built using a dynamic data model and therefore all the historical data can be kept in the system for material tracking and accounting. Figures 5.4 and 5.5 show the functions of image manipulations: image registration in Figure 5.4 and change detection in Figure 5.5.

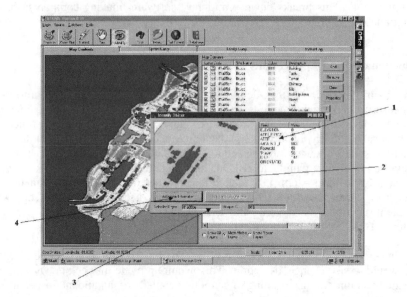

Figure 5.1   An Example of System Interface (Note: 1 – map window, 2 – toolbar, 3 – data control, 4 – facility information, 5 – query facility, 6 – links to documents, 7 – facility ID)

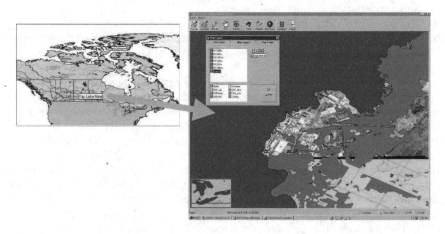

Figure 5.2   Hyper Spatial Data Link

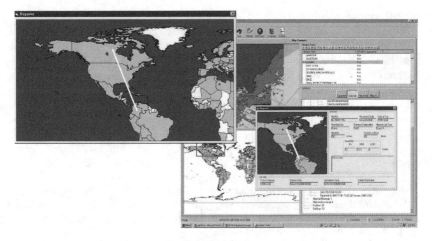

Figure 5.3   Dynamic Tracking of Nuclear Materials

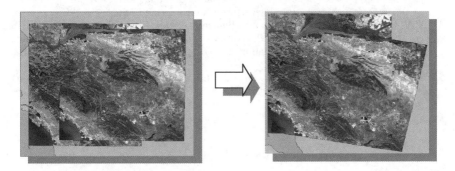

Figure 5.4   Image Registration

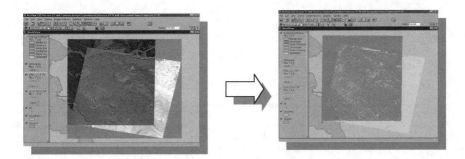

Figure 5.5   Change Detection

Conclusion

Geospatial technology is playing a significant role in the nuclear safeguards community. It has been demonstrated that GeoATOMS™ Offers a unique solution for spatially enabled data management and analysis. It supports spatial and visual representation of data sets, integrated raster and vector management, image manipulation, spatial query and spatial analysis. These tools are of particular importance to nuclear safeguards community as well as for peacekeeping purposes.

Notes

1   The authors would like to thank Jon Ruttle, and Rafael Lucero for their contributions to the system development and programming. Technical support and advice provided by Messrs. Robert Benjamin and Richard Keeffe of the Canadian Nuclear Safety Commission are gratefully acknowledged.
2   Atomic Energy Control Board (AECB), 1998. *Annual Report* 1997–1998. Ottawa, Canada.
3   International Atomic Energy Agency (IAEA), 1997. *Model Protocol Additional to the Agreement(s) between State(s) and the International Atomic Energy for the Application of Safeguards*. Vienna, Austria: International Atomic Energy Agency.
4   C.V. Tao, B. Truong, R. Keeffe, and R. Benjamin. 1998. 'Potential Applications of GIS for Management of Safeguards Information'. Paper presented at the International Seminar on Safeguards Information Reporting and Processing, Vienna, Austria, November 30–December 4, 1998.
5   Robert Hartman. 1997. *Focus on GIS Component Software: Featuring ESRI MapObjects*. Santa Fe, USA. Onward Press.

Chapter 6

Financial Considerations in the Acquisition of High Resolution Commercial Satellite Imagery for United Nations Peacekeeping and Humanitarian Operations

Steve Adam[1]

Introduction

Over the past 30 years, Earth observing satellites have collected remarkable imagery of our planet at greater resolution with each passing decade. Today we stand at the pinnacle of civilian satellite technology with the successful launch of Space Imaging's satellite. Launched on September 24, 1999, it is the world's first commercial high resolution satellite, collecting data at 1 m panchromatic (black/white) and 4 m multispectral.[2] Even more recently, ImageSat's Eros A-1 satellite, with 1.8 m panchromatic data, was successfully put into orbit on December 5, 2000.[3]

High-resolution commercial satellite imagery (CSI) can offer significant advantages to United Nations (UN) peacekeeping missions and other aid organizations operating in regions where timely geographic information is required. For example, CSI can be used to assess threats to forces or other personnel, gather information on refugee movement, airport conditions, road conditions, and verify or discount damage re-ports or other claims made by eyewitnesses or governments.[4]

The concept of the Darwinian imperative, where groups will exploit any advantage available to make gains in their cause, has also been applied to the UN.[5] Although the UN has been described as a potentially slower and more cumbersome adopter of this technology, compared to other more desperate groups such as terrorist organizations, this is one information source the UN should not overlook. Coincidentally, recommendations from the Brahimi report state that:

> Peace operations could benefit greatly from more extensive use of geographic information systems (GIS) technology, which quickly integrates operational information with electronic maps of the mission area, for applications as diverse as demobilization, civilian policing, voter registration, human rights monitoring, and reconstruction.[6]

The UN already offers geographic information on their website,[7] hence, satellite imagery would act as a complement to that data.

Although the advantages and applications of CSI to peacekeeping appear to be enough motivation to initiate the use of CSI, the financial commitment can be imposing. To balance the benefits of CSI with the cost, the question that must be asked is: *What is the financial commitment for purchasing high-resolution satellite imagery to use operationally in peacekeeping and aid missions?*

Scope

This chapter will focus on the financial requirements and considerations necessary to acquire high-resolution commercial satellite imagery. Two themes are illustrated. First, what are the present considerations where only a few satellites are available, and second, issues and advice for organizations planning image acquisitions when there are constellations of satellites.

The term *organizations* refers here to groups such as humanitarian agencies and UN peacekeeping. This does not include military or peacemaking operations since these operations and supporting groups may have already established unique acquisition protocols for CSI or have access to military satellites.

Imagery From Only a Few Orbiting Satellites (Present/Near-Future Situation)

Modern, high-resolution commercial satellite image collection was championed by Space Imaging, which successfully launched its Ikonos-2 satellite (later renamed Ikonos) on September 24, 1999. Although the Russian photographic programs, such as the Cosmos and the Kometa satellites, preceded Space Imaging's launch, their sparse global coverage, low temporal resolution, and limited collection cycle limit their operational use for peacekeeping and humanitarian missions. Nonetheless, the Russian imagery does have a place, primarily as a change detection source. To illustrate the present CSI options, this discussion will be divided into two parts: the use of archived imagery and new acquisitions.

Buying archived imagery: The present

Archived imagery is used in applications where timeliness may not be of primary importance or for change detection investigations. Presently, the three satellite programs which have an active archive are shown in Table 6.1. Eros A-1 was successfully launched on December 5, 2000 but has not been included in this discussion since its archive will remain sparse for many months or more.

Imagery extracted from an archive has many advantages, namely, speed of delivery, knowledge of image condition (i.e. clouds, haze, time of year), and cost. Disadvantages include imagery that is too old, wrong time of the year, cloud cover, or simply unavailable. The latter will continue to be an issue until there is a dense enough constellation of high-resolution satellites to rapidly image the Earth's surface.

The IRS-1 satellites are the most cost effective and provide the largest archive of the three programs listed in Table 6.1. Their 5 m resolution is optimal for delineating roads and large cultural features,[8] but too coarse for finer features such as vehicles, groups of people, and small buildings. For the latter features, the 1 m resolution imagery has been shown to be optimal.[9]

It is evident that the cost of imagery increases with the resolution and, therefore, buyers should take into account what it is they *need* to see, as opposed to *what* they want to see. Ultimately, a user who needs to map roads would like to see houses, however, the cost per unit area for 5 m resolution data is many times cheaper than 1 m data. Some of the early pricing schemes for the satellite data were based on a linear or algorithmic computation comparing resolution. This is not likely to be a viable pricing technique for most commercial products. This scenario is very common and is an important consideration when choosing image sources. Additionally, and more significantly, the range of prices within a single type of imagery reflects the level of processing required. Does your operation simply need a digital *picture*, an image that is simply projected (which is more expensive), or a truly planimetric product from which features can be accurately extracted (which is most expensive)?

Table 6.1 High-Resolution Image Archive (Prices are $US as of January 2001 for imagery outside of North America.)

Company	Satellite	Resolution (m)	Cost/km² ($)	Minimum order ($)	http://
Space Imaging	Ikonos	1 and 4	18–200	1800	www.spaceimaging.com
SPIN-2/ Sovinform-sputnik	Cosmos and Kometa	1 and 2	5–50	None	www.spin-2.com www-com.iasis.svetcorp.net/ index.html www.terraserver.com
Indian Space Agency (Distributed by Space Imaging)	IRS-IC/D	5	1–5	900	www.spaceimaging.com www.isro.org/sat.htm
EarthWatch	Quick-bird-1*	1 and 4	15–65	1000	www.digitalglobe.com

* Quickbird-1 failed to reach orbit. The prices are shown simply for comparison and are what EarthWatch would have listed if the satellite would have successfully reached orbit and began collection.

New image acquisitions: The present

Although the SPIN-2 program periodically puts satellites into relatively short duration orbits to collect imagery, the irregularity of acquisition and delay between acquisition and delivery make it a less reliable program than other orbiting systems. As of winter 2000, this leaves only the Ikonos and Eros A-1 satellites available for new image delivery. Several more satellites are scheduled for launch by the end of 2001. However, technical issues often arise and launch tables change frequently, and therefore it is difficult to predict just how many will be launched successfully into orbit and begin imaging. Hence, as long as there are at least two satellites acquiring imagery the price model shown in Table 6.2 should remain relatively stable. There are still some unknowns in Eros pricing due to the recentness of the launch.

Table 6.2 New Image Acquisition and Satellite Program (Prices are $US as of January 2001 for imagery outside of North America.)

Company	Satellite	Resolution (m)	Cost/km² ($)	Minimum order ($)	Rush tasking fees
Space Imaging	Ikonos	1 and 4	18–300	1800	3000
ImageSat	Eros A-1	1.8	10–?	?	?

One reason for the likely price stability is sufficient demand for imagery to support two different high-resolution satellite companies. For example, effective September 15, 2000 Space Imaging tripled the size of its minimum purchase and instituted additional tasking fees for rush orders. This was done to curtail the minute orders which filled its collection queue. Effectively, this policy promotes larger, more profitable orders and discourages a clientele who require only smaller areas.

Another factor affecting price stability is that Ikonos and Eros A-1 are not as similar as Ikonos and Quickbird-1[10] may have been, since the latter both have similar 1 meter panchromatic and 4 meter multi-spectral sensors. The Eros A-1 data will be delivered to commercial clients with 1.8 m resolution and without the option for multi-spectral coverage. Although 0.8 m does not sound like a large difference in resolution they may effectively be serving two different markets. One additional issue with the Eros A-1 imagery is the lack of metric control: these image data sets will require a densification of ground control in order to create orthorectified quality reference images.

In addition, CSI pricing is related to the concept of *commoditization* of high-resolution satellite imagery, where standard image products are produced and can be compared across different satellites and companies.[11] Commercial satellite imagery is trending towards this condition, but has not yet fully realized it, with so few new satellites in orbit.

Downward pressures on new acquisition pricing will depend on more direct competition, with like products competing for the same users.Perhaps one of the few possible areas of consumer savings in the above price model depends on Space Imaging lowering or discontinuing its tasking fee to remain competitive with

ImageSat. Essentially, the price per unit area of imagery would stay the same but the cost to the user would decrease because the additional fee for custom tasking is reduced or retracted.

Constellations of Satellites: Buying in the Future

Constellations of high-resolution satellites would suggest that the user market is maturing. The advantages of a mature market would include:

1 Robust standards so that image products could be compared across different providers;
2 Responsive distribution networks;
3 Efficient and knowledgeable customer service;
4 Competitive pricing.

If all of the high-resolution satellite launches planned for the next 18 months are successful (possibly five[12]), the preceding section would be modified based on somewhat different commercial competitive conditions. However, it is impossible to predict how many high-resolution satellites will be in orbit in the next two to five years. It is worth noting that since the unsuccessful launch of EarthWatch's EarlyBird satellite in December 1997 (the first commercial high resolution satellite to the launch pad) there have been only two successful commercial high-resolution satellite launches out of six attempts. Furthermore, launches are constantly being rescheduled, delaying the introduction of more satellites to the arena.

Thus, the following section will be relevant in as much as five years from now and the available collection systems on orbit will certainly be different. Nonetheless, it will describe the prevalent issues an organization should address when attempting to acquire high-resolution satellite imagery in a time where numerous options exist. As with the previous section the following discussion is divided into using archived satellite data and acquiring new imagery. New acquisition is further divided into the following considerations: choosing a satellite image provider, purchasing arrangements, and a brief look at the forces which influence price.

Buying archived imagery: In the future

As stated earlier, purchasing archived imagery offers the opportunity for more rapid delivery, knowledge of image condition (i.e. clouds, haze, time of year), and lower cost than new acquisitions. In addition, the disadvantages we experience today, namely an incomplete archive of highresolution imagery, will hopefully be minimized with so many satellites collecting data. An ideal situation would be for a few satellite companies to have many birds. Statistically the Earth can be imaged more efficiently this way than if many companies had just one satellite. The latter case would likely result in most companies focusing on more profitable areas which have a high incidence of resale, such as large urban centers, while neglecting other areas which may have less demand but are still desired.

A large image footprint can also act as a satellite multiplier. For example, Quickbird-1 (which was lost in November 2000) had a 22 km x 22 km footprint, effectively four times the size of its competitor, Ikonos, which has an 11 km x 11 km footprint. Therefore, consumers should be aware of different satellite footprints when assessing potential archive use.

Consumers will benefit from all this data collection because if one distributor does not have the imagery required, the consumer can query another distributor's archive. In fact, a further step is already being taken by a number of companies including ImageNet.com, which is positioning itself to distribute imagery from any source over the internet as an e-commerce transaction, a bold move towards centralized distribution. An added advantage of a major central distributor is that Wal-Mart style volume sales could push the price down.

It is difficult to predict what the cost of archived imagery will be in the future. However, what we have seen with archived aerial imagery is a rapid decline in value (thus the price to be commanded) within a few months of image collection. A similar circumstance may happen with archived imagery if so much of it is being collected. Consumers may also see looser restrictions on minimum area purchases and the addition of 'perks' bundled into the purchase,[13] such as digital terrain model (DTM) of the same area or street vectors.

Acquiring new imagery: Choosing an image provider in the future

An organization is often tempted to simply look for the cheapest product. If commoditization of image products becomes common, then price may be a deciding factor. However, the requirement for new acquisition implies a need for current data. Furthermore, peacekeeping and other operational applications require acquisition and delivery on a time scale more sensitive than most users of new imagery. These factors are resource intensive for a satellite company and as a result, one can almost be certain that in the future, as in the present, new – rapid acquisitions will cost more than imagery from the archive.

For an organization to commit to purchasing more expensive, timely imagery, they should feel assured that their images will be acquired and delivered. In choosing a satellite company there are certain characteristics one should look for:

1   Does the company have many satellites in orbit? This increases the chances of acquiring an image. Note that many satellites in orbit from many different companies can be of little use to a customer who requires a new acquisition. This is because placing the same order with many different companies (to increase your chances) may mean that you have to pay several times for the same image if some, or all, of the companies acquire it. Conversely, business arrangements may permit a buyer to only commit to a satellite collector which is first in collection and de-livery of the desired imagery.

2   Does the company have the facilities or infrastructure to acquire, process, and deliver a new acquisition in the time frame required?

3   Does the company have many other clients (e.g. military) who also require timely imagery? This could mean competition for time on the satellite when it is needed most. Gupta clearly points out that the free market encourages

economic and military powers to monopolize premier remote sensing services.[14] Even if that is not their intent, exclusive arrangements made by powerful groups can affect other commercial clients. This was seen during the summer of 2000 when the Ikonos satellite was overbooked largely with military acquisitions.

Acquiring new imagery: Purchasing arrangements in the future

There are two unique issues regarding purchasing arrangements that should be mentioned in the context of peacekeeping and humanitarian operations. First, peacekeeping and humanitarian missions by nature have proportionately more rapid acquisition and delivery requirements than most applications and therefore, should find some assurance of timely acquisition and delivery. Second, the high profiles of UN peacekeeping and humanitarian missions are effective tools for negotiating an agreement.

Any organization which has made the financial commitment to acquire new imagery and requires a rapid response should look for some form of preferred status/pricing with a satellite company to assure delivery. An effective approach is one that the United States military already uses with Space Imaging, that is, a *negotiated pre-purchase agreement*. Under this scenario, organizations or agencies (singly or jointly) that have responsibility for peacekeeping, disaster relief, or other humanitarian missions would have arranged with the major satellite imaging companies preferred conditions under which they would purchase the satellite image products. For example, over a one-year period, a set amount of image area could be negotiated with a committed dollar amount. In addition, a pre-purchase agreement would allow an aid agency to negotiate for enhanced mapping products such as rectified imagery and the addition of the local DTM.

Such an arrangement provides organizations with some assurance that they will receive timely imagery and also guarantees an income source to the image provider. Effectively, this assurance removes some of the competition for satellite-time a peacekeeping organization would otherwise experience with other buyers because they are promoted to a status slightly greater than the regular commercial customers, as is presently the case with the US military and Space Imaging.

Although UN missions may not require volumes of imagery to make them an attractive client, the marketing value of the imagery's application can be very valuable for a satellite company. UN missions can be leveraged for their extensive media coverage to receive favorable status when negotiating a purchasing agreement. Satellite companies would very likely benefit from this sort of coverage. In addition, the areas of timely interest to peacekeeping organizations also have additional value to the satellite imaging company, such as for sale to news agencies and other regional governments. This should argue for favorable pricing in a pre-negotiated agreement.

Acquiring new imagery: Potential costs and price factors in the future

It is difficult to predict what the price will be when constellations of high resolution imaging satellites are in orbit, however, typical downward pressures on price should see it lower than the present $10/km^2–$200/km^2 (this range represents the range of image products from all companies). The question is, how much lower? The answer to this question depends upon which combination of factors, discussed below, are present.

To make up for a drop in price, a satellite company must increase its sales volume. Satellite companies are presently limited by their number of satellites, on-board storage capacity and density of ground receiving stations. However, this situation should change in the future. As this capacity increases, more orders can be filled and the archive can be continuously replenished. In addition, there may be third party distributors which, through their own volume sales, can offer price savings. An example is Core Software, which is positioning itself to distribute imagery for any vendor across the internet.

To accommodate a drop in price, a satellite company must have lower costs. These costs can be efficiencies in operating, smaller debt load, and lower insurance costs. Insurance can represent between 25 per cent and 30 per cent of the cost of building and launching a satellite. However, the insurance price is not based solely on imaging satellite but on the entire satellite launch industry, which fortunately has had a greater success rate than has the niche imagery satellite sector.

It is also possible that prices may not fall substantially. A comparison to home computer prices may be relevant. Although home computers are many times faster and have greater storage capacity than in the past, one still pays only marginally less than before. Comparably, the new modern home computer appears to be better than those of the past and may also come with peripherals such as a printer and scanner, but the price is not significantly less. One could argue that the same could happen with satellite imagery. The price may drop slightly but you may get more for that price. For example, imagery may cost around $7/km^2 (compared to today's $10/km^2) but a buyer may receive the local DTM for the area, or may not have to pay tasking fees or comply with a minimum order.

Conclusions

It has been stated throughout this chapter that the price of imagery and the number of commercial high-resolution satellites in the future is impossible to predict. For the next few years the price should stay around the $10–15/km^2 mark (for uncorrected imagery), while the commoditization of imagery and the maturity of the market grow. In the short term, the cost of archived imagery will likely remain lower than new acquisitions.

As more satellites are launched into orbit, many factors come into play which will affect the final cost. Overall, there should be a typical downward pressure on price. To best position themselves, the UN and other aid agencies should negotiate a pre-purchase agreement with a satellite company for preferred status and pricing. Although the UN may not request the volume of imagery other pre-purchase arrangements will (i.e. government military), they may be able to leverage their high media profile missions for a favorable agreement.

As briefly illustrated in this chapter and further developed in other chapters in this volume, commercial high-resolution satellite imagery is an effective source of information for UN peacekeeping and other aid organizations. The financial considerations outlined here suggest that CSI is presently, and will continue to be, a cost effective method of acquiring information. As outlined in the Darwinian Imperative, the UN has more to gain from purchasing CSI than it can afford to loose by not purchasing CSI.

Notes

1   The author wishes to thank Alvin Hanks of Chesapeake Analytics (Sunriver, Oregon) for his insightful review and comments. This chapter was also improved through discussions on economics with John Kwan of Canadian Geomatic Solutions Ltd. (Calgary, Alberta, Canada).

2   See www.spaceimaging.com for launch details and product updates.

3   See www.imagesatintl.com for details about the launch.

4   Vipin Gupta, 'New satellite images for sale', *International Security*, Vol. 20, No.1 (Summer 1995), p.114.

5   Mark Stout and Thomas Quiggin (1998), 'Exploiting the new high resolution satellite imagery: Darwinian Imperatives?', *Canadian Security Intelligence Service, Commentary* No.75, p.8. Available at www.csis-scrs.gc.ca/eng/comment/com75e.htm.

6   United Nations, *Report of the Panel on United Nations Peace Operations; Summary of Recommendations*, August 21, 2000, A/55/305-S/2000/809, p.7.

7   Maps and geographic data are found at http://www.un.org/Depts/Cartographic/english/htmain.htm.

8   An excellent example of using IRS-1 5m imagery for road and access mapping is Alberta Environment's (Resource Data Division) provincial map update described in: Ken Dutchak, 'Alberta Access Update Program Using IRS 5.8m Pan Data', 22nd Annual Canadian Remote Sensing Symposium, *Proceedings*, p.183.

9   Gupta, p.102.

10   Details may be found at http://www.digitalglobe.com/index.shtml.

11   Alvin Hanks and Richard Gorecki, this volume, discuss in more detail the idea of imagery commoditization.

12   Jean-Pierre Joseph Paquette, this volume, outlines the launch schedule for future high resolution satellites.

13   Alvin Hanks and Richard Gorecki, this volume, discuss the notion of offering product bundles with satellite image purchase.

14   Gupta, p.115.

Chapter 7

The Use of Commercial Satellite Imagery and Canadian Security Needs

James F. Keeley

The development of a commercial satellite imagery (CSI) industry and its associated services is now commonly noted as a major element in the 'information revolution' sweeping the globe. (Commercial satellite imagery is here defined as unclassified satellite imagery publicly offered for a fee on a routine basis, whether by a public agency or a private firm.) Even without the Internet, access to such imagery by states that do not have their own satellite capabilities, by non-governmental organizations and by other private actors, is affecting the global political system by diffusing access to information. As both a consumer and a producer of imagery, and through its association with the United States, this development has varied and significant implications for Canadian security. This chapter is an effort to draw together and to consider many of these implications. It has two primary but overlapping foci: one is the broad security issues raised by CSI for Canada, particularly in the context of its relations with the United States, and the other is the potential for the use of CSI by the United Nations in support of its peacekeeping operations, or by states in support of such UN operations.

These two foci are to some degree distinct, yet they also overlap significantly. Canada's relations with the US are a cornerstone of our foreign and defence policies, but so, too, is our contribution to international security through activities such as peacekeeping. The use of CSI by the UN or in UN field operations raises a range of issues of significance in their own right, as well as in terms of Canadian support for the UN. At the same time, Canadian policy with respect to CSI has required a degree of co-ordination with the United States.[1] The two overlap as well in terms of Canadian defence requirements, in the question of whether and to what degree Canada responds to the so-called Revolution in Military Affairs (RMA)[2] and the extent to which peacekeeping either furthers or hinders this response. Finally, some of the questions which could arise with respect to UN use of CSI could also speak to concerns which Canada might face in any attempt to exploit the development of CSI in its own response to the RMA.

This chapter will first look in some detail at some issues concerning the UN, CSI and peacekeeping. It will then turn to some issues related to these which arise in the context of broader Canadian security requirements.

The UN, CSI and Peacekeeping

In 1983, the United Nations issued a study of the possibility for an International
Satellite Monitoring Agency (ISMA), which would provide an international satellite
remote sensing capability for verification, monitoring, early warning and
peacekeeping.[3] The report suggested three phases for the development of ISMA:
initially merely the acquisition and use of imagery from existing national sources; a
second phase in which the agency would establish its own ground stations, and a
third phase in which the agency would develop its own satellites, though not
necessarily its own launch capability. While it recognized and built upon the
established importance of national satellite reconnaissance and monitoring systems,
this very ambitious proposal went no further. It did, however, help to establish the
notion of an international remote sensing satellite capability, to be used by
international organizations such as the United Nations. During the 1980s as well,
interest developed in the use of satellite imagery by news media, including, as well,
the possibility of a dedicated capability, 'Mediasat.'[4]

Neither proposal for a dedicated satellite imagery capability went anywhere. But
this did not mean that satellite imagery remained simply the preserve of the
governments of a few highly-capable states. Instead, a developing commercial
satellite imagery industry – including not only satellite owners and imagery
providers, but also service providers of various kinds – has effectively undercut the
need for such expensive, centralized dedicated capabilities. Indeed, Gupta observed
in 1995 that a centralized capability would seem neither necessary nor desirable, as
'[t]he operational beauty of satellite imaging is that it does not require cooperation
with anyone, neither friend nor foe': the politics of international organizations could
thus be avoided.[5]

Others had already noted the potential security implications of the spread and the
commercial availability of satellite imagery.[6] With the developing availability of
CSI and attendant services, and the development of information technology more
generally, the use of CSI has spread from a small group of technologically-capable
states and certain industries to a much wider array of users. In 1990, analyzing the
SPOT imagery catalogue, Peter Zimmerman noted that certain sites appeared to be
significantly 'over-selected'; he inferred from this that SPOT was being 'heavily
used' by intelligence services of states without their own satellite reconnaissance
capabilities.[7] Such imagery has been used by the US in the Gulf War, by West
Germany and Japan; it has been used as well by the news media (e.g. images of
Chernobyl, Kyshtym, Dushanbe, Krasnoyarsk, Dimona, and of Saudi CSS-2
ballistic missile bases).[8] Tomas Ries and Johnny Skorve used LANDSAT imagery
to examine Soviet military installations on the Kola peninsula.[9] Both the Federation
of American Scientists and the Institute of Science and International Security have
released CSI, and interpretations of the images, on their websites, and the
Verification Technology and Information Centre has also used CSI.[10] Gupta and
Pabian examined the possibility of combining CSI and 'open source' media
information to investigate Indian nuclear testing.[11] The Australian Surveying and
Land Information Group posted LANDSAT 7 images of East Timor, including of
fires in Dili, in the turmoil following the independence referendum there.[12] More
recently, Atlantis Scientific Inc. produced digital terrain elevation data of East Timor

for the Canadian Department of National Defence from satellite imagery, in support of a Canadian deployment there.[13] Eurimage provided CSI from LANDSAT and ERS of the Turkish earthquake at a reduced rate.[14] The possible uses of CSI are now being explored by various humanitarian organizations.[15] The International Atomic Energy Agency is moving steadily in the direction of using CSI to supplement its traditional safeguards.[16]

Wider use of satellite imagery, of course, also presents its dangers. Without trained interpretive capabilities, the information presented in an image may not be properly understood: it is one thing to be able to measure a building in an image and another thing to have the much broader knowledge base necessary to understand the significance of the building.[17] This may not, however, prevent the use of such imagery.[18]

The potential systematic acquisition and use of CSI in UN peacekeeping does not entail the development and deployment by the UN of a larger capability along the lines of the ISMA proposal. Gupta's suggestion that such an agency would not actually be needed or useful is thus adopted as a basic premise here. However, his observation on the non-utility of an ISMA-like concept did not address the possible use by the UN itself of CSI. Potential applications for various surveillance systems, not only CSI, have been studied by, among others, the Canadian Department of National Defence, the US Office of Technology Assessment, and the Center for Global Security Research.[19] Gupta and Bernstein, and Gupta and Harris have also studied the possibilities for CSI in a monitoring role.[20] In the Dayton negotiations, the ability of the US to produce and distribute maps based on imagery, showing locations of forces, boundary zones, terrain conditions, etc. was a factor. Aside from providing timely and detailed information for the negotiators, these maps also contained an implied threat: we know where you are, and we know what damage we can do to you.[21] Satellite imagery from various sources – National Technical Means as well as CSI – has been used at times on various UN peacekeeping operations: Smith notes that the UN's Situation Centre has purchased SPOT imagery; Dorn notes that UNEF was shown some US satellite images, and that there was some use of US imagery by UNPROFOR; and Berdal notes the use of LANDSAT imagery by the US 10th Mountain Division in Somalia.[22] At the moment, the UN is looking at the development of a United Nations Geographic Database, which would improve its mapping and data-representation capabilities.[23] This would, of course, link nicely to the availability and the use of CSI as a mapping tool, among other things.

The Brahimi report

With the end of the Cold War, the United Nations experienced an upsurge in the demand for peacekeeping operations. Initially, many of these involved the liquidation of Cold War-related disputes, and were handled with relative success. Then came the Gulf War and, in retrospect certainly, vastly and prematurely ambitious hopes for a UN role in maintaining international peace and security. There followed a series of highly-visible and large-scale failures – in Somalia, the former Yugoslavia and Rwanda in particular – which demonstrated both the larger and more complex demands being made on the UN in its peacekeeping operations, and its very considerable difficulties in meeting these demands. These gave rise to predictable, easy condemnations of the UN as a particularly inefficient, ineffective and incompetent organization – to some degree justified but to some degree also scapegoating exercises which played to domestic political needs and opportunities, and ignored the role of states in setting the limits and shaping the processes of UN responses. There also followed, however, a series of studies, articles, reports and collections of recommendations attempting to analyse more closely the reasons for the difficulties faced in these missions and to suggest remedies.[24]

On March 7, 2000, United Nations Secretary-General Kofi Annan commissioned the most recent of this series of studies. Headed by Lakhdar Brahimi of Algeria, on August 21, 2000 the Panel on United Nations Peace Operations submitted its report, containing over 50 recommendations. While the term 'commercial satellite imagery' does not appear as such in the Report, a number of its recommendations have some bearing, whether directly or indirectly, on the possible use of CSI by the United Nations. Most directly, para. 251 (b) states that:

> Peace operations could benefit greatly from more extensive use of geographic information systems (GIS) technology, which quickly integrates operational information with electronic maps of the mission area, for applications as diverse as demobilization, civilian policing, voter registration, human rights monitoring and reconstruction.

This appeared as part of a larger strategy of improving the UN's information technology (IT) capability, both for Headquarters and for operations in the field, as "a key enabler" of UN objectives in peace and security. The Report emphasized the need for a properly planned and integrated IT structure, and suggested that an Information and Strategic Analysis Secretariat (EISAS), under the Executive Committee on Peace and Security (ECPS), could perform a significant supervisory role in this. It noted as well (para. 221) that the Department of did not have modern means to document ceasefire violations or to monitor these, or movements in demilitarized zones, or the removal of weapons from storage sites.

Other aspects of the Panel's report and recommendations also present potential implications for a United Nations CSI capability. These included the observation that:

> United Nations forces for complex operations should be afforded the field intelligence and other capabilities needed to mount an effective defence against violent challengers.[25]

Other recommendations of the Report touched on areas such as the formation of several coherent, brigade-size units ready for deployment within 30 days. The Report noted a recent tendency for Less Developed Countries to provide the bulk of troops for missions, instead of Developed Countries. There are problems arising from troops arriving in the field ill-equipped or untrained, or without common understandings of mission operations, or common training with other contingents. The development of "coherent brigade-sized forces" would provide troops who had worked together and could meet training, equipment and other standards. As well, the Report argued the need to strengthen support resources for peacekeeping operations in UN Headquarters, including an increase in the number of personnel at Headquarters, especially in the Department of Peacekeeping Operations.

These additional recommendations point to larger command and control issues within UN peacekeeping operations, which form a significant context for the consideration of the use of CSI by the UN. As UN missions become larger and more complex, are deployed in more hostile environments, and become more proactive, the demands for intelligence increase, but the 'fudged' command and control structures typical of UN operations become increasingly stressed. Meeting both the broader command and control needs and more specific intelligence needs of these missions become interlocking requirements.[26]

CSI and UN Peacekeeping

A variety of specific questions must be addressed in order to assess the potential for and the problems entailed in the use of CSI in support of UN peacekeeping.

An initial need is to clarify the current and developing capabilities in the satellite remote sensing field and in the technologies for the manipulation of the resulting information. Only a few years ago, CSI was available at best in the range of 5–10 meter resolution, which would provide some, but limited, usefulness. With the development of 1-meter resolution imagery (such as the IKONOS satellite), RADARSAT, and other sensor capabilities, the possibilities for use have expanded. It has been suggested that, of a fairly standard table of tasks and the necessary spatial resolution to perform them,

> [w]ith the advent of one-meter ground-sample distance (GSD) panchromatic sensors…, nearly 60 percent of the table's military intelligence tasks, and 85 percent of the targeting-related tasks can now be satisfied.[27]

At the same time, the development of communications technology and the hardware and software for imagery analysis, as a part of the larger information technology revolution, have led to both greater ease and greater sophistication of use. Applications in disaster relief are drawing increased attention in the NGO community, while the parallels between fighting forest fires – another potential application for imagery, whether airborne or satellite – and an armed enemy have also been noted.[28]

In approaching the matter of the use of CSI not simply in terms of the imagery itself but also as the centre of a broader system of communications and analytical capabilities, at least three things become apparent. First, there are at least some potential, if still limited, parallels between the demands of peacekeeping and those of managing other activities in which CSI could have applications. Second, the availability of commercial technology – even if it requires some adaptation to UN needs – could be a significant factor in cutting the costs for the acquisition and operation of such a capability. Baines, for example, argues that CSI, and associated interpretation costs, could be reasonably competitive with aerial surveillance.[29] At the same time, CSI presents legal, physical and other financial advantages over aerial surveillance. There is no need to apply for overflight rights over national territory, and satellites, unlike manned or unmanned aircraft, are not exposed to hostile fire and associated loss risks and replacement costs. Williams and Lind, on the other hand, note claims that use of 'commercial off-the-shelf' systems may be cheaper considered individually than military systems, but suggest that they still face problems of compatibility and replacement.[30] Third, while a CSI-based capability may not be "state-of-the-art" as compared to the most highly-advanced militaries, it may still be extremely useful in and of itself.

A second general concern is to establish in greater detail some of the needs of peacekeeping operations themselves with respect to the sorts of information and the applications made possible through the use of CSI. If the demand for intelligence varies with the complexity and the proactive character of the mission, and with the hostility of the environment in which the mission must operate, there may then be variations in the requirements for information from CSI even if all mission types could have potential uses. As well, variation in needs for the phases of the mission and for the nature of the user must be taken into account. In the initial phases of mission planning and preparation, the information would be needed in the UN's New York headquarters. As the force deploys and carries out its mission, how would information needs develop (depending, of course, on the specific mandate of the force as well as mission phase)? Even observation missions could use imagery to map and to help monitor ceasefire lines and buffer zones. More complex missions, whether involving disaster relief, disarmament verification or other operations, could have more and in some cases stiffer requirements. Would CSI compare favourably to other methods for the gathering of imagery?

How such varied needs would be best satisfied raises a third group of concerns. Could the imagery and its analysis be obtained in a timely manner and at an acceptable cost? Would the basic acquisition and analysis be best done by a central unit which would then disseminate the data to commands in the field, or would theatre commands be of a size and have needs sufficient to justify a theatre capacity? What would be the minimum useful size for a CSI 'cell,' as compared, for example, to the size of a given UN operation, and what would be the associated capital and operating costs? What other problems might arise in operating such a unit, whether in the field or at UN headquarters?

The notorious sensitivity of the UN to "intelligence" might also raise problems: states might resist the development of a UN CSI capability in one form or another. This resistance could be either reduced or exacerbated by the connection between the development of such a capability and the broader question of the improvement of the UN's more general command and control capability. If such a CSI capability was politically tolerable, it would still have to be developed and applied within the limits of international law with respect to both remote sensing and the UN Charter.

A UN CSI capability: Better, but no magic bullet

The development of a UN-centred CSI capability is more than an issue simply of imagery. It would have to be linked to broader issues of technology in order to exploit the imagery in the first place: the full impact could not be achieved without this modern technology. As David B. Sandalow, an Assistant Secretary in the US Department of State, has observed,

> The ultimate value of satellite data comes from integration with other technologies of the global information age. Satellite data becomes more useful after it has been analyzed and

fused with other geospatial technologies such as geographic information systems and the Global Positioning System (GPS). This allows for calibration, accuracy, verification and transformation into useful information products. Particularly important is the modeling capability made possible by the fusion of data streams from various sources.[31]

The question of such a capability thus bears on issues of hardware, software, communications equipment, information standards and compatibility, and a variety of other technical issues. These pose significant demands even within the scope of a national military organization.[32] The impact of CSI on the United Nations must therefore be assessed not only merely in terms of the imagery itself, but also in terms of the marriage of that imagery to modern information technology. CSI is of importance not only in itself but also as a platform or base for the use of spatially-represented data more generally. In this sense, the development of a modern CSI capability by the UN means, in essence, its participation in at least some aspects of the Revolution in Military Affairs which some military analysts see happening in at least the most modern armed forces in the world. One broad implication of the Brahimi Report more generally, and not just of the possibilities for the use of CSI, is the necessity of an upgrading of the UN's C4I (command, control, communications, computers and intelligence) capability. To think otherwise is equivalent to proposing to put a 4-cylinder engine on a hand mower.

At the same time, commercial satellite imagery and its associated technologies are not a 'magic bullet', a panacea for all the ills affecting United Nations peacekeeping operations. Information from human sources – HUMINT – is still by far the most important source of information, especially at the level of field operations. There are also significant military and political dangers that could arise from the use of CSI. For example, if it was perceived as a force multiplier, it might be used to justify reductions in peacekeeping manpower, reducing the vital physical presence of peacekeepers. Or, the increasing use of high-technology systems in UN peacekeeping operations – especially in the field – could raise difficulties by increasing the demand for troops capable of using such sophisticated systems.[33] The possible implications here are twofold. On the one hand, a number of states with less sophisticated forces, which might otherwise be quite willing to provide troops for UN operations, could find themselves less called upon, thus reducing in some senses the UN's potential manpower pool for at least some tasks. On the other, would developed states, more likely to have the required forces, be willing to provide them more generously? If they did, would this in turn be a source of concern to Third World states which might not find an outburst of First World peacekeeping activism to be entirely welcome in political terms?[34]

Both technologically and politically, the development of a significant United Nations capability to exploit CSI technology cannot itself address all the problems that the UN faces in its peacekeeping activities. Indeed, the development of such a capability is likely to raise a variety of potentially thorny problems. However, such a capability would mark, or could lead to, a significant improvement in the UN's peacekeeping capabilities more generally. Given that such capabilities are increasingly available in the private sector, to non-government actors, and even potentially to those whom UN peacekeepers might face in the field, there seems to be little point in denying them to the United Nations, and there seems to be much to be gained.

CSI and Canadian Security Interests

Having identified at least some of the issues and problems to be dealt with in developing a UN capability to use commercial satellite imagery, we might then ask how they could be best resolved. In particular, from a Canadian perspective, several additional considerations come into play. First, Canada has an interest in the strengthening of UN peacekeeping, and has declared its general support for the Brahimi Report. Second, we are also interested in the use of satellite (and aerial) imagery and related systems in the context of NATO operations. Third, Canada is an imagery provider, in the instance of RADARSAT, and an imagery service provider. Fourth, Canada is an ally of the United States, and is co-ordinating its policies with those of the US with respect to the availability of CSI.

Canada's ability to address UN requirements and possibilities depends, therefore, not only on technical matters, including its capabilities, but additionally on issues of policy. How far ought Canada be willing to support the development of an autonomous UN CSI capability? If Canada chooses to support such a capability in the UN, how might it best do this? Would a satisfactory or even a superior alternative to the development of a capability lodged within the UN be the development and deployment of a CSI or similar capability located in a national unit on peacekeeping duty? If Canada developed a CSI-related capability, it would be less dependent on US imagery from its National Technical Means. Would this be a necessary or desirable development for at least some purposes, or simply a complication both technically and in our relations with the US? As a producer and a consumer of CSI, how would it deal with issues of 'shutter control'?

The capabilities of the Canadian Armed Forces as such also arise as an issue in the context of the Revolution in Military Affairs. The RMA includes, but is not limited to, increased intelligence and surveillance – broadly, 'battlespace awareness' – capabilities: it also applies to precision weaponry, C4I, and power projection.[35] Some of the questions which the UN might face in the development of its own CSI capability could, however, touch on some RMA-related issues, as is obvious from our discussion thus far. To that extent, the question of a solution for the UN could also be instructive for states less capable than the US.

A further set of considerations arises from the complex intersection of the RMA and low-intensity operations such as peacekeeping. First, commentators have warned that high-technology systems, including intelligence systems, may have limited uses in such operations. The importance of HUMINT in peacekeeping has already been noted.[36] Second, the possibility that such low-intensity operations may be the most frequent form of mission therefore suggests the limited utility of RMA technologies in a common type of operation. Third, this raises a potential tension between the desire of the Canadian Forces to have interoperability with American forces, and its peacekeeping employment, including resource and effort allocation problems between RMA investment and peacekeeping deployments.[37] Fourth, however, just as the US might fear becoming technologically incompatible with 'backward' allies,[38] so increasing the C4I capabilities of the UN to permit it to take advantage of CSI could open an analogous gap between relatively high-technology and low-technology contributors to peacekeeping. 'Medium-technology' states such as Canada could potentially find themselves on both ends of the problems which the RMA poses for multinational operations.

Finally, however, because the Revolution in Military Affairs embraces a range of issues and technologies, there is no inherent reason to believe that all technologies are uniformly problematic for all applications. Overlaps between civilian and peacekeeping applications, and the Brahimi Report itself, suggest that there could be at least some relevance of some technologies and some associated issues to peacekeeping and similar operations. Whether on a technical, organizational, doctrinal or conceptual basis, consideration by Canada of the questions raised by the possibility of a UN CSI capability of some sort could possibly help it avoid, reduce or at least clarify some matters raised by the RMA. There may be no inherent contradiction, within the context of Canadian security interests, between some aspects of the RMA, Canadian peacekeeping and Canadian CSI policy. There may even be some potential for mutual support.

Notes

1   Government of Canada *News Release* No. 153, 'Canada and United States Sign Agreement Concerning Operation of Commercial Remote Sensing Satellite Systems,' June 16, 2000; Barrie McKenna, 'Canada, U.S. strike deal on spy satellite,' *The Globe and Mail*, June 16, 2000, p.B3.

2   See, e.g., Elinor Sloan, 'Canada and the Revolution in Military Affairs: Current Response and Future Opportunities,' *Canadian Military Journal*, Vol. 1, 2000, pp.7–14.

3   United Nations, Department for Disarmament Affairs, *The Implications of Establishing an International Satellite Monitoring Agency*, New York: United Nations, 1983. The ISMA study originated in a 1978 French proposal. In the early 1980s, Canada developed the PAXSAT concept. This, rather than being geared to an overarching, multi-use verification organization, focused on the development of satellite systems for specific treaties. See, e.g., Canada, Department of External Affairs, 'PAXSAT Concept: The Application of Space-based Remote Sensing for Arms Control Verification,' *Verification Brochure* No. 2 Ottawa: Department of External Affairs, n.d.

4   See, e.g., Robert A. McDonald (ed.), *Space Imagery and News Gathering for the 1990s: So What?* Bethesda, Md.: American Society for Photogrammetry and Remote Sensing, 1991.

5   Vipin Gupta, 'New Satellite Images for Sale,' *International Security*, Vol. 20, 1995, pp.124–125.

6   E.g., Ann M. Florini, 'The Opening Skies: Third-Party Imaging and U.S. Security,' *International Security*, Vol. 13, 1988, pp.91–123; Hugh de Santis, 'Commercial Observation Satellites and their Military Implications: A Speculative Assessment,' *The Washington Quarterly*, Vol. 12, 1989, pp.185–200.

7   Peter D. Zimmerman, 'The Uses of SPOT for Intelligence Collection: A Quantitative Assessment,' in Michael Krepon et al. (eds.), *Commercial Observation Satellites and International Security*, New York: St. Martin's Press, 1990, pp.74–77.

8   Michael Krepon, 'The New Hierarchy in Space; Peter D. Zimmerman, 'Remote Sensing Satellites, Superpower Relations, and Public Diplomacy;' Jeffrey T. Richelson, 'Implications for Nations Without Space-Based Intelligence Collection Capabilities,' Zimmerman, "Uses of SPOT;" in Krepon et al., *Commercial Observation Satellites*, pp.16–32, 33–48, 55–73 and 74–77 respectively. A.V. Banner and A.G. McMullan, "Commercial Satellite Imagery for UNSCOM," in Steven Mataija and J. Marshall Beier

(eds), *Multilateral Verification in the Post-Gulf Environment: Learning from the UNSCOM Experience*, Toronto: Centre for International and Strategic Studies, York University, December 1992, p. 155. Florini, "The Opening Skies," pp.103, 111–112.

9   Tomas Ries and Johnny Skorve, *Investigating Kola: A Study of Military Bases using Satellite Photography*, London: Brassey's, 1987.

10   Respectively, http://www.fas.org and http://www.isis-online.org. See also Ann M. Florini and Yahya Dehqandzada, 'Commercial Satellite Imagery Comes of Age,' *Issues in Science and Technology Online* (Fall 1999), http://www.nap.edu/issues/16.1/florini.htm.

11   http://www.auslig.gov.au/acres/referenc/dili.htm. Note that this is found on an Australian government site.

12   Vipin Gupta and Frank Pabian, *Investigating the Allegations of Indian Nuclear Test Preparations in the Rajasthan Desert: A CTB Verification Exercise Using Commercial Satellite Imagery*, Sandia National Laboratories, July 1996; available at http://www.ca.sandia.gov/casite/gupta/index.htm. In 1998, the Canadian government published a bibliography, containing 562 entries, on the use of CSI in verification. Canada, *Security-Related Applications of Commercial Remote Sensing Satellites: A Bibliography, 1955–1997*, Ottawa: Department of Foreign Affairs and International Trade, July 1998.

13   http://www.atlsci.com/news/040200_East_Timor1.html.

14   http://www.eurimage.com.

15   E.g., Einar Bjorgo, 'Digital Imagery in Global Disaster Information, *Bulletin of the American Society for Information Science*, Vol. 26, 1999, http://www.asis.org/Bulletin/Oct-99/bjorgo.html. See also: the United States Institute for Peace 'Virtual Diplomacy' project, http://www.usip.org; the Carnegie Endowment for International Peace 'Transparency and Civil Society' project, http://www.ceip.org; the Nansen Environmental and Remote Sensing Center, http://www.nrsc.no; the ReliefSat project, http://www.nrsc.no/reliefsat; and the ENVIREF project, http://www.enviref.org.

16   On the feasibility of this, see, e.g., Christer Andersson, *Ph 2 Final Report: IAEA Safeguards: Implementation Blueprint of Commercial Satellite Imagery*, SKI Report 00:11, Stockholm: Swedish Nuclear Power Inspectorate, January 2000. See also James F. Keeley and Jason K. Cameron, 'The Need to Know: Commercial Satellite Imagery and IAEA Safeguards,' in Peter Gizewski (ed.), *Non-Proliferation, Arms Control and Disarmament: Enhancing Existing Regimes and Exploring New Dimensions*, Toronto: Centre for International and Security Studies, York University, 1998, pp.13–33.

17   I am indebted to J.P. Paquette for pointing out the difference between analysis and interpretation.

18   See, e.g., the controversy over some of the uses of CSI by the Federation of American Scientists, and some of the claims derived from those uses: Pat Eddington, "Orbital Snooping: Welcome to Amateur Hour," Space News, May 22, 2000, p.14, http://www.fas.org/eye/00052-sn.htm; 'A Response to Pat Eddington's "Orbital Snooping: Welcome to Amateur Hour"' http://www.fas.org/eye/00052-sn-r.htm.

19   S.B. Flemming, *Organizational and Military Impacts of High-Tech Surveillance and Detection Systems for UN Peacekeeping, Project Report 535*, Ottawa: Operational Research and Analysis Establishment, Department of National Defence, December 1992. U.S. Congress, Office of Technology Assessment, *Improving the Prospects for Future International Peace Operations*, OTA-BP-ISS-167, Washington, DC: U.S. Government Printing Office, September 1995. Alex Gliksman (ed.), *Meeting the Challenge of International Peace Operations: Assessing the Contribution of Technology*, Livermore, Calif.: Center for Global Security Research, Lawrence Livermore National Laboratory, June 1998.

20   Vipin Gupta and Adam Bernstein, *Keeping and Eye on the Islands: Remote Monitoring in the South China Sea*, Sandia National Laboratories, May 1999; available at

http://gwis.circ.gwu.edu/~spi/title.htm. Vipin Gupta and LTC George Harris, *Detecting Massed Troops with the French SPOT Satellites: A Feasibility Study for Cooperative Monitoring*, Sandia National Laboratories, January 1999; available at http://www.cmc.sandia.gov/issues/papers/gupta2/index.html.

21 Richard G. Johnson, 'Negotiating the Dayton Peace Accords Through Digital Maps,'"Presentation at a Seminar, 'Virtual Diplomacy – Case Studies,' held by the United States Institute of Peace, Washington, DC, February 18, 1999. http://www.usip.org/oc/vd/vdr/rjohnsonISA99.html. See also Timothy L. Thomas, 'Virtual Peacekeeping: A Military View of Conflict Prevention Through the Use of Information Technology,' U.S. Army, Foreign Military Studies Office, http://call.army.mil/call/fmso/fmso.pubs/.

22 Hugh Smith, 'Intelligence and UN Peacekeeping,' Survival, Vol. 36, 1994, p.185; A. Walter Dorn, 'The Cloak and the Blue Beret: Limitations on Intelligence in UN Peacekeeping, *International Journal of Intelligence and Counterintelligence*, Vol. 12, 1999, pp.427, 428; Mats R. Berdal, 'Whither UN Peacekeeping? *Adelphi Papers* No. 281, October 1993, p.66.

23 Miklos Pinther, 'United Nations Geographic Database,' Presentation at 'Meeting on Cartography and Geographic Information Science,' United Nations, New York, March 28–30, 2000.

24 E.g., Berdal; Alex Morrison (ed.), *The Changing Face of Peacekeeping*, Toronto: The Canadian Institute of Strategic Studies, 1993; U.S. General Accounting Office, *U.N. Peacekeeping: Lessons Learned in Managing Recent Operations*, GAO/NSIAD-94-9, Washington: USGPO, December 1993; Canada, *Towards a Rapid Reaction Capability for the United Nations*, Ottawa: Government of Canada, September 1995; David Cox and Albert Legault (eds.), *UN Rapid Reaction Capabilities: Requirements and Prospects*, Clementsport, N.S.: The Canadian Peacekeeping Press, 1995; U.S. General Accounting Office, *United Nations: Limitations in Leading Missions Requiring Force to Restore Peace*, GAO/NSIAD-97-34, Washington, D.C.: USGPO, March 1997.

25 United Nations, *Report of the Panel on United Nations Peace Operations*, August 21, 2000, A/55/305-S/2000/809, p.x. Hereinafter cited as *Brahimi Report*.

26 Smith, pp.178, 181; Berdal, p.44; John Hillen, *Blue Helmets: The Strategy of UN Military Operations*, Washington: Brassey's, 1988, passim.

27 Lt Col Larry K. Grundhauser, USAF, 'Sentinels Rising: Commercial High Resolution Satellite Imagery and Its Implications for US National Security, *Airpower Journal*, 1998, http://www.usafa.af.mi./inss.

28 See, e.g., John K. Newton, *Autonomous and Remotely Guided Vehicle Market Study*, Edmonton, Alberta: Western Economic Diversification Canada, July 4, 2000, p.24. See also Brad Foster, 'REMSAT Revolutionizes Emergency Management,' *Earth Observation Magazine*, January 2000. http://www.eomonline.com.

29 Phillip J. Baines, 'Spaceborne Imagery: A Universal, Effective, and Cost-Efficient Tool for Ongoing Monitoring and Verification,' in J. Marshall Beier and Steven Mataija (eds.), *Cyberspace and Outer Space: Transitional Challenges for Multilateral Verification in the 21st Century*, Toronto: Centre for International and Strategic Studies, York University, 1997, pp.179, 182.

30 Cindy Williams and Jennifer M. Lind, 'Can We Afford a Revolution in Military Affairs?' *Breakthroughs* (Spring 1999). Available at http://web.mit.edu/ssp/db21/breakthroughs.html.

31 David P. Sandalow, 'Remote Sensing and Foreign Policy,' Presentation at symposium on 'Viewing the Earth: The Role of Satellite Earth Observations and Global Monitoring in International Affairs,' George Washington University, Washington, D.C., June 6, 2000. Available at U.S. Department of State, http://www.state.gov/www/policy_re...000/000606_sandalow_satellite.html.

32   Allen P. Hazlegrove, 'Desert Storm Time-Sensitive Surface Targeting: A Successful
     Failure or a Failed Success?' *Defense Analysis*, Vol. 16, 2000, pp.113–150.
33   Flemming, pp.12, 13–14, 15.
34   Ibid., pp.9–10; the Brahimi Report (para. 103) notes the decline in the percentage of
     troops from developed countries in UN operations in recent years.
35   Sloan, pp.7–8.
36   E.g., Capt. David B. Collins, 'Military Intelligence in Low-Intensity Conflict,' *Military
     Intelligence*, July-September 1991, pp.11–12; Capt. David P. Rababy, 'Intelligence
     Support During a Humanitarian Mission,' *Marine Corps Gazette*, February 1995,
     pp.40–41; Lt. Col. Herschell A. Boyd, 'Joint Intelligence in Support of Peace
     Operations,' Newport, R.I.: Naval War College, June 14, 1996, pp.8–12; Col. D.W.
     Read, 'The Revolution in Military Affairs: NATO's Need for a Niche Capability
     Strategy,' *Canadian Military Journal*, Vol. 1, 2000, p. 21; Lester W. Grau, 'Bashing the
     Laser Range Finder with a Rock,' Military Review, May-June 1997 (available at U.S.
     Army, Foreign Military Studies Office, http://call.army.mil/call/fmso/fmso.pubs/).
37   Sloan, passim.
38   Read, p.17.

Chapter 8

Organizing the United Nations for Commercial Satellite Imagery

James F. Keeley

A variety of detailed and complex technical, financial and legal issues must be resolved before the United Nations will be able to make routine use of commercial satellite imagery (CSI) in support of its peacekeeping operations. In addition, however, various political and organizational issues must be addressed. The former will decide whether such a capability will be permitted at all, much less in any functionally satisfactory way. Subject to the political factor, how the supply, dissemination and use of CSI and related products will be organized raises issues for both UN headquarters in New York and for the structure and operations of field commands. These issues will become still more complex if UN peacekeepers are expected to integrate their activities with nongovernmental organizations (NGOs) active in a 'complex operation' – that is, an operation in which both military and humanitarian aspects are significant.

This chapter will first note the larger contexts within which UN organizational issues regarding the use of CSI must arise. These are, respectively, the political, C4I (command, control, communication, computer and intelligence) capability contexts. It will then draw on some existing information about intelligence and C4I problems and possibilities in UN and other operations to explore briefly five scenarios relevant to the organization of the UN for the use of CSI. In the first two, imagery is essentially under the complete control of states while in the last three some degree of UN capability to acquire and use CSI is assumed.

The Larger Contexts

The fundamental political limitation on the United Nations is the willingness of states to tolerate the acquisition and use of a significant CSI capability by the organization. Many states subject to satellite observation at one time, at least, strongly objected to uncontrolled observation. Most, however, lacked the ability to do anything about it, and ultimately essentially freedom to observe prevailed. There seems to be no inherent legal obstacle in general international law to the collection of CSI, even by international organizations.[1] It is, of course, possible that certain difficulties could still arise with respect to certain practices or actions within either general international law or within the terms of the charter or mandate of authority of a given international organization. For example, if the International Atomic

Energy Agency adopts the use of CSI in its safeguarding activities – a direction in which it is moving – this does not mean it is necessarily free to use such imagery for any and all purposes. It would likely be restricted purely to safeguarding applications, and its ability to disseminate the imagery or information from it to others, for other purposes, would likely be blocked.

In the particular case of associations of sovereign states, more-over, having a legal capacity in theory does not guarantee having in practice either the political support of states or the resources (including financial) that only states may be able to provide for a specific activity. States potentially subject to satellite observation by the UN may hesitate to give it such a capacity. So, too, may states which, through possession of the technology now, may be favoured by its current distribution. Joseph Nye once suggested what he termed 'the Law of Inverse Salience':

> the less important the task politically, either because of its technical nature or limited impact, the greater the prospects for the growth of the [international] organization's authority vis-à-vis the member states. Conversely, the more important the task by nature or impact, the weaker the authority of the organization will be.[2]

The same relationship might be anticipated in the case of independent capabilities wielded by an international organization. Doll and Metz echoed this in 1993:

> For most member states, better a weak, dependent, and pliable UN than a stronger, autonomous one which might act against national interests.[3]

The question of the UN and CSI must also be considered within two additional, nested contexts: the first is the sensitive issue of a UN 'intelligence' capability, while the second and broader concern touches on the UN's C4I capabilities. The effective use of commercial satellite imagery does not simply raise the questions of whether or not such imagery might be available to the UN, or how it should fit into a larger UN 'information' or 'intelligence' capability. These issues themselves must also be located in the still larger context. The UN's C4I capabilities will affect how it could use CSI and, conversely, the effective use of CSI would have profound implications for its C4I capabilities.

For the United Nations, the historical sensitivity of the term 'intelligence' is quite relevant: the collection of 'information' is an absolute necessity in peacekeeping operations, and has occurred, but the creation of a stronger, and in particular a more independent, capability for information-gathering and -analysis may well generate unease among member states. The historical and, now at least, psychological, association of satellite imagery with 'National Technical Means' (NTM) would not be helpful in this regard. Again, Doll and Metz are instructive. They note suggestions that UN enforcement operations

> may not require developing an organic intelligence-gathering capability for the UN, but rather greater intelligence-sharing among the permanent members of the Security Council. In any case, it will remain politically infeasible to collect strategic intelligence at UN headquarters. This means the UN must continue to rely on national suppliers for intelligence.[4]

The political implications of this argument, with its suggestion of dependence on existing state-based intelligence capabilities, are precisely challenged by the possibility of a UN CSI capability. Peace enforcement operations, as they will likely have a very significant element drawn from the permanent five of the Security Council, will differ from peacekeeping or similar complex operations. However, this statement does point to the necessary political question for the Brahimi Report's argument that a greater intelligence capability is needed, both at UN headquarters and in the field:[5] will states now see this need and be interested in addressing it – and if so, how?

Against this posited reluctance to give the UN a strengthened, much less an independent, intelligence capability might be argued the growing use of CSI in particular by private actors and NGOs, the interest shown in its use by the International Atomic Energy Agency as a safeguarding tool and, more broadly, the growing volume and utility of 'open source' information more generally. 'Open source' information may be loosely defined as information which is both publicly available and legally obtained.[6] It thus does not carry the same political burden as information obtained covertly. CSI, being by definition available in a public market, would fit within this definition. As CSI becomes more widely and readily available, along with the hardware and software to exploit it, the logic of denying to the UN a capability increasingly in the hands of everyone else becomes strained. How precisely this imagery and information derived from or based on it might be provided to and used by the UN might still be significant questions, however. What are the problems and possibilities which might arise depending on how that supply and use are organized? Considerable variation is possible here, with significant implications for the UN both in its New York Headquarters and in the field.

Five Scenarios

The scenarios developed here briefly set out five general modes of organization of the UN for the use of CSI. They are used to identify some of the problems which would have to be addressed. There is no suggestion here that any one is necessarily the best approach; rather, each will present its own challenges and requirements.

The first two scenarios draw on examples from past UN operations. They assume that imagery, whether from CSI or from 'National Technical Means' is essentially under the control of states, and is not systematically provided to or processed through the UN. The first scenario is more of a benchmark or reference case, a summary of various past significant complaints about the UN's information capabilities and practices, whether in the field or in UN headquarters in New York. This will be used to identify some basic defects and problems in the UN's C4I capabilities, as they affect intelligence more generally and thus could also bear on the use of CSI. The second scenario is a 'sub-contracting' model – that is, essentially a peacekeeping operation has been 'contracted out' to a particular major player, though other states may also contribute forces and resources. These two scenarios thus correspond to variants within the broader suggestion noted by Doll and Metz above.

The remaining scenarios extrapolate from various recommendations in the Brahimi Report, depending on three patterns for how those recommendations are taken up. All are based on the possession by the UN of an independent ability to acquire and analyze CSI, but they vary in terms of the location of that capability whether in New York or in its theatre commands or both. The key factor underlying these scenarios is the willingness of states to see a strengthening of the UN capability, along lines flowing from the Brahimi Report and, if so, where. In the third scenario, this capability is assumed to reside only in the UN's New York headquarters, with an information feed then flowing to the field or theatre headquarters. The third scenario thus builds on some of the suggestions in the Brahimi Report at the level of the New York headquarters. At the theatre level, however, it assumes dependence on relatively unreformed field commands for relevant functions. The fourth scenario assumes that institution of a capability in a brigade formation structure along the lines suggested in the Brahimi Report is more politically palatable than a significant strengthening of the New York headquarters.[7] In essence, therefore, this attempts to incorporate some aspects of a leading state approach. The final case covers the possibility of an independent UN CSI capability at both the New York and field command levels.

Issues of 'shutter control' are not addressed in any of these cases. As well, assuming the acquisition and use of CSI by the UN at any level does not require a parallel assumption that national units do not have access to their own imagery and derived information. Finally, while we assume that CSI might have applications for a wide array of UN missions, it is possible that both the specific uses and the ability of field units to deploy CSI 'cells' will vary from one mission or mission type to another. For example, while ceasefire observation and buffer zone observation missions might have uses for CSI, some operations of these types could perhaps be too small to justify an organic CSI 'cell' at the field level. Two issues thus arise: first, the minimum useful size for such a 'cell' in the field, given specifics such as mission type and scale, and given the actual uses for the information and the volume of imagery required;[8] and second, whether useful imagery and derived information could be provided in a timely manner from a central unit at New York regardless of mission specifics or scale.

Scenario 1: A composite of bad

There may be instances where the UN has been given satellite imagery (whether from NTM or CSI), or at least information derived from such imagery, at a central or at a theatre level. Dependence on such outside sources – and thus on these sources' willingness and ability to grant or withhold access to such imagery and information – could be a very sore political point even if the utility of the imagery and information is granted. However, merely giving the UN unimpeded access to imagery would in itself be insufficient. Without an organization able to acquire, analyse and deliver the imagery and derived products satisfactorily, access to imagery alone is of little real use. Access to imagery is not enough, and access to appropriate hardware and software is not enough; the organization as such must be capable of exploiting the technology properly. This is not the current case in the United Nations. This initial scenario outlines some of the relevant complaints about the UN's C4I system, to provide a benchmark of some of the problems that must be addressed if a useful UN CSI capability is to be developed.

There are several well-known complaints about the UN's ability to launch and to manage peacekeeping operations in New York, and about the handling of what are essentially intelligence functions in the field. In New York, both the haste with which a mission might be mounted and chronic understaffing undermine the planning and preparation processes. The inability of the UN headquarters to be available for field commands after hours, also noted, may reflect both 'cultural' and resource factors. Although some steps have been taken to address these problems, in terms of information-gathering and -generation the UN is still highly dependent on states. Although an Office for Research and the Collection of Information was created in the UN Secretariat in 1987, this apparently accomplished little and was eliminated as a separate entity in 1992.[9] A Situation Centre was created within the Department of Peacekeeping Operations in the early 1990s, to provide 24 hour/7 days a week contact. This consisted in 1994 of 24 staff, of whom 17 were from North America, Western Europe and Australia,[10] raising a potential issue of Western domination. The Centre has an Information and Research Unit, which Dorn[11] reports in 1999 as consisting of four officers, drawn from France, Russia, the US and the UK, thus raising the same issue. A brief description of the Situation Centre points out its need for maps and GIS capabilities.[12] Commenting on the UN's need for a geographic database at a conference in March 2000, the Head of the UN Cartographic Section noted that not only did the UN still rely largely on paper maps, but also that lack of co-ordination among UN units hinders the use of digital maps even if these are available, and absence of agreements with national agencies limits access to relevant geographic databases.[13]

Additionally, the description of its functions leads one to believe that the Situation Centre is primarily engaged in deriving information for the use of headquarters rather than also providing extensive information for field use.[14] This could corroborate a comment that the information flow in UN operations between the field and headquarters tends to be up rather than down, or 'all suck and no blow'.[15] Such a complaint could apply within the field as well. In terms of conditions in the field, a Swedish Armed Forces publication comments with respect to intelligence that:

> The individual national contingent, although supported in part by senior support organizations, will to a large extent be dependent on its own national assets and expertise.[16]

A Canadian comment on UNPROFOR is also of interest. It states that:

> with the exception of CCUNPROFOR input, United Nations-generated intelligence support was virtually non-existent and of no use to units.[17]

It goes on not only to note a lack of NATO-UN co-operation regarding aerial imagery, but also, respecting imagery exploitation, that:

> Canadian-based intelligence collection resources, including imagery exploitation, were incapable of responding quickly enough to provide timely support to units in-theatre. Generally, units were able to patrol into areas and disseminate information more quickly than imagery assets could be brought to bear.[18]

Merely resorting to national resources is not necessarily a remedy for UN deficiencies.

Intelligence functions in-theatre have thus also been problematic. Both haste and the problems of putting together a multinational mission 'on the fly' may lead commanders to give a higher priority to other concerns. Once established, a field command intelligence unit – however titled – might be incapable of doing much more than summarizing incoming information from deployed units. It might face considerable personnel problems, in terms of both basic competence and the rotation of specific personnel.[19] Specific national units might then develop or draw on their own capabilities but be reluctant to share their information. In the case of Somalia, the US fielded its own Intelligence Support Element, but this was not within the UN chain of command though information from it could be provided to the UN force commander. As a result, some national units in a mission might be better informed than the force commander.[20] The sharing of information derived from national sources (e.g., NTM) could be hindered or at least partially blocked. Dorn has noted that:

> in UNPROFOR, a Canadian peacekeeper with NATO clearance received US satellite photographs (useful to determine his operational deployment) but he was not permitted to show the images to his UN commander, who was a French officer.[21]

These varied problems have been recognized, and at least partially addressed, but much still remains to be done. The Brahimi Report proposes a much-strengthened information capability in New York, through the establishment of an Information and Strategic Analysis Secretariat, established as a subsidiary of the Executive Committee on Peace and Security (EISAS), and the development of Integrated Mission Task Forces.[22] However, it provides no particular recommendations for the structuring of field commands, despite its suggestion of the development of brigade formations. Canada and Norway have recently agreed to try to help improve mission planning in the Secretariat.[23] (Their offers of seconded personnel were apparently turned down.) The use of CSI by the UN could help to reduce some of these problems, such as some of the dependence on member states for information, and could improve aspects of planning, preparation, deployment and operations in the field. It could reduce, although possibly not eliminate, strains within the theatre from some units having an information advantage over the force commander. However, this litany of fundamental problems firmly establishes that merely access to CSI and related technologies for its exploitation will be ineffective in strengthening UN operations without associated significant improvements in UN C4I practice.

Scenario 2: The leading nation

A 'leading nation' model of UN operations has one state take a major role in organizing and managing the operation. For our purposes, this will be taken as a 'sub-contracting' approach, in which the UN is dependent on such a state being willing and able to act.[24] Of course this also assumes that this leader also has the leading intelligence capabilities, if political problems are to be avoided. The 'leading nation' is thus here assumed to be as well the leading intelligence nation.[25] It might seem that such a structure could avoid a number of problems arising in the first scenario. There is, however, potentially less here than meets the eye. Problems in the relations between this leader and the UN, and between this leader and other participating forces must still be addressed. As well, however, smooth operations within the leading nation's forces cannot be assumed.

The first two sets of issues are readily enough identified. UN dependence on state capabilities – and the associated political and control issues this creates – would continue and could even be exacerbated under this model. Far from acquiring greater capabilities, whether for mission planning and preparation or for management of operations, existing UN capabilities in these areas could well atrophy instead. If a leading nation model worked, it would still leave uncovered those operations for which no leading nation, or at least none with the appropriate capabilities, could be found. As for relations between the leading nation and other forces participating in the mission, while there would be an improvement, one presumes, in the central intelligence apparatus in the field and between home capabilities of the leading nation and the field, relations among national units could continue to be a problem. Differentiating among various types and levels of releasability would be needed, to preserve important source and method information. This was an issue in Somalia.[26] In the case of Bosnia, it led to 3 levels of intelligence: national only; NATO releasable; and IFOR releasable.[27] Considerable progress was made in this regard in Bosnia, the US Department of Defense noting at one point that the time for the sharing of imagery intelligence was reduced to 1.5 hours.[28] Interoperability problems may also exist between leading nation technology and that available to other participants.[29] So, too, might problems of differing doctrines, methods and organizations.

The leading nation model points to some potential gains and problems, from a UN perspective, in the use of a CSI capability. The development of a UN CSI capability would enhance rather than undercut, existing UN capabilities. The use of 'open source' imagery could reduce the problems of protecting sources which can hinder the sharing of NTM-based intelligence. Where a leading-nation model was not adopted, the use of CSI might at least reduce, although it would probably not eliminate, the disadvantageous position of a UN theatre commander not from an NTM-capable state. However, problems of organizing both the UN headquarters and the field for the effective use of CSI would still exist – including the problems of technical, doctrinal and other interoperability issues.

These difficulties are underlined by their existence even within a technologically-capable leading nation. The American experience in the Gulf War pointed to precisely such problems, among others.[30] Coia, for example, notes that the Marine Expeditionary Force (MEF) was bitterly dissatisfied with the intelligence support it received. Its supporting intelligence unit deployed at significantly less than full strength, was overwhelmed by information and tended to revert to 'bean-counting and plotting positions,' had to compete with others for access to imagery resources, and had difficulties with its communications systems which affected its ability to supply imagery in hard copy to subordinate units. The imagery provided was often of poor quality, too slow to be useful, or 'often lacked reference grid locations, north arrows, photo interpreters' analytical annotations, and image dates'. At one point, the MEF sent two officers to Washington to find any current imagery they could concerning an Iraqi unit.[31] The development of an Intelligence Support Element, such as was deployed in Somalia, was one response to these problems. This unit apparently numbered about 100 people at most.[32] Even so, there were still problems in Somalia.[33] Some of these were resolved by the time of the US deployment in Bosnia.[34]

A 'leading nation' approach might thus be of value both in practice and as a guide for other modes of organization. Such an approach can resolve some difficulties faced by the UN, but this in turn assumes that the internal operations of the leading nation are adequate, and that its ability to provide information to other participants is adequate. It leaves unresolved at best the questions of UN headquarters capabilities and of what is to be done when no appropriate leading nation offers itself for an operation. A UN CSI capability can directly address some of these issues. However, problems experienced within the leading nation also point to questions which would have to be addressed within a UN CSI capability, too. A resolution of these problems within a UN capability may not reach the highest military standards, and may face problems of interoperability, etc., itself. It may, however, still be good enough to be better than the absence of such a capability.

Scenario 3: A UN headquarters capability

The Brahimi Report, as already noted, presents a number of recommendations for the strengthening of the UN's headquarters capabilities. These include expanding the Department of Peacekeeping Operations, creating an Information and Strategic Analysis Secretariat, and developing Integrated Mission Task Forces for each operation. In presenting his initial proposals for the implementation of the report, the Secretary General stresses that the reforms at the UN headquarters level are to allow the 'better use' of information already within the UN system and of 'open source' information.[35] The implementation proposals also intend to follow up on recommendations in the Report to involve mission leaders 'as early as possible' in the mission planning process.[36] There is also interest in strengthening the UN's ability to access and use geographic database information.[37]

These proposals do not of themselves speak of developing a CSI capability, but it will be assumed here that they could form a basis for one. However, strengthening the UN headquarters in this way does not necessarily imply a parallel strengthening of theatre commands. Thus, this scenario assumes simply a central UN capability, upon which theatre commands would be completely dependent. Even where in some circumstances a field CSI capability might make sense, depending on the scale and nature of the operation, in others it might not. In very general terms, this could correspond to a 'leading nation' model in which field commands and units are dependent on centrally-supplied imagery and analysis services.

The size and staffing practices of such a central unit would be important questions. It would have to be large enough potentially to serve several missions at once: thus, it could require a surplus or 'surge' capacity. The scale of personnel, the terms of their service (e.g., secondment versus direct employment by the UN), and issues of personnel rotation would have to be addressed, as would the required training and skills.

The activities of such a central unit would depend on mission types and phases, and also on the nature of their connection, if any, to field commands. In the preparation and planning phase of a mission, and even into its deployment phase, CSI might be of use in assessing infrastructure (including transportation and communications links), mapping, locating refugee concentrations and planning their management, identifying or planning ceasefire lines and buffer zones, and other functions. Other possibilities, such as searching for mass graves in cases of actual or suspected large-scale human rights abuses, might require coordination with both appropriate field units and separate agencies, such as war crimes investigators.

Where a field operation had no independent CSI capability, then either we must depart from an "all suck and no blow" orientation in order to feed information as needed to the field command, or we should restrict the sort of information acquired through the use of CSI to that directly relevant to UN headquarters and its specific functions. If the centre did provide information services for the field, then obviously that information would have to be timely and appropriate, being both quickly produced and oriented to the needs of the field command. Some of the problems faced by the MEF in the Gulf War become significant in this respect. The logic of running all such imagery through a central unit would hold only if these demands could be met. This model leaves unaddressed questions of how that information might be disseminated and used in the field. Nor are issues of interoperability and other compatibility problems among field units, and the entire question of a field command's C4I capabilities, dealt with.

Scenario 4: An independent field capability

Where Scenario 3 assumes a central capability but no separate field capability, this scenario assumes a field capability only. It appears to be, so to speak, the UN equivalent of the leading nation model in which units in the field directly tap imagery resources. Such an approach could entail the "downloading" of certain functions from the UN centre or, perhaps along the lines suggested in the Brahimi Report, the greater involvement of mission leaders in the planning and preparation phases. It would either leave unaddressed questions of how the centre would get access to needed CSI-derived information, or would depend on a feed from the field command. It would, of course, depend on the feasibility of a CSI feed directly to the field command, 'cutting out the middleman' or the necessity of a capability at the UN centre, and on an operation being large enough to warrant such a separate capability.

Key problems in this scenario would arise in the theatre command's C4I capabilities and in the management of compatibility and interoperability problems within the multinational character of the force. Problems of personnel competence, and vulnerability to the rotation of either or both specific units or specific persons would have to be addressed. A 'military information' unit dependent on multinational staffing could face problems on both accounts, if critiques of past UN missions are accurate, while dependence on a single state to provide a coherent and competent unit for this function could still leave it vulnerable to both unit and personnel rotation, or even the withdrawal of that state from the mission altogether.

One alternative – drawing on a central UN unit for personnel and equipment deployable to the field as needed – might be worth entertaining but, like a central UN capability more generally, this unit would have to be capable of serving potentially several missions at once.

The recommendation within the Brahimi Report for the development of coherent brigade-size formations[38] could provide a structure within which to address some of these problems. Such units, drawing on several states, would train and deploy together. This could permit the development of sufficient familiarity among the units of differing states as to overcome some of the co-ordination problems they might otherwise face. Some interoperability problems, at least, might thus be identified and dealt with in advance. However, if several such units were developed, their training standards and interoperability issues would have to be addressed in a way compatible across brigades as well as within them if co-ordination problems were not simply to appear on a higher level. Moreover, if the capability to use CSI were to be if not uniform then at least roughly comparable across these units, then each would likely require at its command core the presence of troops with the requisite technology and sophistication. Thus, rather than bunching technologically-capable states together, these might have to spread out to cover each such brigade. As well, the ability of the brigade to function would then depend on such states being willing to participate in specific missions. If individual states retain an ability to control their participation in specific deployments, either this could compromise the unit or alternative appropriate participants would need to be available. Again, drawing on some sort of central UN 'pool' could be an alternative here.

The Brahimi Report does not address issues arising in field commands, or in its proposed brigade formations, in any detail. Some information, however, is available on the Standing High Readiness Brigade (SHIRBRIG) recently developed by a number of states.[39] In SHIRBRIG's staffing, however, one finds only eight personnel in G2 (Military Information).[40] Is this large enough to meet intelligence requirements even without an additional capability for CSI? How large would a minimal CSI capability have to be in order to justify deployment at the field level? Would it only make sense for operations above a brigade? As well, these personnel are drawn from a variety of states. One would hope that SHIRBRIG has resolved some of the problems noted in complaints about intelligence units in earlier UN operations, through its co-ordinated standards and training. Additionally, SHIRBRIG participants retain their ultimate national control over their forces.

Outside of the development of a central but deployable pool, this scenario would actually fall somewhat short of a true UN field CSI capability; instead, it would really be based on access to deployed national capabilities placed at the service of the UN. This could increase its attractiveness to states, but at the cost of complications in the real availability and use of such a capability. It would mark a closer co-ordination among states, and to some degree the spreading of a 'leading nation' model, but would not in truth move much beyond that model.

Scenario 5: A full UN capability

This is the most ambitious and complex scenario, and the one in which the UN has the greatest independent capability. It requires a CSI capacity at both headquarters and field levels, with not only some degree of specialization between them but probably also two-way information flows as needed. The relevant uses of and users for imagery and related information would vary with mission phase and type, and with specific information needs of the two levels. Giving both levels a degree of independent capability might reduce timeliness and utility problems, though it could also increase competition for resources and could inevitably be seen as creating a degree of duplication. It would require, of course, a resolution of difficulties at both levels, including difficulties identified in scenarios 2, 3 and 4, and the successful integration of their activities. Development not only of a central CSI capability but also of a pool of deployable personnel and equipment could be a step in this direction. This could help to reduce some problems of communication and interoperability between levels.

Conclusion

All five scenarios present important problems and possibilities for a UN CSI capability, not only in terms of the issues directly related to the use of imagery but also in terms of the larger C4I problems, and some others, that would have to be resolved. Perhaps the most significant scenario, however, is the second – the leading nation model. The three following it could all draw from aspects of this, though the development of coherent but still multinational brigade formations could introduce its own complications, as could the peculiarities of an international organization headquarters. From a technical-organizational point of view, studying issues arising from the use of imagery within a leading nation context – including in its interactions with other participants in a multinational force – could therefore be a particularly rewarding approach. Unfortunately, however, such a model could also generate the greatest political resistance, since it implies the greatest coherence and capability for the UN, and thus potentially the greatest test of Nye's 'Law of Inverse Salience.' Whether a politically-acceptable organization for a UN CSI capability could also meet the technical test of utility thus remains an open question. In that respect, the model of state-based independent field capabilities (scenario 4), combined but not necessarily well-integrated with some degree of a central headquarters capability, or a limited central capacity with little feed to the field (scenario 3), may be the more likely models if the UN has significant access to CSI at all.

Notes

1   Carl Q. Christol, 'The 1986 Remote Sensing Principles: Emerging or Existing Law?' International Institute of Space Law of the International Astronautical Federation, *Proceedings of the Thirtieth Colloquium on the Law of Outer Space,* 1987, Washington, DC: American Institute of Aeronautics and Astronautics, 1988, p.271. See also United Nations, Department for Disarmament Affairs, *Report of the Secretary-General: The Implications of Establishing an International Satellite Monitoring Agency,* New York: United Nations, 1983, pp.51–55.

2   J.S. Nye, *Peace in Parts: Integration and Conflict in Regional Organization*, Boston: Little, Brown, 1971, pp.23–24.

3   William J. Doll and Steven Metz, *The Army and Multinational Peace Operations: Problems and Solutions*. Report of a Roundtable sponsored by the Strategic Studies Institute of the U.S. Army War College and the U.S. Army Peacekeeping Institute, Carlisle Barracks, Pennsylvania, November 29, 1993, p.15.

4   Ibid., p.17.

5   United Nations, *Report of the Panel on United Nations Peace Operations*, August 21, 2000, A/55/305-S/2000/809, p. x. Hereinafter cited as the Brahimi Report.

6   For a more developed definition, see Robert D. Steele, 'The Importance of Open Sources Intelligence to the Military,' *International Journal of Intelligence and Counterintelligence*, Vol. 8, 1995, p.457.

7   I am grateful to John Ferris, Department of History, University of Calgary, for noting this possibility.

8   I am grateful to Mike Schuelter, a graduate student at the Centre for Military and Strategic Studies, University of Calgary, for drawing this question to my attention.

9   Mats R. Berdal, 'Whither UN Peacekeeping?' *Adelphi Papers*, No. 281, October 1993, p.66 footnote 50; A. Walter Dorn, 'The Cloak and the Blue Beret: Limitations on Intelligence in UN Peacekeeping,' *International Journal of Intelligence and Counterintelligence*, Vol. 12, 1999, p.433.

10   Hugh Smith, 'Intelligence and UN Peacekeeping,' *Survival*, Vol. 36, 1994, p.189.

11   Dorn, p.433.

12   Immaculée Uwanyiligira, 'Situation Centre needs.' Presentation at 'Meeting on Cartography and Geographic Information Science,' United Nations, New York, March 28–30, 2000. Available at http://www.un.org/Depts/Cartographic/english/ungis/meeting/.

13   Miklos Pinther, 'United Nations Geographic Database.' Presentation at 'Meeting on Cartography and Geographic Information Science,' United Nations, New York, March 28–30, 2000. Available at http://www.un.org/Depts/Cartographic/english/ungis/meeting/.

14   Uwanyiligira. See also the brief description of the Situation Centre's duties provided in US Army, Joint Warfighting Center, *Joint Task Force Commander's Handbook for Peace Operations*, Ft. Monroe, Va.: Joint Warfighting Centre, June 16, 1977, pp.IV–4–5.

15   Thomas Quiggan, 'Response to 'No Cloak and Dagger Required: Intelligence Support to UN Peacekeeping Missions,' *Intelligence and National Security*, Vol. 13, 1998, pp.203–4.

16   Swedish Armed Forces, *Joint Military Doctrine – Peace Support Operations*, para. 21; available at http://www.mil.se/doctrines/.

17   Canada, Army Lessons Learned Centre, 'Operations in the Former Republic of Yugoslavia,' *Despatches*, Vol. 4, 1996, p.25.

18   Ibid.

19   Paul Johnston, 'No Cloak and Dagger Required: Intelligence Support to UN Peacekeeping,' *Intelligence and National Security*, Vol. 12, 1997, p.109. See also Maj. Raymond J. Leach, '"Information" Support to U.N. Forces,' *Marine Corps Gazette*, September 1994, p.49.

20   Col. Ronald Davidson, *UN Reform – Can It be the Answer to Intelligence Support to UN Peacekeeping Operations?* Carlisle Barracks, Penn.: U.S. Army War College, April 22, 1998, p.8. U.S., Joint Chiefs of Staff, *Joint Doctrine for Intelligence Support to Operations*, Joint Publication 2-0, May 5, 1995, p.VIII–1. Doll and Metz, pp.16–17. See also the description of US operations in Somalia in David S. Alberts and Richard E. Hayes, *Command Arrangements for Peace Operations*, Ft. McNair, Washington, DC: National   Defense   University   Press,   May   1995;   available   at

http://wwwndu.edu/inss/books/capo/capohome.html. They note that 'Both US doctrine and practice prevent the assignment of military intelligence organizations to UN or other non-US commands ...'

21 Dorn, p.428; see also Maj. David L. Shelton, 'Intelligence Lessons Known and Revealed During Operation RESTORE HOPE Somalia,' *Marine Corps Gazette*, February 1995, p.38.

22 Brahimi Report, paras 65–75, 198–217.

23 Canada, Department of Foreign Affairs and International Trade, 'Canada and Norway to Promote Increased Capacity for Rapid Reaction for UN Peacekeeping Missions,' *News Release* No. 102, May 12, 2000.

24 See, e.g., the discussion in James Fergusson, 'A Mile Wide and an Inch Deep: Multilateralism and the Command and Control of Multinational Forces in Peace Operations,' *Multilateral Institutions and Global Security*, Working Paper No. 8, Toronto: Centre for International and Security Studies, York University, June 1988, passim.

25 Smith, p.178.

26 Shelton, p.38.

27 Larry K. Wentz, 'Intelligence Operations,' in Larry Wentz (ed.), *Lessons from Bosnia: The IFOR Experience,* Chapter IV, p. 19. http://www.dodccrp.org/bostoc.htm.

28 US, Department of Defense Background Briefing, 'Intelligence Support to Operation JOINT ENDEAVOUR,' January 18, 1996. Lt Col. George K. Gramer, 'Operation JOINT ENDEAVOR: Combined Joint Intelligence in Peace Enforcement Operations,' *Military Intelligence Professional Bulletin*, No. 4, 1996, available at http://www.fas.org/irp/agency/army/tradoc/usaic/mipb/1996-4/gramer.htm.

29 Wentz, Chapter IV–31. Lt Col. Herschell A. Boyd, Joint Intelligence in Support of Peace Operations, Newport, R.I.: Naval War College, June 14, 1996, pp.13–16.

30 Allen P. Hazlegrove, 'Desert Storm Time-Sensitive Surface Targeting: A Successful Failure or a Failed Success?' *Defense Analysis*, Vol. 16, 2000), esp. pp.123–125. Maj. Raymond E. Coia, 'A Critical Analysis of the I MEF Intelligence Performance in the 1991 Persian Gulf War,' May 22, 1995. Written in fulfillment of a requirement for the Marine Corps Command and Staff College. Available at http://www.fas.org/irp/eprint/coia.htm.

31 Coia, passim.

32 Davidson, p.8.

33 Shelton, passim.

34 But see Wentz.

35 United Nations, *Report of the Secretary General on the implementation of the report of the Panel on United Nations peace operations*, October 20, 2000. A/55/502, paras 42–63. See also Patricia Bliss McFate et al., 'Verification in a Global Context: The Establishment and Operation of a United Nations Centre for Information, Training, and Analysis (CITA),' *Arms Control Verification Studies No. 7*, Ottawa: Non-Proliferation, Arms Control and Disarmament Division, Department of Foreign Affairs and International Trade, February 1996.

36 Ibid., paras 64–65; Brahimi Report, para. 101 (b).

37 See 'Meeting on Cartography and Geographic Information Science,' available at http://www.un.org/Depts/Cartographic/english/ungis/meeting/.

38 Brahimi Report, paras 114–117.

39 See http://www.shirbrig.dk/. Argentina, Austria, Canada, Denmark, Italy, the Netherlands, Norway, Poland, Romania and Sweden are full members; Finland, Spain, Portugal and Slovenia have subscribed to some of the agreements underlying SHIRBRIG.

40 http://www.shirbrig/dk/staff.htm.

Chapter 9

Peacekeeping and Intelligence: Single or Double Bed?

Alex Morrison

Introduction

This chapter will address the role of intelligence in modern-day peacekeeping and, more specifically, how satellite imagery fits into that role. It is written from the point of view of one who has been a peacekeeper in the field. The author also does so from the perspective of one who has spent six years as a military and disarmament affairs advisor at the Permanent Mission of Canada to the United Nations in New York, responsible for arms control and disarmament, international security and negotiating peacekeeping on behalf of Canada, and also as one who for the past six years has been responsible for the education and training, here in Canada, of thousands of civilian and military peacekeepers from over one hundred and fifty countries.

The Pearson Peacekeeping Centre

This chapter will begin with an brief review of the Pearson Peacekeeping Centre. This will allow for an understanding of how this organization contributes to effective peacekeeping. The Centre, or PPC, is not a Canadian government organization, but it is funded mainly by the government. The opinions that stated in this chapter are not necessarily those of the Government of Canada.

The PPC was established by the government of Canada in 1994 to enhance the Canadian contribution to international peace, security, and stability. It was to do so by providing opportunities in research, education and training on all aspects of peacekeeping. It conducts single subject courses – thirteen different ones at the present time – each of which is accredited by a number of Canadian, American and other universities, on various aspects of peacekeeping. It also conducts seminars and round tables. It also houses the Canadian Peacekeeping Press, which puts out about a dozen books a year. PPC designs, conducts, assesses, and refines scenario-based role-playing exercises in Canada and abroad, for civilian and military, large international clients.

The three foundational pillars of the PPC's programs are as follows.

First, its definition of peacekeeping: Actions designed to enhance international peace, security and stability which are authorized by competent national and international organizations and which are undertaken cooperatively and individually by military, humanitarian, good governance, civilian police and other interested agencies and groups.

This is a very wide and deep definition of peacekeeping, and it is meant to be. There are a wide range of terms associated with this term that include peace operations, peace support operations, preventative diplomacy, complex humanitarian emergencies, peace restoration, peace enforcement, and so forth. One day an academic will design a peacekeeping ladder akin to Herman Kahn's forty-rung ladder of nuclear escalation that will include all of these concepts as elements on a peacekeeping spectrum. The PPC does not spend its time trying to determine where each activity fits because it all fits within the wide and deep definition of peacekeeping – knowing, of course, that other people use other terms.

The second pillar of the PPC was established in 1994. It is the concept of the 'new peacekeeping partnership.' The new peacekeeping partnership is the term applied to those organizations and individuals that work together to improve the effectiveness of modern peacekeeping operations. It includes the military; civil police; government and non-government agencies dealing with human rights and humanitarian assistance; diplomats; the media; and organizations sponsoring development and democratization programmes.

The third pillar is the 'peacekeeping umbrella.' This is the notion of a very wide range of actors, functions and challenges, all inextricably linked. The action by any actor in any area has an impact on another and thus generates a considerable complexity in modern peacekeeping. Thus the PPC bases everything it does on the concepts of a wide and deep definition of peacekeeping, the new peacekeeping partnership, and the peacekeeping umbrella.

There is another term that needs to be considered – 'mission reality.' This was coined to replace this pejorative, odious, negative term called 'mission creep.' 'Mission reality' says that in a theatre of operations all of the resources must be used with a high degree of synergy. If this is not done, those engaged in peacekeeping operations are neglecting not only their own people but are also neglecting the people that they are there to help. It is necessary to take the time to explain all of the above because the PPC is in partnership with a very broad range of partners – military and civilian – and no aspect of advancing the cause of modern peacekeeping is beyond the interest or potential engagement of the PPC.

The Issue

Against that background, the precise title of this chapter was chosen to illustrate and emphasize the artificial and unnecessary restrictions within which peacekeepers currently operate. This refers mainly to the United Nations but much of this material applies equally well to lead countries in peacekeeping, to groups of countries, and to other organizations engaged in peacekeeping. Consider, for example:

1   Should there be a singular, insular approach to peacekeeping or should resources be combined for the best possible results?
2   Should information and intelligence be treated as subjects which are never to be brought together under the United Nations umbrella?

3   Should individual nations either refuse to share intelligence or, if it is offered, must bring it in through the back door?
4   Should an arrangement continue which views open cooperation with business in design, development, and enhancement of peacekeeping missions as somewhat unwholesome?

Cooperation must be the governing operating principle in peacekeeping. There are times when it might be appropriate for single disciplines to work alone. Yet there are also situations in which performance will be significantly enhanced by working together. Specific to the theme addressed in this book, the following questions need to be answered:

1   What is the role for commercial satellite imagery? And, what is the role for commercial satellite experts and companies in supporting the entire UN system? And remember that when most of us talk about the UN, we are referring only to that building on the East River in New York, in which representatives of 188 countries talk until their governments tell them what to do. There are also 36 other United Nations agencies that are autonomous, semi-autonomous, fiefdoms, kingdoms – one of those words will apply to one or more of them.
2   What is the role of commercial satellite imagery and companies in ensuring that the entire UN system has the best possible resources at hand when it deploys civilian and military peacekeepers with various command, control and cooperation relationships, in conflict resolution situations?
3   What can business do to ensure its products are developed and distributed with the maximum degree of efficiency and effectiveness?
4   And, what should be the United Nations' reciprocal response?

This chapter will answer some of these questions.

The Dynamic Nature of Peacekeeping and the Need for Intelligence

It must be realized that as the world advances, technology and its applications continue to alter practically every characteristic of the modern world. These changes affect the continuing and pressing need for upgrading personal computers to the kilometres of fibre optic cables that blanket the ocean floor to how wars are fought and peacekeeping operations are conducted. In an article entitled, 'Exploiting the New High Resolution From Satellite Imagery: Darwinian Imperatives?', Mark Stout and Thomas Quiggin state that in addition to the giant leaps forward in modern life, these far-reaching advances in modern technology also apply to conflict.[1] Conflict, and its prevention and resolution, have been transformed and made more complex by these constant waves of innovation. Indeed, as the world faces rapidly modernizing tension and conflict, the role of peacekeeping must strive to keep pace. Just as peacekeeping in years past has been a crucial component of the struggle for peace and world stability, so, too, will it continue to play an important role in the future.

There are three things that are absolutely certain with regard to future conflict resolution. First, peacekeeping will continue to be the international conflict resolution instrument of choice. Second, all of the mechanisms and modalities that have been used in the past will be required in the future. It is wrong to think that there will not be another Bosnia. It is also wrong to think that there will not be another Rwanda or East Timor. Everything that has been done in the past is going to be done again in the future. The third certainty is that in the future there are going to be new challenges, and that these will require new approaches. Those approaches are not yet known because the world has not yet been faced with these new challenges and opportunities. All of this means that the world community needs to be enormously flexible in its approach to conflict resolution.

Walter Dorn and David Bell highlight the weaknesses displayed in the United Nations operation in the Congo almost forty years ago, in order to help derive some conclusions about what is needed for future successes. They write that 'to be effective, peacekeepers in conflict zones must proactively acquire and painstakingly analyze information about conditions in the mission area.'[2] If that statement is combined with the fact that technology has caused a metamorphosis in conflict, it is possible to deduce that changes in the current approach to peacekeeping must be made.

The United Nations and Intelligence

Given the increasing complexities of conflict today, the UN must recognize that to do less means to not provide our peacekeepers with all available and necessary resources. Dorn says that there is a need to de-stigmatize the idea of the United Nations collecting information and turning it into intelligence.[3] He has also written about how Dag Hammarskjöld once remarked that despite the difficulties posed by the absence of an intelligence branch, its omission was necessary to keep the UN's hands clean[4] – as if there was something dirty about using everything at one's disposal to accomplish the objectives of peacekeeping. Dorn and Bell also indicate that the corporate UN has come to see intelligence as a necessary evil.[5] This is borne out by the current complex, dangerous and challenging operations throughout the world. Intelligence is an indispensable good. The UN should be more open and assertive about the need for information when carrying out its operations.

In addition to this, member states should be more agreeable to the establishment of a UN intelligence branch. To many people that may seem like common sense. However many member states disagree because of the risk they see to their national sovereignty.

The United Nations must now reflect on its earlier information-gathering attempts and consider the possibility of creating a permanent agency for the purpose of collecting and analyzing information and turning it into intelligence. The United Nations in the 1980s did not begin to attempt this. There was an office set up under James Jonah, Assistant Secretary General, who is now Minister of Finance in Sierra Leone. Jonah had the responsibility of making sure that the very few staff he had read newspapers, talked to people and wrote some information about what was happening in the world. Yet in the face of these basic actions many of the member states reacted by saying 'No, you're collecting information on what we do, and we will not permit it.' Thus, that very tentative attempt just fell away.

The United Nations would gain many advantages in obtaining and using information for its strategic planning. The cost of all of this, however, is very high. Recognizing that the United Nations has a zero growth budget the question arises as to how the United Nations would find the funds to pay for this very expensive information. In an article entitled 'Battle Strategy Meets Virtual Reality', by Jonathan Shears, the author describes the benefits that could be obtained by any government authority that opts to use satellite technology for strategic planning. He says that if peacekeeping operations are to be executed without loss of life, and with maximum efficiency, good geographical intelligence is essential.[6]

Satellite Imagery

Satellite imagery should be used to assist in the prevention of surprise shifts in world events. However, care is needed because satellites see those things which they are capable of seeing. There are numerous countries that do not want satellites to see 'everything' they are capable of seeing. And there are a lot of countries that do not appreciate that satellites are impartial. For that very reason it is likely that many member states of the United Nations will object strenuously to the use of this type of equipment in peacekeeping. There are countries that would rather have their citizens suffer than to use the benefits bestowed by using satellites and satellite imagery for the common good.

Another benefit of using satellite imagery, is the political legwork that could be saved. Even with access to satellite imagery, there is still a need for people on the ground It may be, however, that the number of people that are required on the ground can be lessened – to what degree remains uncertain – but it can be lessened because of the satellite imagery and the knowledge that it brings.

If the United Nations had its own capability for gathering and analyzing information and turning it into intelligence, it would be freed from relying on its member states for information.

Vipin Gupta argues that if the United Nations had an independent source of information of course it could 'exercise a greater degree of autonomy from the host population.'[7] That is, the countries in which the peacekeeping is taking place. But most peacekeeping needs to take place with the consent of the countries concerned. What does the United Nations do if the countries concerned do not want satellite imagery used over their territory? Does the United Nations state that it is going to use it anyway? Or is it not used and then result in the claim that the United Nations inaction resulted in the direct, or indirect deaths of people?

Peacekeeping, Intelligence and the 2000 Brahimi Report

Other chapters in this collection have argued that the Brahimi Report indicated that the United Nations ought to move into the field of intelligence gathering. The problem is that not every member of the United Nations is as enthusiastic about the totality of the Brahimi Report. The omission of the actual word 'intelligence' in the Brahimi Report is no mistake. Yet the mission of the entity recommended in the Report by Brahimi and his colleagues is clearly the same one that would be assigned to an intelligence agency.

The United Nations must be given the leeway by its member states to establish the ability to satisfy the need of its peacekeepers for accurate intelligence. The Brahimi Report states that 'without such capacity the UN will remain a reactive institution unable to get ahead of daily events and the Executive Committee on Peace and Security will not be able to fulfill the role for which it was created.'[8]

Fifty-five years ago the United Nations was brought together as an organization of the victorious powers of the Second World War, determined, in the words of the preamble of the charter, 'to save succeeding generations from the scourge of war.'[9] That road has been long, but progress has been made. Much of the credit goes to the peacekeeping operations that the UN has conducted over the course of its brief history. This begins in 1956 with the invention of peacekeeping by Lester B. Pearson. Since this time many lessons have been learnt about these missions. These include the reasons for success and the explanations for shortcomings. A glaring weakness in the process of peacekeeping is the lack of a proficient intelligence-gathering arm to supply United Nations personnel in the field with adequate knowledge about the conditions they face. This is a conclusion that is shared in the Brahimi Report.

A Time for Action

If peacekeeping is to be made into a reliable method for conflict resolution, this limitation must be addressed. Men and women cannot continued to be sent into service without the instruments they need to succeed in the task that are assigned to them.

The United Nations and its member states need to have a clear view of conflicts before it, and they, commit lives and resources to remedy the situations. To accomplish this, the need for the United Nations to have the devices necessary to help guide us toward greater peace, security, and greater stability must be recognized. The field of satellite imagery is an option the United Nations must be allowed to explore. It is clear that the UN's pressing need for rapid and accurate intelligence can largely be fulfilled using the technology that high-resolution imagery offers. What remains unclear is whether or not member states will sacrifice their privacy in order for this need to be answered. The United Nations must address the need openly and ask for the methods and modalities to do the job.

An important component of peacekeeping, and one that the Americans in the main are already fortunate enough to have, is well-trained and dedicated personnel. Another equally important piece of the puzzle is adequate knowledge of the crisis that are to be resolved.

The Way Ahead

How then to proceed? First, those who wish to press upon the United Nations the important advantages that instrumentation of this type can bestow must learn to understand the United Nations; its 36 semi-autonomous agencies and must learn to understand the relationship between New York and each of its field missions. The concerns of the member states about sovereignty must be understood, both in terms of inclusion and exclusion. And then there is the question of sharing. Will information that is provided to the UN from a member state be complete, or will it contain only a partial picture?

There is information that is given from one country only to certain other countries. In the case of information acquired through satellite imagery the question then arises as to what happens to this information when it is given to the United Nations for the purposes of peacekeeping operations? There is absolutely no way that the information, once it is given to peacekeepers – whether they are policy makers or practitioners to guarantee that this information will not immediately be transferred to national capitals, and to other parties.

The United Nations has tried to gather intelligence before and this has alarmed Member states when it has tried to collect information from open sources. The best way to proceed with international conflict resolution, and thus the best way to proceed with inculcating people with the desire to have this type of resource is that there must be integration and unification of civilian/military aims and resources.

It is much easier, perhaps much more efficient, for private enterprise to take a lead and then present the United Nations and peacekeeping missions with the concepts and equipment that it needs. There is room for businesses associated with satellite imagery to become more familiar with the work of the Pearson Peacekeeping Centre and to cooperate with it. This would expose the thousands of people from 150 countries who come to the Centre to better understand the benefits of satellite imagery.

Another area that commands attention to this issue are civilian police. The requirement for the participation of civilian police in peacekeeping operations has increased dramatically. There is now room for many thousands of them in the field, but they are not there. They are not there because they are not available because of their expense. The question then arises as to how satellite imagery can help civilian police in engaging in international peacekeeping operations in a more economic manner.

The use of civilian police has been around since the time of the Congo but their use is now becoming more acceptable. It is also becoming more desirable because there are countries that will not tolerate one military death on a peacekeeping mission. Yet there seems to be less concern over the deaths of civilian police on a peacekeeping mission. Another reason that police are becoming more popular is that some countries are using them in multinational support units (MSUs) to carry out tasks that the military would normally carry out. Thus, civilian police will have an ever-increasing range of tasks in international peacekeeping.

There is also a need to think about the educational process in concrete terms. Both the policy makers and the technical personnel need to be convinced of the usefulness of satellite imagery. Technical personnel understand how these work.

Policy makers do not have to understand them, they just have to be convinced that it is a good thing. For example, during the Cuban Missile Crisis the members of the Security Council were strongly impressed by the American photos of the Soviet missiles in Cuba? Technology has come a long way since then. However, there are people who look at satellite imagery today the same way they looked at those photos of those missiles in Cuba. Some will say 'that is absolutely wonderful and that proves our case, and incidentally we really have to do more of this.' There are others who will say, 'we don't want anything to do with that because the use of those things will make it less easy for us to do the types of operations that we want to do.'

These capabilities need to be thought of in concrete terms. There is a need to think of the money required for this technology, and about zero growth in the UN budget. The United States pays 25 per cent of the assessed budget and 30 per cent of the peacekeeping budget. If businesses and/or countries say to the United Nations, 'you don't have to pay anything at all – we are going to give it to you', there will be complaints from some member states. These will be based on the argument that those with the money to provide the imagery will continue to run the UN. The second argument that will be given is that the expertise in this area will continue to accrue and grow in the hands of the people who will give the UN the expertise.

Balance at the UN is very important. It is also necessary to remember that the command and control on peacekeeping missions is different from when a state acts alone. The commander of a military peacekeeping force does not command it. Nobody commands a UN military peacekeeping force. It is a group of national contingents, each with separate terms of reference, each with separate channels of communication to its national government, which operate nominally under somebody who tries to persuade them what to do to accomplish a very large Security Council mandate.

It is necessary to emphasize the collateral benefits, the spin-off benefits of satellite imagery. It is clear that its use can play a large role in detecting incipient conflict, in conflict prevention, in dealing with conflict that has broken out, and in assisting with post conflict implementation and maintenance of peacekeeping agreements.

Conclusions

In order to advance the notion of an intelligence capability for the UN and the possible roles of satellites and other technology the following conclusions must be reached:

1   It is necessary to understand the UN and its agencies, as well as relations between New York and field missions.
2   The concerns of the member states regarding sovereignty both in terms of intrusion and exclusion must be appreciated.
3   There is scope for cooperation with the Pearson Peacekeeping Centre, in terms of research, but also in participation in courses, seminars and exercises in order to better understand the growing complexities of the peacekeeping business.

4   The UN has tried to develop its intelligence capability tentatively – by collecting information from open sources, with the only result that member states were suspicious.

5   There needs to be a practical unity of effort, of civil/military intentions, aims and resources and actions to conduct modern peacekeeping operations.

6   Business must show some initiative, and take a lead and cooperate. This could indeed be a major contribution in the dynamic world of modern peacekeeping.

7   There is a need to understand what is happening with police in regards to peacekeeping operation, and a need to understand how this new technology might assist their involvement.

8   The educational process must be understood in concrete terms – policymakers need clear technical advice.

9   The matter of cost must be understood – should the USA. lead? Will developing countries simply see this as a further loss to the development funds?

10   Are the concerns about the use of information for other purposes real?

11   What happens to intelligence if the command and control of UN peacekeeping missions cannot be improved?

12   Finally, all is not negative. There are a number of spin-off benefits.

It is clear that if civilian and military peacekeepers are not provided with the best possible resources to use in their often risky and dangerous missions, there is an increased chances for loss of life. The mission will not then be as successful as it could be. It is also clear that business and civilian organizations, along with the military, must work together to accomplish the true aim of peacekeeping – the saving of lives and the alleviation of human suffering. The choices, opportunities and possibilities are clear. Our actions must indicate equally as clearly that we will all attempt to respond positively and energetically to the challenges ahead.

Notes

1   http://www.csis-scrs.gc.ca/eng/comment/com75e.html.
2   Walter Dorn and David Bell. 1995. 'Intelligence and Peacekeeping: The UN Operation in the Congo 1960-1964'. http://www.ryerson.ca/~woc/wdorn/wdcongo.htm.
3   Walter Dorn. 'Keeping Tabs on a Troubled World: UN Information Gathering to Preserve Peace'. http://www.pgs.ca/woc/wdorn/wdsecdial.htm.
4   http://www.ryerson.ca/~woc/wdorn/wdcongo.htm.
5   Ibid.
6   http://www.geoplace.com/ge/1997/0197/feature.asp.
7   Vipin Gupta. 'New Satellite Images for Sale: The Opportunities and Risks Ahead'. http://www.llnl.gov/csts/publications/gupta/contents.html.
8   The Brahimi Report. http://www.un.org/peace/reports/peace_operations.
9   The UN Charter, Preamble. http://www.un.org/aboutun/charter.

Chapter 10

Commercial Satellite Imagery, Canadian Security Needs and International Law

Michel Bourbonnière and Louis Haeck

Introduction

The rapid gathering and dissemination of information has become the defining paradigm of our epoch. Space technology occupies an important part of this new reality. In fact, space technology is now a crucial component of our global information infrastructures. Satellites are the space component of our information pipeline. Telecommunication satellites provide an important seamless conduit of data. Military navigational satellites (GPS and GLONASS) provide essential information not only to military operators but also to civil commercial sectors. No one can deny that the air travel industry has greatly benefited from this military technology. Last but certainly not least, earth imaging satellites collect a vast amount of data for military and civilian uses. This economic value, dependence, and hence, the strategic importance of space infrastructure, is easily comparable to that of hydrocarbons and electricity during the nineteenth and twentieth centuries. In fact, information is so quickly permeating our lives, and is doing this to such an extent, that one has to wonder if perhaps, by itself, information is structuring a homogeneous universal ethos.

Revolutions in information concepts are however not unique to our epoch. Gutenberg had created an important revolution with the invention of the printing press, which was perhaps even more disturbing to his period of time than what we are presently experiencing. The printing press created a significant change in the distribution and accessibility of information. The accessibility of books to a large number of people created what can be referred to as the first step to the de-intermediarization of knowledge. That is, as the Bible became more accessible to a greater number of people, the Church lost its privileged position as the keeper and interpreter of knowledge. The relationship between the Catholic Church and its members was to be forever changed.

The development of technology has catalytically affected the process the de-intermediarization of information. In the early 1900s electricity, radio, television, all, again revolutionized society, changing the way in which people and governments would relate to one another. Now cyber-space, global telecommunication networks, new methods of information gathering, some of which are not even on our planet (that is, they are space-based), coupled with the global dissemination of the data and information are again forcing us to adapt,

123

changing the way in which we relate to one another, affecting even our consociations. Thus, governments have also been forced to adjust to a new reality. And according to the nature of the beast, governments adapt by regulating. However, if there is a constant within our history of knowledge and information it is that politics, laws, and issues of national security have been continuously redefined as these concepts are themselves contingent upon technological paradigms. Perhaps, this capacity to adapt to a changing information environment can be qualified as 'information Darwinism'. Those who can adjust the best to their new information environment will not only survive but also prosper. Information and cyber security are a twenty-first century concern. Possible threats to these important national assets will have to be dealt with.

This chapter will analyze Canadian security needs within the specific area of space based earth imaging. But what exactly is meant by 'security'? And how is security, so defined, applicable within a Canadian and information context? In answering these questions and methodologically speaking, the chapter will first briefly expound the international law norms regulating the security of States, namely the right to self-defence, aggression, and threats thereof. Secondly this chapter will then review the interface between these norms and the use of space-based earth imaging technology.

Security threats and international law

Narrowly defined, security requirements can be expressed as concerns with foreign activities which endanger a State's sovereignty and political independence. Classic examples of such threats are armed attacks upon the integrity of a State's territory, or violation of a State's sovereign airspace or territorial waters, usually conducted by a belligerent State. The United Nations Charter recognizes within Article 51 the inherent right of States to individual self-defence against such threats. It must however also be noted that Article 2(4) of the UN Charter also edicts that States must 'refrain in their international relations from the threat or use of force against the territorial integrity or political independence of any state'. Remaining within the narrow definition of security but broadening slightly its scope of applicability, self-defence can also imply collective military actions to defend allies against similar threats. Again, the United Nations Charter recognizes within Article 51 the right of states to collective self-defence against armed attack. Canada as a member of NATO and NORAD has international obligations of collective self-defence with its allies. The United Nations Security Council may also take actions which it deems necessary to maintain or restore international peace and security. Canada in accordance with Article 25 of the United Nations Charter agrees to accept and carry out the decisions of the Security Council in accordance with the UN Charter.

A threat, to be real and credible, has two constituent parts. The first element of a threat is a State's capacity to use force. In this case military strength can be evaluated by obtaining information concerning the size and technological advancement of a belligerent State's military capabilities. The second element of a threat is the intention of a State to use its military capacity to endanger our sovereignty and independence. This capacity can be evaluated by the state's ability and willingness to project force. Threats can be very difficult to evaluate. Correct and precise intelligence is a sine qua non for a state to properly assess threats. To complicate matters, this concept of 'threat' not only includes acts of aggression from other sovereign states but can also include acts of terrorism. The difficulty of assessing threats increases exponentially for information and cyber operations. Future information and cyber military operations constitute a new challenge to allied forces. Important issues will have to be addressed by the international community. For example, how should States react to cyber intrusions? What constitutes an act of aggression in outer space where there are no national boundaries?

Aggression and international law

An act of aggression is defined in international law as being:

> The use of armed force by a State against the sovereignty, territorial integrity or political independence of another State, or in any other manner inconsistent with the Charter of the United Nations, as set out in this definition.[1]

According to the UNGA resolution on aggression, which can be interpreted as being an articulation of customary international law, the following acts are to be considered as aggression: the first use of force by a State; invasion or attack by armed forces of the territory of another State, by land, sea, or air; and military occupation, annexation of territory, bombardment or the use of weapons, blockades of ports or coasts.

These acts do not constitute an exhaustive definition. Thus the Security Council of the UN[2] has the ability to declare other actions as acts of aggression. Furthermore, an act of aggression is a most serious crime of concern to the international community.[3] It is important to note that the threat of the use of force was not included in Article 1 of UNGA 3314.[4] It is also interesting to note that economic coercion was not included within UNGA 3314. Several UN resolutions have however denounced economic coercion as being a threat to the sovereignty of states.[5] Furthermore State aggression can also occur indirectly. As Brownlie wrote:

> Charges of 'aggression' are frequently based on allegations of military aid to, and control over rebels in a civil war. If rebels are effectively supported and controlled by another state that state is responsible for a 'use of force' as a consequence of the agency. Thus aid to rebels by foreign states has been held by the General Assembly to be inconsistent with the principles on the United Nations Charter, with implicit reference to Article 2, paragraphs 2 and 4...[6]

The element of control is an important component when determining state responsibility for indirect acts of aggression. Brownlie astutely criticizes certain UNGA resolutions for not respecting this normative criterion. It is also important to note two presuppositions that permeate the UN resolution. First, in defining aggression the resolution focuses upon the kinetic concept of weapons. Second, the definition assumes that aggression occurs through a physical violation of sovereign territory. Indeed, this concept of aggression remains applicable in our present context, as classical military operations still occur. However, the definition is certainly technologically contingent.

The application of the definition of aggression to information military operations is somewhat problematical. The lacunae of the definition are exemplified in the following examples. A computer virus, logic bomb or Trojan horse, implanted within a nation's computer system, may cause more damage than a gravity bomb. In this case, there is no used nor are borders crossed. Yet damage can be considerable, and not necessarily physical.[7] Similarly, information gathering and dissemination might also be used very aggressively.

It is also interesting to note that the UNGA resolution refers to attacks by land, sea or air, the space and cyber mediums being absent. This, however, must not be interpreted as meaning that that aggression cannot occur either from, within, or to the space or cyber-space mediums. This problem is further compounded by the fact that the means and methods of information attacks do not necessarily originate from foreign governments. The virus was a brilliant example of the havoc which one individual can cause.

Furthermore, the growing commercialization of military technology is also cause for concern posing complex multidimensional legal problems. States are now faced with intricate regulatory issues. Governments must balance divergent interests. On one side, states seek the economic benefits gained from global trade in areas of high technology. On the other hand, regulators realize that there is a need to restrict the access of states of concern and of terrorist organizations to sensitive military technology. This is a classic trade-off which is commonly found in regulations applicable to the arms industry. However, if only it was so simple. The regulatory complexity increases exponentially within a global information based society. First, as information becomes a more important part of threats and of military operations which deal with these threats, other issues surface, becoming important within the regulatory matrix. Such issues include civil rights such as freedom of expression. Regulators must decipher a new equation composed of new variables. Our western governments take pride in being strong democracies. Freedom of speech is a cornerstone of the democratic system. In fact, one can perhaps even argue that freedom of speech and transparency of government action are themselves questions of national security. Second, global trade complicates matters even further. Within a system of global economies, capital flows more freely across international boundaries. Regulations, on the other hand, are confined to their territorial prisons. Our state-centric system assures this. States see extraterritorial regulatory effects as countermanding their sovereign rights. Yet our southern neighbor feels compelled to regulate the activities of its corporate citizenry even beyond its borders. Over-protective regulatory structures can have unintended pervasive effects, perhaps even weakening the competitiveness of important industries, or force capital investments to go elsewhere.

Broadly defined, state security can certainly encompass a wide range of diverse issues besides those which are strictly defined as acts of aggression against the integrity of states, their political independence, or their nationals. Other areas of national security interests can be related to the economic well-being of states. This concept encompasses other sectors, such as industrial development, control of strategic resources, the development of certain industrial sectors, the export of critical military technology, and trade and military relations with allies. However, broadening the definition of national security again increases the level of difficulty of an already complex problem. The danger of a broad definition lies in the fact that mixing trade and weaponry can also create insidious regulatory effects. Commercial policies can easily be cloaked within a penumbra of national security. The exact purpose of a protective regulatory structure might be difficult to decipher. What is the object of protection: is it an industry? is it national security 'qua' national security?

Canadian Security Needs

Using a narrow definition of security, Canada's security needs are easily defined. Canadian security needs occur on two levels. These are, first, the defence of its territory and sovereignty, such as protection against acts of aggression and preserving our independence. Second, within a geopolitical context, its security needs include the application of our foreign policy to promote international peace and security. The best examples of this are: the Canadian participation in international peacekeeping missions, and our engagement within international institutions, which promote global peace and security. The word 'engagement' means more than mere participation.

Using a broad interpretation, our security concerns include other aspects such as the control of key space technology, and creating an economically viable indigenous space industry. Canada's present development strategy concentrates upon the creation of an expertise in certain niche markets, such as space-based earth imaging with the RADARSAT project, and space robotics.

The imagery and spectral data base are important assets in an information based world. Information security has been addressed by NATO by the cryptology available to NATO members. Perhaps the Canadian forces should invest in this expertise securing Canadian information and data bases.

Canadian national security needs

Canada has a unique geography bordering on three oceans and occupying the entire northern part of our hemisphere. Due to its northern latitude, our country has within some regions, periods of complete darkness during half the year, mainly within the high arctic. Canada is also sparsely populated. Within the east, the majority of its population lives within a narrow corridor between Quebec City and Windsor Ontario. Within the western provinces the population is concentrated just north of the Canada–US border. Canada also maintains a relatively small defense budget. Space technology offers Canada a unique opportunity to economically and efficiently manage a vast and diverse territory. The ability to conduct satellite surveillance is critical for Canadian security needs. Space represents the proverbial 'high ground' for military operations. The challenge to our Canadian military is to participate in a very expensive endeavor with a minimal amount of resources. Considering the importance of space, it would perhaps be wise for our government to increase funding for space security operations. There is no doubt that space assets and in particular space-based remote sensing will in the future continue to play an important role for Canada on many levels.

Space-based earth-imaging satellites have considerable implications for national security. Firstly, these assets can provide data on a State's military resources, its natural resources (e.g., water and minerals), its use of resources, the environmental effects of its activities, its agricultural production, among other things. Secondly, Canadian security needs includes access to space based earth imagery, not only for our territorial concerns but also for our military operations abroad where data on other countries are not always accurate or even available. Furthermore during missions abroad, the Canadian forces need a secure access to space imaging data in real time. When operating in foreign missions this can best be assured with a mobile military earth station. The Canadian navy could play an important role in a military space information structure. Some ships should be equipped with the capacity to establish a downlink with RADARSAT and interpret the data.

National security concepts represent one of the most sensitive issues in Canadian-US relations on space-based commercial remote sensing. Canada's announcement of a 3 m resolution capability for its RADARSAT-2 remote sensing satellite caught US attention. The US defence and intelligence establishments repeatedly expressed their concerns, which led to a series of discussions between the two countries.

National defence objectives

The first mission of national defence involves the protection of Canada from a belligerent state. In this case, space imaging can permit the detection of a threat platform carrying weapons, which have the potential to endanger our territory and citizens. Such platforms, being land-, sea- or air-based, fall clearly within the definition of aggression espoused within our corpus of international law. Space-based imagery can help protect Canada against such threats. Its usefulness can be found not only in the detection of such threats but also in the management of the response to these threats.[8] Immediate threats and future threats can be evaluated and the required defensive actions prepared.

A second implication involves Disaster Relief Operations within Canada, such as floods, ice storms, fighting forest fires, etc. DND support to the victims of the Saguenay and Red River floods, as well as the Québec ice storm, are now part of the history of Canada. Satellite surveillance data was used throughout these operations to identify the critical areas that needed the most aid, thereby saving time and effort in the dispatch of the limited military resources available. It was noted, however, that assured access to the requisite satellite imagery could not be guaranteed. There was a serious lack of available local ground stations to receive, interpret and make use of the data, and therefore this resource was certainly not maximized. This is undoubtedly an area where more investment should be made by our Government.

Foreign policy objectives

Space-based earth imaging is a useful tool for intelligence data collection. Briefly stated, this is the supply of strategic information rather than tactical, high-resolution information. A broad range of issues can be addressed, such as a humanitarian crisis posing a threat to international peace and security, treaty compliance verification, and environmental disasters. With real-time global information, situations can be better evaluated and the proper response planned on both the political and military levels.

For example, in October 1998 Hurricane Mitch hurled its devastating power upon Honduras and Nicaragua. The rain caused devastating floods and mudslides. Within Honduras, the Valle de la Sula (Ulua Valley) was particularly hard hit, as this valley contains an extensive river system. The Canadian RADARSAT satellite provided data assisting emergency management response.[9]

The Canadian Forces could provide their expertise in crisis management and disaster recoveries in case of emergencies to developing nations.

Threats can occur at any time. When analyzing the technological options for Canada for space-based imaging, only radar satellite surveillance can provide 24/7 coverage throughout the year. Hence the decision for RADARSAT.

Canada's uses of satellite imagery in support of its national objectives require it to have a degree of self-sufficiency. However the reality is that this technology is mainly American. Although Canada does enjoy close commercial and military ties with our southern neighbor, our strategic interests sometimes diverge. As far as commercial space-based earth imaging is concerned, we have to optimize our commercial and military options. We have to maintain access to this technology, address US security needs, promote our space industries, and assure them a competitive regulatory structure. Policy decisions are not necessarily evident nor are they easy to determine. Commercialization of space technology also creates a new paradigm of civil-military co-operation. This is a strategic investment for Canada on both the military and the industrial levels. It is important to increase the close co-operation between civilians and Canadian military staff working in space applications at all levels. Future co-operation with NATO European space partners should be encouraged, diversifying Canadian military space ventures.

Department of National Defence Space Policy

A Department of National Defence (DND) space policy was issued in September 1998 and is based on the *1994 Defence White Paper*, and the renewal of NORAD. Regrettably the *1994 Defence White Paper* is out of date. There is an urgent need for review by the Canadian Forces of this document. New possible threats must be addressed including, information, space and cyber security concerns.

Recent international military operations have demonstrated the usefulness of space military applications. Space capabilities are now considered to be the key to supporting traditional military operations of maritime, land and air forces, including: command, control and communications; intelligence gathering, surveillance, navigation; mapping; meteorological services and arms control verification.

DND space goals are:

1   To protect national security and sovereignty interests;
2   To protect national interests from threats located in or assing through space;
3   To fulfill Canada's defence commitments by supporting missions and tasks using space technology wherever appropriate.In order to satisfy Canadian space

capability requirements, defence planners should make maximum use of all available civil, governmental and military technologies, and seek opportunities for international cooperation.

Canadian participation in collective space security efforts will help ensure access to allied space intelligence, facilities and data. A strong space relationship developed with the US under NORAD is very important for Canada. The civil sector must realize that military space needs represent an important market for our satellite industry, including both American and European military partners.

Canadian space activities within NORAD will remain within the current primary mission of 'aerospace warning' and 'aerospace control' of North America. Aerospace warning consists of the monitoring of man-made objects in space and the detection, validation and warning of attack against North America, whether by aircraft, missiles, or from space. Aerospace control includes providing surveillance and control of the air and space of Canada and the US.

Some DND space activities may also have potential roles in Ballistic Missile Defence (BMD). The *1994 Defence White Paper* called for the examination of BMD options, focusing on research and building on Canada's existing capabilities in areas such as communications, surveillance and warning. Canada must review its present position on National Missile Defence and also increase its role in information warfare.

Arms Control Verification

With the end of the cold war and the emerging new role of the United Nations, arms control verification could very well become a new 'growth industry'. Satellite surveillance by its nature is able to 'cross borders' and avoid diplomatic obstacles which sometimes impair ground verification. This could be an important market for Canadian commercial space based earth imaging.[10] The Canadian military, as professionals of arms, have the required expertise to excel in arms control verification if given adequate access to space based earth imaging assets. RADARSAT as a dual use satellite could play a significant role on this issue.

Peacekeeping

The role of satellite for peacekeeping is similar to their role in arms control verification. The military information provided to peacekeepers assists in the monitoring of the activities of the belligerents, which in turn assists in the overall security for all concerned. The increased probability of detection when agreements have been contravened ensures compliance and hopefully more appropriate behavior. Space-based earth imaging can also improve UN peacekeeping Rapid reaction capability. Military personnel as 'professionals of arms' are ideally trained to have an important role in operations to support monitoring and Verification of military treaties.

Present Canadian Commercial Space Imagery

The RADARSAT joint venture

Canada is presently operating a Synthetic Aperture Radar (SAR) space-based earth imaging asset. This asset is called RADARSAT-1. From an international perspective, RADARSAT-1 is a joint project between Canada (Canadian Space Agency) and the United States (National Aeronautic and Space Administration-National Oceanographic and Atmospheric Administration). From an internal Canadian perspective, the RADARSAT-1 project is a joint venture involving both the public and private sectors. The Canadian Space Agency (CSA) managed the development of the satellite. The public sector participants included the Canadian federal government and the provincial governments of Québec, Ontario, Saskatchewan, and British Columbia. The private sector participated through RADARSAT International, Inc. (RSI). RSI was established to market, process, and distribute RADARSAT-1 data (CSA, 1999b) and was originally a consortium that included MacDonald Dettwiler, COM DEV, Spar Aerospace (RADARSAT's prime contractor, now called EMS Technologies), and Lockheed Martin Astronautics.

The project cost an estimated total of CDN$620 million, of which CDN$500 million CDN came from the Canadian government; a total of CDN$57 million came from the four provinces; and CDN$63 million came from the private sector. The contributors and participants are entitled to data allocations.[11]

RADARSAT-1's International Steering Committee is its supreme governing body. Its members represent CSA, NASA, and NOAA. This body works through consensus to supervise the operations of RADARSAT-1 and resolve possible conflicts. In May 1999, RSI became a wholly owned subsidiary of MacDonald Dettwiler. RSI is the exclusive distributor of RADARSAT data worldwide. RSI pays a royalty to the CSA for all data and derivative products sold. MacDonald Dettwiler is preparing itself for a public offering to make the company Canadian-owned. If an ownership change does occur, RADARSAT-2 could be exempt from certain US licensing requirements.

RADARSAT: a dual-use space asset

The Canadian armed forces do not have the financial resources necessary for developing and deploying space systems exclusively for their own use. The Canadian market for space-based imaging cannot economically sustain expensive satellites by itself. The match is a natural one. A synergy between civilian and military needs for space-based imagery has been created within the RADARSAT-1 project.

RADARSAT-1 technology can detect valuable information to enable the military to properly detect and evaluate threats. Through RADARSAT-1 imaging, DND can evaluate training activity levels and capacities, changes in training routines, military exercises, construction and/or destruction activities on military bases, transportation activities, ammunition and fuel storage sites, and vehicle convoys on roadways (representing possible unit deployments); even the absence of activity can be militarily significant. RADARSAT-1 data can be used to provide images of air installations and infrastructure and to detect the arrival or departure of large numbers of aircraft, analyze aircraft parking patterns, determine types of aircraft, and observe airport construction. RADARSAT data acquisition is not constrained by time of day, climactic conditions, or obscurants (such as the smoke the massive oil well fires in Kuwait created during the 1990–1991 Persian Gulf War). All this gives military planners great flexibility in gathering intelligence.

Information is fluid and volatile, even more so in battle situations, in which conditions can change very quickly. A key issue in military intelligence is providing real-time information to military personnel in command centers and on the battlefield. Space-based data collection can help achieve this, but a transportable ground station would be needed. To this end, IOSAT, Inc., developed Sentry, a mobile multi-satellite receiving and processing mobile station providing near–real-time image processing and management of large volumes of data. Sentry was successfully tested with RADARSAT-1 data on June 28 1998.

Sentry was used to support operational maritime surveillance during Maritime Combined Operational Training (MARCOT) – UNIFIED SPIRIT 1998.[12] In this military training exercise, one of the largest Canada and other NATO countries have participated in, a large amphibious force (15,000 personnel, 40 warships, and 100 combat airplanes from nine countries) landed on a hypothetical 'enemy' shore. In this case, Newfoundland was 'invaded' from a base in Nova Scotia.[13] RADARSAT-1 was used to monitor the exact positions and courses of both enemy and friendly ships. RADARSAT-1 imagery also helped identify the exact location of the landing forces. The results were conclusive. Once RADARSAT-1 collected the data, they were immediately communicated to the Sentry receiving station. The data were then quickly processed to create an image, which was then interpreted, extracting information that was rapidly transmitted to field commanders in near real time. A mere 25 minutes elapsed between the time RADARSAT-1 collected the imagery and the time the commanders used the results. RADARSAT-1 has also been very useful in Canadian peacekeeping operations, either for preparing maps or monitoring large internal refugee displacements. The satellite's cartographic capacity is also very important to the Canadian military, which is often deployed to locations for which updated maps are not readily available. RADARSAT-1 images give these forces the capacity to create their own maps, thus facilitating peacekeeping and other humanitarian operations. RADARSAT-1 data can also be used to locate elements of infrastructure, such as seaports and pipelines, which can be legitimate military targets during conflicts. The data can also be used to evaluate oil reserves, because oil reservoirs have different radar signatures depending on the amount of oil they contain. RADARSAT-1 imagery can also be very useful to Canada's foreign allies. The US Department of Defense, for example, has moved to acquire imagery from commercial vendors to supplement and compliment its existing capabilities.[14]

National governments are of course concerned that regional rivals or terrorist organizations might make use of these images, given their military value. And some interesting images are already available on the World Wide Web. Military planners must now grapple with the possibility of having to deny an enemy the use of commercial spacebased imagery during conflicts, possibly by neutralizing a satellite that is the property of a neutral state. In some cases, regulatory mechanisms, especially those that would restrict the operation of privately-owned remote sensing satellites, must also take constitutional issues into account. Such issues as freedom of information, expression, and the press are, however, beyond the scope of this discussion.[15]

Hemispheric security concerns, including drug trafficking, can also be addressed through RADARSAT-1 technology. Crops have distinctive radar signatures through which they can be identified. In some areas, drug trafficking is a large-scale operation; the ability to detect the associated infrastructure, such as airfields and warehouses, helps law enforcement agencies accomplish their missions more efficiently.

The US connection

American–Canadian cooperation has been an important and ongoing issue in the development of Canadian remote sensing expertise. Canada was interested in participating in NASA's Earth Resources Orbiting Satellite project (EROS). The Prince Albert Radar Laboratory, with an 84-foot diameter parabolic tracking dish, was offered as a receiving station for the EROS satellite. Unfortunately, the project was canceled. NASA established an alternative program, the Earth Resources Technology Satellite (ERTS), in 1969. Canada attempted to get an arrangement on the ERTS project similar to the one that had been agreed upon for the EROS project. However, despite an appeal to President Nixon's scientific advisor, foreign participation in this project was refused.[16] Finally, the first Canadian surveillance satellite was a joint Canada-USA project in 1976 called HERMES.

An agreement between NASA, NOAA, and CSA provided for the launch of RADARSAT-1. In return for NASA's deployment of the satellite, 15.8 percent of the RADARSAT-1 SAR on-time is allocated to US federal departments and agencies. One of NASA's main requirements in this agreement is the mapping of Antarctica, to be completed within the satellite's five-year life span. This mission, now complete, yielded the first complete mosaic of the continent and its ice shelf. RADARSAT-1 has also yielded valuable data on glaciology and has provided NOAA with useful data for monitoring the northeast US coast.

Finally should Canada continue to privilege its space link with the United States, or rather increase its role within ESA?

Conclusion

Commercial space imagery is an important strategic Canadian assert. It is important as it helps Canada as a part of an information based society, as it helps develop high tech industry, and as it helps Canada assume its security responsibilities both in the national sense and international sense. Canadian space assets are dual use. This is extremely important for a country with a small space programme. Its defence budgets do not allow it to have military imaging satellites. Yet its commercial markets are small and a military client helps to leverage our investments with a very important client. Canada's military must learn to become good businessman and take advantage or their economic clout within the industry. In this sense, military thinking must evolve and adapt to its new dual use environment. The military must also accept that the genie is already out of the bottle, and it is not going back in. If Canada's satellites do not image something in demand, some other satellite will. However orbital parameters are predictable. Commercial satellites are not orbiting secretly. Furthermore it is possible to know when one is being actively sensed. On this issue, optical satellites create more of a problem. Military planners must adapt to this new reality. Resistance is futile, and even more so in this age of information warfare.

Perspectives on regulating this industry must be creative. Canada must balance security in the classic sense of the term, industrial growth, trade relations with the Americans (who have a conservative security outlook), ensure access to US technology, ensure market access, and not have regulatory burden which our competitors do not have on the global market.

Canadian security concerns must be fine tuned with the information, cyber and space reality of our epoch. As the legacy of Gutenberg dictates, the present revolution in military affairs is based on new paradigms of operations. The de-intermediarization of information is an ineluctable fact of our millennium. Military operators must not resist this change, but rather find ways to take advantage of this new reality.

Notes

1   Resolution on the Definition of Aggression 1974, UNGA Resolution 3314 (XXIX). 14 December 1974. G.A.O.R. 29th Sess., Supp. 31. p.142: (1975) 69 A.J.I.L. 480. Hereinafter referred to as "UNGA 3314".
2   Hereinafter referred to as UNSC.
3   Article 5(d) 1998 Rome Statute of the International Crimianl Court reprinted in Adam Roberts and Richard Guelff.ed. *Documents on the Laws of War* (Oxford University Press, third edition) at 673.
4   For a quick review of the doetrinal analysis pertaining to this U.N. Resolution see Bennett, 'A Linguistic Critique of the Definition of Aggression,' *31 German Year Book of International Law* 481 (1988); Brown-John, 'The 1974 Definition of "Aggression:" A Query,' *Canadian Year Book of Internationmal Law* 301 (1977); Garvey, 'The UN Definition of "Agression": Law and Illusion in the Context of Collective Security', 17 *Virginia Journal of International Law* 177 (1977); Stone 'Hopes and loopholes in the 1974 Definition of Aggression,' 71 *American Journal of International Law* 224 (1977). For a similar list of aggression see Article 12 of the International Law Commission's Draft Code of Crimes Against the Peace and Security of Mankind. McCaffrey, 'The Fortieth Session of the International Law Commission,' 83, *American Journal of International Law* 153 (1989).
5   See Article 32 of theCharter of Economic Rights and Duties of States, UNGA Resolution 3281 (XXIX); Declaration of the Principles of International Law Concerning friendly Co-operation Among States, UNGA resolution 2265 (XXV); Declaration on the Inadmissibility of Intervention in Domestic Affairs of states and the Protection of their Independence and Sovereignty, UNGA Resolution 2131 (XX). For an interesting analysis of economic coercion pertaining to using oil as a weapon during the Gulf War see: Almond, 'An Assessment of Economic warfare; developments form the Persian Gulf,' 31 *Virginia Jpournal of International Law* 645 (1991); Edwards 'The

Iraqui oil "weapon" in the 1991 Gulf war: a Law of Armed Conflict Analysis,' 40 *Naval Law Review* 105 (1992).

6   Ian Brownlie *International Law and the Use of Force* p.370. See also Nicaragua v. United States.

7   For an excellent analysis in international law pertaining to these issues see Michael N. Schmitt, 'Computer Network Attack and the Use of Force in International Law; Thoughts on a Normative Framework,' *Columbia Journal of Transnational Law* Volume 37, 1999, Number 3, p.885; see also David Gruber, *Computer Networks and Information Warfare, Implications for Military Operations*, July 2000, Occaional paper No. 17, Center for Strategy and Technology, Air War College; William B. McClure, *Technology and Command, Implications for Military Operations in the Twenty-first Century*, July 2000 Occasional paper No. 15, Center for Strategy and Technology, Air War College.

8   See James Moffat et al. *The Utility of Electro-Optical and Radar Technologyies for Space Based Surveillance*. Unclassified report, Department of National Defence, December 1995.

9   Daniel Giroux. *RADARSAT Background Mission Effects of Hurricane Mitch in Honduras*. Canadian Space Agency report on file with the authors.

10   See Peter Bogden and Walter Dorn. *Controlling the Global Arms Threat*. Toronto: The Canadian Centre for Arms Control and Disarmament, 1991; Walter Dorn. *The Case for a United Nations Verification Agency: Disarmament under Effective International Control*. Ottawa: Canadian Institute for International Pearce and Security, July 1990.

11   RSCA-ML0016-N/C, p.2.

12   See also Canadian Space Agency, 1999.

13   IOSAT, 1998.

14   Joan Johnson-Freese and Richard Hanberg (1997), *Space, the Dormant Frontier: Changing the Paradigm for the 21st Century*, Praeger, Westport, Conn. p.193. W. Ferster (1999), 'U.S. to Buy Private Imagery for Intelligence', *Space News*. April 12, p.1. J. Singer (2000), 'U.S. Spending Plan for Boosting Spy Imagery Called Inadequate', *Space News*. May 8, p. 1.

15   See G.M. Kramer (1989). 'The First Amendment Viewed form Space: National Security Versus Freedom of the Press', ADAS p.339; Thomas S.Martin (1982), 'National Security and the First Amendment: A Change in Perspective', *American Bar Association Journal*. Vol. 68, pp.680–685: Robert P. Merges et al. (1989), 'News Media Satellites and the First Amendment: A case Study in the Treatment of New Technologies', *High Technology Law Journal*. Vol. 1. pp.1–32.

16   Canadian Centre for Romote Sensing, 1998.

Chapter 11

Commercial Satellite Imagery and Canadian National Security

Robert S. Macleod

Introduction

Commercial space-based imagery has become a very important contributing factor to the daily activity of the business community, maritime operations and defence. Canada, one of the first countries to launch a satellite into space, has become a world leader in Synthetic Aperture Radar technology. With the development of RADARSAT-2, Canada is introducing for the first time, ground moving targets indication (GMTI) to space-based radar surveillance. The commercial market for space-based imagery is growing daily, and basically anyone with a credit card can access this capability. On the one hand, this is a tremendous business opportunity, on the other it is a potential threat to national security. Canada's geography and economy makes it imperative that it achieves its fair share of this emerging market; but at the same time, the Canadian government must balance national security interests with economic development.

Commercial satellite imagery is a rapidly growing industry. The products promoted by this industry are no longer designed with the military as the prime customer. Rather, one find examples like the web site www.terraserver.com, where on an average day there are 800,000 page views of available imagery data. They serve 30,000 customers per day, 50 per cent of these are business not government. Terraserver has many different imagery systems feeding their web site (electro-optical, radar, thermal, etc.), downlinked from both space-based and aircraft, and from many nations (US, Canada, UK, France, Russia, India, etc.). Considering Terraserver is only one imagery clearinghouse in the industry, if you could look at worldwide demand for this type of capability, it is not only considerable, but it is an industry that is growing daily. This is an area that Canada needs to be fully engaged in to develop its market share.

Remote sensing serve commercial customers by providing a diverse set of products to include, but not limited to: snow mapping, agriculture monitoring, oil spill monitoring, forestlands management, ice type identification, ice reconnaissance, geological mapping, glacier motion monitoring, flood monitoring, disaster relief, fire fighting, city planning,, and real estate sales. In short, there are vast uses for commercial satellite imagery and anyone with a credit card can have access to it. The problem is that this capability is not always used for peaceful purposes, terrorists or non-friendly nations can take the same products and use them for war planning and other such activities.

Commercial space-based imagery is available throughout the world. Many countries have imagery capabilities of some sort or another, this includes Canada, United States, Britain, Russia, China, Israel, France, India, to name a few. Imagery capability is available in varying forms (electro-optical, radar, thermal, etc.). Resolution can be refined to one-meter for electro-optical and three-meters for radar systems. US law permits commercial sale of imagery no lower than one-meter resolution. Without a doubt, more refined resolution will be available in the near future. However, the US is concerned with the associated national security issues, to both the privacy and protection of its citizens, as well as protection of vital areas of interest, like military installations. The difficulty then becomes the trade off between national security concerns and commercial interests (guardians versus merchants). It is critically important that the correct balance is struck between the guardians' concern for national security interests and the merchants' concern for market share. Nevertheless, the worldwide market is growing for this type of refined space-based imagery, and market share will be pursued by many nations as soon as they can develop and launch this type of capability. Canada needs to be at the forefront of this market niche, by developing technologies, in preparation of meeting this ever-growing market demand. The Canadian government must ensure that the needs of both the guardians and the merchants are addressed in the correct balance so this tremendous opportunity is not overlooked.

As commercial satellite imagery develops, it will be exploited not only by the commercial sector, but most certainly by the military community as well. Canada takes advantage of space-based imagery to support many of its worldwide operations, to include its peacekeeping commitments, in addition to training and daily operations. Canada therefore knows the value of commercial imagery to military operations and is not alone in this recognition. Canada shares many national security and foreign policy interests with its principal ally, the US Within that close relationship, it has worked with the US to ensure that its commercial space-based remote sensing systems do not compromise their shared interests.

Canada, was an early pioneer in developing space capabilities, being one of the first nations to launch a satellite into space with the launch of Alouette in 1962. As the second largest nation in the world, and as a world leader in communications, Canada relies heavily on space capabilities to provide its many sparsely population areas with advanced telecommunications. Canada's involvement in Earth observations from space began with the development of the Prince Albert Satellite Station located in Saskatchewan. It was designed to receive and process data from the Earth Resources Technology Satellite, launched in 1972. Radar Satellite (RADARSAT) capability is vital to Canada because of its large geographical areas that are covered with clouds and ice for extended portions of the year. The data collected helps the Canadian Ice Service to supply daily ice charts, which are critical to Canadian Coast Guard operations, maritime transportation and the fishing industry. MacDonald Dettwiler, a Canadian company, developed the world's first digital Synthetic Aperture Radar processing capability in 1978. This was followed by development of RADARSAT-1 in the early 1980s, which was launched in the mid '90s. This was Canada's first commercial Earth observation satellite, designed to survey environmental changes and support management of ocean activities. It is still today one of the most advanced Earth observation satellites in orbit, providing day-and-night, all-climate imagery to clients worldwide. Canada continues to lead with the development of its MacDonald Dettwiler RADARSAT-2, Canada's second Earth observation satellite, scheduled for launch in 2003. The high resolution provided by RADARSAT-2, with its Synthetic Aperture Radar capabilities will acquire data at horizontal, vertical and cross polarizations over a range of resolutions from 100 to three meters. Some of the new applications offered by RADARSAT-2 will include ship detection, with its ground moving targets indication (GMTI), as well as vegetation and soil monitoring. Once the GMTI capability is validated, in a Department of National Defence experiment, it will then become the world's first space based radar with a GMTI mode. This will significantly enhanced future capabilities for space-based imagery. It will also be a tangible research and development contribution to Canada's allies, at a time when Canada has been criticized for its low military spending.

Canada has long been concerned with protecting the sovereignty of its northern regions and waterways. This is at best, an extremely challenging undertaking. Canada and the US have agreed to disagree on the status of those northern waterways; are they internal waters, as Canada maintains, or are they international waters as the US implies? With global warming opening these waterways for longer periods each year, foreign ships are exploring these areas without permission from Canada. RADARSAT-2 will be able to provide surveillance for this area. This will enhance Canada's capability for monitoring the Arctic Archipelago; nevertheless, monitoring sovereign territory and enforcing that sovereignty are significantly different challenges.

Because of the importance of space-based observations, Canada is working with the United States and United Kingdom to develop systems concepts and help foster technology, research and development capabilities that can support future space-based observation requirements. The aim is to investigate the military value, technical feasibility, and potential cost of space-based surveillance systems for maritime, land and aerospace defence applications. This joint project is looking at space-based radar and electro-optical systems that can provide a cost-effective surveillance coverage in terms of wide area surveillance, detection of GMTI as well as air moving targets indication (AMTI), which will be capable of tracking aircraft anywhere in the world. A constellation of satellites with these capabilities could possibly replace some of today's aging static radars and high-demand airborne sensors.

Once space-based GMTI and AMTI capabilities are fully developed, it will redefine air defence as we know it today. For example, the recent incident with the USS Cole is a clear indication that the future threat is shifting from regional based to include terrorist activities. During the Cold War era, the adversary was clearly identified, its point of origin was defined, and to a large extent its government was stable. A terrorist has no specific regional base, can strike anytime, anywhere and then disperse into many different countries with no affiliation to any single nation. As such, it becomes extremely difficult to defend against this kind of threat.

When we look at national security for Canada, an example of a terrorist threat scenario could be the threat of a weapon of mass destruction delivered via a cruise missile launched from an offshore vessel, whether this be against Canada or Canadian Forces deployed overseas. Recently, proliferation of cruise missile technology has been extensive. Looking at North America as an example, a rogue actor could approach the coast of Canada or the US with a vessel that could launch a cruise missile, and unless there is a capability of not only detecting the launch, but providing continuous tracking of the missile from its point of origin, the likelihood of intercepting the missile is limited. Space-based radar could provide this capability with the data being downlinked into one of North American Aerospace Defence Command's (NORAD's) Air Defence Sectors, thereby considerably increasing the chances of engagement and destruction of the missile before it can reach its intended target. Another example of a threat to Canadian national security, is the aerial counter-drug mission, in which NORAD plays a leading role. Successful accomplishment of this mission could be significantly enhanced if a space-based radar system could track potential drug smuggling aircraft from point of origin in South or Central America continuously to endgame where law enforcement agents arrest the suspects. These are only two examples of how future space-based radar capabilities, employed in conjunction with our allies, and complimentary to our static and airborne surveillance systems, could enhance Canadian national security.

The Gulf War was the first time in history that space-based capabilities were integrated into military operations to such a large degree. Never again will Western Allies engage in combat, or for that matter any type of military operation (peacekeeping, training, etc.), without the support of space-based capabilities. The key aspect of this concept, to the greatest extent possible, is for the allies to fully exploit these capabilities while denying this advantage to the enemy. During the Gulf War, Saddam Hussein was prevented access to space capabilities, specifically satellite imagery, which would have warned him of the allied left-hook maneuver. At the same time the allies took full advantage of what imagery offered, resulting in unparalleled military success.

National security concerns become a serious issue during times of increased tensions and conflict. Should Canada become involved in a conflict under the auspices of the United Nations or NATO, control of access to space-based imagery would become an issue. For example, during the early stages of the Gulf War Saddam Hussein was purchasing SPOT imagery on the commercial market. This problem was resolved by purchasing all available imagery time from the source by the allies, thus blocking the availability of this imagery from Iraq. In a future conflict, availability of space-based imagery could be widespread, especially through the commercial market. This capability could provide an adversary with the ability to identify militarily significant targets as well as providing high-quality situational awareness, order-of-battle, targeting information and battle damage. In order to counter the availability of this product, the first option employed by the allied force will be political, economic or diplomatic. This may even include the allies purchasing all available imagery from the source if political pressure is not successful, and if purchasing the imagery product is feasible. If these methods are not successful, military options may then be considered, to include jamming the source satellite uplinks and downlinks, or destruction of ground stations by use of force. Regardless of the methodology employed to counter the availability of space-based imagery to an adversary, space superiority, similar to air superiority, will be vital to the allied operation.

In the last decade, the type of conflicts Canada has become involved in have been regionally focused, whereby the adversary is operating from a relatively small regional base (Iraq, Bosnia), and the allies have deployed from home units to theatres at great distances. As such, the adversary has not depended as heavily on space-based assets as have the allies. Moreover, Western economies are heavily depended on space-based capabilities for many aspects of daily living; therefore, from a Western Allied perspective, space-based assets will become a centre-of-gravity, requiring protection. Defensive measures will be taken by the allies, to include encryption of information transmitted to and from space, employment of redundant systems, and hardening of satellites to increase survivability. Protection of these vital assets will be a primary concern to the allies, in comparison to the regionally based adversary who may not be as heavily reliant on space-base systems.

Conclusion

In conclusion, commercial space-based imagery is a growth industry. An industry that Canada must ensure, with the help of the Canadian government, that it captures a fair market share. There will have to be a trade off between the economic interests of the merchants, and the national security concerns of the guardians. Canada has become a world leader in the development of space-based GMTI capability, with its RADARSAT 2 project. This will considerably enhance Canada's ability to surveil its vast regions and downlink this information to a number of interested parties, to include the business community, maritime operations and defence. Moreover, if the AMTI aspect of Canada's allied venture can be improved, and employed in conjunction with the GMTI option, it will provide significantly enhanced capability to air defence operations. Additionally, this becomes a very meaningful contribution that Canada is making to allied operations, at a time when Canada has been criticized for its lack of tangible support to military spending. Finally, space as a centre-of-gravity will be a factor in the next major conflict. Space superiority will become as critically important to military combat as air superiority is today.

Chapter 12

Two Steps Back: The Uncertain Promise for the Strategic Use of Commercial Satellite Imagery

Corey Michael Dvorkin[1]

Discussing a topic such as this – the use of commercial satellite imagery for intelligence or strategic purposes – raises a number of interesting contradictions. Satellite imagery and space in general, have been closely guarded topics in military and intelligence circles. In fact, it probably bears remembering that even as recently as eight years ago, the name if not the existence of the National Reconnaissance Office (NRO) was itself classified.[2] While that might lead to assumptions that the commercialization of space and remote sensing is something which has only recently been forced on a reluctant American national security establishment, that is not correct. Even as early as 1984, with the enactment by the US Congress of the Land Remote Sensing Commercialization Act, there was a recognition that industry was moving towards space and that this was something which was potentially of great benefit to the American Government and the US economy.

This chapter will address the American experience in commercializing an earth observation and satellite imagery industry, particularly as it touches on defence and security policy. The US military space program is obviously the largest of any nation, and it is American firms which are leading the charge to the marketplace. The American case is interesting because if the US can successfully reach some sort of accommodation between military, civil and commercial space interests, it stands to achieve enormous benefits. Conversely, the potential national security risks of an unrestrained commercial imaging industry are also significant, and these would fall most heavily on the US While the dynamic between commercial openness and national security has functioned better than may be expected, this chapter proposes that there is a fork in the road ahead and some serious, if not visionary, choices will soon be required.

The United States could potentially reap enormous returns by effectively incorporating commercial imagery into its intelligence and reconnaissance architecture. This is due to a few interrelated factors, but primarily it is because commercial systems are now more capable than they had previously been by several orders of magnitude, and for the first time, the economics of commercial satellite imagery make sense. The economic validity of commercial satellite imagery is becoming increasingly apparent: 1996 was the first year where commercial space revenues surpassed government space expenditures. Commercial growth in space –

and this also includes remote sensing and telecommunications – has seen an annual growth of about 20 per cent for each of the last seven years. This compares to an approximate annual growth rate of 2 per cent on the expenditures of military systems over the same period. The Assistant Secretary of the Air Force for Space has predicted that by 2007, commercial investment in space will outpace DoD space investment by more than ten-fold, some $170 billion commercial against $13–14 billion military.[3] In the same period, commercial satellites are expected to represent about 70 percent of the total placed into orbit.[4]

When contrasted against a long series of mostly flat Pentagon budgets in the previous decade the growth in civilian space industry is even more jarring. Research and development in particular is suffering greatly, with a drop of 8.2 percent in FY 99 alone[5] and, adjusting for inflation, the FY2001 Defense Budget contains the lowest level of R&D funding in 18 years.[6] With such a disparity between commercial and military space funding, it is not difficult to conclude that it does make economic, if not strategic, sense for the US government to leverage off of industry. This chapter will discuss how the US has attempted to achieve that synergy, and will evaluate the degree of success achieved.

Developing a Commercial Satellite Imagery Industry: History, Process and Policy

The policies governing the commercial space industry evolved can be characterized as being an ongoing tug-of-war between unfettered liberalization and absolute control. In looking at this evolution in the United States, there have been two distinct phases in policy development in the last twenty-five years since the first discussions were held on allowing the commercial use of space for imaging purposes. The initial phase, which can have its philosophical roots traced back at least as far as the 1967 Outer Space Treaty, was towards the privatization of space activities, with perhaps, the eventual goal of commercializing those activities. That process eventually reached its fruition sometime in the late 1980s, and it is arguable that since that time, and particularly in the period since 1996, the US government has reversed that trend and now seeks to militarize commercial space activities. Before examining the policy underpinnings of commercial satellite imaging, it is useful to recap how the policies on commercial operation of space systems and the policies regulating satellite imagery evolved separately.

It bears remembering that even in the United States, neither privatization nor commercialization of space was necessarily inevitable. There were no civil satellites in the United States until NASA began its Earth Resources Technology Satellite program in 1969, and the US did not launch its first civil satellite until July 1972. This is some thirteen years after the first launch of a KH-1 military photographic reconnaissance satellite in July 1959.

In fact, many of the early international debates on the use of space centred on whether it should be the exclusive purview of states. In the deliberation of Resolution 1962 (XVIII) of the General Assembly, the Soviets proposed initially that 'all activities of any kind out solely and exclusively by states'. American objections to this proposal were immediate and vocal.[7] Indeed, American objections hinged on the fact that the Soviet proposal would preclude 'the possibility of a Government enlisting the help of a private Corporation or firms, which it might authorize to carry out activities in space subject to continuing Government supervision'.[8] Given that it was in fact a commercial entity, the RAND Corporation, which in 1954 had been the first to suggest the development of a reconnaissance satellite program, the American position is immediately understandable. Finally, in September 1963, the Soviet delegation withdrew their proposal, and agreement was reached.[9] According to the revised Soviet viewpoint, commercial activity could be permitted 'on the condition that such activity would be subject to the control of the appropriate State, and the State would bear international responsibility for it'.[10] This caveat was captured in the language of Article VI of the 1967 Outer Space Treaty. As noted, the early American policy was firmly for 'open skies' for space-based earth observation systems. This is of course consistent with the US government's earlier stance on strategic aerial photography.[11] Undeniably of course the American position was driven partly by self-interest, and not surprisingly, the debates surrounding the legitimacy of satellite reconnaissance remained for some time. Eventually, however, a measure of acceptance emerged, although there is little formal codification of this principle. The only example of this can be found in Article XII of the 1972 ABM Treaty, which prohibited interference with detection by 'national technical means'.[12] That said, the Treaty avoided defining 'national technical means' and said little about how those systems were to operate other than noting they would do so 'in a manner consistent with generally recognized principles of international law'.[13] There was, however, no framework governing the operation of civil or commercial systems. It was not until almost 20 years later that this matter was finally codified when the UN General Assembly adopted 'Principles Relating to Remote Sensing of the Earth from Outer Space' on 3 December 1986.

Again, the debates on the 1986 accord were sharply polarized, and centered around the need for consent by the imaged state.[14] The American position was that collection and distribution of civilian remote sensing imagery should be unrestricted. The Soviet position was that both the acquisition and dissemination of imagery be allowed only with the consent of the state that is overflown; in essence, instilling the need for prior consent. The 1986 UN Principles were a clear victory for the American position. The final text eschewed any such notification, and only accords the sensed state the right to have access to data of its terri-tory 'on a non-discriminatory basis and on reasonable cost terms'.[15] Lacking any more specific requirements or a regime to actively enforce them, satellite operators have been free to interpret this clause in a manner that is most convenient to them. At present, Principle XII is interpreted to mean that a country being imaged is entitled only to a finished imagery product (as opposed to data which could be further processed), only if it aware it is being imaged and only if it explicitly requests a copy. Even then, a state will still not know who requested a specific image of for what purposes.[16]

While the United States government was an early and vocal advocate for allowing the commercialization of space, there were no such industries operating domestically. Some analysts have noted that the United States may have sought to encourage the early creation of a commercial satellite imagery industry, in order to 'accustom people to photographs in space' and help lend legitimacy to US military reconnaissance efforts.[17] Indeed, in a tautological string of circular logic, the US was to argue that since military activities in space were fundamentally identical to civilian activity, and as there was no logical basis for the UN to interfere with those legitimate commercial activities, then military systems should be similarly unregulated. This was expressed by the statement of Senator Albert Gore Sr. to the First Committee of the General Assembly on December 3, 1962. Gore noted that 'no workable dividing-line between military and non-military uses of space exist, and as such, there can be 'no basis for objection to observation satellites'.[18]

The Emergence of a Commercial Satellite Imagery Industry: LANDSAT

LANDSAT, the world's first commercial satellite system, was originally an outgrowth from American intelligence collection programs. As part of an ongoing effort to increase the capabilities of the CORONA system, CORONA Mission 1104 (7 August, 1968) tested infrared film, and colour film was flown later on Mission 1105 (3 November 1968).[19] In 1970, the CIA issued a report to analyze the data received from these two experimental missions and provide an evaluation of the utility of colour imagery. This report noted that while the resolution of colour film was only half as good as black and white film, there was significant potential to use colour film for mineral and resource detection. A second test mission, Mission 1108, was flown 4 December 1969 with colour film in order to test this hypothesis. The results of that study, 'Appraisal of Geologic Value for Mineral Resources Exploration', upheld that earlier finding.[20]

NASA began its Earth Resources Technology Satellite program in 1969, and launched its first satellite in July 1972. For the second satellite in 1975, the name LANDSAT was adopted. LANDSAT used a light-sensitive electronic sensor which was more advanced that the film-return systems of the KH-4B military reconnaissance systems from which it was derived, although its resolution was far lower (80 metres as opposed to 2 metres at the time for CORNOA).[21] Nevertheless, LANDSAT was still a revolution for scientists, educators and government agencies. The LANDSAT program continued to evolve and improve; LANDSAT-3 was launched in 1978 with a resolution of 30 meters.

In an effort to broaden the user base for LANDSAT, in the eventual hopes of creating a commercial industry, the Carter Administration issued Presidential Decision Directive (PDD) 54 in July 1979. This directive charged the government to 'seek ways to further private sector opportunities in civil land remote sensing activities…with the goal of eventual operations of these activities by the private sector'.[22] Towards that end, Carter transferred operations and management of the LANDSAT system to the National Oceanographic and Atmospheric Administration (NOAA) in the Department of Commerce and away from NASA. It was thought that such a move would alter the nature of LANDSAT from the purely scientific and align the program with the needs of industry. Furthermore unlike NASA, NOAA would be at arms length from the research and development, manufacturing and programmatic aspects of LANDSAT. As such, the administration hoped NOAA would be better able to sharply reduce management costs, which were increasingly becoming an issue at NASA, and improve the attractiveness for commercializing the program.

Notwithstanding the changes of PDD-54, over the next decade the impetus to commercialize a remote sensing satellite industry faltered and eventually looked to die out altogether. The Reagan administration had come to office on a platform which prioritized reducing federal spending, and not surprisingly the administration launched headlong into transitioning LANDSAT into the private sector. This shift in policy ignored four feasibility studies commissioned by the US government between 1982 and 1983.[23] Unanimously, these studies concluded that the current commercial market for satellite imagery was seriously underdeveloped, and all cautioned for gradual and incremental commercialization. In much harsher language, the National Academy of Public Administration admonished the Reagan Administration, by concluding that commercialization 'fails to meet sensible criteria of preservation of the national security' and was a 'forced premature privatization of these responsibilities'.

This did not deter the Reagan administration from pushing ahead with its plans for privatization, and Congress approved the Land Remote Sensing Commercialization Act (P.L. 98-365), which has signed into law on July 17, 1984. This Act directed the Secretary of Commerce to assign a contractor to operate the LANDSAT system, and established requirements for establishing a licensing and oversight process for an eventual commercial remote sensing industry. Earth Observation Satellite Company (EOSAT) was selected to be the operator of the LANDSAT network for a ten-year period beginning in October 1985. Under the terms of the arrangement, the American government was to cover the operational costs of LANDSATs 4 and 5 through the end of their operational lives in 1988, and would be given a $295 million subsidy to develop and launch the follow-on LANDSAT-6 and 7.

Almost immediately there were problems. The Reagan administration deleted the funding subsidy to EOSAT in FY87, and as a result EOSAT ceased all marketing and spacecraft development activities in December 1986. Congress later restored just under half of the previously cancelled subsidy, although such funds were contingent on the National Oceanic and Atmospheric Administration devising a new commercialization plan in concert with EOSAT. That plan, submitted to Congress in late 1987, called for EOSAT to only develop one satellite, LANDSAT-6, and allocated in principle a further subsidy of $220 million to EOSAT. Unfortunately, these delays had served to push the timelines beyond where the contingency funding had been set in PL 9.8.-365, which had anticipated that the replacement systems would be operational by 1988. The reality of the matter was, however, that work on those successor systems had not even begun. As a result funding to operate LANDSATs 4 and 5 expired, and NOAA had to direct EOSAT to turn off the satellites in April 1989. The outcry over having the services of the only two civil satellites suspended eventually prompted the National Space Council, chaired by Vice President Dan Quayle, to overrule NOAA and rescind the shutdown order in March 1989. Similar interim funding actions were repeated in 1990 and 1991 in an effort to keep LANDSAT nominally operational and entice EOSAT to stay with the program long enough to launch a successor system.

It was rapidly becoming apparent in government circles that commercialization was faltering. The US government had hoped to spend $295 million to allow EOSAT to develop and launch two follow-on systems, but instead had invested

$245.7 million and EOSAT had only been able to start development on one system. Additionally, attempts by EOSAT to recoup their investment had caused the price of LANDSAT images to rise sharply, which caused a 77 percent drop in imagery purchases between 1984 and 1990.[24] The LANDSAT program might have continued on this haphazard course were it not for two things; the launch by France of its own civil remote sensing satellite, SPOT-1, in February 1986 and the Persian Gulf War of 1991.

The 1990s: The Pendulum Swings

France's 1986 launch of Satellite Pour l'Observation de la Terre, SPOT-1, presented a direct challenge to the United States' commercial monopoly. Unlike LANDSAT, SPOT was not an outgrowth of a military program, but rather true civil-commercial system, eventually attracting investment from French industrial and financial sources, as well as investment from Sweden, Italy, Spain and Belgium. Possessing a nominal 10 m black-and-white and 20 m colour resolution, SPOT-1 was a vast improvement over the 3 m LANDSAT imagery then available. It is not surprising then, that by 1989 SPOT imagery sales surpassed that of LANDSAT.[25]

The impact of SPOT's imagery was immediate. Even more no table than its increased resolution, was the way in which SPOT Image, the corporate agency managing the system, established itself internationally. From the outset SPOT incorporated a dispersed architecture and encouraged the establishment of Direct Receiving Stations, eventually establishing 23 stations in over 17 countries. This was in sharp contrast to LANDSAT data which was all routed through US government agencies. Furthermore, France did not shy away from making data available to countries in regions of tension, and actively pursued establishing stations in Pakistan, South Africa, Saudi Arabia, Israel and Taiwan. In fact, an analysis of the SPOT catalogue notes that the Golan Heights and other sensitive areas are among the most popular targets for clients of SPOT images.[26] There is also circumstantial evidence that Iraq made extensive use of SPOT imagery during the eight-year Iran-Iraq war and later in preparing for the invasion of Kuwait in 1990.[27]

What was also apparent was that satellite imagery was being increasingly moved into the public sphere. During the Cold War, satellite imagery – unlike aerial photography – had never entered the sphere of public diplomacy. As Gerald Steinberg has noted, 'the leaks and propaganda exchanges that characterized formal talks were absent in this case [satellite imagery]' and there is at least some evidence that both the United States and Soviet Union explicitly avoided making public such imagery, which could give cause for developing an anti-satellite capability.[28] Such restraint was not to be forthcoming, however, from the private sector, and by 1985 images of 'secret' Libya, Iran and Soviet facilities were starting to become regular occurrences in both print and television. Perhaps the best example however, of the immediacy of these images was to come in 1986. The explosion of Unit 4 at the Chernobyl nuclear plant in Ukraine resulted in an extensive denial campaign by the Soviet Union, which further sealed off a 100-mile area around Chernobyl and banned foreign travel into Kiev. American intelligence and military satellites began collecting data the day after the Tass news agency acknowledged the accident on April 28, but they were not alone in this endeavour. By April 30th, LANDSAT images ordered by the American Broadcasting Corporation (CBC) of the blazing reactor were shown and these were quickly followed with higher resolution images from SPOT-1.[29]

It was the 1990-91 Persian Gulf War which served to reinforce the linkages between commercial imagery and national security. Analysts have described Desert Storm as the first space war,[30] but what is not as widely known is the extent to which commercial systems supported that effort. These activities covered the full spectrum of space activities including both communications and imagery. Commercial satellite communications accounted for 20 to 25 percent of all satellite communications used, while the US DoD spent at least $5 to $6 million on LANDSAT imagery and the US Defense and Mapping Agency spent a further $5.7 million on SPOT imagery.[31]

While the US had an excellent network of strategic reconnaissance satellites, it found that such imagery was not well suited to the situation at hand. Imagery from national intelligence systems was not at all practical for wide area surveillance, nor for geomatics or mapping purposes. Furthermore, data from intelligence systems could often not be processed and analysed in a timely fashion, and lastly, due to the high level of classification, such national strategic imagery could not be provided to the theatre commander in the field nor could it be routinely shared with the Coalition allies.[32] The commander of air operations in Desert Storm, Lieutenant General Charles Horner, would later conclude that part of the problem was 'the walls of classification the space intelligence community has built around themselves.'[33] The solution to many of those problems lay in commercial imagery.

LANDSAT began imaging the Kuwaiti war zone on the very day Iraq invaded and began immediately providing imagery to the American forces. Fifteen days later, the US Army's XVII Airborne Corps had been provided new maps in preparation for the deployment of its 82nd Airborne Division, and by 1 September, the Army was being provided with three-dimensional digital terrain maps. By 10 January, deployed forces were receiving such data directly from space and able to process it in the field. The official United States Space Command's classified assessment of Desert Storm noted that commercial imagery 'figured prominently' in planning airborne and amphibious operations, in the planning of offensive operations and in the tracking of Iraqi forces.[34]

What was also apparent though, is that if such imagery was available to the US and its allies, it might also potentially be available to Iraq. As LANDSAT is licensed by the US Government through NOAA, Washington was able to deny Iraq access to that source. What was perhaps more worrying to military planners, is that news agencies would purchase satellite imagery in attempt to overcome the restrictions the Pentagon had imposed on reporting. There was no mechanism in place to limit purchases by domestic buyers. Although much of the imaging time over the Persian Gulf had already been purchased by the US military, this was at best an imperfect mechanism of control. According to recently declassified accounts, the US Defense Intelligence Agency 'intervened at the last moment to prevent the release of LANDSAT data of the Kuwait-Iraq/Saudi border to the American news media'.[35] The requested images, showed extensive road building activity by the US that would have clearly indicated US plans for the surprise 'left hook' flanking manoeuvre, and might have given the Iraqis time to prepare for the war-ending assault.

France, the only other nation operating a commercial imagery satellite also had to contend with the problem of releasing information of potential strategic value. As France was a part of the Gulf War Coalition, the board of directors of SPOT-Image came forward and announced their intention to terminate all private commercial sales of Persian Gulf imagery. This policy was not the result of any particular altruism by SPOT-Image, however, but rather a result of the unique circumstances of the Gulf War.[36] In announcing its self-imposed censorship SPOT did not – as had the board governing the INMARSAT satellite communications system – make any connection between its motives and the belief that space should be used exclusively for peaceful purposes. According to Phillipe Renault, Deputy Director-General of SPOT-Image, if EOSAT Corporation has sold LANDSAT imagery to Iraq, SPOT-Image would have done likewise in the interest of business competition.[37]

Both the benefits and risks of commercial imagery had become obvious during the Gulf War. The headquarters of the Air Force Space Command in its own classified lessons learned report recommended that the service 'advocate for an improved MSI [multi-spectral imaging] system' and inferred that it may be appropriate for the DoD to become engaged in setting the 'requirements, funding, [and] operations' of a follow-on LANDSAT-7.[38] As was bluntly noted by US Space Command:

> The United States must maintain its MSI capacity and give the user the type of support he or she needs to use MSI data. Unless action is initiated quickly, the US MSI capability will 'go away'…If this happens, the US war-fighter will be dependent on foreign sources for MSI data. Additionally, the supply of MSI data should be improved so that US military personnel receive the type and quantity of MSI data they need.[39]

However, the LANDSAT program seemed beset by intractable problems and it was doubtful that it could be shored up sufficiently to meet these new demands. What was therefore needed was a new solution: a robust commercial imagery industry, which could be drawn upon as needed to support national security objectives. This conclusion was reinforced in the Wilkening Report which warned that the Cold War security requirements continued to contribute to inefficiencies in the conduct of the nation's space program.[40]

Attempts to redress this problem were not long in coming. In 1992, the House Science Committee drafted the Land Remote Sensing Policy Act, eventually enacted into law as P.L. 102–555, which was designed to 'enable the United States to maintain its leadership in land remote sensing and to establish a new national remote sensing policy'. Drawing from the experience in Desert Storm, and making explicit acknowledgement that 'LANDSAT data are particularly important for national security', the Department of Defense was designated a managing agency, as was NASA. Authority for licensing future systems remained with the Secretary of Commerce. The Act rejected the terms of Reagan's 1984 law and noted that 'the commercialization of the LANDSAT program cannot be achieved in the near future' although commercialization 'should remain a long-term goal of United States policy'.

Amongst the goals of P.L. 102–555, the legislation attempted to once again attract corporate enterprises into the remote sensing field by reducing the barriers to market entry. Despite the changes introduced under the 1984 LANDSAT Act, no US firm had applied for a license to operate commercial satellites, despite the fact that the legal framework for such ventures was firmly in place.[41] Furthermore, by 1992 DoD downsizing was beginning to have serious implications for preserving the industrial base.[42] Legislators quickly seized upon this cause. Citing 'concern about the intelligence industrial base' the Senate Select Committee on Intelligence held a closed hearing on June 10, 1993 to 'learn from government and private sector experts how the entry of US medium resolution imaging technology into the commercial remote sensing market would affect US national security interests and the US intelligence industrial base'.[43]

There were two complementary solutions to resolve this issue in the short-term, and both were tried to varying degrees under P.L. 102–555. The first solution was to diversify the range of activities defence contractors were engaged in, while the second involved the government actively protecting, if not subsidising key industries. Encouraging a commercial satellite imagery would serve to meet both of these ends. Some analysts have noted that the attempt to diversify merely let many of the subsidiary firms already engaged in intelligence-community work transfer data back to the parent corporations for use in the commercial market.[44] As Gerald Steinberg has noted, 'commercial imaging, which was based on technology developed for the US government, would in turn subsidise the government and security community's reconnaissance requirements'.[45] Furthermore, the government would be able to guarantee itself a privileged position without having to assume the risk or cost of research and development. Under P.L. 102–555, if a proposed private satellite system used government funding for research, development or operations the government could set its own special terms on data pricing and distribution.[46]

There was a requirement both to build an industry of satellite imagery providers, and on the other hand, there was a need to build a critical mass of imagery processors and consumers to support these providers. P.L. 102–55 affected changes in both, although by now it was obvious to Congress that the LANDSAT program was not the appropriate method to achieve these goals. As a result, to ensure that 'an advanced land remote sensing system' was developed by 1997, Section 303 of P.L. 102–555 created a 'technical demonstration program', which sought to speed declassifying technology derived from so-called 'US National Technical Means' of intelligence gathering and move it into the private sector in an effort to jump start private industry. These changes had the desired effect; in July 1992, only 2 months before P.L. 102–555 was signed into law by President Bush, WorldView Inc. in partnership with Space Imaging applied for a license to develop its 'EarlyBird' satellite with a 3 m resolution. Others soon followed suit, and between 1992 and 1998 another 11 commercial satellite licenses were granted by the US government.[47]

Such structural solutions would need time to evolve, however, and until they were in place, it would be necessary to ensure the continued survival of the LANDSAT program. The most immediate concern was the resolution of the 'funding and organizational uncertainties' which had dogged the program under privatization. Congress' short-term solution was to try and bring the Pentagon onboard as an underwriter for the LANDSAT program. Under the rubric of P.L. 102–555, DoD was now able to take active part in setting the design requirements for LANDSAT-7.

From the start, however, there were problems: NASA favoured utilizing a less expensive and less complex sensor with a 15 m resolution which had a proven viability, whereas the Pentagon was advocating a new and much more expensive 5 m sensor which could collect strategically significant data.[48] As both agencies were equally responsible for the LANDSAT program, it was not apparent how this competing design requirement would be resolved. When LANDSAT-6 failed to reach orbit on October 5, 1993 the question became moot. In order to maintain continuity of data to the academic and commercial market, the development of LANDSAT-7 was accelerated and NASA insisted that the high cost of developing the Pentagon's High Resolution Multispectral Stereo Imager sensor could undermine the timely completion of the satellite. As a consequence, DoD pulled out of the LANDSAT program entirely.[49] Once again, the spectre loomed that all medium-resolution commercial imagery would have to be procured offshore.

It would still be some years before any American firms would be capable of deploying imaging satellites, and already revolutionary changes in the marketplace were underway. As already noted, SPOT Image was rapidly emerging as the dominant firm, with the launch of SPOT-3 in 1993. Further, the future was crowded with the prospect for competition: France was developing SPOT-4 with double the resolution over the previous generation and Israel, Japan, South Africa, China and India were all working on medium to high-resolution systems.[50] Most devastating however to the US position was the entry of Russia into the commercial space marketplace. Following the dissolution of the Soviet Union, Russia announced in early 1992 that it was joining the commercial space powers. Starting from in late 1987, the Soviet Union had selectively marketed medium-resolution KFA-1000 images purposes under the state-run Soyuzkarta corporation in a half-hearted effort to compete with LANDSAT in the mapping and geomatics market. Now however, Russia was far more serious in its efforts and licensing two commercial firms, Sovinformsputnik and Priroda, to sell high-resolution 2-meter resolution archive data from its KVR-1000 and KFA-3000 intelligence satellites. Furthermore, Moscow announced its intention to make 0.75-meter products available in the future.[51]

In light of the spectre of the US being relegated to a marginal share of commercial reconnaissance it is not surprising that on 9 December, 1993 the Chairman, Vice Chairman and ranking Minority member of the Senate Select Committee on Intelligence wrote to President Clinton and offered their opinion that 'there are substantial commercial opportunities for United States businesses to sell satellite imagery systems and products without in any way placing US intelligence capabilities and methods at risk' and urged the administration to strongly support such sales.[52] Such liberalization was not long in coming and it would in no certain terms signal the intention of Washington to re-establish primacy.

Jumping in With Both Feet: PDD-23

In March 1994 President Clinton issued Presidential Decision Directive (PDD)-23, entitled 'Foreign Access to Remote Sensing Space Capabilities'. While still classified as of mid-2001, some of the key tenets of the PDD were released.[53] PDD-23 stated that its fundamental goal is 'to support and to enhance American industrial competitiveness in the field of remote sensing space capabilities while at the same time protecting US national security and foreign policy interests'.[54] This directive opened even further the potential for high-resolution commercial imagery, but the government would retain the right to monitor both the end-use customer and the nature of the data purchased. Moreover, all commercial systems would use data encryption systems provided by or approved by the US government, with the inference that transmissions could be monitored. With PDD-23, the mechanism of 'shutter-control' – discontinuing imaging during periods of crisis – was established and export controls were now firmly intertwined with national security. PDD-23 lowered the threshold for commercial electro-optical imagery to 1-meter resolution, and synthetic aperture radar (SAR) to a resolution of 5 m, and opened the door, however cautiously, for American dominance of the market.

Directive PDD-23 advocated three different paths by which to jump-start American industry: in allowing the export sales of the satellites themselves, by enabling export sales of imagery, and by committing the US government to a drastic increase in purchases from domestic suppliers. Few nations had at that time the technical capacity to even produce imagery of the resolution which was permitted under PDD-23, much less be able to offer it for sale commercially.[55] For the other space-faring nations, the signing of PDD-23 was a very clear signal that the US rapidly intended to achieve perpetual market dominance. This fact was not lost on the members of the Western European Union (WEU), who at the time had been examining their own needs for dual-use military-civil imaging systems. According to a later study submitted to the WEU Assembly by its Technology and Aerospace Committee, 'directive PDD-23 will doubtless enable the United States to overrun the market for high-resolution satellite imagery'.[56]

Just eleven months after the signing of PDD-23, President Clinton issued Executive Order 12951, which authorized the release of 'certain scientifically or environmentally useful imagery acquired by space-based national intelligence systems known as the Corona, Argon and Lanyard missions'. This unmatched database of more than 800,000 images, collected between 1960 and 1972 would be made available by the US Geological Survey's Earth Resources Observation System's Data Center in Sioux Falls, South Dakota. Therefore almost overnight, an industry of data processors could be created in the United States, with the vast majority of the overhead costs already paid by the Pentagon. It is fair to conclude that industry was being not-so subtly encouraged to follow what could uncharitably be called the 'Microsoft business model': arrive at the market with ideas or products which other paid to develop, use this to secure an overwhelming advantage and utterly crush all com-petition. Furthermore, the American Government would actively help and encourage this.[57]

If 1992 was a period of enormous change for the military industrial base, then 1995 was a period of vast transition for the US intelligence community. It should not have been surprising that the end of the Cold War would bring significant changes for the imagery community. After all, in the years following both World Wars I and II, the American military had dismantled the photographic interpretation institutions that had been built up in the course of those conflicts.[58] While the NRO was never threatened with dissolution, it was already becoming clear that the system of satellites designed to monitor the Soviet Union were not well adapted for many of the emerging challenges. Moreover, while both the enormous expenditures and the veil of absolute secrecy of the NRO were arguably justifiable during the Cold War, it was less certain that either would continue to the same degree in the new post-Col War era. It certainly did not help the imagery community that the post-Cold War era began in scandal. In August 1994 it was discovered that the NRO had misappropriated funds to build itself a lavish new headquarters complex in upstate Virginia, and a year later it became public that the NRO had yet again secreted unspent appropriation funds.[59]

Not coincidentally, there was renewed and focused attention being brought to bear on the need to reform and restructure the intelligence community, and two bipartisan blue-ribbon groups were established to do just that. The Intelligence Authorization Act for Fiscal Year 1995 (Public Law 103–359) created a 'Commission on the Roles and Capabilities of the US Intelligence Community' chaired by Les Aspin, and tasked to develop proposals to overhaul all facets of the intelligence community. The Commission released its report *Preparing for the 21st Century: An Appraisal of US Intelligence* on March 1, 1996.[60] It was followed three months later by a Staff Study written by the House Permanent Select Committee on Intelligence entitled *IC21: The Intelligence Community in the 21st Century.*

There was a remarkable uniformity among the conclusions of the reports. Both cited the need for drastic changes: namely it was felt that the intelligence agencies were too expensive, too narrowly focused on Cold War activities and were not taking advantage of open source material. Furthermore, the intelligence agencies were too concerned with the development of high-technology collection means while little, if any, attention was being paid to analysis and the dissemination of the product to the audience which required it. Finally, the US military was finding itself engaged in Bosnia, Rwanda, Somalia and Haiti; areas that had received scant attention in the silo counting days of the Cold War and the intelligence community had not adapted to even begin facing the challenges of dealing with these new missions.

Moving to a broader commercialization of imagery was an attempt to rectify some of those problems. More sensors in space would allow some of the background missions to get done, while the specialized expertise of the intelligence agencies could be applied to analysis and the generation of intelligence from the information. Preparing for the 21st Century cited the fact that 'the current US capability in space is vulnerable to the failure of any single system' and noted the paucity of systems was due to their 'substantial cost'.[61] In fact a demonstration of this vulnerability had already occurred: in 1985 the US intelligence community had been reduced to a single reconnaissance satellite, when KH-11 satellite number 5507 was lost on launch.[62] More seriously, some five years after the recommendations of the Aspin/Brown report the entire constellation of five US reconnaissance and intelligence satellites failed temporarily due to complications with the 'Year 2000' change-over.[63] The Commission recommended that 'by taking advantage of developments in the commercial satellite industry, the costs and the vulnerability of current capabilities might be further reduced'[64] although, that said, commercial capabilities 'will not obviate the need to maintain separate intelligence systems for the foreseeable future'.[65] The House's IC-21 report upheld those conclusions in recommending that 'commercial imagery needs to be considered as an adjunct to national systems and plans must be put in place to facilitate its use'.[66]

An August 1996 review of the mandate and function of the NRO (led by Admiral David Jeremiah, former Vice Chairman of the Joint Chiefs of Staff) arrived at similar conclusions.[67] Jeremiah recommended that the mission of the NRO be redefined as 'global information superiority' to the US Government as a whole.[68] Additionally, the Panel found that while the NRO remains a key national asset, the shifting expectations of military customers and of policy makers required the NRO to adapt. What was needed was a return to first principles, as the NRO was 'no longer universally accepted as being at the leading edge of technology'.[69]

Already this reorientation was underway, and again it would involve partnership with the private sector. On November 28, 1995 the Administration announced its intention to create a National Imagery and Mapping Agency (NIMA), an organization which eventually came into being 1 October, 1998. NIMA brought together the Defense Mapping Agency, the CIA's National Photographic Interpretation Center, DoD Central Imagery Office and the Defense Intelligence Agency's Office of Imagery Analysis. Such consolidation had first been recommended in 1992 by Secretary of Defense Cheney and Director of Central Intelligence Gates. It was thought that by separating the imagery analysis agency, NIMA, from the agency which procured the satellites, the NRO, increased use would be made of commercial imagery. The hope was that, as NIMA would have no vested interest in the continued building of classified systems, the agency would be free to make enhanced use of commercial systems.

At least initially, there was great enthusiasm that commercialization would shore up the industrial base, while contributing to the intelligence community. This was noted in as many words in a 1998 speech by Keith Hall, Director of the NRO. Addressing an audience of commercial space industry executives, Hall expressed his view that 'commercial ventures will now dramatically accelerate the development of future space programs'.[70] With NIMA now in the lead, the US government and military services began making targeted subsidies to corporations. For example EarthWatch, Space Imaging and OrbImage received grants of between $2 and $4 million to upgrade their ground systems to facilitate the transfer of imagery data from their systems to NIMA.[71] The other services followed NIMA's example. The US Air Force agreed to subsidize OrbImage to develop and deploy the 'Warfighter' hyper-spectral sensor onboard its OrbView-4 satellite. OrbImage would be restricted to selling 8-metre resolution imagery from 'Warfighter' to the US government, but would be free to market lower grade 24-metre imagery commercially. Similarly, the office of Naval Research agreed to provide the Space Technology Corporation with approximately $60 million to develop and deploy the Naval EarthMap (NEMO) satellite, with 30-metre hyper-spectral sensor and a 5-metre panchromatic optical sensor.[72]

There was also somewhat of a cultural shift in the perception of commercial imagery in the military intelligence community. In October 1997, the US Air Force Space Command conducted Operation "Seek Gunfighter". This involved the formation of a 'red team' – a simulated opposing force – which proved its ability to track, in near-real time, the deployment of US Air Force assets relying exclusively on open-source information and commercial satellite imagery.[73]

This, and similar exercises drove home the utility of commercial imagery, and it is perhaps not surprising that NIMA began making regular, although initially modest, purchases of commercial imagery. Just before the release of PDD-23, Rear Admiral Jack Dantone, former director of NIMA expounded on the merits of commercial imagery: 'We're committed to it not because it's the right thing to do politically but because it's the right thing to do. It will probably supplant some of the requirements that we have for other imagery, and that can only be good'.[74] In FY98 NIMA dedicated about $5 million annually to the outright purchase of commercial imagery an amount it promised was sure to increase substantially 'once the 1-meter commercial imagery systems were available', which was expected to be sometime in 1998.[75] Secretary of Defense William Cohen opined that he was committed to increasing the $5 million annual expenditure by 'nearly 800 percent' by 2004.[76] Industry leaders reflected this exuberance. Joe Dodd, vice president for government relations at Orbital Sciences wryly observed in a 1998 interview with *Jane's Defence Weekly*, that 'we were told that if we build it they will come, but we weren't sure ... This is a breakthrough of sorts for us and the industry'.[77]

Undaunted by the LANDSAT-7 experience, industry began to accept 'anchor tenancy agreements as well as co-operative ventures designed to leverage government systems by flying them on commercial platforms' and the commercial imaging industry became increasingly enmeshed with the national security establishment.[78]

Two Steps Back: Export Controls, Shutter-Controls and Broken Promises

Even before PDD-23 was signed however, there was concern within sectors of the American government about the national security implications that the availability of high-resolution imagery and its underlying technology would have. Part of the revolutionary nature of PDD-23 is that not only did it allow the sale of imagery, it also made specific allowance for the sales of actual satellites, as well as the underlying technologies of remote sensing. In seeking to commercialize a remote sensing industry, US firms initially sought to sell complete systems, rather than trying to resolve the subtle and more complex problem of selling the actual imagery. It was felt that the problem of restricting the re-transfer of data was almost intractable; whereas existing export controls for military systems could be adapted to govern sales of a complete system. Certainly, PDD-23 was attempting to correct some of the problems which impeded the successful commercialization of the LANDSAT program, where the burden of record-keeping effectively became an effective barrier to market entry.

These initial attempts to sell whole systems – so-called 'turn-key satellites' – revealed the deep divisions on the subject of commercialization within Washington.

The House's IC:21 study had expressed concern about sharing such high-technology systems even with America's closest European allies, for fear that it would give away American technological advantage. The report noted that PDD-23 was 'on the one hand, promoting commercial systems [as] a priority, while on the other hand, it advocates building a US Government system for foreign military sales ... that would directly compete with those same commercial systems'.[79] Interestingly, it was the American desire to protect an ally, rather than any desire to protect American interests or industry, that eventually restrained the charge to unfettered commercialization.

Just prior to the signing of the Land Remote Sensing Act in 1992, the United Arab Emirates (UAE) submitted an application to purchase an imaging satellite from Litton-Itek Optical Systems. Litton had been seeking permission to sell a two-satellite system called 'Murakaba' to the UAE that would provide 0.8 m resolution. Although the rules had not yet been changed, this offer was seriously considered and favoured by the Commerce Department, which would grant the operating license, and by private industry. Ultimately, it is suspected that heavy Israeli lobbying swayed Washington, and the State Department would eventually block the export license.

In 1994 Israel again sought to restrain US commercial activity when Saudi Arabia sought to purchase a major interest in the Eyeglass satellite system (now known as the OrbView system) built by OrbImaging. Eirad, a corporation nominally owned by Prince Fahd Bin Salman Bin Abdulaziz, sought to build a ground station in Riyadh and purchase exclusive rights to all images of the Middle East in return for its investment in the 1 m resolution Eyeglass system.[80] On August 2, 1994 the Clinton Administration asked Israel not to object to the Orb-Imaging agreement with Saudi Arabia. The matter was however seized upon in the US Senate by Jeff Bingaman, who on October 7, 1994, sent a letter bearing the signature of 63 other Senators to the Secretary of Commerce arguing that the transfer of such a system to Saudi Arabia would be harmful to the US national interest. In May 1995, the Commerce Department and Orbital reached an agreement in which the firm agreed to restrict its imaging of Israel, and a license was approved on that basis.

It soon became apparent that such 'one-off' solutions would not prove practical, when Germany applied to purchase a high-resolution system in April 1995.[81] Space Imaging International, a Lockheed-Martin marketing subsidiary, was proposing to build an observation satellite for Germany. Space Imaging suggested that the sale be brokered as a 'government-to-government' sale, which would therefore exempt Germany from US restrictions on the system. However, Washington would reserve the right to take over operation of the platform during emergencies. There were powerful arguments for agreeing to the sale: Germany was actively being courted by France to join its Helios military satellite program, and US industry was anxious to seize their advantage and keep France from entering the marketplace.[82] On 7th December 1995 at the Franco-German summit in Baden-Baden, Chancellor Kohl and President Chirac agreed on German participation in the Helios II program, rejecting the American offer which was reported to be only half the cost of Helios II.

With little prospect for export sales of systems, industry began looking increasingly at data sales. Under PDD-23 a commercial operator agrees to discontinue or limit data collection – a process colloquially known as 'shutter control' – 'during periods when national security or international obligation and/or foreign policies may be compromised'.[83] Through the latter part of the 1990's, the US government began to take an increasingly broad interpretation of this clause, even going so far as to establish conditions of prior restraint.[84] These restraints undermined commercial confidence that the US government was committed to a commercial remote sending industry.

By 1996, the question of imaging Israel was again at the core of a renewed shutter-control debate. Unsatisfied with the resolution of the Eyeglass decision, Senators Bingaman and John Kyl introduced an amendment to the FY97 National Defense Authorization Act which would prohibit the collection and release of data 'with respect to Israel and any other country or geographic area designated by the President'.[85] In introducing the Amendment, Bingaman indicated that it was simply a matter of 'going the extra mile for Israel's security' and that 'our industry should not try to make profits by providing spy satellite images of Israel to Syria and Libya and Iraq and Iran'.[86]

When passed, the language had been narrowed so as to include mention only restrictions of imaging for Israel. Unfortunately, however, the legislation opened the door for similar prohibitions on behalf of US allies world-wide. Such moves threatened to drastically disrupt the business cases of commercial imagery firms, who had assumed that shutter control would not involve permanent blanket restrictions. For example, both Eyeglass International and Space Imaging had been marketing exclusive regional and territorial licenses with exclusive rights being assigned on a first-come/first-served basis.[87] A state concerned about who was imaging it could either 'buy out' the market by purchasing exclusive rights to its region, or pressure Washington to list it as a restricted region. Already examples of this were occurring.[88] Both solutions went against the formal position of the US Government, which was subsequently adopted by the UN, mandating open-skies, with the free exchange of data on a 'non-discriminatory basis'. Having been effectively told that they could not export satellites, corporations were now seeing roadblocks to even exporting the data.

The satellite firms began to appeal their case in pursuit of open markets. Foremost among their complaints was that while the obligations of the private sector where well defined under PDD-23, the responsibilities of the government were, if anything, less clear. Under PDD-23, the Commerce Department retained responsibility for licensing satellites and approving export agreement, but Commerce must now do so in consultation with the Departments of State and Defense. The 1992 legislation had imposed a 120-day limit for Commerce to consider applications, but there were no time limits imposed for State or Defense to return an answer, thus giving them the power to postpone approval indefinitely if they wished. Equally troubling to commercial firms was that there were no limits to shutter-control; it could potentially be invoked with little cause, it could be left in place permanently and there was little recourse for firms either to appeal the directive or to seek compensation for lost business.

Industry began lobbying heavily to have legislation put in place to define the actual process of commercialization.[89] As it was made clear before Congress in 1997, 'the main thing that the private sector is asking for is {for government} to provide some predictability in the process so that we can go out and get our investors to come in. They {need to} know that their investment is going to be secure and they know what the ground rules are'.[90] Such answers would not be forthcoming however, and the 1998 Commercial Space Act showed the amount of disagreement among policy-makers. The House version of that bill, H.R. 1702, included three sections dealing with revisions to commercial activities in remote sensing, launch services and subsidies for improving ground-infrastructure. The Senate version of the Act, S.1473 dealt only with those latter two topics and omitted any reference to remote sensing. Ultimately it was the Senate's version which was finally signed into law. As such, clarity in the regulatory regime for remote sensing would be delayed until February 2000.

Before such changes could be made, however, events would occur which had the potential to completely derail any chance at commercializing a space industry. The 1999 release of the report of the 'House Select Committee on US National Security and Military/Commercial Concerns With the People's Republic of China' (better known as the 'Cox Commission') set these events in motion. The Cox Commission concluded that permissive management of export laws by the Department of Commerce had created a potential opportunity for China and other unfriendly states to improve their strategic capabilities. There were vocal and frenzied concerns in Washington (especially among some of the more zealous members of the Republican party) that too much technology was out there and drastic, if not draconian, measures needed to be taken. As a result, The Strom Thurmond Defense Act of 1999 called for a vast overhaul of export control legislation and transferred the authority for approving licenses for all space-related hardware away from the Commerce Department by placing them on the Munitions Control List (MCL).

Approval for items on the MCL list rests with the State Department's Office of Defense Trade Controls in consultation with the Pentagon's Defense Threat Reduction Agency (DTRA). Under the revised legislation 'United States business interests must not be placed above United States national security interests'.[91] Essentially, that metric was interpreted by the State Department to mean restrictions were mandatory if the technology had any military application at all – it did not matter if it was not being used in a military system, nor even if it was being exported to a NATO ally. Additional reviews of each license were also to be conducted by the Department of Defense, the National Security Agency, the Secretary of Commerce and the Director of Central Intelligence. Later clarification amended the law so that 'such time is afforded as necessary ... to conduct a review of any license'.[92] Furthermore, the Act excluded license reviews for space-related items from the provisions of Executive Order 12981 of 1995, which set out a 30-day time limit for agency reviews and included a dispute resolution mechanism, without which there was a '"black hole" of interagency review by junior licensing officials'.[93] Even under the best of all possible circumstances, license approval could still be delayed indefinitely: the Office of Defense Trade Controls had 14 license reviewers who in fiscal year 1999 had to attempt to adjudicate some 45,000 license requests valued at $26 billion.[94]

Aerospace exports and the commercialization of space ground to a halt: satellite sales of all types dropped 40 per cent between 1998-2000, with the US share of the industrial space market dropping from 72 to 65 per cent in that same time.[95] Routine approvals of export items were now being held up for months, if not years.

France, Germany, the United Kingdom, Canada and Japan were raising complaints about the difficulty in receiving export licenses for even routine items.[96] Addressing a group of defense and industry officials in November 1999 Deputy Secretary of Defense John Hamre expressed his shock in learning that 'DaimlerChrysler Aerospace has put out a directive to its engineers to [design] American components out of their systems because they ran into too much trouble getting licenses approved'.[97] In perhaps the highest profile example, Canada would in late 1999 cancel a contract valued at more than $74 million with Orbital Sciences of Virginia for the satellite bus for its commercial-civil RADARSAT-2 satellite, after being unable to secure an export license despite more than ten months of effort. The RADRSAT-2 contract would later go to Alenia Aerospazia of Rome.[98]

The United States' other European allies were making similar announcements, and trans-Atlantic defense trade was threatening to break down completely. There were concerns that increased export controls were having exactly the opposite of the desired effect, in that the technology was being developed independently rather than under American control. By way of example, Israel's El-Op Electro-Optcis Industries Ltd. secured a contract in early 2000 to sell a 1-metre resolution satellite camera to South Korea for use on the latter's KOMPSAT-2 system. El-Op secured this contract, which 'involves significant technology trans-fer', over at least six competitors, including Lockheed Martin.[99] Given the special protection Israel receives under the Kyl-Bingaman Amendment, some in the American aerospace sector felt that Israel was exploiting a market that American firms were legally prohibited from pursuing.[100]

The final hope for commercial viability of a remote sensing imagery industry – sales to the US government and military – also failed to materialize. By way of example, in 1997 Orbital Imaging was predicting that sales to the US military and intelligence community would account for about 25 per cent of the firm's revenue.[101] There was indeed a basis for this belief as the 'Commercial Imagery Strategy' developed and approved by NIMA and the NRO committed the government to purchasing almost $1 billion in imagery between 2000–2005. This would be broken down into approximately $320 million for outright imagery purchases, $580 million for geospatial data products and services, and $100 million for infrastructure improvements to better integrate commercial imagery into the government architecture.[102]

Unfortunately, according the Congressionally mandated 'Independent Commission on NIMA,' the 'promising $1 billion for commercial imagery purchases…has subsequently proved to be so much fiction'.[103] Publicly available figures indicate that only some $20–$30 million of the $60 million allocated by lawmakers actually was spent in 1999 on commercial imagery by NIMA, and that level looked to remain flat through Fiscal Year 2001. According to American industrial sources, a government commitment on the order of $50 million a year would be needed to ensure the vendors of sufficient business to enable industry to invest in infrastructure and future system developments.[104]

Industry sources had contended they had been led to believe that the 1 m threshold for imagery would provide an abundant market, and many were expressing outrage that their investments were now imperilled. As an example of the risk being incurred by commercial firms, Space Imaging contends they have spent nearly $1 billion in privately funded R&D and market development for its 1 m IKONOS system.

Speaking in September 2000, Lt. Gen. James King, director of NIMA backtracked on this policy. 'When talking about first generation imagery, the utility can be greatly exaggerated ... NIMA is interested in second generation imaging'.[105] Such statements were outright reversals of the position NIMA had advocated only a couple of years earlier, a fact not unnoticed by industry. Gil Rye, the president of Orbital Imaging, has answered that 'the government does not give us confidence. If they are not going to support the first generation systems [i.e., 1 m], it is difficult for us to rationalize investing private capital in the second generation system'.[106] The level of disagreement between industry and government was even greater however. The three US firms who had 1 m programs underway had all applied to NOAA for licenses to build 0.5 m systems; exactly the kinds of second-generation systems NIMA was now saying were required. The first of those license approvals required almost a year's worth of review by the very intelligence agencies that were publicly supporting them.[107]

The outcry among industry and Congressional leaders eventually succeeded in obtaining some reforms. In February 2000, the White House Office of Science and Technology Policy announced that it had established new benchmarks for licensing, which established clear lines of authority between Departments and a new structured timeline of 120 for complete approval.[108] However, this respite was to be short lived, as government regulations again pushed the commercialization of remote sensing take two steps back.

The 'Interim Final Rule' issued by NOAA on July 31, 2000 acknowledged the 'burdensome and intrusive requirements on applicants/licensees' but strengthened shutter-control to an unbelievable extent, giving the United States unprecedented extra-territorial jurisdiction.[109] Under the revised regulations, satellites were now considered to operate under US law if they were built using more than ten percent funding from foreign investment, if they were launched by a US firm or even if they have a data receiving station in the United States. Additionally, now any system under American jurisdiction must maintain the capability to exercise 'operational control' from US territory such that it would at all times 'have the ability to override all commands issued by any operations center or stations'.[110] Licensed systems are now also directed to use 'government-approved rekeyable encryption on the data-downlink' which would effectively give the US government the ability to lock out commercial operators during times of shutter-control, while directing that 'the loss of anticipated profits and the cost of security measures imposed on all licensees are not reimbursable'. These extra costs and the intrusive demands of the license can only reduce the already declining attractiveness of entering the commercial imagery market.

Conclusion

In the long term, commercialization of a remote sensing industry will almost certainly succeed. Unfortunately, that process is neither likely to be short nor will it be an easy one, but the reality of half-metre imagery cannot be ignored. That said, real and significant impediments exist to be overcome. However, the three paths outlined for commercialization in PDD-23 – sales of satellite systems, foreign data sales and lastly government partnerships – still remain viable.

The United States has more to lose by attempting to impose harsh export control and shutter-control legislation. In fact such draconian measures may actually hasten the situation Washington is seeking to avoid, in that other nations and foreign corporations will develop their own systems, effectively increasing the proliferation of imagery available. The US must resist the temptation to view satellites and their imagery as somehow 'different' than other goods. Even should the US government focus its attention on the security and dual-use aspects of such systems, there are well-understood and effective mechanisms to manage such trade. As such, perhaps the first step towards achieving true commercialization of the industry will be to allow export sales of complete systems to the NATO and other trusted allies. Government-to-government agreements can provide assurances for restrictions on access to the data, and thus avoid the complex problem of controlling the information flow to unknown end-users. Such a move would also potentially instill a measure of redundancy at little cost to the United States. It would however, be of little benefit to American industry, nor in times of crisis would allied systems likely be directly capable of supporting American interests as domestically licensed systems are.

Establishing a true and open market for international imagery sales for commercial purposes is a difficult but not an impossible task, and US industry has amply demonstrated that it is willing to undertake such an endeavour. What has hampered the ability of American firms to secure such sales has been the inconsistent direction of US policy: that there is a lack of co-ordination among concerned agencies in the US government is a vast understatement. As of early 2001, the situation appears to be improving, although it took presidential intervention to correct the situation. It remains to be seen whether that solution will endure in the longer term.

For its part, the US Government has to actually believe in the value of commercial satellite imagery while also recognising its limits. Why NIMA has resisted adopting commercial imagery is not readily apparent, although it could be due to differences in corporate culture. As a system builder and operator, rather than a data processor, the NRO would effectively be putting itself out of business if it embraced commercial imagery, but NIMA's motives are troubling and not easy to define. Repeated studies have advocated that NIMA incorporate commercial imagery to fulfill low-priority needs, and yet, annually NIMA fails to meet even these allocated purchasing levels. Among the justifications offered by NIMA for its refusal to use commercial imagery, is that it is not adequately suitable for strategic purposes. That is at least partially correct. But concurrent with understanding what commercial imagery can do, is the need for legislators to understand what it cannot do. There may be an instinctive reaction on the part of legislators to squelch any attempt to commercialize imagery, but like high-performance computers, military encryption, GPS systems, space launch vehicles, and even the Internet these technologies will reach the private sector. Attempts to prevent this will ultimately be self-defeating, and will almost undoubtedly harm both commercial and security interests. Indeed, it goes contrary to the current trend, which is increasingly seeing government roles, even highly sensitive ones, move into the private sector.[111]

Lastly, industry must accept that this marketplace will remain regulated, probably heavily so. There has not as yet been a case where shutter- control invoked, although there are anecdotal accounts that it was actively considered during the Kosovo crisis of 1999.[112] In many ways, the first actual invocation of shutter-control will prove to be the litmus test for commercialization. However, even below that threshold there remains much work to be done to create an effective policy for regulating the industry. The enormous investment required in launching a commercial imaging satellite has invariably lead to the industrial operators trying to aggressively secure any and all sales they can find to recoup their expenses. Cementing the partnership between industry and government is a good first step towards moderating this trend. However, industry cannot count on the US government to be their anchor tenant while pursuing markets in a manner which some have described as 'irresponsible'. The two-tier system proposed in the July 2000 NOAA 'Interim Final Rules' may be exactly the compromise solution which is needed. Under those rules, the government is able to fund specific sensors for use on commercial systems without giving the government automatic control over all sensors aboard the satellite.

The United States is capable of both dominating and benefiting from the establishment of a commercial remote sensing industry. Whether it is capable of overcoming its internal trepidation to aspire to those goals remains to be seen.

Notes

1   The views in this chapter are those of the author, and do not necessarily represent those of either the Government of Canada or the Department of National Defence.

2   In the words of the Report to the Director of Central Intelligence, DCI Task Force on the National Reconnaissance Office, Final Report, April 1992 (SECRET, 35 pp.) it is acknowledged, however, that 'while the NRO's existence was officially classified it was an "open secret"'. Declassified and reprinted in Jeffrey T. Richelson, *The NRO Declassified*, National Security Archive Electronic Briefing Book No. 35. September 27, 2000. National Security Archive, Washington, DC.

3   Cited in Rachel E. Billingslea, Mathew R. Domsalla and Brian C. Payne, *The National Reconnaissance Office: A Strategy for Addressing the Commercialisation of Satellite Imagery*. Harvard University, John F. Kennedy School of Government. (Cambridge, MA, April 6, 1999), p.17.

4   Robert Berry and Donald L. Croner, 'The Global Relevance of Space: Civil, Commercial and Military', 1998 National Space Symposium, Colorado Springs, CO. 8–9 April 1998.

5   David Mullholland, 'Research Funding Drops More Than $3 Billion', *Defense News*, 15 February, 1999.

6   George I. Seffers, 'Drop in Research Spending Worries Analysts, Industry', *Defense News*, February 21, 2000, p.24.

7   See Dwayne A. Day, John M. Logsdon and Brian Latell, eds. *Eye in the Sky: The Story of the Corona Spy Satellites*. (Smithsonian Institution Press: Washington, DC,1998).

8   Statement by Ambassador Stevenson in the 1st Committee (Political and Security) of the General Assembly on December 4, 1961. Cited by J.A. Johnson, 'Freedom and Control in Outer Space', in Mortimer D. Schwartz, ed. *Proceedings of the Conference*

on Space Science and Space Law, University of Oklahoma 1963 (South Hackensack, N.J., F.B. Rothman, 1964) p.139.

9   It should be noted that by the time the Soviets withdrew their objection to 'espionage satellites' in 1963, they had already launched nine low-resolution reconnaissance satellites, and were only two months away from launching their first high-resolution system, KOSMOS 22. Paul Stares speculates that Soviet photo interpreters could have been unprepared for the level of detail which was visible, and argued for the shift in diplomatic efforts to allow continued access to this strategically significant source of information. See Paul B. Stares, *Space Weapons and US Strategy: Origins and Developments*. (Beckenham, UK: 1985) p.238.

10   U.N. Document A/AC. 105/PV.22, 1966.

11   Eisenhower first introduced this concept during the 1955 Geneva Summit, where it was met with outright distrust. An attempt to re-examine the concept in the UN General Assembly also met with fierce Soviet opposition. Eisenhower was seeking to legitimize strategic aerial reconnaissance as a tool for stability and confidence building. A later proposal in August 1960 by Richard Leghorn (formerly a major participant in the Air Force's photographic programs) was to have the President offer US satellite data to the United Nations, and thereby gain some international legitimacy. Neither plan was ever realized. See Gerald M. Steinberg, *Satellite Reconnaissance: The Role of Informal Bargaining* (New York: Praeger Publishers, 1983) pp.30–35.

12   Treaty Between the United States of America and The Union of Soviet Socialist Republics on the Limitations of Anti-Ballistic Missile Systems. Signed at Moscow, May 26, 1972.

13   That the principles of international law are themselves never defined has been often noted. For an examination of how this influences US domestic policy see Stephen Lambakis, 'The Two Faces of American Defense Space Policy' (Fairfax, VA: National Institute for Public Policy) August 1999.

14   Yahya A. Dehqanzada and Ann M. Florini, *Secrets For Sale: How Commercial Satellite Imagery Will Change the World*. (Carnegie Endowment for International Peace: Washington, DC) 2000, p.31.

15   'Principles Relating to Remote Sensing of the Earth from Outer Space', Principle XII, United Nations General Assembly, New York, December 3, 1986.

16   Op Cit. Dehqanzada and Florini., *Secrets For Sale* p.31.

17   Steinberg, pp.58–59.

18   Cited in Steinberg, p.59.

19   Dwayne Day, 'The Development and Improvement of the CORONA Satellite', in D.A. Day, J.M. Logsdon and B. Latell (eds.), *Eye in the Sky: The Story of the Corona Spy Satellites*. (Smithsonian Institution Press: Washington, DC, 1998). p.82.

20   Report No. 9, KH-4B System Capability: Appraisal of Geologic Value for Mineral Resources Exploration. March 1971, TOP SECRET. Declassified and reproduced in Kevin C. Ruffner (ed),. *CORONA: America's First Satellite Program*. Center for the Study of Intelligence, Central Intelligence Agency (Washington, DC: 1995) pp.317–357.

21   Resolution data from US United States Geologic Survey. See for example, 'CORONA Satellite Photography', http://www.edcwww.cr.usgs.gov/glis/hyper/guide/displ/.

22   Announcement of the President's Decisions Concerning Land Remote Sensing Satellite Activities, The White House. (Washington, DC) 20 November, 1979. The assessment here of the LANDSAT program draws from Appendix B, Dehqanzada and Florini, *Secrets For Sale.*

23   These studies are ECON, Inc, 'Commercialization of the Land Remote Sensing Satellite System: An Examination of Mechanisms and Issues', April 1, 1983; National Academy of Public Administration, 'Space Remote Sensing and the Private Sector: An

Essay', March 1983; Earth Satellite Corporation, 'A Study to Examine the Mechanisms to Carry Out the Transfer of Civil Remote Sensing Systems to the Private Sector', March 28, 1983; and, internal study by the Civil Operational Remote Sensing Satellite Advisory Committee, US Department of Commerce, 1982. Cited in Dehqanzada and Florini, *Secrets For Sale.*

24   'Report 102–593', U.S. House of Representatives, Committee on Science, Space and Technology. May 28, 1992; p.4. Cited in Dehqanzada and Florini, *Secrets For Sale.*

25   'Space Business Indicators', US Department of Commerce, Office of Space Commerce. (Washington, DC: June 1991).

26   Peter Zimmerman, 'From the SPOT Files: Evidence of Spying', *Bulletin of the Atomic Scientists*, Vol. 45, No. 7, July 1989. pp.24–25.

27   An inference is made here; while it is well-documented that images of the battle-area were purchased, SPOT does not release the client who requests the purchase. Zimmerman, op cit., and Robert Wight, 'Private Eyes', *New York Times Magazine*, September 5, 1999.

28   Gerald Steinberg, op cit., p.172.

29   United States Congress, Office of Technology Assessment, *Commercial Newsgathering From Space – A Technical Memorandum*. OTA-TM-ISC-40 (Washington, DC: U.S. Government Printing Office, May 1987) pp.15–35.

30   A point made first by General Merril A. McPeak, Air Force Chief of Staff in his briefing at the National War College, 6 March 1991.

31   Satellite Communications data from Bob Preston, *Ploughshares and Power: The Military Use of Civil Space* (Washington, DC: National Defense University Press, 1994) p.132. LANDSAT figures from U.S. House of Representatives, Committee on Science, Space and Technology, National Landsat Policy Act of 1992, Report 102–539. (Washington, DC: GPO, May 28, 1992) p.26. SPOT-1 data from Steve Berner, 'Proliferation of Satellite Imaging Capabilities: Developments and Implications', in Henry Sokolski, *Fighting Proliferation* (Maxwell Air Force Base, AL: Air University Press, 1996), online version http://www.fas.org/irp/threat/fp/index.html.

32   Even setting aside the stated problems in exploiting national reconnaissance systems, the US military would have found itself hard pressed to utilise such information had it been available. The Air Force's unclassified budget for the Tactical Exploitation of National Capabilities (TENCAP) program was a mere $3-4 million at the time of the Gulf War; by 1995 TENCAP funding was at least ten-fold that amount. Figure from Frank Gallegos, 'After the Gulf War: Balancing Spacepower's Development' (Maxwell Air Force Base, AL: Air University, 1996) p.21.

33   Horner made this statement in April 1995. Gallegos, 'After the Gulf War: Balancing Spacepower's Development', p.5.

34   United States Space Command, 'Operations Desert Shield and Desert Storm Assessment', January 1992. SECRET/NOFORN. pp.39–46. Declassified by the National Security Archives, Washington, DC and released as Document 10, National Security Archives Electronic Briefing Book No. 39, January 17, 2001. http://www.gwu.edu/~nsarchiv/NSAEBB/NSAEBB39/.

35   US Space Command, 'Assessment', January 1992. p.43.

36   Cynthia A.S.McKinley, 'When the Enemy Has Our Eyes', Thesis. School of Advanced Airpower Studies, Air University. (Maxwell Air Force Base, AL: 1995).

37   McKinley. Op cit.

38   Headquarters US Air Force Space Command, 'Desert Storm "Hot Wash"', 12–13 July 1991. SECRET. p.6. Declassified by the National Security Archives, Washington, DC and released as Document 7, National Security Archives Electronic Briefing Book No. 39, January 17, 2001. http://www.gwu.edu/~nsarchiv/NSAEBB/NSAEBB39/.

39   US Space Command, 'Assessment', p.67.

40 *A Post Cold War Assessment of US Space Policy; A Task Group Report.* (Washington, DC: Department of Defense, 17 December 1992) p.23. (Hereinafter 'the Wilkening Report'.)

41 Ann M. Florini and Yahya A. Dehqanzada, 'No More Secrets? Policy Implications of Commercial Remote Sensing Satellites', Carnegie Endowment Working Paper #1, 1999. (Washington, DC: Carnegie Endowment for International Peace, 1999) http://www.ceip.org/files/publications/NoMoreSecrets.asf. Goldman notes that a competitor to LANDSAT had almost emerged, although this venture was driven by oil exploration concerns. When the price of oil collapsed, so too did the attractiveness of oil exploration from space. Nathan C. Goldman, *Space Policy: An Introduction.* (Ames, IA: Iowa State University Press, 1992) pp.181–182.

42 The best works in this field remain Jacques Gansler, *Defense Conversion: Transforming the Arsenal of Democracy* (Cambridge, MA: Massachusetts Institute of Technology Press, 1996) and his earlier *The Defense Industry*, Sixth Edition (Cambridge, MA: Massachusetts Institute of Technology Press, 1989). See also US Congress, Office of Technology Assessment, *Building Future Security: Strategies for Restructuring Defense Technology and Industrial Base* OTA-ISC-539 (Washington, DC: GPO, June 1992); Office of Technology Assessment, *Redesigning Defense: Planning the Transition to the Future U.S. Defense Industrial Base* OTA-ISC-500 (Washington, DC: GPO, March 1991).

43 United States Senate. Senate Report 104-4. Committee Activities of the Senate Select Committee on Intelligence. 104th Congress, 1st Session. (Washington, DC: GPO,1995) pp.18–19.

44 Examples of this symbiotic relationship abound. Jeffrey K. Harris, head of the NRO from 1994-1996 is now president of Space Imaging, the firm managing the 1-metre resolution IKONOS system. Orbital Imaging's president Gilbert Rye was the Director of Space and Intelligence programs on President Reagan's National Security Council. See also William J. Broad, 'Commercial Use of Spy Satellites to Begin; Private Ventures Hope for Profits', *New York Times*, 10 February 1997, p.1.

45 Gerald Steinberg, 'Dual Use Aspects of Commercial High-Resolution Imaging Satellites', Occasional Paper No. 37, February 1998. Begin-Sadat Center for Strategic Studies. Bar-Ilan University, Ramat Gan, Israel. http://www.biu.ac.il/SOC/besa/books/37pub.htm.

46 Scott Pace, Brant Sponberg, Molly Macauley. *Data Policy Issues and Barriers to Using Commercial Resources for Mission to Planet Earth.* RAND Corporation Report DB-247-NASA/OSTP. (Santa Monica, CA: RAND, 1999) p.40.

47 Dehqanzada and Florini, *Secrets for Sale* p.20.

48 Even then, the resolution of 15 m was worse than that available from SPOT. However, the LANDSAT program was operated on a cost-recovery basis, with revenue from image purchases being returned to the Treasury. As such, little funding was available for actual R&D or development.

49 Dehqanzada and Florini, *Secrets for Sale*, pp.43–44.

50 One of the most complete descriptions of these competing systems can be found in Steinberg, 'Dual Use Aspects of Commercial High-Resolution Imaging Satellites'.

51 Vipin Gupta, 'New Satellite Images for Sale', *International Security*, Vol. 20, No. 1, Summer 1995. p.98. Sovinformsputnik uses the brand-name 'Kometa' to designate the commercial satellites carrying the KVR-1000 camera, which is known in military service as the 'Yantar'. Sovinformsputnik has joined with Aerial Images Inc. of Raleigh, NC to market images from KFA-1000 systems under the brand name SPIN-2. Data from the SPIN-2 systems has also been marketed by Microsoft as part of its TerraServer service. Russia has for a number of years made announcements that it will begin releasing the data from its 0.5 m resolution KVR-3000 system, although as of

early 2001, this has not yet come to pass. For the most recent example of announcing a 1 m system see Simon Saradzhyan, 'Russia, Industry Plan Imaging Satellite Launch', *Space News*, March 27, 2000, p.1.

52   Quoted in U.S. Senate, Senate Report 104–4 , p.18.

53   An unclassified summary version was released. The White House, Office of the Press Secretary. Fact Sheet: Foreign Access to Remote Sensing Space Capabilities, March 10, 1994 (Hereinafter 'PDD-23 Fact Sheet'.)

54   PDD-23 Fact Sheet, p.1.

55   According to Jane's Space Directory, the Soviet/Russian KVR-1000 camera, which uses a film-return system, has a ground resolution of 75 cm and the DD-5 digital imaging system is said to have a similar resolution. Both are degraded to a nominal 2 m resolution for commercial sale.

56   Assembly of the Western European Union, Technology and Aerospace Committee. *Space Systems for Europe: Observation, Communications and Navigation Satellites – Reply to the Annual Report of the Council*. Document no. 1643, 18 May 1999. Nn.

57   This is far from a unique occurrence. For an excellent discussion of a related case-study see Glenn R. Fong, 'ARPA Does Windows: The Defense Underpinning of the PC Revolution'. Presentation given at the 41st Annual Convention of the International Studies Association, Los Angeles, CA. March 14–18, 2000.

58   David T. Lindgren. *Trust But Verify: Imagery Analysis in the Cold War*. (Annapolis, MD: United States Naval Institute Press, 2000) p.181.

59   See for example, Pierre Thomas, 'Spy Unit's Spending Stuns Hill', *Washington Post*, August 9, 1994, p.A1+; Walter Pincus, 'Spy Agency Hoards Secret $1 Billion: Satellite Managers Did Not Tell Supervisors of Classified "Pot of Gold," Hill Sources Say', *Washington Post*, Sep 24, 1995, p.A1+; Robert Pear, 'Disclosure of Spy Agency's $1.5 Billion Fund Leads to Shake-Up', *New York Times*, September 25, 1995. p.A12.

60   The 'Commission on the Roles and Capabilities of the U.S. Intelligence Community' was created by Section 904 of the Intelligence Authorization Act for Fiscal Year 1995 (Public Law 103-359). Harold Brown succeeded Les Aspin as Chairman after Aspin's death in 1995.

61   *Preparing for the 21st Century – An Appraisal of U.S. Intelligence* (Washington, DC: GPO. March 1, 1996) p.117. (Hereinafter 'Aspin/Brown'.)

62   Lindgren. p.165.

63   John M. Diamond, 'Re-examining Problems and Prospects in U.S. Imagery Intelligence', *International Journal of Intelligence and Counterintelligence*, Volume 14, No. 1, pp.14–16. Recent press reports have also alleged that a Series 3100 'Lacrosse' radar imaging satellite malfunctioned, causing a major gap in monitoring. Bill Gertz, "12-hour Glitch on Spy Satellite Causes Intelligence Gap', *The Washington Times*. 26 July 2001.

64   Aspin/Brown. p.117.

65   Aspin/Brown. p.120.

66   House of Representatives, Permanent Select Committee on Intelligence. *IC21: The Intelligence Community in the 21st Century*. 104th Congress. (Washington, DC: GPO, June 5, 1996) nn. (Hereinafter 'IC21'.)

67   Report to the Director National Reconnaissance Office. 'Defining the Future of the NRO for the 21st Century'. 26 August 1996. (Hereinafter the 'Jeremiah Report'.) Unclassified Executive Summary of 30 pp. released by the National Security Archives as Document 23, of Jeffrey T. Richelson, *The NRO Declassified*. National Security Archives Electronic Briefing Book No. 35. (Washington, DC: September 27, 2000)

68   Jeremiah Report. p.8.

69   Jeremiah Report, p.23.

70 Keith Hall. Remarks to the National Network of Electro-Optical Manufacturing Technologies Conference. 9 February, 1998. http://www.nro.gov/speeches/Hall9802.html.

71 Dehqanzada and Florini, *Secrets for Sale*, pp.18–19.

72 Florini and Dehqanzada, No More Secrets p.10.

73 Operation "Seek Gunfighter" tracked the practice surge deployment of a US air expeditionary force (AEF) to Bahrain. The 'red team' was able to uncover where the AEF would deploy, its mission and its force composition. Making use of SPOT imagery, 'red team' analysts were able to obtain images of both the departure point and destination, and were able to identify the deployed headquarters location, the logistics and maintenance areas, the personnel tents and the security perimeter. Larry K. Grundhauser. 'Sentinels Rising: Commercial High-Resolution Satellite Imagery and Its Implications for US National Security', *Airpower Journal*, Winter 1998, pp. 65–66.

74 Quoted in Warren Fester, 'NIMA Sets Sights on Commercial Imagery', *Space News*, 30 June 1997, p.4.

75 Figure cited in Dehqanzada and Florini, Secrets For Sale, p.19.

76 William S. Cohen, 'Remarks to the Opening Ceremonies of the National Space Symposium', Colorado Springs, CO. April 5, 1999, p.1. http://www.defenselink.mil/speeches/1999/s19990405-secdef.html.

77 Ryan Bender, 'DoD to make use of commercial satellite images', *Jane's Defence Weekly*, November 11, 1998, p.11.

78 David W. Thompson, CEO of Orbital Sciences Corporation. 'Remarks on U.S. Government Policy – Commercial Space Policies for the Next Administration and Congress'. Speech to the Washington Space Business Roundtable, 7 December 2000.

79 *IC-21*, Chapter 6.

80 Steinberg, 'Dual Use Aspects'.

81 'Lockheed Offers Spy Satellite to Germany', *Space News*, April 3–9, 1995.

82 'Spy Satellites for Sale', *Space News*, March 13–19, 1995.

83 PDD-23 Fact Sheet, p.2.

84 In US law, the conditions needed for the government to exercise prior restraint are quite significant. As such, there is considerable debate whether PDD-23 is in fact constitutional. As of early 2001, no test case has yet been brought before the courts to determine if routine sales of satellite imagery meet the legal threshold of being a 'clear and present danger'. See Jason Bates, 'U.S. Remote-Sensing Controls Worry News Agencies', *Space News*, March 27, 2000, p.6; Joseph C. Anselmo, 'Shutter Controls: How Far Will Uncle Sam Go?', *Aviation Week & Space Technology*, January 31, 2000, pp.55–56.

85 United States Congressional Record, National Defense Authorization Act For Fiscal Year 1997. 'Amendment No. 4321, "To Prohibit the Collection and Release of Detailed Satellite Imagery With Respect to Israel and Other Countries and Areas"'. US Senate, 104th Congress, 2nd Session. June 26, 1996, p.S6924.

86 *Congressional Record*, FY97. June 26, 1996, p.S6924.

87 Vipin Gupta, 'New Satellite Images For sale: The Opportunities and Risks Ahead', Center for Security and Technology Studies #UCRL-JC-118140. Lawrence Livermore National Laboratories. (Livermore, CA: September 28, 1994).

88 The Indian government has purchased exclusive regional rights from IKONOS imagery to its own territory, even going as far as to downgrade its resolution for domestic customers. Similarly, Israel has purchased exclusive rights to the imagery from the EROS-A1 satellite from ImageSat International, the only non-US supplier of 1 m imagery. Moreover, Israel has also supplied ImageSat with 'a list of countries they cannot have any dealings with'. See K.S. Jayaraman, 'India, U.S. Firm Agree to Sale of 1-Meter Imagery', *Space News*, July 17, 2000, p.1. Peter B. deSelding, 'Israel

Approves Sale of Images From Spy Satellite', *Space News*, June 28, 1999, p.7. Also, Barbara Opall-Rome, 'Israel's MoD Strategy Guards Commercial Imagery', *Space News*, February 26, 2001, p.4.

89   See for example, John R. Copple, CEO Space Imaging L.P., 'Comments on Proposed Draft "Commercial Space Act of 1997, S.1473"', Submitted to the Senate Commerce Committee on Science, Technology and Space. Dated February 27, 1998.

90   Testimony of D. James Baker, Undersecretary for Oceans and the Atmosphere, U.S. Department of Commerce. Hearing Before the U.S. House of Representatives, Committee on Science. The Commercial Space Act of 1997, Parts I-III. 105TH Congress, First Session. May 21, 22 and June 4, 1997, p.111.

91   United States Congress. Strom Thurmond National Defense Authorization Act for Fiscal Year 1999. P.L. 105–261. October 17, 1998, Section 1511 (1).

92   U.S. House of Representatives, Admiral James W. Nance and Meg Donovan Foreign Relations Authorization Act, Fiscal Years 2000 and 20001. H.R. 3427, November 17, 1999. 106th Congress, First Session. Adopted into law as part of the omnibus authorization act P.L. 106–113.

93   'U.S. Export Control Policies on Satellites and U.S. Domestic Launch Capabilities'. Testimony of William A.Reinsch, Under Secretary for Export Administration, Department of Commerce. Senate Committee on Foreign Relations, Subcommittee on International Economic Policy, Export and Trade Promotion. June 24, 1999, p.2.

94   Testimony of Eric D. Newsom, Assistant Secretary for Political-Military Affairs, United States Senate, Committee on Foreign Relations, June 24, 1999, p.7.

95   John W. Douglas, President and CEO, Aerospace Industries Association. Testimony before the Committee on Armed Services, United States Senate. February 28, 2000.

96   See among others, 'Intelsat Might Move Out of US', *Space News*, July 5, 1999, p.1; Peter B. deSelding, 'US Export Rules Frustrate Germans', *Space News*, July 5, 1999, p.1.

97   Joseph C. Anselmo, 'Hamre: Export Delays Hurting U.S. Alliances', *Aviation Week & Space Technology*, November 8, 1999, p.34.

98   Peter B. deSelding, 'Alenia Wins Radarsat 2 Contract', *Space News*, January 10, 2000, p.3.

99   Barbara Opall-Rome, 'Israeli Firm to Sell S. Korea 1-meter Satellite Camera', *Space News*, March 20, 2000, p.1.

100   See, for example, Commentary, 'Losing Control', *Space News*, March 20, 2000, p.18.

101   Joseph C. Anselmo, 'Commercial Satellites Zoom In on Military Imagery Monopoly', *Aviation Week & Space Technology*, September 22, 1997, p.78.

102   Commercial Imagery Program, National Imagery and Mapping Agency, 'Frequently Asked Questions, NIMA Use of Commercial Imagery', cited in Douglas B. Rider, 'Establishing a Commercial Reserve Imagery Fleet: Obtaining Surge Imagery Capacity From Commercial Remote Sensing Satellite Systems During Crisis', Thesis. Air Command and Staff College, Air University. AU/ACSC/152/2000-04. (Maxwell Air Force Base, AL: April 2000) p.16.

103   The Independent Commission on the National Imagery and Mapping Agency. *The Information Edge: Imagery Intelligence and Geospatial Information in an Evolving National Security Environment*. Final Report, December 2000, p.16.

104   Joseph Dodd, 'Alternatives for Integrating Commercial High-Resolution Imaging Satellites in the Future Architecture'. Unpublished white paper (ORBIMAGE, Inc. Dulles, VA: no date). Cited in Douglas B. Rider, 'Establishing a Commercial Reserve Imagery Fleet.

105   Jason Bates, 'Imaging Craft of Limited Utility, NIMA Chief Says', *Space News*, September 25, 2000, p.3.

106 Gil Rye. Presentation at the conference Space at the Crossroads: Military Use of Commercial Space. U.S. Senate, Russell Caucus Room. Washington, DC. September 14, 2000. Author's notes.

107 Vernon Loeb, 'U.S. Is Relaxing Rules on Sale of Satellite Photos', *Washington Post*, December 16, 2000, p.A03.

108 The White House, Office of Science and Technology Policy and the National Security Council. Fact Sheet Regarding the Memorandum of Understanding Concerning the Licensing of Private Remote Sensing Satellite Systems. February 2, 2000. http://www.licensing.noaa.gov/moufactsheet.htm.

109 *Federal Register*, Vol. 65, No. 147 July 31, 2000. pp.46822–46837.

110 *Federal Register*, Vol. 65, No. 147 July 31, 2000. pp.46834.

111 So-called 'privatization' or 'alternate service delivery'. For a related case in the intelligence community see Vernon Loeb, 'NSA to Turn Over Non-Spy Technology to Private Industry', *Washington Post*, June 7, 2000. p.A29. According to Loeb, the NSA would eliminate the jobs of some 1,200-1,500 employees and a further 800 contractors, to outsource its non-classified information technology activities. This ten-year effort was estimated to be worth as much as $5 billion.

112 According to an account in *Aviation Week & Space Technology*, 'during the NATO bombing of Serbian troops in Kosovo, a junior officer in the US–European command called for imposing shutter control over Europe on Space Imaging's first Ikonos satellite. The proposal is believed to have made it all the way up to the Joint Chiefs of Staff, but became moot when the spacecraft was destroyed in a launch mishap on Apr. 27'. Joseph C. Anselmo, 'Shutter Controls'.

Chapter 13

Access Control of Remote Sensing Satellites

Dana G. Clarke

Introduction

Space Imaging's introductory images of Washington were stunning. With the unaided eye one could see the scaffolding that then surrounded the Washington Monument and count the individual vehicles on the surrounding roads, readily distinguishing between smaller cars and larger trucks. Released on 12 October 1999, the Washington images were the first taken by Space Imaging Inc.'s new Ikonos satellite, capable of imaging items as small as 1 meter in size from its orbit 680 kilometers above the earth.[1] They introduced the world to the emerging capabilities of commercial remote sensing satellites, which were once the preserve of classified national intelligence systems.

Space based imagery has been used by the United States (US) since the first successful 'Corona' programme mission, Discovery 14, returned its film payload on 18 August 1960. Although its pictures were somewhat fuzzy and offered a resolution of about 8 meters, it was the harbinger of what was to come. The Corona programme was to take some 800,000 images and last until 1972. Corona was the key strategic intelligence resource of the United States a dozen of the most difficult years of the Cold War of the US intelligence and yet the best resolution achieved by the programme's satellites was only two meters, half of that offered by today's Ikonos system.[2]

Today's Challenge

Today the classified systems have certainly passed that of available commercial systems, but the latter, the capabilities of which surpass what was available for much of the Cold War, clearly are of value to military planners. Today, even militaries that have access to more capable systems, such as the US Army, make use of commercial imagery. It has proven an excellent resource for such tasks as mapping, but it is also favoured for its releasability to the lowest levels, even to the public, as it is derived from unclassified sources rather than a highly sensitive national resource. The imagery from the latter may not be releasable to the tactical commander on the ground, let alone to civilian agencies such as the United Nations (UN).

Ikonos, with a nominal 1 meter imaging capability is indicative of the anticipated proliferation of advanced new sensing systems on the immediate planning horizon. Orbital, the operator of the Ikonos, have applied to the Department of Commerce for a license to build and operate a .5 meter panchromatic satellite. Earthwatch, after the unfortunate loss of its Earlybird and Quickbird 1 satellites, is planning a 2001 launch for its 1 meter panchromatic Quickbird 2 satellite. Space Imaging is planning to offer 1 meter panchromatic and 4 meter multi-spectral imaging capability on its Orbview 3 and 4 satellites, with the latter adding an 8 meter hyperspectral sensor. Both Orbview 3 and and Orbview 4 are planned to be launched in 2001. France plans to launch SPOT-5 in 2002 with a 2.5 meter panchromatic and 10 meter multi-spectral sensors and the ability to take stereo pairs. The latter capability will facilitate the creation of digital terrain elevation models. In early 2003, Canada plans to launch the 3 meter Synthetic Aperture Radar (SAR) RADARSAT-2 satellite. All told there are approximately 20 civil and commercial earth imaging satellites planned for launch in the next five years.[3]

There is little doubt that, given unrestricted access to modern commercial imagery and the skilled image and intelligence professionals who could exploit it effectively, the resulting products could be invaluable to UN field forces. Geomatic mapping and intelligence products alike would help the range of UN operations from humanitarian relief to peace enforcement. Emerging and planned commercial systems, such as .5 meter electro-optical and the new SAR systems that are on the immediate horizon, promise even greater utility. That promised utility however, has attracted the concern of a growing number of governments concerned with safeguarding their national security interests. This concern is being manifested in an increasing regime of restrictions designed to ensure that users, be they commercial or civil, or domestic or international, do not have unlimited access.

The advances in commercial space remote sensing systems, their increasing proliferation and the global access that characterizes commercial systems spoke to the need for government oversight. The challenge for governments is how to reconcile the need to safeguard national security and foreign policy interests of the state with the UN 'Principles Relating to Remote Sensing of the Earth From Space'. These principles, adopted by the General Assembly in 1986, provide that all remote sensing should be done for the benefit of all countries. They also declare that data should be made available from the sensing to the sensed state without discrimination and at reasonable cost.[4] The further challenge is how to balance those state interests with the compelling need to foster a healthy domestic space industry.

The Development of Access Controls

The United States, with the world's most developed space industry, was the first to take on the challenge. The 1992 Land Remote Sensing Policy Act opened the door to commercial operators. It also clearly established that 'No person who is subject to the jurisdiction or control of the United States may, directly or through any subsidiary or affiliate, operate any private remote sensing space system without a license pursuant to section 201'.[5] The licensing regime, administered by the Department of Commerce's National Oceanic and Atmospheric Administration

(NOAA), allows the US Government to place limitations on the performance and operation of imaging systems and on the distribution of the resultant imagery.

There are two basic functions of a government-imposed access control system for commercial remote sensing satellite systems. The first function is to protect national security by denying access to information that may pose a threat should it be available to potential adversaries. The second function is to guarantee that the government will have priority access to the system's capabilities during times of crisis.

The first function, controlling access, could best be served by simply limiting a commercial system's capabilities to a level where they would not be a concern. For example data from the 15 meter panchromatic and 30 meter infrared resolutions of the US Landsat 7 are unlikely to be considered a potential threat. The designed 8 meter SAR capability of Canada's RADARSAT-1 satellite was likewise not considered a threat. However, the capabilities of a 1-meter panchromatic system such as Ikonos and the planned 3 meter SAR RADARSAT-2, are clearly of value to military planners. By imposing limitations on the performance of the spacecraft and the overall system, a government can readily limit its security concerns. As both Ikonos and RADARSAT attest however, governments must also consider the economic and other effects that limiting domestic industry might have. By sponsoring a leading-edge domestic industry, one can exercise a measure of control over the industry, while effectively discouraging foreign commercial competition by establishing a dominant market presence. In allowing the operation of advanced systems, the government can also have the best capabilities available to itself to augment the national security or civil systems it may have.

To be commercially effective, remote sensing systems must be able to offer system capabilities that are better than, or at least highly competitive with, competing systems. Because the physical characteristics of satellites cannot be changed after launch and the lifespan of major satellites is generally several years, satellite operators would like to place the best possible systems on orbit. Even though Governments may be reluctant to allow full commercial exploitation of a technologically advanced system, they can choose to authorize the design and operation of such systems. As an alternative to limitations on designed performance, restrictions can be placed on the dissemination of information. This is inherently more flexible, in that the commercial operator can typically expect to be able to sell the full capabilities of the system to authorized government customers yet still sell data that is commercially competitive on the global market. As competing foreign systems become more advanced, the government can amend the rules governing the commercial operator to allow continued competitiveness.

In response to pressing national security or foreign policy situations, the government may wish to further limit the collection and dissemination of remote sensing data. It can reserve the right to impose additional temporary restrictions under such circumstances. This is commonly referred to as 'shutter control'. Shutter control could be exercised in the form of prohibitions on the collection of data over a specified geographic region, or limitations on the throughput time (the time between collection of data and its delivery to the customer) that would mitigate the potential tactical value of an image. Shutter control measures might also include further restricting the technical performance of a system, perhaps for a specified region. They may also further restrict the dissemination of information, prohibiting distribution to certain customers. The business implications of imposing an interruption to normal commercial services could be significant and therefore shutter control would only be imposed under exceptional circumstances.

The second function of a government-imposed access control system is to guarantee the government preferential access to the system's capabilities. This is particularly important if the system has unique capabilities and can be used to meet time sensitive requirements, such as providing imagery that could assist in reacting to a natural disaster or a regional security crisis. 'Priority Access', as it is normally termed, is less controversial in that it would typically guarantee the operator a contracted fee for the exercise of such access. This is not to indicate that such a policy is benign to the commercial operator, however. In invoking Priority Access, established and/or higher-paying customers may be bumped to the detriment of the operator's commercial relationships. This argues for judicious controls on the invocation of Priority Access. In the US, the key policy documents with respect to space based commercial remote sensing are the *Land Remote Sensing Act of 1992*, as amended by the *Commercial Space Act of 1998*, and the 1994 *Presidential Decision Directive 23* (PDD 23). Together they establish the intent of the US Government to both foster the development of a dominant space-based remote sensing industry and to regulate that industry. The *Land Remote Sensing Act* invests the Secretary of Commerce with the authority to regulate space based commercial remote sensing systems. The *Commercial Space Act* directs the Secretary of Commerce to publish the information required to apply for a license in the *Federal Register*. In turn, the *Federal Register* lays out the rules and regulations for the operation of remote sensing systems. With respect to what it terms 'new or advanced systems', such as SAR or hyperspectral satellite systems, the prescribed conditions include potential limitations on operating parameters. For SAR systems these could include restrictions such as on maximum (or best) resolution, geolocational accuracy, and acceptable grazing angles.[6]

Canadian Efforts

RADARSAT-1 was launched in 1995 as a Canadian Government civil programme to meet the needs of for remote sensing data of Canada's vast territory and of the globe. The monitoring of environmental change and natural resources were the principal impetus behind the RADARSAT system. Its success has helped create a leading commercial value-added industry in Canada and has helped convince the Government of Canada that there is the potential to develop a world class and thriving commercial space-based earth remote sensing industry in Canada. This has shaped Government objectives for the RADARSAT-2 programme, which is touted as a commercial satellite although more than 75 percent of the up-front funding and of the risk is being shouldered by the Government. The Government foresees the Private Public Partnership (PPP) as being a stepping-stone to the full commercialization of the remote sensing industry.

The commercialization of the space-based earth remote sensing industry has forced the Government of Canada to consider the need for legally established controls on the collection and dissemination of data, something that was not required in the case of the Government-owned RADARSAT-1 system. The need for such controls was also under-scored by the considerable improvements in performance that the new radar satellite promised over its predecessor.

Under the leadership of the Department of Foreign Affairs and International Trade (DFAIT), an interdepartmental working group was established to consider the need for access control provisions for RADARSAT-2. Representation was sought from all departments and agencies with a stake in either the RADARSAT-2 project or the wider legal or remote sensing issues. Participants included the Canadian Space Agency (CSA) as the principal proponent of Government civil and commercial space policy and the programme manager. The Department of National Defence, Industry Canada, Natural Resources Canada, the Solicitor General's Office, and the Department of Justice were among those represented.

Beginning from comprehensive background papers prepared by DFAIT, the working group systematically considered the implications of the operational characteristics of RADARSAT-2, the need for access control, potential control models, and the supporting framework that would be necessary for controls. The deliberations began in earnest in early 1998 and continued through early 1999. Having determined that controls were necessary, DFAIT led the effort to prepare a Memorandum to Cabinet. The resulting Cabinet decision was announced on 9 June 1999. It established the Government of Canada's intent to control Canadian -owned or -operated commercial remote sensing satellites. The backgrounder that formed part of the announcement set out 'principles' to guide the drafters of the formal Government policy and the supporting legislative framework. It also set out the responsibilities and obligations of the owner, new legislation and set out guidelines for commercial owners and operator.[7]

A key feature of the new policy includes the assertion that the Government reserves the right to approve commercial remote sensing systems on an individual basis. It also reserves the right for the Government to interrupt normal commercial service in situations where 'the availability of data may be detrimental to Canada's national security and foreign affairs interests' and to impose access controls 'which may consist of spatial, temporal, performance or customer-specific denials or restrictions, or combinations thereof, as deemed necessary on a case-by-case basis'.[8] The Government also reserves the right to demand 'Priority Access' to the system. This is essentially the right to priority service over all customers, commercial or government, again when significant national security or foreign policy interests warrant.

The Government's Access Control Policy will also impose obligations on the commercial owner or operator. Key provisions include requirements to:

1   register and receive Government approval for commercial satellite remote sensing systems and to not make unauthorized changes following approval;
2   maintain records of all satellite tasking and make them available to the Government;
3   meet all import and export obligations;
4   not transfer ownership without Government approval;
5   maintain positive control of the satellite from Canada such that it remains under Canadian jurisdiction at all times, including ensuring that the satellite

uplink provides for the Government to exercise sovereign control over the satellite if necessary, and a downlink format that allows the Government exclusive access to satellite data when required;

6   use Government approved cryptographic devices to prevent un-authorized access;

7   acknowledge that only the safety of the satellite itself has higher priority than a duly authorized tasking under the provisions of Access Control;

8   notify DFAIT when it intends to enter into 'significant or sub-stantial agreements' with foreign customers;

9   in accordance with the United Nations Resolution 41/65, to make available to any government data that has been collected concerning its territory, as long as doing so is not detrimental to Canada's national security and foreign affairs interests;

10   to provide periodic reports to ascertain compliance with the Access Control policy and to submit to duly authorized audits, investigations and cease and desist injunctions; and

11   before destroying any data, offer it to the Government of Canada at the cost of reproduction and transmission.[9]

Those familiar with the US licensing regime will recognize that many of the provisions are similar in intent to those specified by the US Department of Commerce as can be seen in the US *Federal Register*.[10] This reflects a close study of the US regulations before developing the Canadian policy, consultations with the US to learn from their experience in developing access control criteria, and most importantly, similar security concerns. Consultations were also effected with other nations but the US regulations were the most fully developed and most closely paralleled Canadian requirements. Most current 'commercial' remote sensing satellites are still government owned or sponsored and therefore under direct government control. As more commercial capabilities develop internationally, other nations will be confronted with developing their own regulatory policies.

The application of the Canadian Access Control policy is expected to be customer-based to the maximum extend possible. Government customers can expect to be able to access the full capabilities of the system commensurate with their requirements. The Canadian remote sensing industry can expect wide access to system capabilities to meet the needs for finished products by Government and commercial customers. Allied governments willing to respect Canadian concerns about the dissemination of data may also be provided with considerable access to system capabilities, as may certain established and trusted customers with legitimate requirements. In general, customers should expect wide access to data equivalent to that provided by the current RADARSAT-1 system, as well as access to many of the features of RADARSAT-2, albeit with some restrictions.

Intergovernmental Cooperation

Following the 9 June 1999 announcement of the Government's intention to regulate commercial remote sensing satellites, discussions began in earnest to negotiate an intergovernmental agreement with the United States. On 16 June 2000 the Minister of Foreign Affairs, Lloyd Axworthy and US Secretary of State Madeleine Albright signed such an agreement. Its aim was cited as being 'to ensure that commercial remote sensing satellite systems will be controlled in each country in such a manner as to protect shared national security and foreign policy interests while promoting the commercial benefits to be derived from these systems'.[11] As related in the press release, recognizing the increasing commercialization of the satellite remote sensing industry, the agreement commits both countries to extensive consultations on its control.

The need for an intergovernmental agreement arose principally from three factors. The first was certainly a desire to coordinate policies to best protect shared security and foreign policy concerns. The second two were somewhat more pragmatic. The use of American technology in the design of the RADARSAT-2 spacecraft, meant that the United States Government was looking for assurances that such technologies would be effectively controlled. Without such assurances the satellites owner MacDonald Dettwiler and Associates Ltd (MDA) of Richmond, British Columbia, as well as the Canadian Space Agency, could not be confident that they would receive, in a timely manner, the requisite Technical Assistance Agreements (TAA) to permit the development of the RADARSAT-2 spacecraft. The final and most perplexing factor was that MDA was then a wholly-owned subsidiary of Orbital Sciences Corp., an American company. The American parent also owned major data distribution rights. This created a situation where the US Department of Commerce considered that it could claim the authority to regulate and license RADARSAT-2. A formal agreement on Canadian control of the satellite forestalled potential concerns that the US might attempt the extraterritorial application of its law.

Conclusion

Notwithstanding the development of access controls in Canada and the United States, both Governments face the continuing challenge of balancing the desire to promote their domestic space industries while addressing the need to safeguard their national security and foreign policy interests. Although governments provide today's greatest customer base for remote sensing products, the industry sees a potentially greater commercial market for a broad range of advanced data products. This places considerable pressure on governments to progressively limit the regulation of the remote sensing industry. Indeed, both the United States' and Canadian Governments acknowledge that licensing parameters will evolve as international competition threatens domestic industries. A reactive approach rigorously applied may lead, however, to the eventual erosion of competitiveness in favour of international competitors.

Canada's Access Control Policy seeks to find the balance between the competing security and foreign affairs interests on one hand and the satellite and remote sensing industries on the other. Through encouraging the development of the most capable systems and encouraging the broad range of government customers to exploit the potential of such systems, it hopes to foster the development of a vibrant leading edge Canadian capability. Canada's Access Control regime should be permissive in that it can allow trusted customers greater access to system capabilities, while restricting the availability of information to those without a legitimate need or of questionable reliability. More importantly, the access control restrictions can evolve in response to changes to the geopolitical and economic environment. By putting in place a flexible access control regime, Canada is trying to ensure that balance is maintained and that industry's interests remain in the forefront.

Notes

1   Space Imaging Inc. online at www.spaceimaging.com/newsroom/releases/ 1999/firstimage.htm, 13 Dec 00.
2   William E. Burrows, *This New Ocean: The Story of the First Space Age* (New York: Random House, 1998), pp.228–236; and National Reconnaissance Office, online at http://www.nro.mil/corona/facts.htm.
3   Environmental Remote Sensing Center, *Earth Observation Satellites Future* (Madison: University of Wisconsin, 2000) online at www.ersc.wisc.edu/ersc/Resources/ EOSF.html. See also Canadian Space Agency, *Global Space Sector Market Trends and Drivers: Year 2000 Edition* (Montreal: Canadian Space Agency, 2000), pp.36–40.
4   United Nations, 'Resolution 41/65. Principles Relating to Remote Sensing of the Earth from Outer Space,' 3 Dec 1986, online at http://www.unesco.org/webworld/ com/compendium/2501.html, 16 January, 2001.
5   United States, H.R.6133: *Land Remote Sensing Policy Act of 1992*, online at: http://www.nnic.noaa.gov/refs.htm.
6   Department of Commerce, *Federal Register*: Part IV Department of Commerce National Oceanic and Atmospheric Administration: 15 CFR Part 960 Licensing of Private Land Remote -Sensing Space Systems; Interim Final Rule. np. 31 July 2000, p.46826.
7   Department of Foreign Affairs and International Trade, 'Canada to Control Imaging Satellites,' *News Release* No. 134, np. 9 June 1999, online at http://www.dfait-maeci.gc.ca.
8   Ibid.
9   Ibid.
10   U.S. Department of Commerce, *Federal Register*: Part IV Department of Commerce National Oceanic and Atmospheric Administration: 15 CFR Part 960 Licensing of Private Land Remote -Sensing Space Systems; Interim Final Rule. np. 31 July 2000, pp.46822–46837.
11   Department of Foreign Affairs and International Trade, 'Canada And United States Sign Agreement Concerning Operation of Commercial Remote Sensing Satellite Systems' *News Release* No. 153, np. 16 June 2000, online at http://www.dfait-maeci.gc.ca.

Chapter 14

Blue Eyes: Surveillance Satellites and UN Peacekeeping

Ulric Shannon[1]

Proposals for a global surveillance satellite regime have circulated for decades, but have never become reality. Yet security and defence scholars have resurrected the issue every time the international political and strategic context in which such proposals operate has changed in a significant way. This book has acknowledged the most recent wave of sometimes revolutionary changes in the international political landscape and has asked whether a global approach to satellite technology is not again a relevant concept.

The scope of these changes cannot be overstated. Of direct relevance to the subject of this book, the privatization of surveillance satellite technology since the Gulf War (to use a convenient benchmark) has challenged old orthodoxies about the benefits of a capacity for global monitoring. But during this same period other variables have been transformed as well. It is necessary now to think about this very particular and esoteric technology in the context of the emergence of complex crises which require an equally complex military, political, and humanitarian response; the identity crisis which currently afflicts United Nations peacekeeping in the wake of high-profile failures; changing definitions of state sovereignty, including at the Security Council; and the enduring question of whether powerful states can be enticed into relaxing their proprietary grip on national technical means in the interest of collective security.

These issues are of particular relevance to the increasingly popu-lar proposition that satellite imagery should become a staple of UN peacekeeping. But before addressing the question of how, one must first ask the question of whether. Does modern peacekeeping really have an identifiable need for overhead surveillance, particularly of the kind provided by satellites? This is, after all, a different world from the one in which the idea of an International Satellite Monitoring Agency (ISMA) was first floated. Verification, while still important, is no longer an appropriate tool for the majority of the inchoate conflicts that are now the Security Council's daily bread. The complex crises of the type witnessed in Sierra Leone, Kosovo and East Timor, which are likely to be emblematic of peacekeeping in the foreseeable future, are a world apart from UNEF II (Sinai) and UNDOF (Golan), a cornerstone of which was aerial and satellite imagery provided by the United States. Confidence building, which is the essence of traditional peacekeeping and the key value-added of overhead imaging, seems almost quaint in the context of the failed states and imploding societies into which UN forces are being deployed with increasing regularity.

The reality is that the kind of armed conflict which satellite surveillance is best suited to address – namely, involving regular forces, conventional hardware, with movements and tactics following from strategy – is becoming a rarity, at least at the Security Council. At first glance, it may in fact seem that sophisticated surveillance platforms are particularly out of step with the small-bore irregular warfare and civil violence that accounts for so much of the peacekeeping agenda. In addition, the range of different UN missions, and of mission needs, means that tactical improvements – even dramatic ones – will not be felt with equal effect across all areas of peacekeeping activity.

Yet, in a period when UN peacekeeping has been subjected to unprecedented criticism for its ineffectiveness, particularly in contrast with the successful operations undertaken by multinational coalitions, the UN does not have the luxury of waiting for a panacea. Any improvement, however incremental, has merit. In the case of satellite technology, potential benefits to peacekeeping can be inferred in the area of cost savings, force safety, and more comprehensive peacekeeping. A question of primary importance is whether commercial sources of imagery are more appropriate to the task of enhancing the practice of peacekeeping than traditional national technical means. These issues are addressed in the following sections, leading to a discussion of the political obstacles to the use of satellite technology in a UN context.

Cost Savings

The late-1990s trend which saw a significant decline in the number of UN missions and deployed personnel is conclusively over. Over the last two years, the UN has authorized large and costly missions in Kosovo, East Timor, Sierra Leone, the Democratic Republic of the Congo, and now Ethiopia and Eritrea, which have more than tripled the number of military and police personnel on UN duty, from a low of 12,000 in June 1999 to 38,000 in November 2000. For Canada – one of the few countries that pay their UN bills on time and in full – this has meant a threefold increase in our peacekeeping assessments, from \$33 million in FY98-99 to perhaps more than \$100 million in FY00-01.[2]

Some states have reacted to the steepening bill by quietly applying downward pressure on the authorized force levels of new UN operations, often with little concern for the consequences this has on mission effectiveness. Others states have advocated that some current peacekeeping missions be merged, or otherwise rationalized. In this environment, any innovation which holds out the hope of allowing the UN to do more with fewer people is sure to be pursued aggressively.

For years, satellite imagery has been proposed as a possible force multiplier for peacekeeping. But the idea that this technology has the potential to allow the UN to rationalize some of its more personnel intensive operations remains an unverified proposition, and the present reality of peacekeeping is not cause for optimism in this regard. While it is theoretically true that overhead imaging could duplicate some of the more basic monitoring functions currently carried out by peacekeeping personnel, a preliminary survey reveals that few UN missions nowadays consist predominately of this kind of activity. Traditional observation and reporting now forms the core of fewer than half a dozen peacekeeping operations, including Cyprus (unga), Lebanon (UNIFIL), Croatia (UNMOP), and India/Pakistan (UNMOGIP).

While the Department of Peacekeeping Operations could certainly examine the merits of using overhead imaging in these missions as a means of rationalizing personnel, the potential economies involved are modest at best. Leaving aside UNIFIL, which is kept well staffed for largely political reasons (and whose mandate may terminate soon anyway), these missions represent only about 1,300 of the 38,000 uniformed personnel currently deployed by the UN. The bulk of the remainder are employed in complex, multi-disciplinary missions that frequently involve rebuilding failed states from the ground up, for which monitoring is of limited relevance.

It is precisely this characteristic of modern peacekeeping that has fed much of the skepticism about the role of satellite imagery in UN operations. A 1992 study by Canada's Department of National Defence (DND), for example, raised doubts about the cost savings associated with the use of satellite imagery as a substitute for peacekeepers, stating that there were untold hidden costs involved in replacing people with systems. The study was referring specifically to the national investments required in establishing sophisticated surveillance platforms – an issue whose time has passed, perhaps, with the emergence of commercial imagery. But another concern was the truism that there is no technological substitute for qualified peacekeeping personnel on the ground.[3]

The intervening years have probably served to support this contention. The UN's involvement in increasingly complex crises means that much more is expected of peacekeepers nowadays than could possibly be accomplished by systems that, after all, are less intelligent than a human. As the DND study found, the real value of peacekeepers lies in their ability to conduct field diplomacy and defuse potential problems before they can escalate. UN personnel today routinely operate in volatile situations where confidence-building among local parties has taken on political, economic, ethnic, religious, and other dimensions. This requires much more than just verifying the absence of impending military aggression (whether through direct monitoring or through remote sensing), and it requires a presence in numbers.

If the cost savings offered by satellite imagery remain questionable in the UN context, this is even truer where commercial data is concerned. At present, the private imagery market remains subject to certain monopolistic tendencies that have kept satellite photographs very expensive (e.g., for 1-metre resolution, US $3,000 per purchase, with minimum orders of $10,000). For cash-strapped organizations such as the UN, the terms of acquisition, from a standpoint solely of cost-effectiveness, will remain prohibitive until the market liberalizes further.

Force Safety

As the rebel attacks on UN personnel in Sierra Leone demonstrated, peacekeeping remains an extremely hazardous profession. Since 1948, 1,528 uniformed personnel have died in the line of duty, one-third from violence and much of the balance from accidents.[4] In recent years, the protection traditionally afforded to peacekeepers as neutral guests has eroded as the Security Council has indulged in a more active approach to peacekeeping that occasionally strays into peace enforcement. Given also the often anarchic situations of societal implosion into which UN personnel are increasingly being deployed, observers have concluded that the practice of peacekeeping is not about to get any safer, and have begun searching for solutions.

One emerging pole of consensus is that the UN should start treating peacekeeping missions as national defence establishments treat any military operation, by massing sufficient force and adopting strong rules of engagement with a view to deterring aggression. The core principle of this vision is that peacekeepers should never be left vulnerable, and should have a capacity to protect themselves when the attitude of hitherto consenting parties shifts in a negative way. This summer, the UN Panel on Peace Operations (the 'Brahimi Panel') gave its measured endorsement to this vision, stating that 'United Nations forces for complex operations should be afforded the field intelligence and other capabilities needed to mount an effective defence against violent challengers.'[5] Proponents of satellite technology have seized on this approach and have averred that this surveillance offers the UN just such a capability to better assess, and therefore better address, the threat situation faced by its personnel.

The adoption of a manifestly tactical approach to peacekeeping, and any ancillary embrace of relevant technology such as satellite imaging, would pose a revolutionary challenge to current practice within the UN system. The unfortunate reality is that the Security Council is seldom given the freedom to think in military terms, even when dealing with questions of collective strategy and the role therein of a UN armed presence. For reasons that are explored later in this chapter, large segments of the UN membership have consistently elected to keep the Security Council in something of an information vacuum on operational issues, and have resisted any initiative to give the Secretariat the capacity to provide informed military advice to the diplomats.

As a result, the Security Council has frequently found itself deploying peacekeepers into dangerous situations without even a basic understanding of local conditions. One Permanent Representative has stated that:

> the Council was never told where the rebel Revolutionary United Front forces could be found in Sierra Leone, was never briefed, at any point, as to what parts of Eritrea that Ethiopia had occupied or vice versa, was never informed of the location of camps housing paramilitaries within East Timor, and was never shown a map illustrating the ethnic break-down of localities in Kosovo.[6]

While this blackout is evidence primarily of the UN Secretariat's inability to adequately assimilate open-source data, it also points to a systemic failure to even attempt to take advantage of information technology, of which overhead imaging is but one example.

The emergence of commercial satellite imagery has the potential to help end this self-imposed embargo on strategically- and tactically significant information, but only if the benefits can be conclusively shown to transcend the political obstacles. While the safety of UN personnel remains the most effective selling point in this regard, however, there has yet to be a compelling elaboration of the practical applications of satellite technology in improving the security of peacekeepers. A preliminary appraisal suggests that these benefits are likely to be modest.

Much of the threat to UN personnel today is disparate, unpredictable, and often indistinguishable from common civil violence. The peacekeepers killed in Sierra Leone and East Timor were targets of opportunity, and from a tactical standpoint it is unlikely that these loosely-organized ambushes could even have been detected from above. The conundrum is that dense or otherwise opaque terrain, which harbors the greatest threat from hostile forces, is precisely the type of environment that is least amenable to overhead imaging. The UN Mission in the Democratic Republic of the Congo (MONUC), for example, may face the greatest potential danger of any UN operation, with at least 18 distinct armed factions active in the country, half of whom are not signatories to the cease-fire agreement that MONUC is mandated to implement – all in a country that has once before been a veritable graveyard for peacekeepers and one Secretary-General. Yet it is not clear that surveillance technology could appreciably improve the security of UN personnel in the DRC, given that the terrain is so utterly impenetrable (and the field of vision so limited) that western militaries have assessed that there is no point in equipping military observers deployed there with binoculars.[7]

While the tactical applications of overhead imaging remain limited, however, the technology may have a more relevant contribution to make to the safety of personnel writ large, in terms of pre-deployment reconnaissance. Satellite data is increasingly being used by western defence establishments to assess the infrastructural and other realities – and therefore some of the environmental threats – that their personnel will face in host countries. While human intelligence remains the most reliable source of this kind of information, it has frequently proved faulty or insufficient in the context of UN peacekeeping, sometimes with dire consequences – hence the need for a high-tech complement.

It may seem incongruent that in an age of a Revolution in Military Affairs, basic details such as climate or topography could be readily misapprehended. But in recent years peacekeepers have frequently been deployed with inappropriate apparel or with vehicles ill-suited to the terrain, and more often still with useless maps (or none at all), including in mined areas. The UN's seemingly chronic unfamiliarity with terrain and road conditions may be partly responsible for making road accidents the greatest killer of peacekeeping personnel.

More serious mistakes about other basic environmental realities have placed peacekeepers in direct danger, and speak to the need for better technical intelligence. For example, blind spots about movements of internally-displaced persons leading up to the 1995 crisis at Kibeho, Rwanda – primarily a failure of human intelligence – landed UN personnel in the middle of firefights between Rwandan armed forces and fugitive génocidaires who had infiltrated the IDP columns.[8] In Croatia, Canadian military personnel were likely exposed to contaminated soil because of incomplete knowledge about nearby industrial activities; as a result, a Department of National Defence board of inquiry concluded that deployed contingents needed 'human and technical means to collect, process and analyze intelligence and provide resources to assess pre-deployment environmental threats.'[9]

The expanding use of national technical means as part of a more exhaustive reconnaissance process makes blunders such as these far less likely – at least for states fortunate enough to possess the relevant technology. But increasingly, the bulk of peacekeeping is being carried out by developing states that lack an indigenous imaging capacity, meaning that the median quality of UN pre-deployment reconnaissance may actually decrease in the future. This risks exposing a greater number of peacekeeping personnel to preventable threats and, over time, eroding the confidence of troop-contributing states in the relative safety of UN service.

In his seminal Agenda for Peace (1992), Secretary-General Boutros Boutros-Ghali decreed that 'innovative measures will be required to deal with the dangers facing United Nations personnel'.[10] One such initiative could be the development of an in-house reconnaissance capability within the UN Secretariat that would provide basic information to prospective troop-contributing states, particularly those lacking national technical means. One component of this reconnaissance unit could be satellite imagery either contributed by member-states or acquired through commercial sources, and interpreted strictly in the interest of force safety. This type of arrangement would merely regularize the sharing of relevant data among troop-contributing states with uneven intelligence resources, as the US has done with peacekeeping partners in Bosnia and Somalia.

The political hurdles that await such proposals, however, are considerable. As is addressed more extensively later in this essay, the willingness of the UN membership to enhance peacekeeping is fickle at best, and ambitious proposals such as these are particularly frowned upon. This summer – eight years after the UN Secretary-General endorsed the development of innovative approaches to improving the safety of the organization's personnel – the Brahimi Panel examined the issues raised in this section and drew separate conclusions about extant deficiencies in information-gathering and in the protection of UN personnel, without venturing a link between the two. This was a clear setback for advocates of better intelligence and improved force safety in UN peacekeeping, and suggests that consensus on the usefulness of overhead imaging remains illusory.

Comprehensive Peacekeeping

In recent years, the mandate of UN peacekeeping has broadened to include tasks well beyond neutral interposition between warring states. Peacekeepers are now expected to play a role in support of the political, economic, humanitarian, and legal imperatives of the Security Council – including, sometimes, the complete reconstruction of failed states – and in this regard require more comprehensive intelligence. Three areas in particular where the UN's agenda has expanded, and where overhead imaging could be a key source of information, are sanctions enforcement, support for UN war-crimes tribunals, and humanitarian operations.

Sanctions

The use of satellite data in enforcing UN sanctions has a checkered history, a function of the organization's dependence on ad hoc national contributions of intelligence. The most celebrated case study remains UNSCOM, which benefited from US imaging in dismantling the Iraqi non-conventional arsenal in furtherance of Security Council resolutions. During its short but storied life, UNSCOM also highlighted some of the political obstacles – linked to widely-shared suspicions about 'western' technology – that await any proposal to make satellite imaging a regular part of the UN toolkit.

More recently, the Security Council has wrestled with how to use overhead imaging in enforcing sanctions in Sierra Leone and Angola. Here, there has been less resistance to the proposition that the UN should benefit from aerial surveillance in addressing the illicit sources of support for groups like the RUF and UNITA; beyond the universally recognized depravity of these movements, this supportive attitude may be due in large measure to the manifest consent of the governments concerned to a surveillance role for the UN, which was not the case for UNSCOM.

But here the real failings in the relationship between the UN and its most influential members have shown through. In contrast with their support for UNSCOM, some of the permanent members of the Security Council have reportedly been reluctant to share national intelligence with the sanctions committees charged with exposing the sources of support for the RUF and UNITA. This is a function less of indifference toward the sanctions measures imposed on these rebel movements – in fact, the US has led the assault on the RUF's Liberian backers – than of their traditional reluctance to disclose anything that could betray the caliber, or perhaps more relevantly the limitations, of national technical means.

In the absence of superpower contributions of surveillance data, and recognizing that the UN has no indigenous surveillance capacity to monitor sanctions-busting by the RUF and UNITA, the Security Council effectively turned the problem over to sub-regional organizations including the Economic Community of West African States (ECOWAS) and the Southern African Development Community (SADC). In separate resolutions in April and July of this year, the Security Council emphasized the need to deter cross-border trafficking in diamonds, weapons, and fuel, and identified extant deficiencies in air-traffic monitoring in West and southern Africa. But the Council could do little besides urging ECOWAS and SADC to consider the introduction of measures to improve the detection of illegal flight activities in their respective regions.[11]

The problem, of course, is that these sub-regional organizations have even less capacity to acquire, interpret and use sophisticated data than the UN. Devolving the matter to less capable organizations has done little to address the UN's institutional inability to secure consistent contributions of national technical means from its permanent members. And while commercial imagery could represent an alternate source of surveillance information, and a more apolitical one at that, it is difficult to see how the UN could regularize its use given the ad hoc nature of sanctions work by the Security Council and the inherent reluctance of the organization to seek out inculpatory information about any of its members.

Tribunals

A related field of activity requiring tools for monitoring and investigation is support for war-crimes tribunals. In recent years, the UN has taken on this responsibility in the Balkans, Rwanda, East Timor, and now Sierra Leone, and has shown itself amenable to the use of new techniques. Satellite imaging is relevant in this regard because it has the capacity to reveal the presence of mass graves – some applications are reportedly capable of detecting the presence of decomposing bodies – and can be instrumental evidence as to when atrocities were committed. It can also reveal who controlled a particular area when the crimes were committed, and point in the direction of the perpetrators.

To date, satellite imagery used in investigating war crimes has derived from national technical means, chiefly those of US intelligence agencies. As in the case of sanctions, this approach also has a checkered history and is evidence of a need for the UN or some of its agencies to have an independent imaging capability. The case of the International Criminal Tribunal for Yugoslavia (ICTY) is quite instructive in this regard.

A passive consumer of satellite imagery insofar as it relies on whatever contribution of data western governments are prepared to make, the ICTY has had a mercurial relationship with its most important benefactor, the American government. In recent months, the US has provided crucial satellite photographs as evidence in the landmark trial of General Radislav Krstic, the highest-ranking Bosnian Serb ever tried by the ICTY and the first man ever prosecuted for genocide.[12] Beyond the more obvious benefits, a conviction, it is hoped, will also encourage states to regularize their support for war-crimes tribunals, including through overhead imaging.

But this example of positive collaboration between the American government and the ICTY is only a snapshot in time. In recent years, the US has also been accused of failing to cooperate with ICTY prosecutions of Croat military officials. Specifically, in May 1996 ICTY investigators requested the US government to provide eight satellite images taken during a 1995 Croatian bombing offensive against Serb civilians in the Krajina region of Croatia, which resulted in the ethnic cleansing of 100,000 Serbs. The US government never responded to the request, and as a result Croat military officials slated for prosecution by the ICTY were never indicted.[13] This followed allegations that US spy satellites had also recorded Serb mass murders in the Bosnian town of Brčko in 1992, but that Washington kept quiet for over a year as officials pondered the implications of disclosing this information.[14]

The sub-optimal use of imaging in support of war-crimes tribunals is a reflection not of the technology but of underlying political motives. While a tribunal process supported through voluntary contributions of national intelligence data has been shown to be viable, the highly expedient nature of this support (or absence thereof) does little for the legitimacy of the endeavor. This may therefore represent a potential niche market for commercial satellite imagery, which in the hands of a non-governmental benefactor could be perceived as freer from political influence, and therefore more credible, than national technical means. It is as yet unclear who such a purchaser might be, however. While human-rights organizations have been strong advocates of overhead imaging as a means of accountability, none has expressed an interest in taking on the responsibility of providing this kind of data. The tribunals themselves, as subsidiary bodies of the UN, remain subject to the will of the membership and are limited in how independently they can pursue inputs from without; it is unlikely that they will choose to expend their meagre political capital on unproven commercial applications of the technology.

Humanitarian assistance

The use of satellite technology in humanitarian assistance is well established, and was showcased most recently during flood-relief efforts in Mozambique. The principal benefit that aid agencies derive from the technology is the ability to establish 'ground truth' about a number of variables, including the exact location, size, and growth rate of refugee camps, the condition of roads and airstrips for relief purposes, locations for food drops, and mine fields. Given time, some humanitarian agencies hope to perfect their use of imaging and apply it to the planning of more sustainable refugee camps, and to streamlining the repatriation of displaced persons.[15]

But as in the case of war-crimes tribunals, the use of national technical means in humanitarian applications is also subject to manipulation for political reasons. In December 1996, for example, the US State Department released selected satellite images of the refugee situation in eastern DRC, under pressure from aid groups who felt that Washington was ignoring a deepening humanitarian crisis. The UN's interpretation of the images was that they revealed the presence of approximately three-quarters of a million Rwandan Hutu refugees. The US, for its part, had a radically different interpretation of the same images, and maintained that the refugees in question had returned to Rwanda and that there was therefore no need for an assistance force, which Canada had offered to lead. The American view eventually outlasted events on the ground; US military officials were later to boast that the selective disclosure 'prevented the unnecessary deployment of a multinational force'.[16]

Aid organizations have understandably grown leery of the political character of national contributions of imagery, and have begun to turn to private sources. Most recently, UNHCR, the UN Department for Humanitarian Affairs (UNDHA), and the International Federation of Red Cross have expressed serious interest in working with imaging firms. Many aid agencies, however, remain wary of commercial providers. According to one scholar, 'Satellite image applications have had a tendency to be oversold, and the earth observation community must be careful not to promise too much to relief agencies with very limited budgets'.[17] It is unlikely, in fact, that humanitarian organizations will become regular customers of commercial imagery unless the marketplace expands and allows prices to stabilize to a level that aid agencies can afford.

Obstacles

Having established that there is indeed a need, albeit limited, for satellite imagery as a complement to UN peacekeeping efforts, it is now necessary to turn to some of the obstacles that will complicate putting this into practice.

First and foremost is resistance originating with the UN membership. The current reality is that, for diverse and often conflicting reasons, a significant array of states would likely object to the regular use by the UN of satellite imagery, irrespective of how it was acquired or how much peacekeeping might stand to benefit. This is a function of the fact that UN member states do not share an equal enthusiasm for making UN peacekeeping more effective, with many in fact seeing it as quite inimical to their own interests.

The United States, for example, has articulated a clear vision of international security in which meaningful peacekeeping is to be carried out by multinational non-UN coalitions, with the UN serving as the forum for second-tier security concerns. (The increasingly rigid attitude of the US on the question of its arrears is quite telling in this regard.) This vision is very much based on a hardening of American views about UN capabilities and the place therein of information technology. In the US orthodoxy, the Revolution in Military Affairs is best segregated from the UN's inchoate pursuit of collective security, and left to military alliances such as NATO and coalitions of like-mindeds. For the UN to begin independently using tactical hardware such as surveillance technology would not only usurp these alliances, it would also lead the UN even further astray from its founding principles.

It was not always this way, of course. In September 1992, in a speech before the General Assembly, President Bush expressed his government's intention to share surveillance data with the UN as a matter of policy, in the interest of effective peacekeeping.[18] This was thirteen months before 18 Army Rangers were killed in Somalia in a US-commanded operation that American policy-makers have retroactively come to blame on the UN. The American attitude toward the UN has never been the same. During his Millennium Assembly speech this past September, President Clinton underscored this reality by expressing his willingness to share satellite data with the UN – but only on environmental issues. In a speech that acknowledged the need to enhance peacekeeping, President Clinton spoke of his intention to provide the UN with satellite pictures of endangered forests but studiously avoided any mention of parallel support in the area of tactical intelligence.[19]

This is not to suggest that the US is alone in wanting to circumscribe the UN's use of satellite imagery. The unfortunate fact is that much of the rank and file of the UN membership shares this view. It is important to remember that during the 1980s, developing countries, which make up a majority of the General Assembly, were not at all supportive of proposals for an International Satellite Monitoring Agency (ISMA). While the Cold War superpowers deservedly took much of the blame for smothering ISMA in the crib, the UN membership in general was guilty of damning the proposal with faint praise. It is instructive that since the end of the Cold War, the idea of an ISMA has not been revived by the General Assembly.

These states are certainly not motivated by malice, and upon reflection their concerns are understandable. Satellite imagery is indelibly identified as western technology, which developing states associate with intrusive intelligence gathering and the erosion of sovereignty. The use of overhead imaging in UNSCOM, and subsequent disclosures about a US intelligence presence on the inspection team, have already darkened the name of this frequently benign technology, in the same way that the Global Positioning System is equated with smart bombs and the Gulf War by much of the developing world. In addition, what western observers usually treat as advantages of surveillance technology are often perceived elsewhere as liabilities. For example, the fact that satellites can gather data without the consent of the countries sensed is a major selling point for proponents of these systems, but for a majority of states the complete blindness of the technology to national sovereignty concerns is nothing short of a poison pill.

This will have a direct impact on how satellite imaging is judged by the UN, particularly for applications relating to peace and security. For, while it is true that national sovereignty is eroding as a core principle of the Security Council, and that developing states have acquiesced in this change, it remains a slow process and one that is not keeping pace with the development of satellite technology.

The point was driven home this spring, when the Security Council toyed briefly with the idea of placing the civil war in Sudan on its agenda but backed off under pressure from non-aligned states. Many facets of the Sudanese civil war could be usefully addressed with the help of overhead imaging; commercial imagery of the country has already been examined by Norwegian-based aid groups to assess the refugee situation.[20] The political reality, however, is that while imaging technology may have much to reveal about Sudan, the Security Council has already foresworn discussing the country's war, to say nothing of examining the Swedish data. This asymmetry between the technology and the politics that inform its use is stark evidence of the hurdles that overhead imaging will face at the UN.

Beyond the issue of sovereignty, the equally immutable concern of developing states over their potential marginalization within the UN system may also trump the benefits of overhead imaging. In fact, the question of satellites and peacekeeping may play out in much the same way as have staffing issues in the Department of Peacekeeping Operations. Two years ago, the UN Secretariat agreed to end the practice by which countries – invariably western states – would contribute highly qualified personnel, free of change, to UN departments such as DPKO. The concern of developing countries was that this led to an overrepresentation of westerners in important positions within the UN system, because other countries were not in a position to make contributions of gratis personnel.

By all accounts, this fixation over the complexion of UN staff has robbed the organization of valuable assets and undermined the quality of policy and analysis. Yet the Secretariat has consistently stood by its decision to give representational concerns precedence over effectiveness, and there is every reason to believe that it would take a similar approach to exclusive technology such as satellite surveillance. Whether a contribution of national technical intelligence or a subsidy of commercial data, satellite imagery remains a tool that is beyond the reach of all but a few countries. The remainder are extremely sensitive to the role that this disparity plays in the emergence of a two-tier system of peacekeeping, in which developing countries are increasingly playing a subordinate role they view as undignified. In the interest of what it perceives as the greater good, the UN Secretariat may elect to forsake this useful but potentially divisive technology.

Ultimately, however, the most serious obstacle to the use of satellite imagery by the UN is also the most obvious: Who will pay? As was discussed earlier, the technology remains expensive, and in an era of zero-growth for the UN's regular budget the mere fact that overhead imaging can make peacekeeping safer or more effective is not likely to hold much sway. Unless it can be proven that this technology represents potential cost savings – a dubious proposition, as I outlined earlier – it will be extremely difficult to achieve a consensus view that satellite imagery is necessary and should be paid for with assessed contributions. As for the possibility of states donating imagery (whether from national or commercial sources) on a regular basis, the problem of unequal representation leading to marginalization, outlined above, remains a fundamental hurdle.

Finally, one peculiar but nevertheless relevant question is whether the Security Council's own broadening definition of peacekeeping, to include peace enforcement under Chapter VII of the UN Charter, would not unduly complicate the acquisition of commercial satellite information. Each imaging company is subject to a corporate charter governing the use of its data, and it is not a given that these conventions necessarily recognize the legitimacy of peace enforcement operations. The charter for the communications satellite Inmarsat, for example, refers to peaceful uses by the UN, and had to be revised several times before it could be said with confidence that the system could be used in support of Chapter VII operations.[21]

Conclusion

While there are real and potential benefits to be derived from using commercial satellite imagery in the context of UN peacekeeping, they are modest and should not be mistaken for a panacea. Principally, some improvements are possible in the area of force safety, particularly as regards pre-deployment reconnaissance and the identification of environmental threats. Overhead imaging could also be used to positive effect in areas of UN activity that frequently overlap with peacekeeping, including the enforcement of better targeted (and therefore more humane) sanctions; support for war-crimes tribunals; and improvements in the delivery of humanitarian assistance.

Resistance to the regular use of satellite imagery in UN peacekeeping and related activities is likely to be strong. Peacekeeping is often but one front in the battle for supremacy at the UN between the 'haves' and the 'have-nots', and any proposal that emphasizes exclusive assets such as sophisticated technology risks compounding this polarization and ultimately perishing from it. If there is scope for swaying the skeptics at the UN – be they in the General Assembly, the Secretariat, or the permanent membership of the Security Council – this will probably require that the UN be persuaded to use the technology in selected applications, sufficiently to demystify the technology for non-aligned countries and prove cost-effective for the exchequer states.

This last element, ultimately, is the most critical. An iron-clad case will have to be made that commercial imagery represents cost savings; merely holding out the promise of better or safer peacekeeping likely will not be sufficient. At present, this is a difficult proposition because of extant rigidities in the imagery marketplace. But with at least eight new high-resolution commercial satellites scheduled for launch in the next three years, increased liberalization is expected to result in lower prices. Hopefully, this will also contribute to the emergence of a constituency within the UN system that sees more clearly the larger benefits of the technology.

Notes

1   Ulric Shannon is the Security Council desk officer in the Regional Security and Peacekeeping Division of the Canadian Department of Foreign Affairs and International Trade. He holds graduate degrees in international relations and security studies, and specializes in peacekeeping and security in Africa. The views expressed in this essay are personal and do not necessarily reflect those of the Canadian government.

2   United Nations. 'UN Summary of Contributions to Peacekeeping Operations', 16 November 2000; Department of Foreign Affairs and International Trade (Canada), relevant Treasury Board submissions, 1998–2000.

3   S.B. Flemming. *Organizational and Military Impacts of High-Tech Surveillance and Detection Systems for UN Peacekeeping*, Project Report 535, Ottawa: Operational Research and Analysis Establishment, Department of National Defence (Canada), 1992, pp.6–14.

4   United Nations. 'Peacekeeping: Fatalities', available at http://www.un.org/Depts/dpko/fatalities/.

5   United Nations. *Report of the Panel on United Nations Peace Operations*, S/2000/809, 21 August 2000, p.x.

6   United Nations Association of the United States of America. 'Enhancing UN Peacekeeping Capability: a UNA-USA Policy Roundtable', New York, 5 July 2000, available at http://www.unausa.org/issues/peace/705/htm.

7   Personal conversations with officials from the Department of National Defence (Canada).

8   Philip Gourevitch. *We Wish to Inform You that Tomorrow We Will be Killed with our Families: Stories from Rwanda*, New York: Picador, 1998, p.190.

9   Department of National Defence. *Croatia Board of Inquiry: Final Report*, p.27, available at http://www.dnd.ca/boi/engraph/report_e.asp.

10   Boutros Boutros-Ghali. *An Agenda for Peace: Preventive Diplomacy, Peacemaking and Peace-keeping*, New York: United Nations, 1992, p.39.

11   Security Council Resolution 1295 (2000) on sanctions measures against UNITA, adopted 18 April 2000, and 1306 (2000) on the illicit diamond trade in Sierra Leone, adopted 5 July 2000.

12   BBC News Online. 'Bosnian Serb Accused of Genocide', 13 March 2000, available atnews.bbc.co.uk/hi/english/world/europe/newsid_676000/676297.stm.

13   Raymond Bonner. 'War Crimes Panel Finds Croat Army "Cleansed" Serbs', *New York Times*, 21 March 1999.

14   Andrew Ross. 'Never Say Never Again: New Evidence Suggests Early U.S. Knowledge of Serb Atrocities', *Salon*, 2 May 1996, available at http://www.salonmag.com/news/news960502.html.

15   Einar Bjorgo. 'Very High Resolution Satellites: A New Source of Information in Humanitarian Relief Operations', *Bulletin of the American Society for Information Science*, October 1999, available at http://www.asis.org/Bulletin/Oct-99/bjorgo.html.

16   Jo Ellen Fair and Lisa Parks. 'Inspecting African Bodies: Television News Coverage and Satellite Imaging of Rwandan Refugees', paper presented at Sixth Annual African Studies Consortium Workshop, 2 October 1998, available at http://www.sas.upenn.edu/African_Studies/Workshop/joelisa98.html.

17   Bjorgo, op. cit.

18   President George Bush. 'Address by the President of the United States of America to the 47th Session of the United Nations General Assembly', *USUN Press Release* 84 (92), 21 September 1992.

19   President Bill Clinton. 'Remarks to the Security Council', Office of the Press Secretary, 7 September 2000, available at http://www.state.gov/www/regions/africa.

20 ENVIREF, a Norwegian consortium of refugee-relief groups, has a particular interest in the use of satellite data in humanitarian applications. (See http://www.enviref.org).
21 Lt.-Cdr. J. Todd Blac. 'Commercial Satellites: Future Threats or Allies?', *Naval War College Review*, Winter 1999, at http://www.nwc.navy.mil/press/Review/1999/winter/art5-w99.htm.

Chapter 15

Canada and Commercial Satellite Imagery: Technology in Search of a Foreign Policy

Rob Huebert[1]

Commercial satellite imagery (CSI) has a wide range of new and exciting uses for Canada. As discussed in other chapters in this book, Canadian peacekeeping and peace enforcement operations stand to make considerable gains through the utilization of CSI. CSI is also playing an increasingly important role in determining the impact of climate change on Canada.

It is evident that CSI requires a complex mix of industry and government in order to establish the technology and to fully use it. The partnership between the Canadian Space Agency and MacDonald Dettwiler and Associates Ltd. (MDA) to develop the RADARSAT 1 and 2 demonstrates the need for cooperation between the two. The fact that Canada has subsequently relied on the United States to launch the satellite underlines the international need for bilateral cooperation. The recent agreement reached between Canada and the United States on the operation of commercial remote satellite systems serves to underscore the reality that Canada cannot operate such systems in isolation.

The challenge increasingly facing the Canadian Government is how to manage the various actors and requirements to produce a coherent foreign and defence policy. At the same time, the government must remain sensitive to the problems that they will create. The objective of this chapter is to consider these challenges.

Challenges of New Technology in Canadian Foreign Policy: The Problem

One of the key elements in understanding the development of Canada's CSI policy is recognizing the importance of the United States. As the leading nation in space technology, the United States plays a central role in the development of Canadian space policy in general. There are two specific components to the Canadian-American relationship and commercial satellite imagery. First, Canada relies on the United States for both technological and launch support. While it is possible for Canada to develop its own capabilities, to do so would be extremely expensive and, therefore, unlikely. Until the end of the 1980s, the United States was the only nation to which Canada could turn to for such support. Canada would not turn to the USSR for security reasons. Likewise, the Europeans and the Japanese were only then developing their own capabilities.

At the same time, Canada has had to be sensitive to the United States' security interests. Since Canada would not develop its own capabilities and could not find alternative assistance, it has had to comply with American security requirements with little room for negotiation. This has not been a major issue since Canada and the United States share the same security viewpoint on most issues. However, Canada has had to take special care in the use of its own satellites. Specifically, Canada has been required to enter into agreements commonly referred to as 'shutter control', which control the images that Canada can take, and to whom it can sell them. While this is not an insurmountable problem for Canada, it does complicate the Canadian use of CSI. Nevertheless, Canada has needed to ensure that its own interests are protected.

The development of a Canadian policy towards CSI has also been strongly shaped by the Canadian space policy. While many Canadians have grown up sharing the American vision of space exploration moulded by the early moon missions, successive Canadian Governments have refused to enunciate a holistic Canadian space policy that incorporates both security and civilian issues. Despite the fact that Canada was the third nation in the world to place a satellite in orbit, and that numerous government studies called for an independent Canadian Space Agency since the end of the 1960s, one was not developed until 1989. Furthermore, even when the Space Agency was created, it was specifically restricted from dealing with security issues. This separation between security interests and civilian interests imposed numerous challenges on policy-makers given that the development of SAR technology on the RADARSAT satellites offered both civilian and military applications.

Since the end of the 1960s, Canadian policy has been that space is to be used for only 'peaceful purposes'. With this policy in place, Canada was reluctant to dedicate the money necessary for an independent, national space capability for fear that there may be military applications in these capabilities. The dedication to the peaceful use of space, while a noble sentiment, was not completely consistent with Canadian policy. Canada was, and continues to be, a full member of NATO and NORAD, both of which were directed against the threat of an aggressive USSR. Both military alliances were anchored by the nuclear deterrent of the American ICBM and SLBM forces. The ballistic missiles that propelled these weapons were developed through the American space programme.

These developments ultimately led Canada to develop a policy by which it needs to rely on both private industry and the American Government to acquire a powerful capability that is designed for civilian purposes but carries with it security and foreign policy implications. The Canadian Government is now attempting to come to terms with these challenges. This chapter will examine how Canada has found itself in this set of circumstances and what it is doing.

Historical Development of Canadian Space Policy

Following the end of the Second World War, the Canadian Government continued its cooperation with the United States in space and rocket research into the development of ballistic missile technology. In 1947 the principal Canadian scientists were consolidated into the tri-service Defence Research Board (DRB).[2] They pursued a wide range of projects including: upper atmosphere studies, satellite design and construction, communications, rocketry design and testing, and ballistic missile development.[3] The Canadian space programme continued to grow between 1957 and 1967. Though substantial basic science was pursued, a significant proportion of the work was geared towards the security needs of both Canada and the United States. On September 28, 1962 Canada had become the third nation to launch a satellite when it placed the Alouette satellite into space. Although it was launched with American assistance, the satellite itself was Canadian designed and built.[4] By 1967 Canada had designed and launched the Black Brant rocket and seemed poised to develop the ability to launch its own satellites.[5]

In May 1966, the Science Secretariat of the Privy Council Office commissioned the first comprehensive study of the Canadian upper atmosphere and space program.[6] Chaired by John Chapman (hence known as the Chapman Report), the study provided an in-depth examination of the Canadian space program.[7] The study noted that while Canada had become a significant 'space' nation it was facing several major challenges. First, the report noted that the 'lack of a central organization for space activities was unfortunate'.[8] It also noted that the scale of the Canadian space program was substantially lower on a GNP basis than other industrial nations.[9] The report did note the important progress that Canada had made but warned of future problems. Specifically,

[t]he absence of a national mission-oriented agency with overall responsibility for upper atmosphere and space activities in Canada has resulted in fragmented programs, divided responsibility, and serious omissions in planning. These deficiencies are bound to become more serious in the future, and could lead to tragic consequences for Canada in loss of technological opportunity, and in gradual erosion of national control over natural resources and domestic communications.[10]

Following the completion of the report, the Science Council of Canada prepared a report on the development of the Canadian space program.[11] It offered several recommendations and findings. Most importantly it called for the establishment of a space agency for the:

advancement of Canadian capability in the science and technology of the upper atmosphere and space; for furthering the development of Canadian industry in relation to the use of the upper atmosphere and space; and for the planning and implementation of an overall space program for Canada.[12]

The report stated that the creation of such an agency was not meant to be a substitute for the space program of the Department of Defence. It also stated that the agency should be free 'under suitable circumstances, to undertake work on behalf of the defence agencies'.[13]

However, by the end of the 1960s, the momentum for developing such an agency or a coherent space policy disappeared. Pierre Trudeau's government made two decisions that effectively redirected and reduced the existing space capabilities. The first decision was to redirect the scientific pursuits to industrial applications.

In 1967, the Federal Government made a decision to redirect Canada's space activities from purely scientific pursuits (exemplified by the Alouette and ISIS programs) to the applied. Specifically, this meant that Canada's principle objective in space would be the application of technology and science to domestic telecommunications and resource-survey problems. This decision terminated the Alouette-ISIS program with ISIS-2 and led to a serious decline in space-science activity in the late 1970s.[14]

At the same time, the government also decided that the existing Canadian space program was becoming too focused on military requirements. In 1966, 41 per cent of the Canadian space programs were military-related. American assistance provided an additional 20 per cent that were shared spaced projects that were almost all military oriented. Another 11 per cent of Canadian funding was for joint military-civilian projects. Thus almost 75 per cent of Canadian space expenditures had some degree of military orientation.[15]

By 1969, although the Trudeau government did not officially cancel the existing Canadian space programs, it began to starve them of funds. All military related space projects were either terminated or substantially reduced.[16] The government also transferred the control of space research and development from the Department of Defence to the Communications Research Centre of the Department of Communications.[17] In 1970, the Canadian Government decided that all future communication work would be undertaken by this new department. This communication work was incorporated into the government's sole satellite project, which was known as the Anik series.[18]

Although the government was transferring control of space programs, it refused to create a specific space agency. Instead it established an Interdepartmental Committee on Space 'to review and coordinate Canadian space activities and resources and to consider plans and policy'.[19] In keeping with the government's desire to remove all security connections from its space policy, the Department of Defence was not included on the committee.

The committee failed to meet its mandate to promote and coordinate the Canadian Space Program. Several experts and bodies testifying before the Standing Committee on Research, Science and Technology on the Study of Canada's Space Program in 1987 severely criticized the ICS. The Aerospace Industries Association of Canada (AIAC) stated:

> The Interdepartmental Committee on Space (ICS) is expected to coordinate Canada's efforts. It is not expected to manage them. In fact, nobody in Canada manages a truly national space program. Each department involved in space looks after its own projects. This fragmentation is demoralizing to the space industry, because government, after all, is not only its partner, but also one of its biggest customers. And it is confusing to Canada's interdepartmental partners and customers, who must deal with several different government departments which damage Canada's image in the world community.[20]

L.W. Morely who was the founding director of the Canada Centre for Remote Sensing at York University and who served on the committee for a decade was particularly critical:

For 10 years I suffered as a member of the Interdepartmental Committee on Space, and I do not think there was a more ineffectual committee in the whole government.[21]

A Canadian policy for space was adopted in 1974. It called for the transfer of government research into industry. In direct contradiction to the recommendation of the Chapman Report, the 1974 policy stated that Canada was to rely on foreign launches and abandon any effort to maintain an indigenous Canadian capability. Finally, the policy also stated that Canada's activities should contribute directly to national goals.[22] However, the report did not explain how this was to be accomplished nor did it suggest that foreign or security interests be included in these national goals.

The launch of the Anik satellites were completed in 1976 and the government decided against the further development of a national satellite program.[23] Instead it focused on the development of the Remote Manipulator System (the Canadarm on the American space shuttle).

At the same time that Canada was winding down its national space program, it was also becoming increasingly dependent on foreign sources for remote sensing. The Chapman Report had stated that Canada needed to develop its own means of remote sensing to facilitate Canadian interests, specifically surveillance of the Canadian north and resource development. However, rather than develop its own capability, the Canadian Government entered into an agreement in 1971 with the United States which provided that it would receive American data in exchange for research and equipment.[24] This agreement was renewed in 1975.

In December 1981, the Canadian Government announced a new space plan for the period 1982-1983 to 1984-1985. The policy had two major premises: first, the use of space can contribute to the attainment of social, cultural and economic goals and, second, economic benefits are to be obtained through the creation of a strong, domestic, space industry.[25] The plan was based on four main elements. First, Canada needed to continue to explore new applications of space technology. Second, a domestic prime contractor was required for the development and construction of satellites. Third, international relationships were to be strengthened. Fourth, technology development had to be a central goal of any new developments. The government allocated $475.8 million allocated over 4 years (or approximately $115 million annually) in order to achieve these objectives.[26] The government was essentially following the policy established in 1967, which was that the development of industrial capability was the primary purpose of the Canadian space program. The report commented only briefly on the development of Canadian foreign policy[27] and there was no mention of Canadian security policy and space.

Ultimately, Canadian space capability diminished. The Trudeau Government's policy was to remove the military component from space issues but no real effort was ever made to develop a civilian Canadian equivalent to NASA. While space policy was removed from the control of the Department of Defence, the new lead departments, the Department of Communications and the Department of Energy, Mines and Resources, were not provided with the necessary resources nor were they particularly interested in developing a leadership role for space policy. In addition, the general public in both the United States and Canada lost some enthusiasm for space activity during the 1970s. The net effect was that Canada lost most of its space capabilities. Those companies that retained some interest in space had expertise that was largely based on the military projects of the 1950s and 1960s.[28]

The 1971 Canadian White Paper on Defence named the surveillance and protection of Canadian land space as its top priority. However, there is little to indicate that the government attempted to develop a space policy for surveillance. From the beginning of the 1970s to the mid-1980s, there was little evidence that the Canadian Government gave much thought or credence to the development of a space policy that would be explicitly tied to either defence or foreign policy. This began to change in 1983 with the American government's announcement that it wished to develop a space based system to protect the United States against a Soviet nuclear attack – the Strategic Defence Initiative (SDI) (also known in the popular press as Star Wars). The change of the Canadian Government in 1984 also precipitated a willingness to re-examine the Canadian position.

Following the American announcement of SDI, strong opposition to any Canadian cooperation or participation in SDI developed in Canada. When the Reagan Administration invited Canada to participate, the Mulroney Government considered, but declined, the invitation. However, Canadian companies were granted permission to participate.[29] The request ignited a renewed debate on space policy not only amongst the general public but also within the Canadian Government. Both the House of Commons Standing Committee on External Affairs and National Defence and the Senate Special Committee on National Defence undertook studies in 1986 and 1985 respectively that called for the development of a national, military space program.[30]

The Canadian Government released its policy paper on space in May 1986. The paper's substance was somewhat limited. As did the preceding policy reviews, it called for better coordination of Canadian space projects that had survived the 1970s. However, the policy paper was important in that it provided the first real effort to develop a coherent policy on space. The decision was finally made in 1989 to create the Canadian Space Agency. Its mandate was:

> [t]o Promote the Peaceful use and Development of Space, to advance knowledge of space through science and to ensure that space science and technology provide social and economic benefits for Canadians.[31]

At the same time, the Department of National Defence also began to develop a new set of policies.[32] In July 1989, the Chief of Review Services tabled a report on Canada's defence space program.[33] This report led to the creation of the Space Defence Working Group (SDWG), which developed a comprehensive space policy.[34] Subsequently, the Directorate of Space Development (D Space D) was created in 1997and placed under the Deputy Chief of the Defence Staff (DCDS) (the third-highest ranking officer in the Canadian Forces).[35]

In March 2002 it was reported that the Department of Defence is now planning to develop its own surveillance satellite system, named 'Polar Star'.[36] Much of the system is classified, but news reports suggest that it will make use 'of images gathered by sophisticated commercial satellites that can observe objects on the ground as small as three metres in length'.[37] This suggests that it will be using SAR since this is the resolution that RADARSAT-2 is expected to be capable of. The system is estimated to cost between $596 and $684 million (Cdn). It is not publicly known if the money has been approved.

Thus, by the 1990s, Canada had begun to re-examine and redevelop its space policy to include a security component. Efforts were undertaken to coordinate and develop actions that would serve Canadian interests. However, these efforts were constrained by limited resources. In a time when other issues such as health care, education and the deficit were the priorities for most Canadians and decision-makers there was little room for the development of a comprehensive and expensive space policy. However, the Canadian Government has now focused its attention on the development of niche capabilities, cooperation with other state partners (primarily the United States and the European Space Agency) and the private sector. The main characteristic of Canadian space policy was its focus on the private sector. While there was some renewal of security considerations in the use of Canadian space, they were not funded well and remained rudimentary. Furthermore, these efforts were separate from Canadian space policy in general.

Having examined the general evolution of Canadian space policy as it pertains to security considerations, we will now address the more specific development of the RADARSAT program. The main issue to be considered is how the Government of Canada has attempted to reconcile the need to cooperate with the United States and to meet private industry requirements with the need to ultimately incorporate Canadian foreign and security needs into a very powerful instrument.

The Development of RADARSAT 1, 2 and 3

In the mid-1970s, Canada began to cooperate with the United States in developing synthetic aperture radar (SAR). This is a powerful, microwave instrument that sends and receives signals that can penetrate clouds, haze, smoke and darkness.[38] The major advantage of SAR is its ability to 'see' through bad weather and darkness. SAR is a very powerful tool despite the fact that the images need to be interpreted and the images themselves have a slightly lower resolution capability than optical imagery. Canada is one of the world leaders in the development of the technology and has been successful in developing its commercial application. However, the Government of Canada has not fully used this advantage in terms of national policy and specifically has not utilized it to its fullest potential for Canadian security needs.

Canada became a world leader in the development of SAR through its initial cooperation with the United States' SEASAT (sea satellite) and through an airborne SAR program called SURAT (surveillance satellite).[39] SEASAT was the first Earth-orbiting satellite designed for the remote sensing of the Earth's oceans and it deployed the first space-borne SAR. The satellite was launched on June 28, 1978. It had the capability to take imagery that had a 25 metre resolution. SURAT was an interdepartmental program established in 1977 by the Canadian Government. Both SAR and SURAT were the first steps towards the creation of an operational surveillance satellite system.[40] Canadian industry was involved in SEASAT from the beginning by developing the first digital SAR processor to manage SEASAT SAR data.[41] Unfortunately, the SAR operated for only 105 days until a massive short circuit ended its mission.[42]

In the early 1980s, the Canadian Government made the decision to develop a satellite that could utilize SAR. It was initially supposed to be a joint, international project with the United States and the United Kingdom.[43] Quebec, Ontario and Saskatchewan, and Canadian aerospace private companies, were also included as partners. The United States and the United Kingdom were expected to provide the bulk of the funding, but did not do so.[44] As the project proceeded, the satellite capabilities were eventually reduced in order to respond to the United States' and the United Kingdom's withdrawal from the project. Optical sensors were deleted and the planned life cycle of the satellite was reduced from 10 years to 5 years. (However, the satellite has already exceeded the expected life cycle and continues to operate.) This reduced the program's costs from $978 million (Cdn) to $635 million. Even with these reductions, the continuation of the program was in question in 1987. However, the Standing Committee on Research, Science and Technology, which conducted an examination of Canadian space policy in 1987, had as its first recommendation the continuation of the RADARSAT program.[45]

The Canadian Government had to increase its funding and try to find new partners after the United Kingdom and the United States withdrew their participation. Ultimately, British Columbia and additional private interests joined the project. Industrial partners included Spar Aerospace (prime contractor), MDA, SED Systems, CAL Corporation, COM DEV, Fleet Industries, IMP and FRE Composites.[46] The federal government provided $500 million (Cdn), the four provinces provided $57 million (Cdn) and the private sector provided $63 million (Cdn).

The Canadian Government entered into an agreement with the United States to launch the satellite. On February 27, 1991, a Memorandum of Understanding (MOU) was reached between the Canadian Space Agency, NASA and the National Oceanic and Atmospheric Administration.[47] The agreement was enacted through an exchange of notes on November 12, 1991. The most important elements of the MOU established that NASA would launch the satellite in return for access to the imagery. Under Article 8.1(ii), the available SAR data acquisition time would be allocated 'in proportion to the value of their contribution to the space segment and the ground support equipment and the mission control system, the launch and the associated launch services'.[48]

The launch date of the RADARSAT-1satellite was delayed until November 4, 1995. After it was launched, it was placed in a sun-synchronous (dawn-dusk) orbit at a height of 800 kilometres. The satellite has the ability to narrow or broaden the size of its imagery between 45 to 500 kilometres and can focus its resolution to between 8 to 100 metres. It covers the Arctic daily and most of Canada every three days. The data that it receives can be down linked in real time or stored on the onboard tape recorder and downloaded when the satellite come within range of a receiving station. There are two receiving stations in Canada (Prince Albert, Saskatchewan and Gatineau, Quebec). Canada also has agreements with receiving stations across the globe to allow downlinking from locations outside of Canada.[49]

Even before RADARSAT-1 was successful, plans were in place to develop an even better capability with RADARSAT-2. The Canadian Government entered into negotiations with MDA to construct and manage this project. A tentative agreement was created on March 2, 1998, and finalized on December 18th of the same year.[50] As work progressed the following year, MDA acquired RADARSAT International, which was the company that distributes the RADARSAT imagery.[51] The Government of Canada is contributing $225 million (Cdn) and MDA is providing $80 million (Cdn).[52] Pursuant to the agreement, MDA will provide Canada with $225 million (Cdn) worth of imagery from the satellite which means that the Canadian Government will recoup its expenditure through the supply of imagery.

While work continued on RADARSAT-2, negotiations for an expected launch in 2002 proceeded between the Canadian Space Agency and NASA. However, it soon became apparent to the Americans that the satellite was going to have exceptional capabilities. It had improved polarization that aids in the identification of surface features. Most importantly, the satellite's resolution is being improved to between 100 to 3 metres. The satellite's detailed resolution has caused the greatest concern to the United States.[53] As a result, NASA has deferred the launch of the satellite.

The Americans were concerned about the potential accuracy of the new system. At a top resolution capability of 3 metres, the satellite would have important military applications. The imagery would be able to isolate individual ships and large structures in all weather conditions and during the day and at night. Given these abilities and the fact that the imagery will be for sale on the international market, the Americans became worried. Their main fear was that a state or group opposed to the United States might buy imagery of the United States and/or its allies and use it for military purposes. For example, the Iraqi Government could attempt to buy imagery of American forces in the Gulf region. Such intelligence could be invaluable. If the satellite and the distribution of the imagery was directly controlled by the Canadian Government, it is likely that the American Government would not have been as concerned as it was. However, since the satellite was operating on a commercial basis, the possibility arose that states unfriendly to either the United States or Canada could arrange to purchase imagery to be used against either. Thus the Americans made it clear that they would launch the satellite only if they had insurances in place to protect their security interests.

The Canadian Government entered into negotiations with the American Government to address this matter. The negotiations led to a bilateral agreement regarding the operation of Canadian commercial satellites, which was signed by Canadian Foreign Affairs Minister Lloyd Axworthy and US Secretary of State Madeline Albright on June 16, 2000.[54] The agreement focuses on the RADARSAT-2 but can be extended to other satellites as agreed to by the two countries. The key article (Article 1) of the agreement states that:

> The Parties agree to ensure that such commercial remote sensing systems will be controlled by each Party in a comparable manner in order to protect and serve shared national security and foreign policy interest.[55]

Pursuant to the agreement, Canada agrees to implement controls over the use of RADARSAT-2. Two annexes are included in the agreement. The first outlines Canada's access control policy. It provides the means by which the government will act to oversee the use of RADARSAT-2 and, more importantly, the process by which the government will 'invoke, modify or revoke' shuttle control – i.e., what pictures can and cannot be used and who has access to them. A second confidential annex outlines how Canada implements control with regard to the operator (MDA).

The agreement is interesting in that the emphasis is on Canada and not the United States. While the agreement opens the option of applying the agreement to other satellite systems there is no specific mention of applying it to existing American commercial satellite systems. The agreement is also unique in that it clearly links Canadian security and foreign policy with RADARSAT-2. Nowhere else in any Canadian Government statement or policy is this link explored.

Immediately following the official signing of the agreement, Boeing won the contract to launch the satellite.[56] It will use a Delta II rocket which will be launched at the Vandenberg Air Force Base in California. The launch date has already been delayed from 2002 to 2003, though even this date is not certain.

Even though RADARSAT-2 has not yet been launched, MDA is now developing plans for RADARSAT-3. On February 20, 2001, MacDonald Dettwiler and Associates and the Canadian Space Agency announced the commencement of a feasibility study for RADARSAT-3.[57]

The imagery produced by RADARSAT has had a wide range of uses by a wide range of clients. It has been used for ice surveillance in the north, as well as by shipping companies in North America, Europe and Asia and by government agencies in both North America and Europe with ice reconnaissance and mapping mandates. It has also been used for the mapping and planning of land use,[58] which include the use of agricultural monitoring in Canada and the United States and the monitoring of forests. RADARSAT imagery has also been used in the study of climate change.[59] It has also proven to be of use for humanitarian aid and disaster monitoring.[60] It has proven particularly useful during floods and has been used to monitor flooding in Italy, the United States, Honduras, China, Quebec and Manitoba. In short, RADARSAT imagery has proven itself to be a very versatile and useful tool.

However, the Canadian Government's efforts to transfer the program into private hands has meant that MDA may pursue business that could run counter to Canadian national interests. While the agreement with the United States suggests that RADARSAT-2 will be controlled more rigidly, there is no indication that the Canadian Government has been willing to make such concessions in the use of RADARSAT-1. An incident in the summer of 2002 illustrates how the Canadian Government has not fully appreciated the security ramifications of a commercial entity having such a powerful tool at its disposal.

One of the current foreign customers of RADARSAT imagery is the Danish Meteorological Institute (DMI). In July 2002, it signed an 18 month, $1.4 million (Cdn) contract for the imagery that 'will be used to create ice charts and reports for ships navigating the ice-infested Greenland Sea'.[61] This will include navigation in the waters of Greenland and Canada.[62] The sale of the imagery fits the mandate of MDA and provides a needed source of income. The problem is that this information may have been used in the summer of 2002 to undermine Canadian sovereignty in the Canadian Arctic. While the information is still sketchy, there is mounting evidence that the Danish Government sent an ice-strengthen frigate into disputed waters.[63] Hans Island is a small island between the northwest tip of Greenland and Ellesmere Island over which both Denmark and Canada claim sovereignty. While the island is insignificant, its location is important. The existing maritime boundary between Canada and Greenland may change depending on who has sovereignty over the island. The Danish vessel sailed into these disputed waters possibly to bolster the Danish claim. The Canadian Government issued a diplomatic note of protest in response to this voyage.

Since the Canadian Government has encouraged RADARSAT to be developed as a private interest, MDA needs clients such as the Danish Government. However, in this case, MDA's interests are not the same as those of the Government of Canada. Currently, the Canadian Government has limited ability to control to whom the data is sold. The agreement with the Americans is for RADARSAT-2. When that agreement comes into effect it is possible that the Canadian Government will become more sensitive to the security and sovereignty ramifications of the imagery. Given that the Canadian Government has shown little interest in considering RADARSAT in a security context, it does not seem likely to act even with the agreement in place. Ultimately, Ottawa will have to be sensitive to the business needs of MDA. As a private company, it must ensure that sales become profitable. If this is not the case, the company will not be able to maintain the program.

RADARSAT and Canadian Foreign and Security Policy

The preceding discussion illustrates two important points. First, RADARSAT provides a very powerful but expensive tool that is increasingly finding new applications. This discussion has listed only a few of the uses that are now being employed. When RADARSAT-2 is launched, it will substantially improve this already outstanding capability.

Second, while RADARSAT's potential as a tool for the Canadian Government should be clear, it does not appear that the government realized it immediately. The Canadian Government considered RADARSAT in the context of national security only when the United States became concerned about the satellite's resolution ability. The government's primary focus is to place the overall program into the hands of private industry. If the Canadian Government had been willing to retain greater control of RADARSAT, then the issue of shuttle control would be more manageable. However, this would have required a willingness to accept the costs of the RADARSAT programs and to view them as a foreign and defence asset.

Successive Canadian Governments since the late 1960s have shown incredible reluctance to linking the use of its space assets to its security policy. This is a shortsighted policy that is hindering Canadian national interests. It is even more troubling when the Canadian Government's only effort to actually link its security policy to commercial satellite imagery occurred only at the insistence of the American Government. As RADARSAT's capabilities continue to improve, so will its applicability as an instrument to protect and enforce Canadian security. Hopefully, the traditional Canadian Government indifference to space will not blind it to a more vigorous future role.

Notes

1   The author would like to thank Shabnam Datta and James Keeley for their insightful comments in developing this chapter.
2   D.J. Goodspeed, *A History of the Defence Research Board of Canada* (Ottawa: Queen's Printer, 1958).
3   Andrew Godefry, 'Is the Sky Falling? Canada's Defence Space Programme at the Crossroads', *Canadian Military Journal* vol.1, 2000, p.54.
4   John Kirton, 'A Renewed Opportunity: The Role of Space in Canadian Security Policy', in David Dewitt and David Leyton-Brown (eds), *Canada's International Security Policy*, Scarborough: Prentice-Hall, 1995, pp.111–112.
5   Godefry, 54.
6   Science Council of Canada, *Report #1: A Space Program for Canada*, Ottawa: Queen's Printer, July 1967, p.2.
7   J.H. Chapman, P.A. Forsyth, P.A. Lapp and G.N. Patterson, *Upper Atmosphere and Space Programs in Canada, Special Study #1*, Science Secretariat Privy Council Office, Ottawa: Queen's Printer and Controller of Stationary, February 1967.
8   Chapman, p.101.
9   Ibid., pp.91–92.
10   Ibid., pp.109–110.
11   Science Council of Canada, *Report #1: A Space Program for Canada*.
12   Ibid., p.5.
13   Ibid., p.5.
14   Standing Committee on Research, Science and Technology on the Study of Canada's Space Program, *Canada's Space Program: A Voyage to the Future, Report of the Standing Committee on Research, Science and Technology on the Study of Canada's Space Program* (June 1987), p.2.
15   Kirton, p.114.
16   Godfrey, p.54.
17   Department of National Defence, *The CRAD Space R&D Program, Space R&D Planning Committee*, January 1993, quoted in Kirton, nt7.
18   Kirton, p.115.
19   Terrance Jamieson, *The Canadian Space Research Program -Science and Technology Division*, Research Branch, Library of Parliament BP-121E,Ottawa: Minister of Supply and Services Canada, February 15, 1985, p.3.
20   Standing Committee on Research, Science and Technology on the Study of Canada's Space Program, p.25.
21   Ibid., p.25.
22   Jamieson pp.3–4.
23   Kirton, p.115.
24   Ibid., p.116.
25   Ministry of State, Science and Technology Canada (MOSST), *MOSST Back-ground Paper: The Canadian Space Program Plan for 1982/83 – 1984/85* (Ottawa: Minister of Supply and Services, December 1981), p.2.
26   MOSST, pp.2–7; appendix II.
27   Ibid., p.5.
28   Kirton p.116.
29   Joel Sokolsky, 'The Bilateral Defence Relationship with the United States', in David Dewitt and David Leyton-Brown (eds), *Canada's International Security Policy*, Scarborough: Prentice-Hall, 1995, p.179.
30   House of Commons, Standing Committee on External Affairs and National Defence, NORAD 1986 – *Report of the Standing Committee on External Affairs and National*

Defence, February 14, 1986; and Senate, Special Committee of the Senate on National Defence, *Canada's Territorial Air Defence – Report of the Special Committee of the Senate on National Defence*, January 1985.

31 Canadian Space Agency, *Mission and Mandate,* March 16, 2000 [http://www.space.gc.ca/asc/eng/default.asp] (September 8, 2002).
32 Godefroy, p.56.
33 Department of National Defence, *A Canadian Military Space Strategy*, Ottawa: Chief of Review Services, July 1989.
34 Department of National Defence, *Space Policy*, Ottawa: DND, 1992.
35 Godefroy p.56.
36 David Pugliese, 'Forces Could Spend $684M on Spy Satellite', *National Post* March 23, 2002, p.5.
37 Ibid.
38 Canada Centre for Remote Sensing, *Radarsat Overview* April 10, 2001 [http://ccrs.nrcan.gc/ccrs/tekrd/radarsat/specs/radovere.html] (June 5, 2002).
39 RADARSAT-2, *RADARSAT Program Background* June 1, 1999 [http://mda.ca/radarsat-2/background/index.shtml] (June 5, 2002).
40 Natural Resource Canada, Canada Centre for Remote Sensing, CCRS Scientific Publications DataBase – A.L. VanKoughnett, R.K. Raney, and E. Langham, *The Surveillance Satellite Program and the Future of Microwave Remote Sensing, update* September 10, 2002, [http://www.ccrs.nrcan.gc.ca/ccrs/misc/publica_e.html] (September 8, 2002).
41 RADARSAT-2, *RADARSAT Program Background*.
42 SEASAT *1978 Overview* February 10, 1999.
[http://soutport.jpl.nasa.gov/scienceappa/seassat.html] (September 8, 2002).
43 Standing Committee on Research, Science and Technology on the Study of Canada's Space Program, p.9.
44 Ibid.
45 Ibid., p.15.
46 Canada Space Agency, *RADARSAT Background*, updated February 25, 1999, [http://www.space.gc.ca/csa_sectors/earth_environment/radarsat/radarsat_info/backgr/default.asp] (June 27, 2002).
47 United Nations Treaty Series 'Exchange of notes Constituting an agreement for cooperation in the RADARSAT Programme (with Memorandum of Understanding of February 1991). Washington November 12, 1991)' vol. 1883 I-32041, 1995.
48 Ibid.
49 Canada Space Agency, *RADARSAT Background*.
50 MacDonald, Dettwiler and Associates, RADARSAT-2 Home '1998 News', (up-dated May 30, 2002) [http://www.mda.ca/radarsat-2/news/1998.shtml] (June 5, 2002).
51 RADARSAT-2, 'MacDonald Dettwiler to Acquire RADARSAT International ', RADARSAT-2 *Press Release* February 15, 1999 [http://mda.ca/radarsat-2/new/pr19990215001.html] (June 5, 2002).
52 MacDonald, Dettwiler and Associates, RADARSAT-2 Home 'RADARSAT-2 Press Release', (December 18, 1998) [http://www.mda.ca/radarsat-2/news/pr1998121801.html] (June 5, 2002).
53 Ann Florini and Yahya Dehqanzada, 'No More Secrets? Policy Implications of Commercial Remote Sensing Satellites', Transparency and Civil Society – Working Paper Number 1, Carnegie Endowment for International Peace, July 1999, p.12.
54 Government of Canada, 'Canada and United States sign Agreement Concerning Operation of Commercial Remote Sensing Satellite Systems', New Release no.153 June 16, 2000.
55 Canada, 'Telecommunications – Agreement between the Government of Canada and the

Government Concerning the Operation of Commercial Remote Sensing Satellite Systems (with Annex)', Treaty Series 2000/14 June 16, 2000.

56 Boeing, 'Boeing Wins Contract to Launch RADARSAT-2 in 2003', *News Release* June 28, 2000, [http://www.boeing.com/news/releases/2000/news_release_000628h.html] (September 10, 2002).

57 MacDonald, Dettwiler and Associates, 'Canadian Space Agency and MDA begin Work on RADARSAT-3 Mission Feasibility', RADARSAT-2 Home, *News*, (February 20, 2001) [http://www.mda.ca/radarsat-2/news/pr2001022002.html] (June 4, 2002).

58 Canada Space Agency, *RADARSAT Background*, updated February 25, 1999, [http://www.space.gc.ca/csa_sectors/earth_environment/radarsat/radarsat_info/backgr/d efault.asp] (June 27, 2002).

59 Space Daily, 'Radarsat Cuts Through Cloud to see Arctic Ice', June 21, 2000 [http://www.spacedaily.com/news/arctic-00a.html] (August 23, 2002).

60 Canada Centre for Remote Sensing, Remote Sensing in Canada – on line, 'RADARSAT Mapping for Humanitarian Aid', vol. 25, 1997 (updated March 7, 2002), [http://www.ccrs.nrcan.gc.ca/ccrs/comvnts/rsic/2501/2501ap1_e.html] (May 12, 2002); Canada Centre for Remote Sensing, Remote Sensing in Canada – on line, 'Disaster Monitoring,',   vol.27,   1999   (updated   February   19,   1999), [http://www.ccrs.nrcan.gc.ca/ccrs/comvnts/rsic/2701/2701ap1_e.html] (May 12, 2002).

61 MacDonald, Dettwiler and Associate 'MDA Helps Ships Navigate Icy North Atlantic', *News Index* July 30, 2002 [http://www.mda.ca/news/pr/pr2002073001.html] (September 9, 2002).

62 RADARSAT-2, 'MDA Renews Contracts in Canada and Denmark for Safe Ship Navigation Through Icy Waters', *RADARSAT-2 Press Release* September 6, 2001 [http://mda.ca/radarsat-2/new/pr2001090602.html] (June 5, 2002).

63 Sharon Hobson, 'Canadian Navy Back in Arctic Waters', *Janes Defence Weekly*, August 28, 2002, p.7.

Conclusion

James F. Keeley and Rob Huebert

This volume addresses a variety of issues raised by the development of commercial satellite imagery. It has focused on two broad sets of issues in these chapters: first, the usefulness of CSI for peacekeeping and peacemaking operations; and second, the implications for Canada in its multiple roles as a producer of satellite imagery, a consumer, a state with a significant and traditional interest in peacekeeping and peacemaking and in the improvement of UN performance in peacekeeping and peacemaking, and both an ally of and a state technically dependent on the United States. These intertwine, since any Canadian response on peacekeeping and peacemaking issues would have implications for and would have to be compatible with its multiple roles. The continuing improvements in and the growing use of commercial satellite imagery are considerable, and only some of the possibilities have been touched on. These implications are even greater if satellite imagery is linked with other developments in computer, information, and communications technology.

The United Nations, Imagery and Peacekeeping

Canada has a traditional association with United Nations peacekeeping and peacemaking operations. This, together with an active Canadian presence in the commercial satellite imagery sector makes a focus on the peacekeeping and peacemaking uses of CSI a natural question, especially in light of both recent critiques of UN operations and Canadian and other proposals to improve UN peacekeeping and peacemaking. While the focus on UN peacekeeping and peacemaking may initially seem quite narrow – for all its considerable complexity and ramifications – it may also serve as an introduction for a wide range of other uses and issues. The imagery, the uses, the delivery systems, the technical, legal, organizational and cost issues that arise in the context of UN operations bear some resemblance to the sorts of questions that have arisen and will arise in a wider set of contexts, ranging from national and international disaster relief, to refugee management, to nuclear and other safeguarding or disarmament measures, to coalition operations involving states of differing levels of technical sophistication, to the application of CSI in the military operations of individual states. The claim here is not that these varied activities are all basically alike. It is, rather, that they are sufficiently alike that two additional consequences relevant to peacekeeping and peacemaking arise:

1   Problems, approaches and solutions in these other areas may have analogues in
     the peacekeeping and peacemaking area, just as problems, approaches and
     solutions in peacekeeping and peacemaking may have analogues in these other
     areas;
2   As practical steps are taken to exploit CSI in these other areas, its application
     should become less unusual, less exotic, and less likely to arouse the unease of
     states, and this might possibly smooth its application, in both practical and
     political terms, in the peacekeeping and peacemaking area.

Alex Morrison's chapter sets the stage for consideration here of imagery,
intelligence and peacekeeping; it notes both the desirability of and some of the
problems facing, the use of commercial satellite imagery by the UN, and the
larger issue of 'intelligence' in UN operations. Ulric Shannon's chapter also
plays a crucial role. It serves as a foil for many of the other chapters in this
volume, setting out a variety of concerns that must be addressed, above all in
peacekeeping and peacemaking applications, but which also can and would be
raised for other applications. To the degree that these problems can be addressed
in one context, the chances increase of their being addressed in others. To the
degree that the use of CSI becomes more acceptable in one context, the more
resistance to its uses in other contexts might be reduced. So, identifying and
responding to these concerns is both a practical and a political necessity. In
responding, however, certain lines of approach might seem advisable. Taken
together, these create not only a strategy of argumentation but also a research
agenda:

1   At a certain level, it is easy to treat satellite imagery as 'magic': as Arthur C.
     Clarke has remarked, 'any sufficiently advanced technology is indistinguishable
     from magic'. But even magic has its rules and its limits. The dangers of
     overselling CSI are considerable, and may lead not only to a sense of
     disappointment when the true complexities, costs and constraints are displayed,
     but also to an unwillingness to approach the use of CSI as above all a practical
     issue, posing problems which can be addressed on a practical level. To avoid
     overselling, therefore, the real limits and difficulties in applying CSI must be
     acknowledged squarely and then be addressed in terms of practical solutions.
     This necessity of demystifying satellite imagery does not arise for those
     technically versed in it, but it does arise for others.
2   Once addressed squarely, it may become apparent that some concerns are real,
     some concerns might be based on misapprehensions which can be corrected,
     and finally that some concerns may serve in whole or in part as surrogates for
     others. In particular, real, misapprehended and simply mistaken financial and
     technical concerns, and some raised almost 'off the cuff', may be surrogates for
     more fundamental political objections, whether to spending money or to giving
     especially an intergovernmental organization significantly more effective
     and/or more independent capabilities. Once the surrogates are addressed, these
     objections will remain and may prove fatal in their own right. Or, it may then
     be possible to address and resolve them, as well.

Shannon's chapter outlines some of the practical and political difficulties of using commercial satellite imagery in support of United Nations peacekeeping and peacemaking.

Cost, cost-effectiveness and trade-offs

The cost of an imagery capability of any sort for the United Nations will be an assured source of resistance to its acquisition. In connection with this, questions of cost-effectiveness will be raised. There will also be hopes for a trade-off: that the expenditures on such a capability could be offset by related savings elsewhere. Absent such a trade-off possibility, the prospect of an imagery capability will be much less attractive.[1] It is therefore of considerable importance to address these issues effectively, to separate the real from the misunderstood and the surrogate.

Costs for an imagery capability are often presented in terms of the cost of imagery alone. This, of course, is potentially misleading if variations in imagery costs are not noted, and insufficient if necessary services and capabilities are omitted. As shown, imagery costs may vary substantially, depending on the resolution of the image and on whether the needed information can be derived from archived imagery or if new imagery must be acquired. Different suppliers may charge different rates; these rates will themselves vary in addition depending on such factors – for new imagery – as the speed with which the imagery must be obtained by the user. A quote of a single cost per image as an illustration of costs is not sufficient to provide good guidance, though it would seem to provide a handy initial benchmark.

Additional considerations come into play. The issue is not simply what a single, representative, image might cost, but also the volume of imagery required per year. The possibilities of various contracting arrangements with suppliers must also be considered in this context. Further, if the case of a UN in-house analytical and interpretive capability is considered, the hardware, software and personnel must be considered. Here, the volume of imagery will play a part in dictating the likely size of an imagery unit. Fortunately, some estimates have been made for the case of an imagery capability to assist in monitoring the Comprehensive Test Ban Treaty, and there are estimates for an IAEA imagery unit. These are based on estimates of volume for certain kinds of imagery, and the requisite unit to handle the estimated volume.

In 1994, Nardon provided an estimate for the costs of an imagery unit to assist in monitoring the Comprehensive Test Ban.[2] Nardon estimated a need for 860 images per year, and used SPOT's rate of US$3,300 per image, to derive a total imagery cost of US$2,838,000 per year. Personnel costs for analysis for this many images were estimated at US$1,620,000 per year. Total costs were thus estimated at US$4,458,000 per year, not including indirect costs, equipment, administration and office space. The cost of acquiring the necessary equipment was estimated at US$375,000-550,000. All told, the cost was estimated as running at approximately US$6,500,000 per year. In that same year, Cleminson produced another set of estimates for imagery monitoring of the CTBT.[3] Working on the basis of 600 images per year, at US$3,200 per image, he thus estimated the annual imagery costs at US$1,920,000. Assuming operating costs of US$430,000 per year and personnel costs of US$1,578,000, and allowing a 30 per cent "increment," his total estimate of yearly costs was US$4,400,000. He did not estimate capital costs. In his cost-benefit analysis of a possible commercial satellite imagery unit for the IAEA, Andersson[4] provided three scenarios, at 121, 245 and 297 images per year. Assuming an ability to 'bundle' imagery and assuming also a discount as a "large and reliable customer", he provided three different estimates of yearly imagery acquisition costs, based on slightly different costs per image for the three scenarios: US$444,675, US$903,044 and US$ 1,031,481. (The average costs across the three scenarios would be US$3,616 per image.) He estimated the total yearly cost to the IAEA at US$840,000-1,700,000 depending on the scenario.

Clearly, estimates of both imagery volume and imagery price are significant factors in any serious cost estimation process, and imagery volume in turn drives estimates for the annual costs of hardware, software and personnel. Andersson further noted that:

> All these expectations of reduced prices for the Agency are highly dependent on ingenious negotiation with the suppliers of satellite imagery. We cannot emphasise enough the necessity of a resolute purchasing process.[5]

At the same time, the estimated cost of imagery could well be substantially lower than the US$3,200-3,701 suggested across these various studies. J.P. Paquette estimates current imagery costs at US$600-3,800 per image, with, of course, the lower-resolution LANDSAT imagery being the least expensive. Costs for the other satellites he reviews average out at roughly US$3,000 per image. If the cost of usable imagery were to fall significantly below that, the cost of imagery acquisition at least could fall by several hundred thousand dollars per year. If the cost of necessary equipment and software also falls, then that portion of overall costs would also be subject to downward pressures. Against this possibility, however, must be set Steve Adam's warning that the commoditization of imagery would depend on the development of significant numbers of satellites capable of producing similar imagery: price competition might then arise within groups of like products.

These estimates are at best hypothetical and merely illustrative. The central point of these estimates is that they suggest both the array of factors which must be taken into account, and that a capacity to handle even an apparently significant number of images per year would not on its face be prohibitive. The acquisition and use of commercial satellite imagery would not seem to be inherently outrageously expensive, at least in absolute terms. The next step for a serious cost analysis would be to examine further imagery acquisition costs, including by the types of imagery needed, and the likely volume of imagery required per year.

A further issue, found in both Adam's chapter and that by Al Hanks and Richard Gorecki, and noted explicitly by Andersson, is the terms on which a user might acquire imagery. Various possibilities exist here, with implications that, for some users, might go beyond pricing alone.[6] Another issue to consider, from a supply perspective, would be the possibility of using an image broker rather than contracting directly from an imagery provider. Other possibilities arise if, through the purchase of certain equipment, a field command can draw images directly from a satellite overhead, and then perform the necessary analysis and interpretation itself.[7]

Beyond that, a more political question looms: how much are states willing to pay for such a capacity? This is precisely where questions of cost-effectiveness and of trade-offs will come into play. There are, however, some crucial bases for both of these to be addressed, if they are to be other than general, ungrounded and possibly surrogate concerns. First, a sound, even if general, estimate of costs must be provided. As noted above merely quoting cost per image is completely unsatisfactory and inadequate in this regard. Second, common but possibly misleading twists in the usual presentation of cost-effectiveness and trade-offs must be confronted.

Cost-effectiveness is hard enough to estimate when costs are unclear. It is even harder when criteria for effectiveness are unspecified. Further, 'cost-effectiveness' is often a code word for cost-cutting, even though, logically, increased expenditures at the margin may sometimes buy a more than proportionate increase in effectiveness. It is not inconceivable that a stronger UN ability to plan and direct mission deployments, to discover and direct assistance to refugee populations, to devise and monitor buffer zones, and to oversee disarmament agreements, could save costs. It is even more conceivable that a UN more capable in these specific undertakings could be more effective in saving lives and in managing conflict situations and complex humanitarian operations – with savings that are human (including in the ranks of UN peacekeepers) and political as well as economic. First, however, arguments of cost-effectiveness must be disentangled from sub-texts of cost-cutting.

Trade-off arguments are seemingly linked to cost-effectiveness, with their explicit hope of offsetting increases in some expenditures through reductions elsewhere. Here, again, however, the phrasing of the issue may be also misleading. Trade-offs imply a zero-sum relationship between factors, but that relationship may be more complex. In the case of imagery, it implies that imagery is a perfect substitute for other resources, such as people on the ground: if imagery is a force-multiplier, the use of imagery must be justified in terms of permitting a reduction in ground forces. While it is true that imagery may be able to substitute for certain functions of people in the field, however, this overlooks the possibility that field forces perform functions which imagery cannot perform, or perform as well, and that imagery as a capability may find its more significant pay-off in interacting synergistically with, rather than merely as a substitute for, other capabilities. Cost-effective synergies – imagery permitting the more effective use of other capabilities – may be an alternative line of argument.

In the case of peacekeeping and peacemaking, nothing can match the physical presence of a UN force, as a sign and symbol of concern, as a conflict mediator even in small, daily frictions, as a controlling or calming presence, and as an interpositioning factor between two hostile forces. A pure trade-off argument ignores this and, if implemented, could jeopardize vital functions of a peacekeeping and peacemaking force. The argument also ignores the possibility that imagery could make UN field forces more effective in these various functions, increasing their capabilities and therefore potentially adding to the UN's ability to control and avoid the risks and costs of conflict.

Specific applications of commercial satellite imagery in peacekeeping and peacemaking operations

What of specific uses of commercial satellite imagery in particular kinds of UN peacekeeping and peacemaking operations? One likely possibility is that imagery needs could vary significantly depending on the phase and type of mission, as well as by specific tasks within a mission. For example, missions or tasks requiring high resolution imagery, or frequent imaging of a locale, would be more costly: not only because of the higher costs associated with higher resolution and the larger number of images, but also if a premium had to be paid to ensure securing the images in a timely manner. Certain kinds of buffer zone, disarmament or disaster monitoring tasks could present some combination of these requirements. Conversely, other uses might need only initial imaging, to establish basic features of terrain, infrastructure, population zones and the like. Some of these needs could possibly be satisfied by lower-resolution or even archived imagery, with reduced costs by comparison. Or, as suggested in the chapters, such lower-resolution imagery could itself be used to locate areas requiring further examination, so that a full scan at high resolution would not be needed.

While this question presents considerable scope for detailed, technical discussion, it may well be precisely the least debatable point. Satellite imagery, including imagery of lower resolution than that now currently available commercially through the IKONOS 1 m system, has long been available to states for their own purposes, including both intelligence in general terms and support to their forces. The Gulf War – in which commercial imagery as well as imagery derived from National Technical Means played a significant role – is now commonly regarded as a harbinger of the future. The chapters by MacLeod, and by Bourbonnière and Haeck note some of the near- or real-time possibilities for military use. The notion that, technically, these applications might be suitable for national militaries, and even by non-state agencies outside of UN peacekeeping and peacemaking, but are not suitable for this specific application seems hard to defend. The technical requirements for resolutions to perform various tasks are well known, and it would seem that many of these tasks can be carried out with resolutions over 1 m. There are real difficulties here in developing an adequate system to supply imagery and its products as needed, when needed and where needed, as the US discovered in the Gulf War. These, however, are auxiliary concerns, however significant: the basic utility of the imagery seems unimpeachable.

The approximate resolutions at which various surface features can be detected and generally identified will vary considerably, depending on the nature of the object. An apparently standard – or at least widely-cited – list[8] provides the following figures:

1   Surface terrain: 90 m for general identification, 4.5 m for more precise determination.
2   Urban areas: 60 m for detection, 30 m for general identification.
3   Ports and harbours: 30 m for detection, 15 m for general identification.
4   Railroad yards and shops: 15-30 m for detection, 15 m for general identification.

5   Coasts and landing beaches: 15-30 m for detection, 4.5 m for general identification.
6   Surface vessels: 7.5-15 m for detection, 4.5 m for general identification.
7   Roads: 6-9 m for detection, 6 m for general identification.
8   Airfield facilities: 6 m for detection, 4.5 m for general identification.
9   Bridges: 6 m for detection, 4.5 m for general identification.
10 Troop units, in bivouac or on road: 6 m for detection, 2 m for general identification.
11 Aircraft: 4.5 m for detection, 1.5 m for general identification.
12 Minefields: 3-9 m for detection, 6 m for general identification.
13 Communications: 3 m for detection, 1-1.5 m for general identification.

As the available resolution increases, still further information can be derived from the image.

Hall-Beyer notes that some surface features may be observed using even very low resolution imagery (250-1000 m). From Paquette's chapter, one might conclude that the LANDSAT series of satellites might be of some value down to possibly item 6 on the list, at least for detection. RADARSAT could be of use, in fine mode, down to item 7 or even beyond. SPOT would be of use, in panchromatic mode down to item 6. IRS-1 C/D, at 5 m panchromatic, could be of use down to item 10. The KVR-1000 would be of use to item 13 and below. IKONOS-2, at 1 m panchromatic and 4 m multispectral, would be of use over this range as well. This does not, however, account for additional factors, such as contrast, which could give additional information even for larger resolution images. Paquette argues that even the lower-resolution satellites he surveys could be of use for mapping, including of rail and road networks, identifying zones of destruction, some assessment of urban and agricultural areas, tracking large groups of refugees, and some change detection. As resolutions improve, their ability to perform these tasks correspondingly is also improved. The SPIN-2 series (including the KVR-1000 satellite) and IKONOS-2 would, of course, be able to provide much greater detail for these tasks, and IKONOS-2 in particular could be used to assess some military features, and infrastructure damage.

How might these varied capabilities be matched to mission tasks, types and phases? This could be, at first glance, a far more complex issue. Rehbein[9] suggests a fairly straightforward classification of operations, in terms of the potential utility of American intelligence assets:

1   Indications and early warning.
2   'Pre-deployment planning to select the location of UN field headquarters, access to major transportation routes, status of the belligerents' forces, terrain, etc.'
3   Security of UN forces.
4   Monitoring ceasefires and disengagement agreements, including 'shaming' those who cheat.
5   Withdrawal.

He notes the possible applications of commercial satellite imagery, but suggests significant limitations in their larger resolutions, affordability, UN force capabilities, and timeliness.[10]

Others have produced more detailed and complex studies of mission types or of UN tasks, but not necessarily oriented to intelligence issues. Diehl et al.[11] suggest an initial 12 categories:

1 Traditional peacekeeping and peacemaking, to separate combat-ants in a ceasefire through the deployment of troops.
2 Observation of ceasefires or humanitarian situations by a smaller number of personnel.
3 Collective enforcement to restore international peace and security.
4 Election supervision, including monitoring a ceasefire, disarmament and elections in internal war situations.
5 Humanitarian assistance during conflicts, including transporting and distributing relief supplies.
6 State- or nation-building, including restoring law and order, and reconstruction of infrastructure and administration.
7 Pacification, especially in the face of severe human rights abuses, by suppressing domestic disturbances.
8 Preventive deployment.
9 Arms control verification, including monitoring of troop withdrawals.
10 Protective services, including establishing safe areas.
11 Intervention in support of democracy, which may include overthrowing a government or providing support for it.
12 Sanctions enforcement.

They find, however, that these cluster into a smaller number of more general types: monitoring (types 2, 4 and 9), damage limitation (types 5 and 8), restoration of civil societies (types 6, 7, 10, and 11) and coercion (types 3 and 12), as well as ceasefire operations.[12] Johnson provides another cut at the problem, clustering the various tasks which peacekeeping and peacemaking missions might be called upon to perform.[13] This approach finds certain tasks recurring over a wide array of specific cases, such as:

1 Observing and reporting on developments.
2 Supplying military information and liaison.
3 Monitoring the activities of combatants or belligerents.
4 Monitoring conditions in a potential conflict area.
5 Assisting in conflict diffusion, stabilization and resolution.
6 Investigation of complaints and violations.

Almost all of these tasks involve information gathering.[14] Further the range of tasks surveyed tend to cluster. Four such clusters are the following:

1 Humanitarian relief operations, providing convoy escorts, monitoring refugee flows, conducting field operations.
2 Supervising the demilitarization of forces, assisting in troop withdrawals, encouraging the resumption of normal relations.
3 Supporting the development of civil authority, assisting in weapon collection

and confiscation, monitoring the withdrawal of forces, observing and report violations.

4   Stabilizing conflict, monitoring disengagement forces, assisting weapon collection and confiscation, and clearing mines.[15]

These various suggestions help to reduce lengthy lists of specific tasks to more generic undertakings, but clearly a more specific consideration of CSI capabilities and task requirements would be required to construct a detailed assessment of the needs-capabilities match. Initially, at least, it would seem that some significant undertakings could be met by the use of commercial satellite imagery, but these might vary in their demands for resolution, frequency of re-imaging and speed of delivery of a product.

Further refinement would direct us to consider both mission phase and the location of the user. Different needs arise for the planning and deployment phase as compared to the phase of force presence, for example, and potentially between the UN Headquarters and the field command headquarters. In the field, HUMINT (human intelligence) is the dominant useful mode, but this need not exclude imagery of various sorts for certain tasks. Key problems here would be not only the speed with which imagery could be acquired, analysed, interpreted and delivered to a user, but also the capability of that user to handle the resulting product. The development of transportable ground stations could ease a technological difficulty,[16] as could the development of more powerful software and more portable hardware, but if a field force did not have an integral imagery 'cell', it would still be dependent on the supply of products from elsewhere, with possible attendant delays and other difficulties.

While UN Headquarters could also have a need for high-resolution, frequent imagery for task performance during missions – particularly if the field unit depended on it for the resulting information – it might also have a substantial use for imagery for less-demanding tasks. Initial mapping and planning for a mission might be able to draw on lower-resolution imagery, and need it with less frequency.

System and Organization Issues

Assuming that, in rough terms, both the cost and the potential specific applications of commercial satellite imagery are not considered problematic, the more technical specifics of the system for their acquisition, analysis, delivery and use must still be addressed. The experience of the US in the Gulf War underlines the fact that these issues are by no means insignificant.

Arrangements for the acquisition of imagery could vary considerably, including the sort of arrangement detailed by Hanks and Gorecki for illustrative purposes, use of an imagery broker, or direct access by a field unit using a transportable station. This last also presents an alternative to the dependence of a theatre command on UN headquarters for imagery products and services, and thus moves us into the internal organization of the user, not only the nature of the supplier/user link. As pointed out in Keeley's chapter on the organization of the UN for imagery, various models could be applied, depending on what capabilities are available to UN headquarters and to field units. These could include variations on a 'leading nation' model, including one in which the whole question of a UN capability is bypassed in favour of specific states organizing their own imagery supplies, whether to UN headquarters in New York or to a field command. This possibility would, of course, continue the dependence of the UN on certain states, with the attendant political difficulties. It might also, however, address certain other political concerns of states currently possessing the technology.

Hanks and Gorecki, as well as Tao and Truong more indirectly, also raise significant technical questions of system capabilities. This is where we have to outline some of the system requirements for acquisition, analysis and delivery. In some cases, at least, the necessary hardware and software to support imagery and imagery product delivery, analysis and interpretation is becoming more readily available, and perhaps less dependent on a central service provider. Hall-Beyer's examination of the availability and use of low-resolution imagery suggests similar implications. The necessity of integrating commercial satellite imagery with modern computing and communications technology is underscored by this.

Tao and Truong's illustration of the content and organization of a GIS system for IAEA safeguarding demonstrates not only the technical possibilities of such modern systems but also their potential as information management and decision support tools. The Brahimi Report has noted the desirability of developing GIS applications to support peacekeeping and peacemaking. The Cartographic Section of the UN is already working towards this, as part of the larger project of constructing a UN geographic database.[17] Development of a stronger UN GIS capability makes sense as an adjunct to the best use of imagery, and development of at least some sort of imagery capability, whether through direct purchase or through arrangements with national suppliers, makes sense as an addition to a GIS capability. Once such a capability is developed, moreover, the basis exists for an in-house imagery unit of at least some sort, as an additional resource in the planning and management of peacekeeping and peacemaking operations.

Learning from and working with NGOs and other UN agencies

Various non-governmental organizations, and certain other United Nations agencies, have become interested in or have developed uses for, commercial satellite imagery for their own purposes. This provides a rich field for both co-operation and co-ordination on the one hand, and learning from their experience in creating a peacekeeping and peacemaking capability on the other.

There are a number of overlaps in information needs between aid and humanitarian agencies (including both NGOs and UN agencies) and the military side of peacekeeping and peacemaking operations. Assessing infrastructure, locating populations, assessing camp locations, examining environmental conditions, are among these areas.[18] Digital Elevation Models which can be used for humanitarian purposes may also have applications for peacekeeping and peacemaking, such as assessing visibility from various points and establishing locations for communications.[19] Other possible applications are obvious from the discussion above, and from the chapters by Paquette and Hall-Beyer.

This overlap in information needs could also generate some movement (though also some difficulties) in other areas of civil-military co-operation in complex operations. The co-ordination of civilian and military efforts in peacekeeping and peacemaking missions is increasingly recognized as both a vital area and one which needs work. Information-sharing is a significant aspect of both the problems and the potential for this co-operation and co-ordination. Overlapping needs is only one aspect of the possibilities here. Because nongovernmental organizations and other agencies may vary considerably in their technical sophistication and in their systems compatibilities, there are significant hurdles in devising common or at least compatible requirements and capabilities, and then in developing systems which can serve these. Some experience has been gained in this regard in the creation of a Geographic Information Support Team in Kosovo, among UN agencies and donors, to test the possible collaborative use of GIS. Imaging could be of value both in itself and as a base for such a shared system.[20] In overcoming the technical difficulties, several purposes could be served on a very practical level: closer integration among these various actors; development and testing at various levels of possible technical and organizational solutions; and dealing with the problem of co-ordinating among users of differing levels of technical sophistication and of differing system types. The problems faced by military and civilian organizations in dealing with each other in complex operations could be very like some of the problems internal to the military component, at least as far as the use of commercial satellite imagery is concerned.

Further important lessons might be learned by studying the use of commercial satellite imagery by other UN agencies, such as the High Commissioner for Refugees and the Food and Agriculture Organization. The UNHCR has a Geographic Information and Mapping Unit, and has been drawing on imagery (both aerial and satellite) for several years.[21] The FAO has developed and used the ARTEMIS (A[frica] Real Time Environmental Monitoring Information System), using satellite data, since 1988. It has developed contracts and agreements with SPOT and NASA, and has a system to provide data and products by electronic means to its headquarters, to the field and to researchers.[22]

Of particular importance in these various applications by other UN agencies is the simple fact that they are being developed and used. Although for many agencies the cost and the political and technical issues involved may be daunting,[23] it is notable that political obstacles which states can present to the use of such imagery seem to be getting overcome, in much the same way that use of commercial satellite imagery by the IAEA – in a much more sensitive area – seems to be going forward. Politically, technically and organizationally, the experiences of these other agencies, and the growing experience of civilian-military cooperation in complex operations, may be of value as a demonstration of possibilities, as a test-bed for modes of approach, and as a method of increasing state comfort with the use of commercial satellite imagery.

The political factor: The art of the acceptable

The technical, legal, organizational and financial issues to be resolved in obtaining a UN capability for the use of commercial satellite imagery in support of its peacekeeping and peacemaking operations cannot be dismissed. Yet the problems in these areas, once identified, can be worked through, though some compromises will be required. These are not insurmountable obstacles to the significant and regular use of commercial satellite imagery in UN peacekeeping and peacemaking operations. The ultimate controlling factors will be the political, ruling both the shape and the very feasibility of any imagery capacity in UN peacekeeping and peacemaking.

Addressing the political factor requires engagement on a number of fronts, and on a number of issues. Two apparently narrow questions which are sure to be raised concern legality and confidentiality. From Jakhu's chapter, it might be anticipated that no general legal obstacle would exist to the acquisition and use of commercial satellite imagery by an international organization. Indeed, the fact that other actors in the UN system are already making use of this imagery underlines that this is not likely to be a serious legal issue. It may, however, have serious political aspects, given the likelihood of a short psychological leap from commercial imagery to National Technical Means and from peacekeeping and peacemaking to 'military operations', and the historic UN allergy to 'intelligence'. Protections against misuse, however defined by sensitive states, would have to be built in. In any event, the fact that the same imagery could be readily available to the public would seem to make the matter moot. Confidentiality concerns might also benefit from an examination of how the problem is handled in other agencies, such as the International Atomic Energy Agency. Why would the IAEA be able to overcome these problems, yet the UN Secretariat – or at least the Department of Peacekeeping Operations – might not? The underlying question is basically political: for which purposes, and why, are states willing to tolerate an increase in the information capability of an international organization, and an increase in its organizational independence? Larger questions of UN staffing practices are also raised: here the real issues are the willingness of the Secretariat to institute proper personnel policies, and of member states to tolerate this where the proper functioning of the organization requires it. Again, this is not seen as being an insurmountable problem at the IAEA.

Yet this line of response itself indicates how readily the issues broaden. Even in technical and organizational terms, the implications spread widely and rapidly. Keeley argues, for example, that the question of an adequate system for CSI use connects quite directly to several broader issues of UN organization and capability – questions which are at the heart of the Brahimi Report. How the UN organizes itself, and organizes and manages peacekeeping and peacemaking missions, pose significant problems for peacekeeping and peacemaking operations. These problems, including not only staffing and management in UN headquarters but also participation and command organization in the field, could present serious obstacles to effective CSI use. The old systems engineer's adage – 'you can't change only one thing' – comes readily to mind.

At broader levels, the underlying issues are, first, the question of UN 'intelligence', and secondly, the ultimate issue of UN effectiveness. For the first, 'no intelligence in peacekeeping and peacemaking' is surely a peculiar principle, the acceptance of which in one sense itself lends to the double entendre. It is in any event a principle somewhat honoured in the breach in reality. If people wish to avoid the term, all well and good. Euphemisms are meant, after all, to ease discomfort even when their meanings are crystal clear. Politically sensible yet operationally adequate limitations on UN information-gathering and analytical capabilities might yet be possible. The most basic question, however, is exactly whether states are willing to accept a more effective UN. An independent UN CSI capability of any sort might be unacceptable to a wide range of states which fear the implications of information they cannot control, not least as it could contribute to a loss of control over the UN more generally.

In narrower terms, one might look for resistance to a UN CSI capability from two opposing groups: those who enjoy information dominance, and those who have feared it. This complicates any response, as it would seem that remedies acceptable to the one group would almost automatically appear threatening to the other. Those who have information dominance, based on superior space-imaging capabilities and other, associated, technologies, and who are coming to value information dominance as an increasingly central factor in military superiority, would be reluctant to see this advantage dissipated. Those who are the looked-upon, and who are as yet lagging in the ability to access and exploit the new imagery technology, might conversely fear being placed at an even greater disadvantage – a particular concern if they see themselves as likely either to be marginalized in the UN by the introduction of this capability or subject to the tender ministrations of a UN dominated by those capable of exploiting it.

Neither position, however, may quite do justice to the complexities presented by the growing availability of commercial satellite imagery, nor to the limits it could face. The lead that high-technology states might enjoy in the Revolution in Military Affairs – if this is indeed what we face – may be somewhat eroded by the diffusion of space-imaging and associated technologies, as well as by the spread of information technologies more generally, but it will not be completely threatened. The RMA touches on a wide array of technologies working in concert; satellite imagery is only one of these. Moreover, denial of a CSI capability to the UN will not appreciably slow the rate of diffusion. On the other hand, high-technology states, through regulatory means and international public or private consortia, may still be able to exercise some influence on terms of access and use, as Jakhu, Dvorkin and Clarke suggest.

For those who fear information dominance, the diffusion of CSI access, and to a lesser degree of the capabilities themselves, should be a mitigating factor: they themselves might anticipate being able to make greater use of it, making it thereby perhaps less mysterious and threatening. Over time, and indeed as other actors – states, firms, NGOs and other UN agencies – make increasing use of it, the aura of National Technical Means which affects thinking about CSI should dissipate at least to some degree, and make more rational assessments and responses possible. Rather than being an invitation to marginalization – which would seem to depend on a more vigorous Western engagement in the dirty end of peacekeeping and peacemaking than currently seems likely – participation in peacekeeping and peacemaking operations with a significant CSI component could be seen as an opportunity to increase their familiarity with this technology. Anticipating being the sensed in a UN intervention might still be a dampening consideration, but here also the diffusion of CSI capabilities plays a role: even if the UN as such is denied the necessary capabilities, individual states are not, and might still supply appropriate products and information to the UN or to at least some participants in UN operations. Again, denying the UN this capability does not seem to be a particularly effective response.

The most general response to these 'information dominance/dominated' fears is thus that denial of a CSI capacity to the UN neither really addresses the problem nor adequately takes into account the implications of the diffusion of technology. Denying the UN a capacity in peacekeeping and peacemaking will not stop its use by other actors – including other UN agencies – but will merely inflict a technological disadvantage on the organization on top of its other significant limitations in a crucial function. Given the possibility of the supply of at least some CSI-based information products to the UN, or to participants in UN operations, by some states, and the increased access to CSI by other, non-state, actors, the rationale for denial is hard to see.

If the fear is of increased UN independence as a consequence of such a capability, this also may be misplaced, or at least more complex than at first it seems. Even with some in-house capability to access and use CSI imagery and related products, the UN would still be subjected to significant limitations: it would not be an uncontrolled user. Nor, more generally, can the UN be seriously thought of as an actor which transcends its membership, the sovereign states of the world. But many absolutely or even relatively uncontrolled users do exist, and their numbers are growing daily. Is a controlled, regulated UN capacity to be preferred to UN incapacity in what could be an increasing free-for-all? The answer is not obviously no.

Canadian Interests and Commercial Satellite Imagery

What are the challenges faced by Canada as it attempts to adjust to the advantages and challenges of the commercial satellite imagery. Canada is a middle power that is technically advanced. However, its resources are not unlimited. Its geography is immense with much of its northern regions. It has played a pivotal role in the overseas UN peacekeeping and peacemaking deployments, while at the same time has increased its participation in coalition military actions overseas. At the same time, it has continually reduced the budget to its military. Of all the contradictions of Canadian foreign and defence policy in the 1990s, one of the most paradoxical is its development of its space policy and more specifically its policy towards the support of its domestic commercial satellite imagery industry and its use of its product.

Through its alliances in NATO and NORAD Canada has benefited from the security use of space since the end of the Second World War. Its commitment to deterrence was based on the existence of American military communication and surveillance satellites as well as the rockets used to support the American ICBM and SLBM fleets. However, successive Canadian governments have refused to acknowledge this dependency. Instead official Canadian space policy has been focused on the support of it commercial space industries and the development of niche market capabilities. This has resulted in the development of a highly sophisticated and capable industry in the area of CSI. However, it is the effectiveness of these commercial systems that now require the Canadian Government to develop a security policy regarding the use of CSI. The recently concluded RADARSAT-2 agreement with the United States has forced the Canadian government to give security consideration to how this imagery is to be used and who is able to purchase it. It is somewhat ironic that the original efforts of the earlier Canadian Government to decouple its space policy from security considerations have resulted in the creation of an industry that now requires precisely such thoughts.

It is clear that in terms of the potential use that CSI has for use as a tool for international security issues, be they with the United Nations or for national interests the time has arrived for a comprehensive reexamination of Canadian space policy. Such an examination must include the use and future development of CSI.

Notes

1   This was the pattern of concerns as well for the IAEA in its examination of the possible use of commercial satellite imagery.

2   Laurence Nardon, *Test Ban Verification Matters: Satellite* Detection. London: Verification Technology Information Centre, November 1994, pp.30–34.

3   F.R.Cleminson, 'The Application and Cost-Effectiveness of Overhead Imagery in Support of the Verification of a Comprehensive Test Ban'. In Steven Mataija (ed.), *Non-Proliferation and Multilateral Verification: The Comprehensive Test Ban Treaty* (CTBT). Toronto: Centre for International and Strategic Studies, York University, 1994, pp.102–103.

4   Christer Andersson, *IAEA Safeguards: Implementation Blueprint of Commercial Satellite Imagery, Ph. 2 Final Report. SKI Report 00:11*. Stockholm: Swedish Nuclear Power Inspectorate, January 2000, pp.71–90, 93.

5   Ibid., p.82.

6   See, e.g., Stephen T. Denker, 'Trust Me – I'll Deliver': Acquisition Approaches to Guarantee Commercial Companies Deliver Critical Space Products in Time of Crisis. Research Report, Air Command and Staff College, Air University, USAF, April 1998.

7   One such system is the Eagle Vision system (and later models) developed for the United States. It provides a capability for 'in-theater, real-time acquisition and processing of commercial satellite imagery into formats required by users.' It is air-transportable and compatible with a number of commercial remote sensing satellites. Yves Lafeuillade, 'A Multisatellite Transportable Station: An Invaluable Tool for Crisis Management', EURISY Conference on The Use of Satellites and Integrated Technologies for Humanitarian Purposes, Varese, Italy, September 19–20, 2000. http://demining.jrc.it/aris/events/eurisy/index.htm.

8   Vipin Gupta, 'New Satellite Images for Sale', *International Security*, Vol. 20, No. 1 (Summer 1995), p.109.

9   Robert E. Rehbein, 'Informing the Blue Helmets: The United States, UN Peacekeeping and peacemaking Operations, and the Role of Intelligence', *Martello Papers No. 16*, Kingston, Ont.: Centre for International Relations, Queen's University, 1996, pp.24–25.

10   Ibid., p.81.

11   Paul F. Diehl, Daniel Druckman and James Wall, 'International Peacekeeping and peacemaking and Conflict Resolution: A Taxonomic Analysis with Implications', *Journal of Conflict Resolution*, Vol. 42, 1998, pp.39–40.

12   Ibid., pp.45–46.

13   Thomas H. Johnson, 'The Task Structure of International Peace Operations', Paper presented at the 1998 Annual Meeting of the International Studies Association, Minneapolis.

14 Ibid., pp.28–29.
15 Ibid., p.29.
16 See note 7 above.
17 See the website for the United Nations Geographical Information Working Group, at http://www.un.org/Depts/Cartographic/ungis/ungis.htm.
18 Enviref, Progress Report No. 1, January-June 1999, pp.12–14. http://www.enviref.org. O.M. Johanessen, Ø. Dalen, T. Rost, E. Bjørg, G. Andersen and M. Babiker, 'ENVIREF: Environmental Monitoring of Refugee Camps Using High-Resolution Satellite Imagery', EURISY Conference on The Use of Satellites and Integrated Technologies for Humanitarian Purposes, Varese, Italy, September 19–20, 2000. http://demining.jrc.it/aris/events/eurisy/index.htm.
19 Carlos Ordoñez, 'Use of elevation data in humanitarian relief operations', *ENVIREF, Demonstration and Evaluation Workshop Report*, February 2001. http://www.enviref.org.
20 See the United States Institute of Peace 'Virtual Diplomacy' project, particularly the following: 'Taking It to the Next Level: Civilian-Military Co-operation in Complex Emergencies', http://www.usip.org/oc/vd/vdr/nextlevel.html; Col. Michael J.Dziedzic and Dr. William B. Wood, 'Kosovo Brief: Information Management Offers a New Opportunity for Cooperation between Civilian and Military Entities', http://www.usip.org/oc/vd/vdr/dziedzic-wood.html; United States Institute of Peace, 'Promoting an Information-Sharing Regime in Peace Support and Humanitarian Operations', http://www.usip.org/oc/vd/vdilpo-share/vdiplo-share.html.
21 Abraham Abraham, 'Welcoming Remarks for ENVIREF demonstration-workshop', *ENVIREF, Demonstration and Evaluation Workshop Report*, February 2001. http://www.enviref.org.
22 Jelle U. Hielkema, 'FAO Spatial Information Applications for Early Warning for Food Security: The ARTEMIS System', EURISY Conference on The Use of Satellites and Integrated Technologies for Humanitarian Purposes, Varese, Italy, September 19-20, 2000. http://demining.jrc.it/aris/events/eurisy/index.htm.
23 E. Bjørgo, 'Digital Imaging in Global Disaster Information', *Bulletin of the American Society for Information Science*, Vol. 26, No. 1 (October/November 1999), http://www.asis.org/Bulletin/Oct-99/bjorgo.html. François Grunewald, 'From Airborne Images to Ground-Truthing in Turbulent Times: Potentials, Myths and Dangers of New Satellite Technologies from the NGO Perspective', EURISY Conference on The Use of Satellites and Integrated Technologies for Humanitarian Purposes, Varese, Italy, September 19–20, 2000. http://demining.jrc.it/aris/events/eurisy/index.htm. Bjørgo reports that an arrangement has been reached between SPOT and some UN agencies which results in significantly reduced costs.

Bibliography

Abraham, A. (2001), 'Welcoming Remarks for ENVIREF demonstration-workshop', *ENVIREF, Demonstration and Evaluation Workshop Report*, February http://www.enviref.org.

Adams, T.R. (1968), 'The Outer Space Treaty: An Interpretation in Light of the No-Sovereignty Provision', *Harvard International Law Journal*, vol. 9.

'Address by Dr Helmut Kohl', *European Space Agency Bulletin*, no. 58, May 1989.

Agreement between the United States National Oceanic and Atmospheric Administration and the European Organisation for the Exploration of Meteorological Satellites on an Initial Joint Polar-Orbiting Operational Satellite System, signed November 19, 1998.

Alberts, D.D. and Hayes, R.E. (1995), *Command Arrangements for Peace Operations*, National Defense University Press, Washington, D.C.

Almond, H.H. (1991), 'An Assessment of Economic Warfare: Developments from the Persian Gulf', *Virginia Journal of International Law*, vol. 31.

Andersson, C. (2000), 'Ph. 2 Final Report: IAEA Safeguards: Implementation Blueprint of Commercial Satellite Imagery', *SKI Report 00:11*, Swedish Nuclear Power Inspectorate, Stockholm, January.

Anselmo, J.C. (1997), 'Commercial Satellites Zoom In on Military Imagery Monopoly', *Aviation Week & Space Technology*, September 22.

Anselmo, J.C. (1999), 'Hamre: Export Delays Hurting US Alliances', *Aviation Week & Space Technology*, November 8.

Anselmo, J.C. (2000), 'Shutter Controls : How Far Will Uncle Sam Go ?', *Aviation Week & Space Technology*, January 31.

'Ariane Sends French Spysats Into Orbit', http://www.spacedaily.com/spacecast/news/ariane-99x.html.

Assembly of the Western European Union, Technology and Aerospace Committee (1999), *Space Systems for Europe : Observation, Communications and Navigation Satellites – Reply to the Annual Report of the Council. Document No. 1643*, May 18.

Baines, P.J. (1997) 'Spaceborne Imagery: A Universal, Effective, and Cost-Efficient Tool for Ongoing Monitoring and Verification,' in J.M. Beier and S. Mataija (eds), *Cyberspace and Outer Space: Transitional Challenges for Multilateral Verification in the 21st Century*, Centre for International and Strategic Studies, York University, Toronto.

Banner, A.V. and McMullan, A.G. (1992), 'Commercial Satellite Imagery for UNSCOM', in S. Mataija and J.M. Beier (eds), *Multilateral Verification in the Post-Gulf Environment: Learning from the UNSCOM Experience*, Centre for International and Strategic Studies, York University, Toronto.

Bates, J. (2000), 'Data Delivery Drives Remote Sensing Industry', *Space News*, December 30.

Bates, J. (2000), 'GM Officials Consider Sale of Hughes', *Space News*, October 23.

Bates, J. (2000), 'Imaging Craft of Limited Utility, NIMA Chief Says', *Space News*, September 25.

Bates, J. (2000), 'Kodak Aggressively Chasing New Market in Remote Sensing', *Space News*. August 28.

Bates, J. (2000), 'NOAA Lifts Cap on Foreign Investment in Satellite Imaging', *Space News*, August 14.

Bates, J. (2000), 'U.S. Remote-Sensing Controls Worry News Agencies', *Space News*, March 27.

Bennett, (1988), 'A Linguistic Critique of the Definition of Aggression', *German Yearbook of International Law*, vol. 31.

Bekdil, B.E. and Enginsoy, U. (2000), 'U.S. Satellite Operator Offers Imagery to Turkey', *Space News*. September 11.

Bender, B. (1998), 'DoD to make use of commercial satellite images', *Jane's Defence Weekly*, November 11.

Berdal, M.R. (1993) 'Whither UN Peacekeeping?' *Adelphi Papers No. 281*.

Berner, S. (1996), 'Proliferation of Satellite Imaging Capabilities: Developments and Implications" in H. Sokolski, *Fighting Proliferation*, Air University Press, Maxwell Air Force Base, AL. http://www.fas.org/irp/threat/fp/index.html.

Berry, R. and Croner, D.L. (1998), 'The Global Relevance of Space: Civil, Commercial and Military', 1998 National Space Symposium, Colorado Springs, CO.

Billingslea, R.E., Domsalla, M.R. and Payne, B.C. (1999), *The National Reconnaissance Office: A Strategy for Addressing the Commercialisation of Satellite Imagery*, John F. Kennedy School of Government, Harvard University, Cambridge, MA.

Bjorgo, E. (1999), 'Digital Imagery in Global Disaster Information', *Bulletin of the American Society for Information Science*, vol. 26, http://www.asis.org/Bulletin/Oct-99/bjorgo.html.

Bjorgo, E. (1999), 'Very High Resolution Satellites: A New Source of Information in Humanitarian Relief Operations', *Bulletin of the American Society for Information Science*, vol. 26, http://www.asis.org/Bulletin/Oct-99/bjorgo.html.

Blac, J.T. (1999), 'Commercial Satellites: Future Threats or Allies?' *Naval War College Review*, Winter. http://www.wc.navy.mil/press/Review/1999/winter/art5-w99.htm.

Black, Ian (2000), 'Serb Genocide Trial Starts in the Hague', *The Guardian*, March 14.

Boeing (2000), 'Boeing Wins Contract to Launch RADARSAT-2 in 2003', *News Release* June 28, http://www.boeing.com/news/releases/2000/news_release_000628h.html.

Bogden, P. and Dorn, W. (1991), *Controlling the Global Arms Threat*, The Canadian Centre for Arms Control and Disarmament, Toronto.

Bonner, R. (1999), 'War Crimes Panel Finds Croat Army "Cleansed" Serbs'. *New York Times*, March 21.

'Bosnian Serb Accused of Genocide'. *BBC News Online*, March 13, 2000. http://news.bbc.co.uk/hi/english/world/europe/newsid_676000/676297.stm.

Bourbonnière, M. and Haeck, L. (2001), 'Canada's Remote Sensing Program and Policies', in J.C. Baker, K.M. O'Connell and R.A. Williamson (eds.), *Commercial Observation Satellites: At the Leading Edge of Global Transparency*, RAND, Santa Monica, California.

Boutros-Ghali, B. (1992), *An Agenda for Peace: Preventive Diplomacy, Peacemaking and Peace-keeping*, United Nations, New York.

Boyd, H.A. (1996), *Joint Intelligence in Support of Peace Operations*, Naval War College, Rhode Island, June 14.

Broad, W.J. (1997), 'Commercial Use of Spy Satellites to Begin; Private Ventures Hope for Profits', *New York Times*, February 1997.

Brown-John, C.L. (1978), 'The 1974 Definition of "Aggression": A Query', *Canadian Yearbook of International Law*, vol. 15.

Brownlie, I. (1963), *International Law and the Use of Force by States*, Clarendon Press, Oxford.

Brownlie, I. (1998), *Principles of Public International Law*. Clarendon Press, New York.

Burrows, William E. (1998), *This New Ocean: The Story of the First Space Age*, New York: Random House.

Bush, G. (1992), 'Address by the President of the United States of America to the 47th Session of the United Nations General Assembly', *USUN Press Release* 84 (92), September 21.

Campbell, J.B. (1996), *Introduction to Remote Sensing*, The Guilford Press, New York.

Canada (1995), *Towards a Rapid Reaction Capability for the United Nations*. September.

Canada (2000), 'Canada and United States sign Agreement Concerning Operation of Commercial Remote Sensing Satellite Systems', *News Release no. 153*, June 16.

Canada (2000), 'Telecommunications – Agreement between the Government of Canada and the Government Concerning the Operation of Commercial Remote Sensing Satellite Systems (with Annex)', *Treaty Series* 2000/14 June 16.

Canada, Atomic Energy Control Board (1998), *Annual Report 1997-1998*. Ottawa.

Canada Centre for Remote Sensing (2001), *Radarsat Overview* April 10, http://ccrs.nrcan.gc/ccrs/tekrd/radarsat/specs/radovere.html.

Canada, Department of External Affairs (n.d.), 'PAXSAT Concept: The Application of Space-based Remote Sensing for Arms Control Verification', *Verification Brochure, no. 2*, Department of External Affairs, Ottawa.

Canada, Department of Foreign Affairs and International Trade (1998), *Security-Related Applications of Commercial Remote Sensing Satellites: A Bibliography, 1955-1997*.

Canada, Department of Foreign Affairs and International Trade (1999), 'Canada To Control Imaging Satellites', *News Release no. 134*, Ottawa. June 9.

Canada, Department of Foreign Affairs and International Trade (2000), 'Canada and Norway to Promote Increased Capacity for Rapid Reaction for UN Peacekeeping Missions,' *News Release no. 102*, Ottawa.

Canada, Department of Foreign Affairs and International Trade (2000), 'Canada and United States Sign Agreement Concerning Operation of Commercial Remote Sensing Satellite Systems', *News Release no. 153*, Ottawa, June 16.

Canada, Department of National Defence (1989), *A Canadian Military Space Strategy*, Ottawa: Chief of Review Services, July.

Canada, Department of National Defence (1992), *Space Policy*, Ottawa: DND.

Canada, Department of National Defence, Space R&D Planning Committee (1993), *The CRAD Space R&D Program*, January.

Canada, Department of National Defence (2000), *Croatia Board of Inquiry: Final Report*, Ottawa. http://www.dnd.ca/boi/engraph/report_e.asp.

Canada, Department of National Defence, Army Lessons Learned Centre (1996), 'Operations in the Former Republic of Yugoslavia', *Despatches*, vol. 4, No. 1.

Canada, Natural Resources Canada, Canada Centre for Remote Sensing (2002), CCRS Scientific Publications DataBase – VanKoughnett A. L. , Raney R. K., Langham E. *The Surveillance Satellite Program and the Future of Microwave Remote Sensing, update* September 10, http://www.ccrs.nrcan.gc.ca/ccrs/misc/publica_e.html.

Canada, Parliament, House of Commons, Standing Committee on External Affairs and National Defence (1986), *NORAD 1986 – Report of the Standing Committee on External Affairs and National Defence*, February 14.

Canada, Parliament, House of Commons, Standing Committee on Research, Science and Technology on the Study of Canada's Space Program (1987), *Canada's Space Program: A Voyage to the Future: Report of the Standing Committee on Research, Science and Technology on the Study of Canada's Space Program*, June.

Canada, Parliament, Senate, Special Committee of the Senate on National Defence (1985), *Canada's Territorial Air Defence – Report of the Special Committee of the Senate on National Defence*, January.

Canada, Ministry of State, Science and Technology Canada (MOSST) (1981), *MOSST Background Paper: The Canadian Space Program Plan for 1982/83 – 1984/85*, Ottawa: Minister of Supply and Services, December.

Canada Space Agency (1999), *RADARSAT Background*, updated February 25, http://www.space.gc.ca/csa_sectors/earth_environment/radarsat/radarsat_info/backgr/default.asp.

Canada Centre for Remote Sensing, 'Fundamentals of Remote Sensing – Tutorial'. http://www.ccrs.nrcan.gc.ca/ccrs/eduref/tutorial/indexe.html.

Canada Centre for Remote Sensing (1997), 'RADARSAT Mapping for Humanitarian Aid', *Remote Sensing in Canada – on line*, vol. 25, April. http://www.ccrs.nrcan.gc.ca/ccrs/comvnts/rsic/2501/2501ap1_e.html.

Canada Centre for Remote Sensing (1999), 'Disaster Monitoring', *Remote Sensing in Canada – on line*, vol. 27, February. http://www.ccrs.nrcan.gc.ca/ccrs/comvnts/rsic/2701/2701ap1_e.html.

Canadian Space Agency (2000), *Global Space Sector Market Trends and Drivers: Year 2000 Edition*, Montreal: Canadian Space Agency.

Chapman, J.H., P.A. Forsyth, P.A., Lapp, P.A., and Patterson, G.N. (1967), *Upper Atmosphere and Space Programs in Canada, Special Study #1*, Science Secretariat Privy Council Office, Ottawa: Queen's Printer and Controller of Stationary, February.

Chesapeake Analytics, Inc. (2000), 'Ecommerce in Remote Sensing', Draft Report, October.

Chesapeake Analytics, Inc. 'Market Intelligence Brief: Geospatial Image Data Management Systems' Rev. 10/00.

Christol, C.Q. (1988), 'The 1986 Remote Sensing Principles: Emerging or Existing Law?' *Proceedings of the Thirtieth Colloquium on the Law of Outer Space, 1987*, International Institute of Space Law of the International Astronautical Federation, American Institute of Aeronautics and Astronautics, Washington, D.C.

Cleminson, F.R. (1994), 'The Application and Cost-Effectiveness of Overhead Imagery in Support of the Verification of a Comprehensive Test Ban'. In Steven Mataija (ed.), *Non-Proliferation and Multilateral Verification: The Comprehensive Test Ban Treaty (CTBT)*. Toronto: Centre for International and Strategic Studies, York University.

Clinton, W.J. (2000), 'Remarks to the Security Council', Office of the Press Secretary, September 7. http://www.state.gov/www/regions/africa.

Cohen, W.S. (1999), 'Remarks to the Opening Ceremonies of the National Space Symposium', Colorado Springs, CO. April 5. http://www.defenselink.mil/speeches/1999/s199990405-secdef.html.

Coia, R.E. (1995), 'A Critical Analysis of the I MEF Intelligence Performance in the 1991 Persian Gulf War', written in fulfillment of a requirement for the Marine Corps Command and Staff College. May 22. http://www.fas.org/irp/eprint/coia.htm.

Collins, D.B. (1991), 'Military Intelligence in Low-Intensity Conflict', *Military Intelligence*, July-September.

Commentary, 'Losing Control', *Space News*, March 20, 2000.

Convention on International Civil Aviation, signed December 7, 1944.

Copple, J.R. (1998), Comments on Proposed Draft Commercial Space Act of 1997, S.1473, submitted to the Senate Commerce Committee on Science, Technology and Space. February 27.

Cox, D. and Legault, A. (eds) (1995), *UN Rapid Reaction Capabilities: Requirements and Prospects*, The Canadian Peacekeeping Press, Clementsport, N.S.

Davidson, R. (1998), *UN Reform – Can It be the Answer to Intelligence Support to UN Peacekeeping Operations?* U.S. Army War College, Carlisle Barracks, Penn.

Day, D.A., Logsdon, J.M. and Latell, B. (eds) (1998), *Eye in the Sky: The Story of the Corona Spy Satellites*, Smithsonian Institution Press, Washington, DC.

'Declaration of the First Meeting of Equatorial Countries', in N. Jasentuliyana and R.S.L. Lee (eds) (1979), *Manual on Space Law*, vol. II.

Dehqanzada, Y.A. and Florini, A.M. (2000), *Secrets For Sale: How Commercial Satellite Imagery Will Change the World*, Carnegie Endowment for International Peace Washington, DC.

Denker, Stephen T. (1998), 'Trust Me – I'll Deliver': *Acquisition Approaches to Guarantee Commercial Companies Deliver Critical Space Products in Time of Crisis*. Research Report, Air Command and Staff College, Air University, USAF, April.

de Santis, H. (1989), 'Commercial Observation Satellites and their Military Implications: A Speculative Assessment', *The Washington Quarterly*, vol. 12.

DeSelding, P.B. (1999), 'Israel Approves Sale of Images From Spy Satellite', *Space News*, June 28.

DeSelding, P.B. (1999), 'US Export Rules Frustrate Germans', *Space News*, July 5.

DeSelding, P.B. (2000), 'Alenia Wins Radarsat 2 Contract', *Space News*, January 10.

Diamond, J.M. (2001) 'Re-examining Problems and Prospects in U.S. Imagery Intelligence', *International Journal of Intelligence and Counterintelligence*, vol. 14.

Dickinson, E.D. (1920), *The Equality of States in International Law*. Arno Press, New York.

Diehl, Paul F., Druckman, Daniel, and James Wall, James (1998), 'International Peacekeeping and peacemaking and Conflict Resolution: A Taxonomic Analysis with Implications', *Journal of Conflict Resolution*, Vol. 42.

Doll, W.J. and Metz, S. (1993), *The Army and Multinational Peace Operations: Problems and Solutions, Report of a Roundtable sponsored by the Strategic Studies Institute of the U.S. Army War College and the U.S. Army Peacekeeping Institute*, Carlisle Barracks, Pennsylvania, November 29.

Dorn, W. 'Keeping Tabs on a Troubled World: UN Information Gathering to Preserve Peace'. http://www.pgs.ca/woc/wdorn/wdsecdial.htm.

Dorn, W. (1990), *The Case for a United Nations Verification Agency: Disarmament under Effective International Control, Working Paper 26*, Canadian Institute for International Peace and Security, Ottawa, July.

Dorn, W. (1999), 'The Cloak and the Blue Beret: Limitations on Intelligence in UN Peacekeeping', *International Journal of Intelligence and Counterintelligence*, vol. 12.

Dorn, W. and D. Bell (1995), 'Intelligence and Peacekeeping: The UN Operation in the Congo 1960-1964'. *International Peacekeeping*, Vol. 2. http://www.ryerson.ca/~woc/wdorn/wdcongo.htm.

Dutchak, K. (n.d.), 'Alberta Access Update Program Using IRS 5.8m Pan Data', *22nd Annual Canadian Remote Sensing Symposium Proceedings*.

Dziedzic, Col. M.J. and Wood, Dr. W.B. 'Kosovo Brief: Information Management Offers a New Opportunity for Cooperation between Civilian and Military Entities', United States Institute of Peace 'Virtual Diplomacy Project', http://www.usip.org/oc/vd/vdr/dziedzic-wood.html.

Eddington, P. (2000), 'Orbital Snooping: Welcome to Amateur Hour', *Space News*, May 22.

Edwards. (1992), 'The Iraqi oil "weapon" in the 1991 Gulf war: a Law of Armed Conflict Analysis', *Naval Law Review*, vol. 40.

Enviref (1999), *Progress Report No. 1*, January-June, http://www.enviref.org.

Environmental Remote Sensing Center (2000), 'Earth Observation Satellites Future', Madison: University of Wisconsin, http://www.ersc.wisc.edu/ersc/Resources/EOSF.html.

Fair, J.E. and Parks, L. (1998), 'Inspecting African Bodies: Television News Coverage and Satellite Imaging of Rwandan Refugees', paper presented at Sixth Annual African Studies Consortium Workshop, October 2. http://www.sas.upenn.edu/African_Studies/Workshop/joelisa98.html.

Federation of American Scientists, 'A Response to Pat Eddington's 'Orbital Snooping: Welcome to Amateur Hour', http://www.fas.org/eye/00052-sn-r.htm.

Fergusson, J. (1988), 'A Mile Wide and an Inch Deep: Multilateralism and the Command and Control of Multinational Forces in Peace Operations', Multilateral Institutions and Global Security, *Working Paper no. 8*, Centre for International and Security Studies, York University, Toronto. June.

Ferster, W. (1997), 'NIMA Sets Sights on Commercial Imagery', *Space News*. June 30.

Ferster, W. (1999), 'U.S. to Buy Private Imagery for Intelligence', *Space News*. April 12.

Fitzmaurice, G. (1957), 'The General Principles of International Law Considered from the Standpoint of the Rule of Law'. *Recueil des cours*, vol. 92.

Flemming, S.B. (1992), *Organizational and Military Impacts of High-Tech Surveillance and Detection Systems for UN Peacekeeping, Project Report 535*, Operational Research and Analysis Establishment, Department of National Defence, Ottawa.

Florini, A.M. (1988), 'The Opening Skies: Third-Party Imaging and U.S. Security', *International Security*, vol. 13.

Florini, A.M. and Dehqandzada, Y. (1999), 'Commercial Satellite Imagery Comes of Age', *Issues in Science and Technology Online*, Fall. http://www.nap.edu/issues/16.1/florini.htm.

Florini, A.M. and Dehqanzada, Y.A. (1999), 'No More Secrets? Policy Implications of Commercial Remote Sensing Satellites', *Carnegie Endowment Working Paper #1*, Carnegie Endowment for International Peace, Washington, D.C.

Fong, G.R. (2000), 'ARPA Does Windows: The Defense Underpinning of the PC Revolution', presentation given at the 41st Annual Convention of the International Studies Association, Los Angeles, CA.

Foster, B. (2000), 'REMSAT Revolutionizes Emergency Management', *Earth Observation Magazine*. January. http://www.eomonline.com.

'France begins work on Helios reconnaissance satellite', *Aerospace Daily*, vol. 141, no. 34, February 20, 1987.

Gabrynowicz, J.I. (2000), 'Expanding Global Remote Sensing Services', in *Proceedings of the Workshop on Space Law in the Twenty-First Century*, International Institute of Space Law with the UN Office for Outer Space Affairs.

Gallegos, F. (1996), *After the Gulf War: Balancing Spacepower's Development*, Air University, Maxwell Air Force Base, AL.

Gansler, J. (1989), *The Defense Industry*, Sixth Edition Massachusetts Institute of Technology Press, Cambridge, MA.

Gansler, J. (1996), *Defense Conversion: Transforming the Arsenal of Democracy*,: Massachusetts Institute of Technology Press, Cambridge, MA.

Garvey, J.I. (1977), 'The U.N. Definition of "Aggression": Law and Illusion in the Context of Collective Security', *Virginia Journal of International Law*, vol. 17.

Gaudrat, P. and Tuinder, H.P. (1997), 'The Legal Status of Remote Sensing: Issues of Access and Distribution', in G. Lafferanderie and D. Crowther (eds.), *Outlook on Space Law over the Next 30 Years*.

Gertz, Bill (2001), '12-Hour Glitch on Spy Satellite Causes Intelligence Gap', *The Washington Times*, July 26.

Giroux, D. (n.d.) *RADARSAT Background Mission Effects of Hurricane Mitch in Honduras*, Canadian Space Agency Report.

Gliksman, A. (ed.) (1998), *Meeting the Challenge of International Peace Operations: Assessing the Contribution of Technology*, Center for Global Security Research, Lawrence Livermore National Laboratory, Livermore, California, June.

Godefry, A. (2000), 'Is the Sky Falling? Canada's Defence Space Programme at the Crossroads', *Canadian Military Journal* vol.1.

Goedhuis, D. (1960), 'The Question of Freedom of Innocent Passage of the Space Vehicle of One State Through the Space Above the Territory of Another State which is not Outer Space', Colloquium on the Law of Outer Space.

Goldman, N.C. (1992), *Space Policy: An Introduction*, Iowa State University Press, Ames, IA.

Goodspeed, D.J. (1958), *A History of the Defence Research Board of Canada*, Ottawa: Queen's Printer.

Gorove, Stephan (1991), *Developments in Space Law : Issues and Policies*, Utrecht Studies in Air and Space Law, vol. 10.

Gourevitch, P. (1998), *We Wish to Inform You that Tomorrow We Will be Killed with our Families: Stories from Rwanda*, Picador, New York.

Gramer, J.K. (1996), 'Operation JOINT ENDEAVOR: Combined Joint Intelligence in Peace Enforcement Operations', *Military Intelligence Professional Bulletin*, no. 4. http://www.fas.org/irp/agency/army/tradoc/usaic/mipb/1996-4/gramer.htm.

Grau, L.W. (1997), 'Bashing the Laser Range Finder with a Rock', *Military Review*, May-June. http://call.army.mil/call/fmso/fmso.pubs/.

Gruber, D. (2000), 'Computer Networks and Information Warfare, Implications for Military Operations', *Occasional paper no. 17*, Center for Strategy and Technology, Air War College, July.

Grundhauser, L.K. (1998), 'Sentinels Rising: Commercial High Resolution Satellite Imagery and Its Implications for US National Security', *Airpower Journal*, Winter. http://www.usafa.af.mil/inss.

Grunewald, François (2000), 'From Airborne Images to Ground-Truthing in Turbulent Times: Potentials, Myths and Dangers of New Satellite Technologies from the NGO Perspective', EURISY Conference on The Use of Satellites and Integrated Technologies for Humanitarian Purposes, Varese, Italy, September 19-20. http://demining.jrc.it/aris/events/eurisy/index.htm.

Gupta, V. (1994), *New Satellite Images for Sale: The Opportunities and Risks Ahead. Report No. UCRL-JC-118140*. Livermore, CA.: Lawrence Livermore National Laboratories, September 28.

Gupta, V. (1995), 'New Satellite Images for Sale', *International Security*, vol. 20.

Gupta, V. and Bernstein, A. (1999), *Keeping an Eye on the Islands: Remote Monitoring in the South China Sea*, Sandia National Laboratories, May. http://gwis.circ.gwu.edu/~spi/title.htm.

Gupta, V. and Pabian, F. (1996), *Investigating the Allegations of Indian Nuclear Test Preparations in the Rajasthan Desert: A CTB Verification Exercise Using Commercial Satellite Imagery*, Sandia National Laboratories, July. http://www.ca.sandia.gov/casite/gupta/index.htm.

Gupta, V. and Harris, G. (1999), *Detecting Massed Troops with the French SPOT Satellites: A Feasibility Study for Cooperative Monitoring*, Sandia National Laboratories. http://www.cmc.sandia.gov/issues/papers/gupta2/index.html.

Hall, K. (1998), 'Remarks to the National Network of Electro-Optical Manufacturing Technologies Conference'. February 9. http://www.nro.gov/speeches/Hall9802.html.

Haley, A.G. (1963), *Space Law and Government*.

Hanley, C. (2000), 'Regulating Commercial Remote Sensing Satellites Over Israel: A Black Hole in the Open Skies Doctrine?' *Administrative Law Review*, vol. 52.

Hartman, R. (1997), *Focus on GIS Component Software: Featuring ESRI Map Objects*, Onward Press, Santa Fe, New Mexico.

Hazlegrove, A.P. (2000), 'Desert Storm Time-Sensitive Surface Targeting: A Successful Failure or a Failed Success?' *Defense Analysis*, vol. 16.

Hillen, J. (1988), *Blue Helmets: The Strategy of UN Military Operations*, Brassey's, Washington.

Hobson, S. (2002), 'Canadian Navy Back in Arctic Waters', *Jane's Defence Weekly*, August 28.

Iannotta, B. (2000), 'Landsat 7 Satellite Maintains Resolution Quality', *Space News*. August 7.

Ianotta, B. (2000), 'Several Firms Promote Global Distribution of Landsat 7 Data', *Space News*. August 7.

Iannotta, B. (2000), 'Remote-Sensing System to Help Fight Forest Fires', *Space News*. August 28.

'India Authorized to Build 1-Meter Imaging Satellites', *Space News* 2000.

'India's Futile Imagery Policy', *Space News*. July 24, 2000.

'Intelsat Might Move Out of US', *SpaceNews*, July 5, 1999.

International Atomic Energy Agency INFCIRC/540 (1997), *Model Protocol Additional to the Agreement(s) between State(s) and the International Atomic Energy for the Application of Safeguards*, International Atomic Energy Agency, Vienna, Austria.

International Civil Aviation Organization (1986), *ICAO Doc. C-WP/8158*, January 15.

International Court of Justice (1951), 'Anglo-Norwegian Fisheries Case', *Reports of Judgements and Advisory Opinions*.

International Law Commission (1980), *UN doc. A/CN.4/334/Add.2*.

International Law Commission (1982), *UN doc. A/ac.105/C.2/SR.369*.

Jakhu, R.S. (1982), 'The Legal Status of the Geostationary Orbit', *Annals of Air and Space Law VII*.

Jamieson, T. (1985), *The Canadian Space Research Program*, Science and Technology Division, Research Branch, Library of Parliament BP-121E, Ottawa: Minister of Supply and Services Canada, February 15.

Jayaraman, J. (2000), 'Antrix Sets its Sights on Commercial Satellite Market', *Space News*. August 7.

Jayaraman, K.S. (2000), 'Indian Imagery Business Expected to Boost Profits', *Space News*, August 7.

Jayaraman, K.S. (2000), 'India, U.S. Firm Agree To Sale of 1-Meter Imagery', *Space News*, July 17.

Jelle U. Hielkema (2000), 'FAO Spatial Information Applications for Early Warning for Food Security: The ARTEMIS System', EURISY Conference on The Use of Satellites and Integrated Technologies for Humanitarian Purposes,

Varese, Italy, September 19–20. http://demining.jrc.it/aris/events/eurisy/index.htm.

Jenks, C.W. and Larson, A. (ed.) (1965), *Sovereignty within the Law*. Oceana, Dobbs Ferry, NY.

Jensen, J.R. (2000), *Remote Sensing of the Environment: An Earth Resource Perspective*, Prentice-Hall, Upper Saddle River N.J.

Johanessen, O.M., Dalen, Ø., Rost, T., Bjørg, E., Andersen, G. and Babiker, M. (2000), 'ENVIREF: Environmental Monitoring of Refugee Camps Using High-Resolution Satellite Imagery', EURISY Conference on The Use of Satellites and Integrated Technologies for Humanitarian Purposes, Varese, Italy, September 19-20, http://demining.jrc.it/aris/events/eurisy/index.htm.

Johnson, J.A. (1964) 'Freedom and Control in Outer Space', in M.D. Schwartz, (ed.), *Proceedings of the Conference on Space Science and Space Law*, University of Oklahoma 1963, F. B. Rothman, South Hackensack, N.J.

Johnson, R.G. (1999), 'Negotiating the Dayton Peace Accords Through Digital Maps', presentation at a Seminar, 'Virtual Diplomacy – Case Studies,' the United States Institute of Peace, Washington, D.C. February 18. http://www.usip.org/oc/vd/vdr/rjohnsonISA99.html.

Johnson, Thomas H. (1998), 'The Task Structure of International Peace Operations', Paper presented at the 1998 Annual Meeting of the International Studies Association, Minneapolis.

Johnson-Freese, Joan, and Handberg, Richard (1997), *Space, the Dormant Frontier: Changing the Paradigm for the 21st Century*, Praeger, Westport, Conn.

Johnston, P. (1997), 'No Cloak and Dagger Required: Intelligence Support to UN Peacekeeping', *Intelligence and National Security*, vol. 12.

Keeley J.F. and Cameron, J.K. (1998), 'The Need to Know: Commercial Satellite Imagery and IAEA Safeguards,' in P. Gizewski (ed), *Non-Proliferation, Arms Control and Disarmament: Enhancing Existing Regimes and Exploring New Dimensions*, Centre for International and Security Studies, York University, Toronto.

Kirton, J. (1995), 'A Renewed Opportunity: The Role of Space in Canadian Security Policy', in David Dewitt and David Leyton-Brown eds. *Canada's International Security Policy*, Scarborough, Ont.: Prentice-Hall.

Kramer, G.M. (1989), 'The First Amendment Viewed from Space: National Security Versus Freedom of the Press', *ADAS*.

Krepon, M. (1990), 'The New Hierarchy in Space', in M. Krepon et al. (eds), *Commercial Observation Satellites and International Security*, St. Martin's Press, New York.

Lachs, M. (1972), *The Law of Outer Space: An Experience in Contemporary Law-Making*. Sijthoff, Leiden.

Lafeuillade, Yves (2000), 'A Multisatellite Transportable Station: An Invaluable Tool for Crisis Management', EURISY Conference on The Use of Satellites and Integrated Technologies for Humanitarian Purposes, Varese, Italy, September 19-20. http://demining.jrc.it/aris/events/eurisy/index.htm.

Lambakis, S. (1999), *The Two Faces of American Defense Space Policy*, National Institute for Public Policy, Fairfax, VA.

Laurini, R., and Thompson, D. (1992), *Fundamentals of Spatial Information Systems*, Academic Press Inc., San Diego, California.

Leach, R.J. (1994), '"Information" Support to U.N. Forces', *Marine Corps Gazette*, September.

Lillesand, T.M. and Kiefer, R.W. (2000), *Remote Sensing and Image Interpretation*, John Wiley and Sons, Toronto.

Lindgren, D.T. (2000), *Trust But Verify: Imagery Analysis in the Cold War*, United States Naval Institute Press, Annapolis, MD.

'Lockheed Offers Spy Satellite to Germany', *Space News*, April 3-9, 1995.

Loeb, V. (2000), 'NSA to Turn Over Non-Spy Technology to Private Industry', *Washington Post*, June 7, 2000.

Loeb, V. (2000), 'U.S. Is Relaxing Rules on Sale of Satellite Photos', *Washington Post*, Dec. 16.

'Losing Control', *Space News*. March 20, 2000.

Lunetta, R.S. and Elvidge, C.D. (1998), *Remote Sensing Change Detection*, Ann Arbor Press, Chelsea, Michigan.

Martin, Thomas S. (1982), 'National Security and the First Amendment: A Change in Perspective', *American Bar Association Journal*. Vol. 68.

Matte, N.M. (1982), *Aerospace Law: Telecommunications Satellites*. Butterworths, Toronto.

MacDonald, Dettwiler and Associates (1998), *RADARSAT-2 Home* 'RADARSAT-2 Press Release', December 18, http://www.mda.ca/radarsat-2/news/pr1998121801.html.

MacDonald, Dettwiler and Associates (2001), 'Canadian Space Agency and MDA begin Work on RADARSAT-3 Mission Feasibility', *RADARSAT-2 Home, News*, February 20, http://www.mda.ca/radarsat-2/news/pr2001022002.html.

MacDonald, Dettwiler and Associates (2002), 'MDA Helps Ships Navigate Icy North Atlantic', *News Index*, July 30, http://www.mda.ca/news/pr/pr2002073001.html.

MacDonald, Dettwiler and Associates (2002), *RADARSAT-2 Home* '1998 News', (updated May 30, 2002), http://www.mda.ca/radarsat-2/news/1998.shtml.

McCaffrey, S.C. (1989), 'The Fortieth Session of the International Law Commission', *American Journal of International Law*, vol. 83.

McClure, W.B. (July 2000), 'Technology and Command, Implications for Military Operations in the Twenty-first Century', *Occasional paper no. 15*, Center for Strategy and Technology, Air War College.

McDonald, R.A. (ed.) (1991), *Space Imagery and News Gathering for the 1990s: So What?* American Society for Photogrammetry and Remote Sensing, Bethesda, Maryland.

McDougal, M.S., Lasswell, H.D., and Vlasic, I.A. (1964), *Law and Public Order in Space*. Yale University Press, New Haven.

McFate, P.B. et al. (1996), 'Verification in a Global Context: The Establishment and Operation of a United Nations Centre for Information, Training, and Analysis (CITA)', *Arms Control Verification Studies, no. 7*, Non-Proliferation, Arms Control and Disarmament Division, Department of Foreign Affairs and International Trade, Ottawa.

McKenna, B. (2000), 'Canada, U.S. strike deal on spy satellite,' *The Globe and Mail,* June 16.

McKinley, C.A.S. (1995), 'When the Enemy Has Our Eyes', Thesis, School of Advanced Airpower Studies, Air University, Maxwell Air Force Base, AL.

Merges, Robert P. et al. (1989), 'News Media Satellites and the First Amendment: A Case Study in the Treatment of New Technologies', *High Technology Law Journal*, Vol. 1.

Meyers, Richard B. (Gen.) (1999), 'Moving Towards a Transparent Battlespace', Defense Review Magazine, Spring, http://www.spacecom.af.mil/usspace/defrev.htm.

Meyers, Richard B. (Gen.) (1999), Written Testimony Presented to the Senate Armed Services Committee Strategic Forces Subcommittee, March 22. http://www.spacecom.af.mil/usspace/speech14.htm.

Moffat, J. et al. (1995), *The Utility of Electro-Optical and Radar Technologies for Space Based Surveillance*, Department of National Defence, Ottawa.

Morrison, A. (ed.) (1993), *The Changing Face of Peacekeeping*, The Canadian Institute of Strategic Studies, Toronto.

Muller, J.P., Doll, C. and Elvidge, C. (2000), 'Nighttime 36-band MODIS data for mapping global urban population, GDP and CO_2 emissions'. http://ltpwww.gsfc.nasa.gov/MODIS/MODIS.html.

Mullholland, D. (1999), 'Research Funding Drops More Than $3 Billion', *Defense News*. February 19.

Nardon, Laurence (1994), *Test Ban Verification Matters: Satellite Detection*. London: Verification Technology Information Centre, November.

Newton, J.K. (2000), *Autonomous and Remotely Guided Vehicle Market Study*, Western Economic Diversification Canada, Edmonton, Alberta, July 4.

Nye, J.S. (1971) *Peace in Parts: Integration and Conflict in Regional Organization*, Little, Brown, Boston.

Opall-Rome, B. (2000), 'Israeli Firm to Sell S. Korea 1-meter Satellite Camera', *Space News*, February 26.

Opall-Rome, B. (2001), 'Israel's MoD Strategy Guards Commercial Imagery', *Space News*, February 26.

Opall-Rome, B. (2000), 'ImageSat International Plans Initial Public Offering', *Space News*. August 14.

Ordoñez, Carlos (2001), 'Use of elevation data in humanitarian relief operations', *ENVIREF, Demonstration and Evaluation Workshop Report*, February. http://www.enviref.org.

Pace, S., Sponberg, B. and Macauley, M. (1999), *Data Policy Issues and Barriers to Using Commercial Resources for Mission to Planet Earth, Report DB-247-NASA/OSTP*, RAND Corporation, Santa Monica, CA.

Pear, R. (1995), 'Disclosure of Spy Agency's $1.5 Billion Fund Leads to Shake-Up', *New York Times*, September 25.

Pincus, W. (1995), 'Spy Agency Hoards Secret $1 Billion: Satellite Managers Did Not Tell Supervisors of Classified 'Pot of Gold,' Hill Sources Say', *Washington Post*, September 24.

Pinther, M. (2000), 'United Nations Geographic Database', presentation at 'Meeting on Cartography and Geographic Information Science', United Nations, New York. March 28-30. http://www.un.org/Depts/Cartographic/english/ungis/meeting/.

Porter, M. (1985), *Competitive Advantage*. Harvard Business School Press, Cambridge, Mass.

Preston, B. (1994), *Ploughshares and Power: The Military Use of Civil Space*. National Defense University Press, Washington, D.C.

Pugliese, D. (2002), 'Forces Could Spend $684M on Spy Satellite', *National Post* March 23.

Pugliese, L. (2000), 'Canada Plans to Triple its Military Space Spending', *Space News*. November 6.

Quiggan, T. (1998), 'Response to "No Cloak and Dagger Required: Intelligence Support to UN Peacekeeping Missions"', *Intelligence and National Security*, vol. 13.

Rababy, D.P. (1995), 'Intelligence Support During a Humanitarian Mission', *Marine Corps Gazette*, February.

RADARSAT-2 (1999), *RADARSAT Program Background* June, http://mda.ca/radarsat-2/background/index.shtml.

RADARSAT-2 (1999), 'MacDonald Dettwiler to Acquire RADARSAT International', *RADARSAT-2 Press Release* February 15, http://mda.ca/radarsat-2/new/pr19990215001.html.

RADARSAT-2 (2001), 'MDA Renews Contracts in Canada and Denmark for Safe Ship Navigation Through Icy Waters', *RADARSAT-2 Press Release* September 6, http://mda.ca/radarsat-2/new/pr2001090602.html.

'Radarsat Cuts Through Cloud to see Arctic Ice', *Space Daily*, June 21, 2000, http://www.spacedaily.com/news/arctic-00a.html.

Ramey, Robert A. (2000), 'Armed Conflict on the Final Frontier: The Law of War in Space', *Air Force Law Review*, vol. 48.

Read, D.W. (2000), 'The Revolution in Military Affairs: NATO's Need for a Niche Capability Strategy', *Canadian Military Journal*, vol. 1, No. 3.

Rehbein, Robert E. (1996), 'Informing the Blue Helmets: The United States, UN Peacekeeping and peacemaking Operations, and the Role of Intelligence', *Martello Papers No. 16*, Kingston, Ont.: Centre for International Relations, Queen's University.

Richelson, J.T. (1990), 'Implications for Nations Without Space-Based Intelligence Collection Capabilities,' in Michael Krepon et al. (eds.), *Commercial Observation Satellites and International Security*, New York: St. Martin's Press.

Richelson, J.T. (2000), *The NRO Declassified, National Security Archive Electronic Briefing Book no. 35*, National Security Archive, Washington, DC.

Rider, D.B. (2000), 'Establishing a Commercial Reserve Imagery Fleet: Obtaining Surge Imagery Capacity From Commercial remote Sensing Satellite Systems During Crisis', Thesis, Air Command and Staff College, Air University, Maxwell Air Force Base, AL.

Ries, T. and Skorve, J. (1987), *Investigating Kola: A Study of Military Bases using Satellite Photography*, Brassey's, London.

Roberts, A. and Guelff, R. (eds.) (2000), *Documents on the Laws of War,* Oxford University Press.

Ross, A. (1996), 'Never Say Never Again: New Evidence Suggests Early U.S. Knowledge of Serb Atrocities', *Salon*, May 2. http://www.salonmag.com/news960502.html.

Ruffner, K.C. (ed.) (1995), *CORONA: America's First Satellite Program*, Center for the Study of Intelligence, Central Intelligence Agency, Washington, DC.

Rye, G. (2000), Presentation at the conference Space at the Crossroads: Military Use of Commercial Space, U.S. Senate, Russell Caucus Room. Washington, DC. September 14.

Sabins, F.F. (1997), *Remote Sensing: Principles and Interpretation*, W. H. Freeman and Co., New York.

Sandalow, D.P. (2000), 'Remote Sensing and Foreign Policy', presentation at symposium on 'Viewing the Earth: The Role of Satellite Earth Observations and Global Monitoring in International Affairs' George Washington University, Washington, D.C., June 6. http://www.state.gov/www/policy_re...000/000606_sandalow_satellite.html.

Saradzhyan, S. (2000), 'Russia, Industry Plan Imaging Satellite Launch', *Space News*. March 27.

Schmitt, M.N. (1999), 'Computer Network Attack and the Use of Force in International Law; Thoughts on a Normative Framework', *Columbia Journal of Transnational Law*, vol. 37.

Schwartz, M.D. (1998), 'Green wave photography', *Nature*, vol. 394.

Science Council of Canada (1967), *Report #1: A Space Program for Canada*, Ottawa: Queen's Printer, July.

SEASAT 1978 (1999), *Overview* February 10, http://southport.jpl.nasa.gov/scienceappa/seassat.html.

Seffers, G.I. (2000), 'Drop in Research Spending Worries Analysts, Industry', *Defence News*. February 21.

Shears, Jonathan (1997), 'Battle strategy meets virtual reality', *GeoEurope*, http://www.geoplace.com/ge/1997/0197/feature.asp.

Shelton, D.L. (1995), 'Intelligence Lessons Known and Revealed During Operation RESTORE HOPE Somalia', *Marine Corps Gazette*, February.

Shorb, Denise N. (1999), 'Space Technology Enhances Allied Force Bomber Missions', *Air Force News*, April 14.

Singer, J. (2000), 'Sensor May Lengthen Life of Missile Warning Satellites', *Space News*. November 6.

Singer, J. (2000), 'U.S. Spending Plan for Boosting Spy Imagery Called Inadequate', *Space News*. May 8.

Sloan, E. (2000), 'Canada and the Revolution in Military Affairs: Current Response and Future Opportunities', *Canadian Military Journal*, vol. 1, No. 3.

Smith, H. (1994) 'Intelligence and UN Peacekeeping', *Survival*, vol. 36.

Sokolsky, J. (1995), 'The Bilateral Defence Relationship with the United States', in David Dewitt and David Leyton-Brown (eds.), *Canada's International Security Policy*, Scarborough, Ont.: Prentice-Hall.

'Spy Satellites for Sale', *Space News*, March 13–19, 1995.

Staelin, D.H. and Kerekes, J. (1997), 'Remote Sensing Capabilities' in D.G. Dalmeyer, and K. Tsipis (eds), *Heaven and Earth: Civilian Uses of Near Earth Space*, Kluwer.

Stares, Paul. B. (1985), *Space Weapons and US Strategy : Origins and Developments*, Beckenham, UK.

Steele, R.D. (1995), 'The Importance of Open Sources Intelligence to the Military', *International Journal of Intelligence and Counterintelligence*, vol. 8.

Steinberg, G. (1998), 'Dual Use Aspects of Commercial High-Resolution Imaging Satellites', *Occasional Paper no. 37,* Begin-Sadat Center for Strategic Studies, Bar-Ilan University, Ramat Gan, Israel.

Steinberg, G.M. (1983), *Satellite Reconnaissance: The Role of Informal Bargaining*, Praeger Publishers, New York.

Stone, J. (1977) 'Hopes and loopholes in the 1974 Definition of Aggression', *American Journal of International Law*, vol. 71.

Stout, M. and Quiggin, T. (1998), 'Exploiting the new high-resolution satellite imagery: Darwinian Imperatives?' *Canadian Security Intelligence Service Commentary, no. 75.*

Swedish Armed Forces, *Joint Military Doctrine – Peace Support Operations.* http://www.mil.se/doctrines/.

Tao, C.V., Truong, B., Keeffe, R. and Benjamin, R. (1998), 'Potential Applications of GIS for Management of Safeguards Information', paper presented at the International Seminar on Safeguards Information Reporting and Processing, Vienna, Austria.

Teorey, T. (1999), *Database Modeling and Design*, Morgan Kaufmann Publishers, Inc., San Francisco, California.

Thomas, P. (1994), 'Spy Unit's Spending Stuns Hill', *Washington Post*, August 9.

Thomas, T.L. 'Virtual Peacekeeping: A Military View of Conflict Prevention Through the Use of Information Technology', U.S. Army, Foreign Military Studies Office. http://call.army.mil/call/fmso/fmso.pubs.

Thompson, D.W. (2000), Remarks on U.S. Government Policy – Commercial Space Policies for the Next Administration and Congress, Speech to the Washington Space Business Roundtable, December 7.

Treaty Between the United States of America and the Union of Soviet Socialist Republics on the Limitation of Ballistic Missile Systems, May 26, 1972.

Treaty on Principles Governing the Activities of States in the Exploration and Use of Outer Space, including the Moon and Other Celestial Bodies. (In force October 10, 1967.)

United Nations, *doc A/AC.105/PV.22* (1966).

United Nations, *doc A/AC.105/C.2/L.99* (1974).

United Nations, 'Peacekeeping Fatalities'. http://www.un.org/Depts/dpko/fatalities.

United Nations (1983), *Report of the Secretary-General: The Implications of Establishing an International Satellite Monitoring Agency*, Department for Disarmament Affairs, United Nations, New York.

United Nations (2000), *Report of the Panel on United Nations Peace Operations, A/55/305-S/2000/809*. August 21.

United Nations (2000), *Report of the Secretary General on the implementation of the report of the Panel on United Nations peace operations, A/55/502*. October 20.

United Nations (2000), 'UN Summary of Contributions to Peacekeeping Operations', Department of Foreign Affairs (Canada), relevant Treasury Board submissions, 1998–2000.

United Nations, 'Meeting on Cartography and Geographic Information Science', http://www.un.org/Depts/Cartographic/english/ungis/meeting.

United Nations, Department for Disarmament Affairs (1983), *The Implications of Establishing an International Satellite Monitoring Agency*, United Nations, New York.

United Nations, General Assembly (1962), *Res. 1803/XVII*, 'Declaration on Permanent Sovereignty over Natural Resources'.

United Nations, General Assembly (1965), *Res. 2131/XX*, 'Declaration on the Inadmissibility of Intervention in Domestic Affairs of States and the Protection of their Independence and Sovereignty'.

United Nations, General Assembly (1970), *Res. 2265/XXV*, 'Declaration of the Principles of International Law Concerning Friendly Co-operation Among States'.

United Nations, General Assembly (1974), *Res. 3281/XXIX*, 'Charter of the Economic Rights and Duties of States'.

United Nations, General Assembly (1974), *Res. 3314/XXIX*, 'Definition of Aggression'.

United Nations, General Assembly (1986), *Res. 41/65*, 'Principles Relating to Remote Sensing of the Earth from Outer Space'. December 3.

United Nations, Security Council, *Res. 1295* (2000), April 18, 2000.

United Nations, Security Council, *Res. 1306* (2000), July 5, 2000.

United Nations (1995), Treaty Series 'Exchange of Notes Constituting an agreement for cooperation in the RADARSAT Programme (with Memorandum of Understanding of February 1991). Washington November 12, 1991)' vol 1883 I-32041.

United Nations Association of the United States of America (2000), 'Enhancing UN Peacekeeping Capability: a UNA-USA Policy Roundtable', New York. July 5. http://www.unausa.org/issues/peace/705/htm.

United States Air Force Space Command. (1991), 'Desert Storm Hot Wash', in *National Security Archives, Electronic Briefing Book No. 39*, Washington, D.C. January 17, 2001.

United States Air Force Space Command (January 1992), 'Operations Desert Shield and Desert Storm Assessment', in National Security Archives, *Electronic Briefing Book No. 39*, Washington, D.C., January 17, 2001.

United States Army, Joint Warfighting Centre (1997), *Joint Task Force Commander's Handbook for Peace Operations*, Joint War Fighting Centre, Ft. Monroe, Virginia.

United States, Congress (1992), *Land Remote Sensing Policy Act of 1992, Public Law 102-555*.

United States, Congress (1996), *National Defence Authorization Act for Fiscal Year 1997* (S. Rep. No. 104-278, 104th Cong., 2nd Sess. s. 1745) s. 1044, Authorizing Appropriations for Fiscal Year 1997 for Military Activities of the Department of Defence, for Military Construction, and for Defence Activities of the Department of Energy, to Prescribe Personnel Strengths for such Fiscal Year for the Armed Forces, and for Other Purposes.

United States Congress. (1998), *Strom Thurmond National Defence Authorization Act for Fiscal Year 1999. P.L.105-261*.

United States, Congress (1998), *Commercial Space Act, H.R. Bill 1702*.

United States, Congress, House of Representatives (1999), *Admiral James W. Nance and Meg Donovan Foreign Relations Authorization Act, Fiscal Years 2000 and 2001*. H.R. 3427, 106th Congress, first session.

United States, Congress, House of Representatives, Committee on Science, Space and Technology (1992), *National Landsat Policy Act of 1992, Report 102-539*.

United States, Congress, House of Representatives 6133: *Land Remote Sensing Policy Act of 1992*: http:// www.nnic.noaa.gov/refs.htm.

United States, Congress, House of Representatives, Committee on Science (1997), Testimony of D.J. Baker, Undersecretary for Oceans and Atmosphere, Department of Commerce, The Commercial Space Act of 1997, Parts I-III, 105th Congress, first session. May 21 and 22 and June 4.

United States, Congress, House of Representatives, Permanent Select Committee on Intelligence (1996), *IC21: The Intelligence Community in the 21st Century*, 104th Congress, Washington, D.C.

United States Congress, Office of Technology Assessment (1987), *Commercial Newsgathering From Space – A Technical Memorandum, OTA-TM-ISC-40*, Washington, D.C.

United States, Congress, Office of Technology Assessment (1991), *Redesigning Defense: Planning the Transition to the Future U.S. Defence Industrial Base, OTA-ISC-500*, GPO, Washington, D.C.

United States Congress, Office of Technology Assessment (1992), *Building Future Security: Strategies for Restructuring Defence Technology and Industrial Base, OTA-ISC-539*, Washington, D.C.

United States Congress, Office of Technology Assessment (1995), *Improving the Prospects for Future International Peace Operations, OTA-BP-ISS-167*. Washington, D.C.

United States, Congress, Senate (1995), *Committee Activities of the Senate Select Committee on Intelligence, Senate Report 104-4*, 104th Congress, 1st Session, Washington, D.C.

United States, Congress, Senate (1996), 'To Prohibit the Collection and Release of Detailed Satellite Imagery With Respect to Israel and Other Countries and Areas', *National Defense Authorization Act For Fiscal Year 1997, Amendment no. 4321*, United States Congressional Record, US Senate, 104th Congress, 2nd Session.

United States Senate, Committee on Foreign Relations, Subcommittee on International Economic Policy, Export and Trade Promotion (1999), Testimony of E.D. Newsome, Assistant Secretary for Political-Military Affairs June 24.

United States, Congress, Senate, Committee on Foreign Relations, Subcommittee on International Economic Policy, Export and Trade Promotion (1999), 'U.S. Export Control Policies on Satellites and U.S. Domestic Launch Capabilities', testimony of William A. Reinsch, Under Secretary for Export Administration, Department of Commerce June 24.

United States, Senate, Armed Services Committee (1997), 'A Broad Range of Missions: Army Posture Statement for Fiscal 1998', February 25.

United States Department of Commerce, Office of Space Commerce (1991), 'Space Business Indicators', Washington, D.C. June.

United States Congress, Senate, Armed Services Committee (2000), Testimony of J.W. Douglas, February 28.

United States, Department of Commerce, National Oceanic and Atmospheric Administration (2000), 'Interim Final Rule', *Federal Register*, vol. 65, no. 181. pp. 56241–56242.

United States, Department of Commerce, National Oceanic and Atmospheric Administration (2000), 'Interim Final Rule on Licensing of Private Land Remote-Sensing Space Systems', *Federal Register*, vol. 65, no. 18. pp.

United States, Department of Defense (1992), *A Post Cold War Assessment of US Space Policy; A Task Group Report*, Washington, D.C. December 17.

United States Department of Defense. (1996), 'Intelligence Support to Operation JOINT ENDEAVOUR', *Background Briefing*, Washington, D.C. January 18.

United States, General Accounting Office (1993), *U.N. Peacekeeping: Lessons Learned in Managing Recent Operations, GA/NSIAD-94-9*. USGPO, Washington, D.C.

United States, General Accounting Office (1997), *United Nations: Limitations in Leading Missions Requiring Force to Restore Peace, GAO/NSIAD-97-34*. USGPO, Washington, DC.

United States Geological Survey, 'CORONA Satellite Photography.' http://www.edcwww.cr.usgs.gov/glis/hyper/guide/displ/.

United States, Independent Commission on the National Imagery and Mapping Agency (2000), *The Information Edge: Imagery Intelligence and Geospatial Information in an Evolving National Security Environment*. December.

United States Joint Chiefs of Staff (1995), *Joint Doctrine for Intelligence Support to Operations*, Joint Publication 2-0. May 5.

United States, President (1994), 'U.S. Policy on Foreign Access to Remote Sensing Space Capabilities'. *PDD-23*, March 10.

United States, White House (1979), *Announcement of the President's Decisions Concerning Land Remote Sensing Satellite Activities*. November 20.

United States, White House, Office of the Press Secretary (1994), *Fact Sheet: Foreign Access to Remote Sensing Space Capabilities*. March 10.

United States, White House, Office of Science and Technology Policy and the National Security Council (2000), *Fact Sheet Regarding the Memorandum of Understanding Concerning the Licensing of Private Remote Sensing Satellite Systems*. February 2.

'US Firms Enter Race to Build Spy Satellite for Turkey', *Space News*, 2000.

United States Institute of Peace, 'Promoting an Information-Sharing Regime in Peace Support and Humanitarian Operations', http://www.usip.org/oc/vd/vdilpo-share/vdiplo-share.html.

United States Institute of Peace 'Virtual Diplomacy' project, 'Taking It to the Next Level: Civilian-Military Co-operation in Complex Emergencies', http://www.usip.org/oc/vd/vdr/nextlevel.html.

Uwanyiligira, I. (2000), 'Situation Centre needs', presentation at 'Meeting on Cartography and Geographic Information Science', United Nations, New York, March 28–30. http://www.un.org/Depts/Cartographic/english/ungis/meeting.

Vienna Convention on the Law of Treaties, signed May 23, 1969.

Vlasic, I.A. (1965), 'The Growth of Space Law 1957–65: Achievements and Issues', *Yearbook of Air and Space Law*.

Vlasic, I.A. (ed.) (1968), *Explorations in Aerospace Law: Selected Essays by John Cobb Cooper 1946-1966*. McGill-Queen's University Press, Montreal.

Vlasic, I.A. (1979), 'Principles Relating to Remote Sensing of the Earth from Space', in J. Nasentuliyana and R.S.K. Lee (eds) (1979), *Manual on Space Law*.

Vlasic, I. (1995), 'Space Law and the Military Applications of Space Technology', in *Perspectives on International Law*.

Wentz, L.K. 'Intelligence Operations,' in Larry Wentz (ed.), *Lessons from Bosnia: The IFOR Experience*, http://www.dodccrp.org/bostoc.htm.

Wight, R. (1999), 'Private Eyes', *New York Times Magazine*. September 5, pp. 50-55.

Williams, C. and Lind, J.M. (1999) 'Can We Afford a Revolution in Military Affairs?' *Breakthroughs*, Spring. http://www.mit.edu/ssp/db21/breakthroughs.html.

World Meteorological Congress (1995), 'WMO Policy and Practice for the Exchange of Meteorological and Related Data and Products Including Guidelines on Relationships in Commercial Meteorological Activities'. CG XII, 12th Meeting.

Zimmerman, P. (1989), 'From the SPOT Files: Evidence of Spying', *Bulletin of the Atomic Scientists*, vol. 45, no. 7.

Zimmerman, P.D. (1990), 'Remote Sensing Satellites, Superpower Relations, and Public Diplomacy', in M. Krepon et al. (eds), *Commercial Observation Satellites and International Security*, St. Martin's Press, New York.

Zimmerman, P.D. (1990), 'The Uses of SPOT for Intelligence Collection: A Quantitative Assessment', in M. Krepon et al. (eds), *Commercial Observation Satellites and International Security*, St. Martin's Press, New York.

Additional Internet Sources

Atlantis Scientific, Inc., http://www.atlsci.com.

Australia, Australian Surveying and Land Information Group. http://www.auslig.gov.au/acres/

Canadian Center for Remote Sensing, http://ccrs.nrcan.gc.ca.

Canadian Space Agency, http://www.space.gc.ca.

Carnegie Endowment for International Peace, 'Transparency and Civil Society' project, http://www.ceip.org.

DigitalGlobe, http://www.digitalglobe.com.

ENVIREF, http://www.enviref.org.

Environmental Remote Sensing Center, http://www.ersc.wisc.edu/ersc.

EOS AM-1 central location for technical documentation: http://terra.nasa.gov.

EOS AM-1 direct broadcast documentation: http://rsd.gsfc.nasa.gov/eosdb.

ERMapper (freeware): http://www.ermapper.com/cgi-bin/products/index.cfm?prodid=148.

EROS data gateway: http://edcimswww.cr.usgs.gov:80/~imswww/pub/imswelcome/plain.htm.

ESRI Inc. (freeware): http://www.esri.com/software/arcexplorer/index.html.

Eurimage, http://www.eurimage.com.

Federation of American Scientists. http://www.fas.org/

ImageSat International, http://www.imagesatintl.com.

Institute for Science and International Security. http://www.isis-online.org.

MODIS image gallery (slow loading):
http://modarch.gsfc.nasa.gov/cgi-bin/texis/MODIS/IMAGE_GALLERY/
modimgview/allimages.html.

MODIS products and science program:
http://ltpwww.gsfc.nasa.gov/MODIS/MODIS.html. Connect to Data, then Data
Products Description.

Nansen Environmental and Remote Sensing Center, http://www.nrsc.org.

NCSA: http://www.ncsa.uiuc.edu. For image file reading software, use the NCSA
search engine to find 'HDF-EOS.'

NOAA data archive: http://saa.noaa.gov.

NOAA GOES information: http://www.goes.noaa.gov/index.html.

PCI Inc. (freeware):
http://www.pcigeomatics.com/product_ind/freeview.html. Calculator for finding
when satellites are above the horizon (i.e., when images will be acquired and
when direct broadcast can be downloaded):
http://earthobservatory.nasa.gov/MissionControl/overpass.html.

RADARSAT International, http://www.rsi.ca.

ReliefSat, http://www.nrsc.org/reliefsat.

Sovinformsputnik, http://www-com.iasis.svetcorp.net.

Space Imaging, http://www.spaceimaging.com.

SPOT Image, http://www.spotimage.fr.

Standing High-Readiness Brigade (SHIRBRIG), http://www.shirbrig/dk/.

Terraserver, http://www.terraserver.com.

United Nations Geographical Information Working Group,
http://www.un.org/Depts/Cartographic/ungis/ungis.htm.

United States Geological Survey, LANDSAT 7, http://landsat7.usgs.gov.

United States Institute for Peace, 'Virtual Diplomacy' project, http://www.usip.org.

United States, National Reconnaissance Office, http://www.nro.mil.

Z/I Imaging Corporation, http://www.ziimaging.com.

Index